Microsoft Hyper-V Cluster Design

Plan, design, build and maintain Microsoft Hyper-V Server 2012 and 2012 R2 clusters using this essential guide

Eric Siron

[PACKT] enterprise 🕸
PUBLISHING
professional expertise distilled

BIRMINGHAM - MUMBAI

Microsoft Hyper-V Cluster Design

First published: October 2013

Production Reference: 1171013

Published by Packt Publishing Ltd.
Livery Place
35 Livery Street
Birmingham B3 2PB, UK.

ISBN 978-1-78217-768-5

www.packtpub.com

Cover Image by Aniket Sawant (aniket_sawant_photography@hotmail.com)

Credits

Author

Eric Siron

Reviewers

Vinicius R. Apolinario

Edvaldo Alessandro Cardoso

Vicente Rodriguez Eguibar

Acquisition Editor

Sam Wood

Lead Technical Editor

Madhuja Chaudhari

Technical Editors

Sandeep Madnaik

Aman Preet Singh

Ankita Thakur

Project Coordinator

Leena Purkait

Proofreaders

Paul Hindle

Simran Bhogal

Ameesha Green

Indexers

Mehreen Deshmukh

Mariammal Chettiyar

Priya Subramani

Rekha Nair

Monica Ajmera Mehta

Graphics

Ronak Dhruv

Disha Haria

Production Coordinator

Manu Joseph

Cover Work

Manu Joseph

About the Author

Eric Siron has over fifteen years of professional experience in the information technology field. Eric has architected solutions across the spectrum, from two-user home offices to thousand user enterprises. He began working with Microsoft Hyper-V Server, version R2 in 2010, and has focused on Microsoft virtualization technologies ever since. He is currently employed as a Senior Systems Administrator at The University of Iowa Hospitals and Clinics, in Iowa City, Iowa, and is a regular contributor to the Hyper-V blog hosted by Altaro Software.

To my daughter, who always inspires me to be better today than I was yesterday. To my wife, who never stops supporting my writing, but ensures that I take breaks so that I don't miss out on the inspiration. To my dad, who brought home the VIC-20 that started me on my career path. I would like to thank all my associates at Altaro Software for providing me with a space to share my thoughts. A special thanks to Pete Bernardy for providing emergency research in the nick of time.

About the Reviewers

Vinicius R. Apolinario has worked with IT for more than 10 years, working with Microsoft Products, managing servers and the environments within small, medium, and large companies. He has a strong background in managing Microsoft Servers such as Active Directory, Exchange, and other Windows Server Components. He is also a Microsoft Certified Trainer and System Engineer on Windows Server 2012 and Private Cloud. Besides being a Microsoft Certified Professional, he holds a Cloud Computing Certification from Exin and teach classes on this technology.

Today, he works for Microsoft Brazil as a Technical Evangelist focused on Infrastructure. As part of his job, he does presentations for partners and customers about products such as Windows Server, Hyper-V, System Center, and Windows Azure. Before this role, he worked at Microsoft Brazil as a member of the Windows Server and Private Cloud Product Team as Technical Specialist. He is the owner of the blog ADM de Redes (`www.admderedes.com.br`) (PT-BR) where he shares his knowledge with other professionals.

Before reviewing this book, he participated on the review of the Windows Server 2012 Hyper-V Cookbook.

> Working on a project like this is always a challenge to maintain balance between my professional and personal life. The support from my wife was extremely important. Her support on everything I do is the most important thing I have. I cannot forget to thank her for being on my side all the time, and always pushing me to achieve the very best. I want to also thank my colleagues for supporting me during this period and my manager for understanding the importance of this project.

Edvaldo Alessandro Cardoso is a virtualization and management subject matter and enthusiast, author, and Evangelist. He works at Insight Enterprise as a Practice Manager for Cloud and Emerging technologies, leading award winning IT projects in key areas involving Cloud, Virtualization, Security, Messaging, and Hosting within the IT, Health, and Government industries.

Microsoft's Most Valuable Professional in virtualization since 2009, his product skill set includes Microsoft infrastructure technologies such as O365, Hyper-V, System Center, Windows Server, SQL Server, Active Directory, Exchange, SharePoint, IIS, and Forefront. He also has sound knowledge of Quest Migration Manager, Linux Infrastructure, Networking, Security Solutions, and VMware in complex and large scenarios.

He is a well-known speaker at IT-related events and author of the book *System Center Virtual Machine Manager 2012* (`http://www.packtpub.com/microsoft-system-center-virtual-machine-manager-2012-cookbook/book`), and technical reviewer of the *Windows 2012 Hyper-V Cookbook*, and *VMware 5.1 Cookbook*.

You can also check out his personal blog where he talks about Microsoft Virtualization and System Center at `http://cloudtidings.com/`, or follow him on twitter at `@edvaldocardoso`.

> I would like to thank my wife, Daniele, and my kids Matheus, Lucas, and Nicole for their support and for being my inspiration. I love you all.

Vicente Rodriguez Eguibar is the co-founder of Eguibar Information Technology S.L. Company, dedicated to give IT Consultancy and Services, focusing on corporate directories, networking, virtualization, migration, and IT optimization. He has been director in this company for the last four years, providing services and solutions to Fortune 500 international companies. He has traveled to several countries in Asia, Europe, and America, supervising and managing projects for different companies.

His technical background started in 1993 as an IT trainer. He has also worked in many different positions such as a system operator, technical project manager, and senior consultant for many international companies. Back in Mexico, where he was born, he was certified by Microsoft as Product Specialist, being one of the first people to obtain this certification in Mexico.

At the beginning in Mexico, he administered and managed computer systems for several industrial companies in the automotive sector. Following his performance in Mexico, the CIO office asked him to to design and manage the international communication network and corporate directory for their formal company. After managing this position for three years, he was hired by a German car manufacturing company to design the global corporate directory, being in this position for three years. When the German car manufacturing company sold the IT section to a German telecommunications company, he was appointed to design IT Architecture Infrastructures for external customer companies and government agencies. His last position before creating his own company was for an international call center corporation, where he was in charge to design, deploy, and migrate to the corporate directory, messaging system, and virtualization strategy.

He wrote *Instant Hyper-V Server Virtualization Starter*, published by Packt Publishing in 2013.

To my wife, my parents, family, and friends; thanks to all, but this work is dedicated to Ivan. I love you son.

---

www.PacktPub.com

Support files, eBooks, discount offers and more

You might want to visit www.PacktPub.com for support files and downloads related to your book.

Did you know that Packt offers eBook versions of every book published, with PDF and ePub files available? You can upgrade to the eBook version at www.PacktPub.com and as a print book customer, you are entitled to a discount on the eBook copy. Get in touch with us at service@packtpub.com for more details.

At www.PacktPub.com, you can also read a collection of free technical articles, sign up for a range of free newsletters and receive exclusive discounts and offers on Packt books and eBooks.

http://PacktLib.PacktPub.com

Do you need instant solutions to your IT questions? PacktLib is Packt's online digital book library. Here, you can access, read and search across Packt's entire library of books.

Why Subscribe?

- Fully searchable across every book published by Packt
- Copy and paste, print and bookmark content
- On demand and accessible via web browser

Free Access for Packt account holders

If you have an account with Packt at www.PacktPub.com, you can use this to access PacktLib today and view nine entirely free books. Simply use your login credentials for immediate access.

Instant Updates on New Packt Books

Get notified! Find out when new books are published by following @PacktEnterprise on Twitter, or the *Packt Enterprise* Facebook page.

Table of Contents

Preface

The world of virtualization continues to expand, and the reach of Microsoft's Hyper-V hypervisor continues to expand with it. This book seeks to reach beyond simple, single-host hypervisor deployment, and provide guidance on clustering hosts together for redundancy, performance, and more thorough utilization of resources.

A design goal of this book is to avoid imposing the author's personal preferences, whether through passive (*I always/I never*) or aggressive (*you must/you should not*) sentences. The goal of this book is to provide you with information about Hyper-V, expose you to real-world pros and cons of decisions, and allow you to apply your own intelligence to design a system that meets your unique needs.

What this book covers

Chapter 1, Hyper-V Cluster Orientation, introduces the foundational concepts of Hyper-V Server in a Failover Cluster environment, and how to begin deployment planning.

Chapter 2, Cluster Design and Planning, outlines a path to determining the requirements for a new cluster in a specific environment.

Chapter 3, Constructing a Hyper-V Server Cluster, steps through configuring nodes and joining them into a Hyper-V Server cluster.

Chapter 4, Storage Design, takes a detailed look at the storage options for virtual machines in a cluster.

Chapter 5, Network Design, examines the possibilities for a Hyper-V Server cluster network, including redundancy and load-balancing.

Chapter 6, Network Traffic Shaping and Performance Enhancements, builds on the architectural networking concepts with the introduction of advanced settings and performance enhancements.

Chapter 7, Memory Planning and Management, explains how Hyper-V Server uses memory and provides guidance on proper configuration.

Chapter 8, Performance Testing and Load Balancing, presents holistic and specific methods to determining how well your system performs. It then guides you through balancing virtual machines across cluster nodes.

Chapter 9, Special Cases, looks at deployments that will need special attention and less common uses for Hyper-V Server clusters.

Chapter 10, Maintaining and Monitoring a Hyper-V Server Cluster, introduces methods to keep a Hyper-V Server cluster current and to watch it for problems.

Chapter 11, High Availability, describes high availability and illustrates how a cluster of Hyper-V Servers can achieve it.

Chapter 12, Backup and Disaster Recovery, rounds out the discussion of Hyper-V Server in a cluster with coverage of the technologies needed for protection and recovery.

What you need for this book

This book has been written to work solely with the tools that are bundled in Windows: the original Windows Server 2012 and Hyper-V Server 2012 products, as well as the R2 releases of those operating systems.

If you will be following the graphical interface instructions for the 2012 release, at least one copy of Windows Server 2012 or Windows 8 is required. If you will be following the graphical interface instructions for the 2012 R2 release, at least one copy of Windows Server 2012 R2 or Windows 8.1 is required.

Who this book is for

If you are an experienced Windows Server administrator, this book is ideal for you. You should have a solid understanding of basic networking concepts and terminology. You should also have a foundational understanding of Active Directory and how to manipulate its objects. You should be comfortable with common Windows tools and technologies, such as Disk Management and the Windows Firewall.

Previous hypervisor and clustering experience is not essential, although familiarity with related terminology is helpful.

Conventions

The product names of the technologies referenced in this book tend to be very long, and they can be tedious for both reader and author. When a specific product is intended, it is generally spelled out completely. "2012" may be used to refer to both Windows Server 2012 and Hyper-V Server 2012. "R2" may be used to refer to both Windows Server 2012 R2 and Hyper-V Server 2012 R2. "Windows Server" may be used to refer to either version of Windows Server. "Hyper-V" and "Hyper-V Server" may be used to refer to either version of Hyper-V Server. The context was carefully considered any time a shortened product name was used.

In this book, you will find a number of styles of text that distinguish between different kinds of information. Here are some examples of these styles, and an explanation of their meaning.

Code words and PowerShell parameters in the text are shown as follows: "Other available QoS parameters are `MinimumBandwidthAbsolute` and `MaximumBandwidth`".

Any command-line input or output is written as follows:

```
(Get-VMSwitch vSwitch).DefaultFlowMinimumBandwidthAbsolute
```

New terms and **important words** are shown in bold. Words that you see on the screen, in menus or dialog boxes for example, appear in the text like this: "Upon clicking on **Finish**, the discovery will run."

> Warnings or important notes appear in a box like this.

> Tips and tricks appear like this.

Reader feedback

Feedback from our readers is always welcome. Let us know what you think about this book—what you liked or may have disliked. Reader feedback is important for us to develop titles that you really get the most out of.

To send us general feedback, simply send an e-mail to `feedback@packtpub.com`, and mention the book title via the subject of your message.

If there is a topic that you have expertise in and you are interested in either writing or contributing to a book, see our author guide on www.packtpub.com/authors.

Customer support

Now that you are the proud owner of a Packt book, we have a number of things to help you to get the most from your purchase.

Downloading the example code

You can download the example code files for all Packt books you have purchased from your account at http://www.packtpub.com. If you purchased this book elsewhere, you can visit http://www.packtpub.com/support and register to have the files e-mailed directly to you.

Errata

Although we have taken every care to ensure the accuracy of our content, mistakes do happen. If you find a mistake in one of our books—maybe a mistake in the text or the code—we would be grateful if you would report this to us. By doing so, you can save other readers from frustration and help us improve subsequent versions of this book. If you find any errata, please report them by visiting http://www.packtpub.com/submit-errata, selecting your book, clicking on the **errata submission form** link, and entering the details of your errata. Once your errata are verified, your submission will be accepted and the errata will be uploaded on our website, or added to any list of existing errata, under the Errata section of that title. Any existing errata can be viewed by selecting your title from http://www.packtpub.com/support.

Piracy

Piracy of copyright material on the Internet is an ongoing problem across all media. At Packt, we take the protection of our copyright and licenses very seriously. If you come across any illegal copies of our works, in any form, on the Internet, please provide us with the location address or website name immediately so that we can pursue a remedy.

Please contact us at copyright@packtpub.com with a link to the suspected pirated material.

We appreciate your help in protecting our authors, and our ability to bring you valuable content.

Questions

You can contact us at questions@packtpub.com if you are having a problem with any aspect of the book, and we will do our best to address it.

1
Hyper-V Cluster Orientation

Microsoft Hyper-V Server 2012 or its R2 successor in a Microsoft Failover Cluster configuration is one of the most powerful infrastructure tools available for system administrators. It provides an inexpensive solution that combines all the benefits of virtualization with the resiliency and resource-spreading capabilities of clustering. While the technologies can provide substantial advantages, designing and implementing a Hyper-V Server failover cluster is not a trivial undertaking.

Before you can begin designing your cluster, it's important to orient yourself to the scope of the task that you're committing to. It is imperative that you master the fundamentals of the technologies involved in a Hyper-V Server cluster. You must also thoroughly understand the problem that you are using a Hyper-V Server cluster to solve. Based on that problem, you must define a clear set of goals that such a system must achieve in order to serve as a proper solution. You will then design a cluster that can meet those goals. After that, you can build, test, and deploy your Hyper-V cluster.

By the end of this chapter, you will have learned about:

- The proper terminology related to Hyper-V Server
- The specific meaning of clustering in a Microsoft environment
- How to begin a cluster project planning document
- The options available within a Hyper-V Server cluster
- The physical components that are necessary for a Hyper-V Server cluster
- Knowledge that you'll need to begin designing your Hyper-V Server cluster

Terminology

Due to an overlap of terms and some misperceptions about the ways that the Hyper-V Server product is delivered, terminology is a common sticking point even for people who have been working with the technology for some time. The following table provides accurate but short definitions for the most commonly misunderstood terms in relation to Hyper-V Server and clusters. These definitions will be expanded upon in detail throughout the course of this book, so don't worry if they are confusing at first:

Term	Definition
Hypervisor	A hypervisor is an operating system that manages other operating systems. The primary responsibility of the typical operating system is to allocate and manage resources for applications. In the context of a hypervisor, "applications" are guest operating systems.
Microsoft Hyper-V Server	This is a full-featured hypervisor from Microsoft. Available as a standalone, no-charge product that includes a reduced-functionality image of Windows Server for the purpose of managing the hypervisor. It is also available as a role within Microsoft Windows Server.
Server Core	A specific installation method of Windows Server from version 2008 onward. This mode does not include a graphical interface. It is a fully licensed copy of Windows Server. Hyper-V is available as a role within Server Core.
Host	A physical computer with a hypervisor installed.
Guest	Another term for virtual machine, although it is commonly used to refer to the operating system within a virtual machine.
Management Operating System	The operating system that is allowed to control the hypervisor installation. In any Hyper-V Server installation, Hyper-V Server is always the hypervisor and Windows Server is always the management operating system. This is also sometimes called a *parent partition* or *host operating system*, although those terms are falling out of favor.
Cluster	In the context of Hyper-V Server, a cluster refers to hosts joined together using Microsoft Failover Clustering to provide Hyper-V Server services.
Node	A single physical computer that is a member of a cluster.
Live Migration	A Hyper-V-specific implementation of relocating a running virtual machine from one node to another without detectable downtime for the services on that virtual machine or external consumers of those services.
Quick Migration	A Hyper-V-specific implementation of relocating a virtual machine from one node to another. This method involves gracefully stopping the virtual machine in some fashion and starting it again at the destination.

Term	Definition
Saved State	A condition in which a virtual machine's operations have been paused. The contents of its system memory are copied to a disk file and the virtual machine is placed in a non-running condition.

> The term *Hyper-V Core* and its variants should not be used. Hyper-V Server is one product and Server Core is a particular mode for the Windows Server product. Combining their labels leads to confusion and should be avoided.

Clustering in a Microsoft environment

The generic term **clustering** in computer terminology refers to any method that groups multiple computers together to provide a particular service. The common reason this is done is to introduce high availability and/or distribution of resources. For the purposes of this book, clustering leverages multiple physical computers to provide a hosting service for virtual machines. All of this is transparent to the consumers — both technological and human; the machines themselves and the clients that rely on them operate as though the cluster and virtualization components were non-existent. Users employ the exposed services no differently than they would if they were directly installed on a traditional physical deployment. An example of a user accessing a website hosted on a virtual machine is shown in the following image:

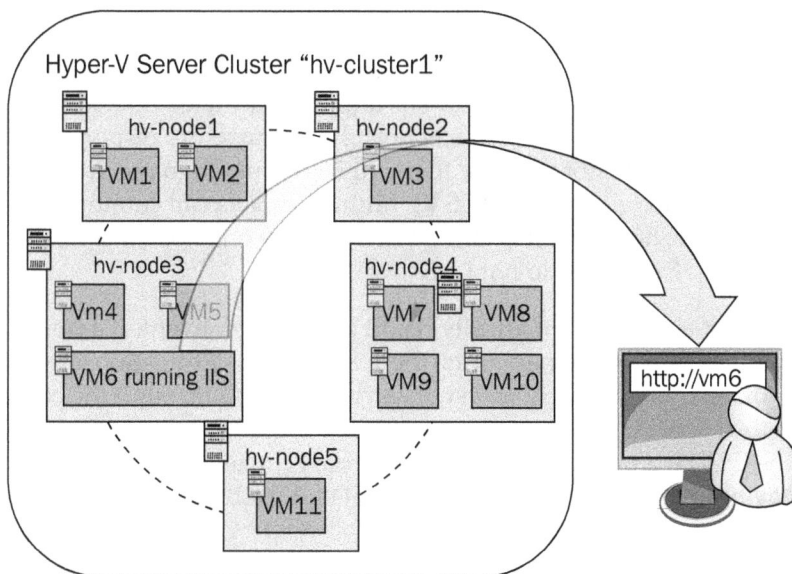

If you're coming to Hyper-V Server clustering with experience in another hypervisor technology, there are substantial differences right from the start. Chief among these is that a Hyper-V Server cluster is composed of two major technologies. The first technology is, obviously, Hyper-V Server. The second technology is Microsoft Failover Clustering. There is significant interplay and cooperation between the two, but they are distinct. This duality of technologies can lead unaware users to draw false conclusions and fall into traps based on incorrect assumptions. It can also cause confusion for newcomers to Hyper-V Server and Microsoft Failover Clustering.

Microsoft clusters are always considered failover clusters. A single virtual machine does not coexist across cluster nodes. All of the resources belonging to any given virtual machine are contained in or accessed through only one node at a time. The cluster system handles system failures by automatically moving—failing over—virtual machines from an ailing node to others that are still running. This does not necessarily mean that other cluster nodes are idle; they can run other virtual machines.

The basic process by which Microsoft Failover Clustering operates is somewhat node-centric. Each node is responsible for three basic resource types: **roles**, **storage**, and **networks**. A clustered role is a service being presented and protected by the cluster. Each virtual machine (and accompanying resources) is considered a role. A virtual machine and its details must be stored in a location common to all nodes; each node is responsible for maintaining connectivity to that storage. Finally, each node must have access to the same networks as the other nodes.

Because of the failover nature of the cluster, roles and storage have *owners*. At any given point in time, one node is responsible for each individual instance of these resource types. A virtual machine's owner is the physical host it is currently running on (or would be responsible for starting it if the virtual machine is offline). A storage location's owner is the physical host that is currently responsible for I/O to that location. A special storage type that will be discussed in much more detail later is the **Cluster Shared Volume (CSV)**. Multiple nodes can communicate with a CSV simultaneously; however, it is still owned by only one node at a time (called a **coordinator node**). Networks do not have owners.

A failure does not always automatically result in a failover event. If a node has difficulty accessing storage or networks, there are various mitigation strategies it can take. If connectivity to a CSV is lost, it can reroute I/O through the coordinator node. If it is the coordinator node, it can transfer ownership to another node that can still reach the CSV. If a node loses connectivity on a cluster network but can still use others, it may be able to use those for cluster-related traffic.

If a failure that requires a node to stop participating in the cluster does occur, there are a few things that happen. First, if the node is still functional but detects a problem, it determines whether or not it can continue participating in the cluster. The primary failure that triggers this condition is loss of communications with the other nodes. If a node can no longer communicate with enough other nodes to maintain **quorum** (a concept that will be thoroughly discussed in *Chapter 11, High Availability*), it attempts to gracefully shut down its virtual machines so that their files can be accessed by other nodes. Ordinarily, quorum is achieved by 50 percent of the nodes plus one tiebreaker being active. The nodes that still have quorum may not be aware of why the node is missing, but they will notice that it is no longer reachable. They will begin attempting to start virtual machines from missing nodes almost immediately upon loss of connectivity. If there is no way for sufficient nodes to form a quorum, the entire cluster will stop and all clustered virtual machines will shut down.

Create a project document

Before you jump into the technology, build a document to outline your project. Even if you're in a small environment, there is great benefit in using a project planning document. Otherwise, your cluster's initial build and growth may be organic in nature — meaning that it will grow and change in response to immediate needs and concerns rather than following a predictable path. Such a cluster may not be appropriate for the loads you'd like it to handle. A planning document can be a simple free-form text sheet that you create in Notepad and use like a scratch pad or it could be a formally-defined organizational document built in Microsoft Word. Among other uses, this document will help you create a focus for the project so that as you work, you can more easily stay true to the initial vision.

If you don't have a formal process in place for design documents, then a suggested format for your document is to format it in three parts: an Overview section, a Purposes section, and a Goals section. The overview should contain a very brief explanation of what Hyper-V and Failover Clustering are and what your organization can expect to achieve by implementing them. This portion can help you to clarify the involved technologies for yourself and others. The *Purposes* section indicates the specific reasons that your organization is undertaking the project. The *Goals* section delineates the ways that the project is expected to meet those purposes. In a smaller environment, combining these two sections may be preferable. Also, unless you have a strict formal organizational structure for the document that precludes this, it's a good idea to include a notes section. You can use that section as a place to track ideas and links for subjects that you discover as your project progresses but which you cannot immediately investigate. If your organization has a policy that governs format and you aren't allowed to place these notes directly in the master planning document, create your own document and ensure that it stays in close proximity to the formal work.

Purposes for a Hyper-V Server cluster

There are several common reasons to group Hyper-V Server hosts into a cluster, but each situation is unique. Your particular purpose(s) will be the primary determinant in the goals you set for your cluster project. The following subsections will talk about the common purposes for building a cluster. Those that you include in your document should be specific to your environment. In a planning document, generic topics belong in the overview portion.

As you consider the technologies and solutions available in Hyper-V Server and Failover Clustering, remember that you are not required to utilize all of them. It's easy to get caught up in the flash and glamor of exciting possibilities and design a system that solves problems your organization doesn't actually have — usually with equally unrealistic price tags and time demands. This practice, infamously known as *over-architecting*, is a non-trivial concern. Whatever you build must be maintained into perpetuity, so don't saddle yourself, your co-workers, and your organization with complexities without a clear and demonstrable need.

High availability

One of the most common reasons to build a Hyper-V Server cluster is to provide high availability to virtual machines. **High availability** is a term that is often misunderstood, so ensure that you take the time to truly understand what it means and make sure you can explain it to anyone else who will be a stakeholder or otherwise involved in your cluster project. High availability is often confused with fault tolerance. A truly fault tolerant solution can handle the failure of any single component without perceptible downtime to the consumers of the service it is providing. Hyper-V Server has no built-in method to make the product completely fault tolerant. It is possible to leverage supporting technologies to provide fault tolerance at most levels, and it is possible to use Hyper-V Server as a component to provide fault tolerance for other scale-out technologies, but Hyper-V Server alone is not a fault tolerant solution.

In contrast to fault tolerance, Hyper-V Server provides high availability. This term means a few things. First, to directly compare it to fault tolerance, it provides for very rapid recovery after a major fault. Second, it grants the ability for planned moves of services without perceptible downtime for those services. The primary reason for this is planned maintenance of underlying hardware and supporting software. Of course, it can also be leveraged when a fault occurs but the system is able to continue functioning, such as when an internal drive in a RAID 1 array fails.

Hyper-V's high availability features do not grant virtual machines immunity against downtime. Approaches that may provide application-level immunity will be covered in *Chapter 11, High Availability*.

The most important distinction between fault tolerant and high availability in Hyper-V Server is that if a failure occurs that causes a Hyper-V Server host computer to fail without warning, such as a blue screen error, all of its virtual machines will crash. The Failover Cluster component will immediately begin bringing failed virtual machines back online on surviving cluster nodes. Those virtual machines will act the same way a physical installation would if its power had been removed without warning.

The following image is a visualization of Hyper-V Server in a cluster layered on fault tolerant subsystems. Despite the fact that the cluster's constituent components have suffered a number of failures, the virtual machines are still running (although likely with reduced performance):

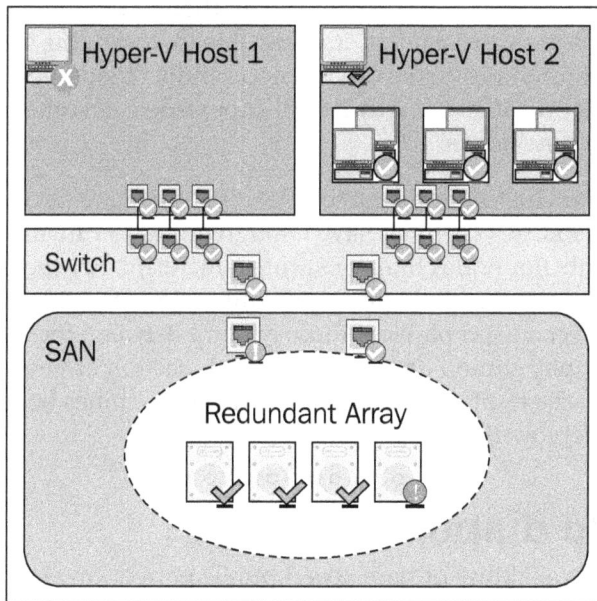

The subject of high availability will be explored more thoroughly later.

High Availability Printing

In Windows Server versions prior to 2012, you could create clusters specifically for the Windows print spooler service. While functional, this solution was never particularly stable. It was quite complicated and required a significant amount of hands-on maintenance. Print drivers provided by the hardware manufacturer needed to be specifically designed to support clustering, certain uses required administrative scripting, and problems were difficult to isolate and solve. In Windows Server 2012, Microsoft now defines **High Availability Printing** as a print spooler service running on a highly available virtual machine. You can no longer establish the print spooler itself as a clustered resource.

Balancing resources

The second most common reason to employ a Hyper-V Server cluster is to provide distribution of resources across multiple physical computers. When all of the nodes in a Hyper-V Server cluster are operational, you have the cumulative entirety of all their physical resources at your disposal. Even though the involved technology specifically mentions the word *failover*, it is possible to design the system in such a fashion that not all hosted resources can be successfully failed over. Virtual machines can be configured to prioritize the way they'll supersede each other when there is contention for limited resources.

When designing your cluster for resource balancing, there are two extremes. For complete high availability, you must have enough nodes to run all virtual machines on the smallest number of nodes that constitute a majority. For the highest degree of resource distribution, you must maximize the utilization of each node. In most cases, you'll gauge and select an acceptable middle ground between these two extremes. Your chosen philosophy should appear in the Goals section of your planning document. It's also wise to plan for additional virtual machines beyond those that will exist at initial deployment.

Geographic dispersion

With the increased availability of high speed public networking solutions across geographically dispersed regions, implementations of multi-site clusters are becoming more feasible. With a multi-site cluster, you can provide high availability even in the event of the loss of an entire physical site. These types of solutions are still relatively young and uncommon. Hyper-V Server does require a substantial amount of expensive supporting technology to make this possible, so ensure that you know all the requirements prior to trying to create such a system. These requirements will be discussed in greater depth in *Chapter 9, Special Cases*.

Natural replacement for aging infrastructure

Traditionally, organizations will purchase server hardware and software on an as-needed basis and keep it until it can no longer serve the purpose for which it was designed. A Hyper-V Server cluster is a natural place for their replacements to be created. Instead of provisioning new hardware to replace old equipment on a one-to-one basis, new hardware is only purchased when the capacity of an existing cluster is no longer sufficient.

Not only does employing a Hyper-V Server cluster slip nicely into the current hardware replacement stream, it can also completely reshape the way that hardware refreshes are handled. By decoupling hardware upgrades and replacements from software roles, an organization can upgrade software without waiting for a hardware refresh cycle. Without the dependency of software, the hardware can be replaced on any schedule that the organization desires; in some cases, and with careful planning, hardware can be upgraded without impacting hosted services. When a service impact is unavoidable, it is still likely to be substantially less intrusive than the normal physical-to-physical transition.

Test, development, and training systems

One of the defining features of a virtualized environment is isolation. Virtual machines are very effectively walled off from each other and the rest of your network unless you intentionally go through the steps to connect them. The ease of deploying new systems and destroying them once they've outlived their purpose is another key characteristic. Taken together, this facilitates a variety of uses that would be far more difficult in a physical environment. Of course, Hyper-V Server can provide this type of environment without a cluster. For some organizations, one or more of these roles are significant enough that they are just as demanding as production. For organizations at the opposite end who could never justify an entire cluster for such a purpose, the extra capacity extant in most clusters will almost undoubtedly provide enough room for a small test environment.

If you've never been in a position to be able to consider these uses before, you can create environments to test trial software releases without placing them on production systems. You can examine a suspicious application in an ephemeral sandbox environment where it can do no lasting harm. You can also duplicate a production system to safely test a software upgrade. You can even copy or emulate an end-user computer to train new users on a line-of-business application. Since all of these systems are as isolated from your live systems as you make them, the benefits provided by a testing environment and the ease with which a virtualization system can deliver it make this more of a strong point than might be obvious at first.

Cloud hosting

A term that has grown more rapidly in popularity than in comprehensibility is *cloud*. This term has so many unique definitions that they could be collected into a cloud of their own. With the 2012 release of server software products, Microsoft is pushing forward with the term and seems to be attempting to satisfy as many of the definitions as it can. One of the core technologies that they are pushing as a major component of their "cloud" solution is Hyper-V Server, especially when used in conjunction with Failover Clustering. Narrowing the scope of cloud to Hyper-V Server and Failover Clustering, what it means is that you can design an environment in which you can quickly create and destroy complete operating system environments as needed without being concerned with the underlying support structure. In order to create a true cloud environment using Microsoft technologies, you must also use **System Center Virtual Machine Manager 2012 (SCVMM)** with Service Pack 1 for a Hyper-V Server 2012 deployment or SCVMM 2012 R2 for a Hyper-V Server 2012 R2 deployment. With this tool, you'll be able to create these virtual machines without even being involved in which cluster node they begin life on. This nebulous provisioning of resources in an on-demand fashion and conceptually loose coupling of software and hardware resources is what qualifies Hyper-V Server as a component of a cloud solution.

Another aspect that allows Hyper-V Server to be considered a cloud solution is its ability to mix hardware in the cluster. As a general rule, this is not a recommended approach. You should strive to use the same hardware and software levels on every host in your cluster to ensure compatibility and smooth transitions of virtual machines. However, an organically growing cluster that is intended to function as a cloud environment can mix equipment if necessary. It is not possible to perform Live Migrations of virtual machines between physical hosts that do not have CPUs from the same manufacturer. Migrations between hosts that have CPUs that are from the same vendor but are otherwise mismatched may also present challenges to seamless migration. If your goals and requirements stipulate that extra computing resources be made available and some possible downtime is acceptable for a virtual machine that is being migrated, heterogeneous cluster configurations are both possible and useful.

Using Hyper-V Server to provide a cloud solution has two major strategies: *public clouds* and *private clouds*. You can create or expand your own hosting service that involves selling computing resources, software service availability, and storage space to end users outside your organization. You can provide a generic service that allows the end users to exploit the available system as they see fit, or you can choose to attempt to provide a niche service with one or more specialized pre-built environments that are deployed from templates. The more common usage of a Hyper-V Server cloud will be for private consumption of resources. Either usage supplies you with the ability to track who is using the available resources. This will be discussed in the following section.

Resource metering

A common need in hosted environments is the ability to meter resources. This should not be confused with measuring performance. The purpose of resource metering is to determine and track who is using which resources. This is commonly of importance in pay-as-you-go hosting models in which customers are only billed for what they actually use. However, resource metering has value even in private deployments. In a purely physical environment, it's not uncommon for individual departments to be responsible for paying for the hardware and software that is specific to their needs. One of the initial resistances to virtualization was the loss of the ability to determine resource utilization. Specifically in a Hyper-V Server cluster where the guest machines can travel between physical units at any time and share resources with other guests, it's no longer a simple matter of having a department pay for a physical unit. It also may not fit well with the organization's accounting practices to have just a single fund devoted to providing server hardware resources regardless of usage. Resource metering is an answer to that problem; usage can be tracked in whatever way the organization needs. These results can be periodically recorded and the individual departments or users can be matched to the quantity of resources that they consumed. This enables a practice commonly known as chargeback, in which costs can be precisely assigned to the consumer.

Hyper-V Server allows for metering of CPU usage, memory usage, disk space consumption, and network traffic. Third-party application vendors also provide extensions and enhancements to the basic metering package.

VDI and RemoteFX

Virtual Desktop Infrastructure (**VDI**) is a generic term that encompasses the various ways that desktop operating systems (such as Windows 8) are virtualized and made accessible to end-users in some fashion. VDI in Hyper-V Server is enhanced by the features of **RemoteFX**. This technology was introduced in the 2008 R2 version and provided superior video services to virtual desktops. RemoteFX was greatly expanded in Hyper-V Server 2012, especially when combined with Remote Desktop Services. A full discussion of these technologies is not included in this book, but if you intend to use them, they and their requirements must form a critical part of your planning and design. The hardware requirements and configuration steps are well-documented in a TechNet wiki article viewable at:

```
http://social.technet.microsoft.com/wiki/contents/articles/16652.
remotefx-vgpu-setup-and-configuration-guide-for-windows-server-2012.
aspx
```

Be open to other purposes

The preceding sections outlined some of the most common reasons to build a Hyper-V Server cluster, but the list is by no means all-inclusive. Skim through the remainder of this book for additional ideas. Look through community forums for ways that others are leveraging Hyper-V Server clusters to address their issues.

Goals for a Hyper-V Server cluster

Once you have outlined the reasons to build a Hyper-V Server cluster, the next step is to identify how your organization intends to benefit from the technology. Before you can fully flesh this portion out, you need to identify how the technology can and cannot be applied to your specific environment. The driving factor behind the work that builds this section is ensuring that expectations of the system are realistic. This is an exploratory process that includes a substantial number of activities.

Identify the resources that cannot be virtualized

Not every application can run in a virtualized environment. A very common reason is a dependence upon a piece of hardware that cannot be virtualized. Anything that requires access to a PCIe slot, a serial device, or a specific piece of parallel-connected equipment will likely be difficult or impossible to virtualize. As it fits within the Microsoft paradigm, a virtualized operating system needs to be portable between hosts without specific ancillary configuration requirements from one host to the next. These types of devices preclude that portability. Fortunately, there are ways to accommodate some types of hardware, such as USB devices. There will be a section on that later.

Consult with application vendors

Application vendors, even Microsoft, may require a specific environment for their software in order to continue providing support. There are many reasons why a software company may not wish to certify their applications on a Hyper-V Server cluster, so you'll need to contact those whose products you use to ensure that you'll continue to have access to the needed support lines.

Even if your vendors have already certified their applications on a standalone Hyper-V Server host, it does not necessarily follow that they will extend that support to a cluster environment. One such example is Microsoft Lync Server. Technologies like Live Migration appear to have no downtime because the normal disconnect time is less than the standard TCP/IP timeout. Even though it's brief, there is a break in service. This can cause problems for some applications.

Microsoft's application-specific support policy in regards to virtualization is viewable on their knowledgebase at `http://support.microsoft.com/kb/957006`.

Involve internal stakeholders

There are some non-technical investigations to be made. Clustering of physical resources expands the reach of your hardware that is dedicated to virtualization. An argument can be made that the traditional reasons to segregate resources onto separate hardware platforms are no longer relevant. You might be able to inspire other departments to join in on the project. This could bring additional resources and an interest in some of the more advanced technologies that Hyper-V Server and Failover Clustering have to offer. There may also be internal reasons to bring others onboard.

Define phases and timelines

Like any other major project, a Hyper-V Server cluster deployment is performed in phases. Each phase is composed of a number of subsections and steps. Setting timelines for these phases helps to frame the project for others, establishes reasonable expectations, and adds another dimension of focus to the project that can help keep it from falling to the wayside or getting mired in side projects. Typical phases for this type of project include planning, design, initial setup, pre-deployment testing, deployment, resource creation and migration, post-deployment testing, and maintenance. Each of these phases should be clearly indicated in the project document with an outline of what events each phase will include. Each phase outline should also include some rough dating for expected completion.

Perform further research

One phase that typically doesn't appear in the project document is the one that you may be in right now: the *Discovery* phase. This may appear in a different organizational document—perhaps one intended to track activity in the Information Technology department. The Discovery phase is essentially the development of the Goals and Purposes phases. A formal description of it might be a *feasibility study* in which you attempt to determine if a cluster of Hyper-V Servers is the right solution for your organization. Use the Discovery phase to address the problem of, "We don't know what we don't know."

To start, at least skim through the other chapters of this book and familiarize yourself with the concepts. It is highly recommended that you obtain a copy of Hyper-V Server or a trial of Windows Server and install and cluster it on a group of test computers. Look to Internet sources and forums for ways that others are exploiting these technologies in their organizations. Ask questions. Watch for any issues that others have had to determine if there are any pitfalls you need to be aware of before starting your own project. Don't restrict yourself to Hyper-V and Windows Server resources; forums and user groups for software you intend to virtualize can also be invaluable sources of insight.

Define success metrics

With a project of this scale, it is rarely sufficient to declare that the project has been successful based on any single factor. Use the project document to list the events that must occur in order for the project to be considered a success. It is advisable to break these up into *Critical* and *Desirable* groups. Normally, a project is not considered to be successfully completed when all items marked Critical have been satisfied, but when unfulfilled Desirable items do not impede progress.

Success metrics should be very specific in nature. Don't simply use entries like, "High availability is functional." Instead, use entries such as, "All virtual machines can be Live Migrated from Host 1 to Host 2". Also, define metrics that cover all aspects of the installation. Use things such as, "Can transfer ownership of all Cluster Shared Volumes from Host 2 to Host 4". Depending upon your organizational needs and processes, it is acceptable to use a shorter list of generic success metrics on your official document that refer to a more specific set of metrics kept separately.

Measure and predict your workload

If at all possible, you should know as early as possible what sort of computing resources will be required by the applications that you'll be placing in your cluster. How well you need to plan for this depends somewhat on the resources you have available. If you have the financial and technical resources available to add new nodes on demand, you can quickly scale a Hyper-V Server cluster out to handle new or unforeseen demands. In all other cases, proper advance planning can ensure that you don't underpower or overpower your systems.

If you're going to be virtualizing an existing physical workload or converting from another hypervisor deployment, you can gather performance metrics to help you determine how to build out your new systems. *Chapter 8, Performance Testing and Load Balancing* covers how to track performance for your cluster, and the same concepts and techniques can be applied to standalone computing systems. The most useful information will be around CPU consumption, memory usage, disk space, and disk IOPS (input/output per second). While it is tempting to just add all current dedicated resources (such as CPU counts and total RAM usage), these numbers are almost always artificially high because few computer systems fully utilize their hardware resources. Also keep in mind that if you will be relocating some systems from older hardware, advances in technology may require fewer resources to provide comparable performance. Track resource utilization over a period of time that includes a typical workload. Of course, since you are using virtual machines, you'll have the ability to add or remove CPU and memory resources and expand disk space with very little impact, so mis-provisioning is usually not a serious risk.

If your new cluster will include a new software deployment for which you have no existing implementation and therefore you cannot track live performance metrics, consult with the software vendor. Keep in mind that it is normal for software vendors to overestimate the actual amount of hardware that their systems require, but they may not support their applications on anything less.

Only allow changes during the planning phase

As you and other stakeholders learn more about the technologies and how they can apply to your environment, your goals and purposes will no doubt be expanded. Set a definite end point at which changes to the project's scope will no longer be accepted. Otherwise, you'll run the risk of *scope creep*, in which a project continually grows until it is no longer manageable. If further changes are desired but not required for the success of the project, they can be placed into a separate project to be completed after successful completion of the current endeavor. If you have no official guidelines, a logical point at which to cease allowing project changes is at the halfway mark of the time allotted to the *Design* phase.

Looking forward to the Design phase

Once you have set reasonable purposes and goals for your cluster project, the next phase involves designing the system that will achieve them. At a high level, this is little different from designing a system that is intended to host a single-purpose service in a non-virtualized environment. You first identify the expected load and then architect a solution that can comfortably bear it. You no doubt already have some idea of the volume of computing resources that will be demanded of your cluster. However, the nature of clustering does require some more understanding before you can begin outlining components to purchase.

Many of these concepts may seem obvious to you as a computing professional, but the early phases of a project will usually require the involvement and sometimes oversight from less technically proficient members of the organization. It is certainly not required that they become subject-matter experts, but they must be made aware of the general needs of the project so that they are not surprised when the requests for resources, time, and capital expenditures begin. Several items will need to have attention drawn to them in the early phases. Specific inclusion of those items in the project planning document is optional based on the needs of your organization and the overall size of your project. You might consider a *Solution Summary* section that briefly itemizes the components of the solution without providing any particular details. If your project is small enough or if there won't be many reviewers of the document itself, you may choose to skip including this section in favor of the more detailed list that will inevitably be included in the Design portion. However, the more simplistic layout may need to be built for presentations, and it can even be used as a basic checklist for the Design phase.

Host computers

A cluster involves multiple physical computer systems. As mentioned in the cloud discussion earlier, it's not absolutely required that each host be identical to the others, but it is certainly desirable. Virtual machines that move across differing hardware may suffer a noticeable performance degradation if the target doesn't have the same capabilities or configuration as the source. Where possible, these hosts should be purchased together prior to initial implementation. Adding nodes to a cluster requires more effort after that cluster has gone into production. Unlike a typical single-server physical deployment, it is common for the combined power of a cluster to provide significantly more computing resources than are actually required to provide the included services. This is because part of the purpose of a cluster is to provide failover capability.

Also, Hyper-V Server host by nature needs to run more than one operating system concurrently, so these systems may require more CPU cores and RAM than your organization is accustomed to purchasing for a single system. If possible, modify your organization's existing provisioning standards to accommodate the differences for virtualization hosts.

Storage

An element that clustering introduces is the need for *shared storage*. While it is technically possible to build a cluster that does not use shared storage, it is not practical. Out of the three main components of a virtual machine, the CPU threads and memory contents can only exist on one node at a time, but they can be rapidly transferred to another node. In the event of a host crash, these contents are irretrievably lost just as they would be if the machine were not virtualized. In a high availability solution, these are considered acceptable losses. However, the long-term data component, which includes configuration data about the virtual machine in addition to the contents of its virtual hard drives, is a protected resource that is expected to survive a host crash — just as it would be in a non-virtualized environment. If that data is kept on internal storage in a host that fails, there will be no way for another host to access it without substantial effort on the part of an administrator.

The files that comprise a highly available virtual machine must be placed in a location that all cluster nodes can access. There are some special-case uses in which only a subset of the nodes are allowed to access a particular storage location, but a virtual machine cannot be truly considered to be highly available unless it can run on more than one cluster node.

Cluster Shared Volumes

Shared storage involves both physical devices and logical components. The preferred way to logically establish shared storage for clustered Hyper-V Server computers is by using Cluster Shared Volumes (CSV). The name more or less explains what it does; it allows volumes to be shared across the nodes of a cluster. Contrast this to the traditional volume which can only be accessed by one computer at a time. In the term CSV, *Volumes* specifically refers to NTFS volumes. You cannot use any other format type (FAT, NFS, and so on) with a CSV (the new ReFS format is acceptable in 2012 R2, as will be discussed in *Chapter 4, Storage Design*).

In more technical terms, CSV is powered by a filter driver that a node uses to communicate with NTFS volumes that might also be accessed by other nodes simultaneously. The technical details of CSVs will be examined in much more depth in later chapters.

SMB shares

A powerful feature introduced with Windows Server 2012 is Version 3.0 of Microsoft's **server message block (SMB)** technology. Because it is typically used on file shares, SMB is usually thought of in terms of storage. In actuality, it is a networking protocol. Its applications to storage are why it is mentioned in this section. For one thing, Cluster Shared Volume communications between nodes are encapsulated in SMB. However, you can now create a regular SMB share on any computer running Windows Server 2012 or later and use it to host the files for a Hyper-V Server virtual machine. Hardware vendors are also working to design systems that provide SMB 3.0 shares. Many will use an embedded installation of Windows Storage Server; others will follow Microsoft's specification and design their own systems.

Mixing SMB 3.0 and CSV

You will cover the specific method(s) of provisioning and using storage during the Design phase, but the possibilities and applications need to be made clear as early as possible. Unless they're on a clustered file server, you cannot create a CSV on an SMB 3.0 share point, and creating an SMB 3.0 share on a CSV does not expose the existence of that CSV in a way that Hyper-V Server can properly utilize. However, a Hyper-V Server cluster can run some virtual machines from CSVs while running others on SMB 3.0 shares. The initial impact this has on planning is that if you have complex needs and/or a restrictive budget, there is no requirement to decide between a **storage area network (SAN)** or less expensive methods of storage. You can have both. If any of these concepts or terms are new to you, read through *Chapter 4, Storage Design*, before making any storage decisions.

The following image shows a sample concept diagram of a cluster that mixes storage connectivity methods:

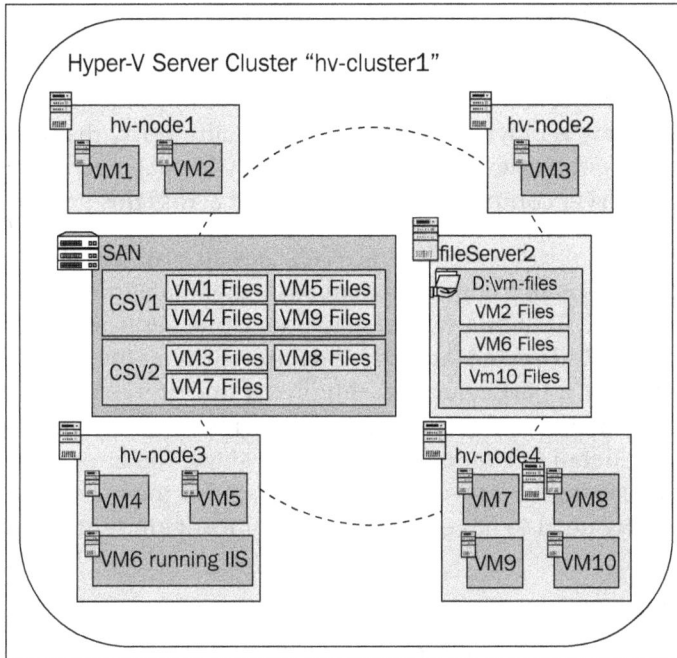

Hyper-V Server Cluster "hv-cluster1"

Networking

The networking needs of a Hyper-V Server cluster node are substantially different from those of a standalone system. A cluster node running Hyper-V Server involves three distinct networking components.

- Management
- Cluster and Cluster Shared Volume communications
- Live Migration traffic

Management

Management traffic involves regular communications to and from the management operating system of the variety that any Windows Server system would use. Examples include connections for Remote Desktop Connection clients, remote management consoles, monitoring tools, and backups that operate within the context of the management operating system. This connection is used as the host's identifier within the cluster and will be the target for cluster management software. Usually, the events that will generate the most bandwidth on this connection are file transfers to and from the host (such as .ISO files to be connected to virtual machines) and backup traffic moving from the hypervisor to a backup server on another computer.

Cluster and Cluster Shared Volumes

The individual nodes of a cluster need to communicate with each other directly, preferably over a network dedicated to inter-node communications. The traffic consists of "heartbeat" information in which the nodes continually verify that they can see each other. Information about cluster resources, specifically virtual machines in the case of a cluster of Hyper-V Server computers, is synchronized across this network.

Communications related to Cluster Shared Volumes also utilizes this network. In normal operations, this is nothing more than basic metadata information such as ownership changes of a CSV or a virtual machine. However, some conditions can trigger what is called **Redirected Access Mode**, in which all the disk operations for the virtual machines on a particular node involving one or more CSVs are routed through the node(s) that own the affected CSV(s). This mode and its triggers will be looked at in greater detail in later chapters. At this stage, the important information is that if you will be using CSVs, you need to prepare for the possibility that cluster communications may need to have access to a significant amount of bandwidth.

Live Migration

A **Live Migration** involves the transfer of the active state of a virtual machine from one node to another. There is a small amount of configuration data that goes along, but the vast majority of the information in this transfer is the active contents of the virtual machine's memory. The amount of bandwidth you make available for this network translates directly into how quickly these transfers occur. The considerations for this will be thoroughly examined later. For now, understand that this network needs access to a substantial amount of bandwidth.

Subnetting

Each of these traffic types must be isolated from the others on their own subnets with the possible exception of cluster communications. This is a requirement of Microsoft Failover Clustering and, for the most part, cannot be circumvented. In some organizations, this will involve calling upon a dedicated networking team to prepare the necessary resources for you. Until you enter the actual Design phase, you won't be able to tell them much beyond the fact that you'll need at least two, and probably more, subnets to satisfy the requirements. However, unless you intend to isolate your Hyper-V Server hosts and/or you expect your cluster to have enough nodes that it might overwhelm currently allocated ranges, the subnet that contains your management traffic can be an existing IP infrastructure. Depending on the capability of your networking equipment and organizational practices, you may also choose to place your IP networks into distinct **virtual LANs (VLANs)**.

The VLAN is a networking concept that has been in widespread use for quite some time, and it is not related to hypervisors or virtual machines. Windows Server's networking stack and Hyper-V's virtual switch are fully capable of handling traffic in separate VLANs. This book will explain how to configure Hyper-V accordingly, but your network equipment will have its own configuration needs. Work with your networking team or provider if you need guidance.

Virtual machine traffic

A fourth traffic type you must design for is that used by the virtual machines. Unlike the traffic types mentioned previously, this is not a cluster-defined network. In fact, Microsoft Failover Clustering in 2012 is not at all aware of the existence of your virtual machine network setup. R2 adds visibility for protection purposes, but it is not a true cluster network. Virtual machine traffic is controlled entirely by Hyper-V Server via the virtual switch. It is recommended that you use at least a one gigabit network adapter for this role, but it is possible for it to share with a cluster role if necessary. If using gigabit adapters, Microsoft only supports this sharing with the management role and only in a particular configuration. The actual amount of bandwidth required will depend on how much your virtual machines need. You will revisit this during the Design phase.

Virtual machine traffic does not require a dedicated subnet. Any virtual machine can access any subnet or VLAN that you wish.

Storage traffic

iSCSI is a commonly used approach to providing access to shared storage for a Hyper-V Server cluster environment. If you're not familiar with the term, iSCSI is a method of encapsulating traditional **Small Computer Systems Interface** (**SCSI**) commands into IP packets. SCSI in this sense refers to a standardized command set used for communications with storage devices. If you will be using iSCSI, it is recommended that this traffic be given its own subnet. Doing so reduces the impact of broadcast traffic on I/O operations and provides a measure of security against intruders.

If your storage system employs multi-path or you have multiple storage devices available, you will occasionally see recommendations that you further divide the separate paths into their own subnets as well. Testing for the true impact of this setup has not produced conclusive results, so it is likely to require more effort than it's worth. Unless you have a very large iSCSI environment or a specific use case that clearly illustrates the rationale for multiple iSCSI networks, a single subnet should suffice.

SMB 3.0 traffic should also be given its own subnet. Like iSCSI, SMB 3.0 can take advantage of multiple network adapters. Unlike iSCSI, using multiple paths to SMB 3.0 storage requires one subnet per path.

Physical adapter considerations

It is recommended that you provide each traffic type with its own gigabit adapter. If necessary, it is possible for the roles to share fewer adapters, all the way down to a single gigabit network interface card. This can cause severe bottlenecks and Microsoft will only support such role-sharing in specific configurations. If you will be using ten-gigabit adapters, the recommendations are much more relaxed. These are important considerations early on as it's not uncommon for a Hyper-V Server host to have more than six network adapters. Many organizations are not accustomed to purchasing hardware with that sort of configuration, so this may require a break from standardized provisioning processes.

All physical adapters are not created equally. While the only base requirement is to use gigabit adapters, other features are available that can provide enhanced network performance. One of these features is **VMQ (virtual machine queue)**, which allows a guest to bypass some of the hypervisor's processing for incoming traffic. More recent technologies that Hyper-V Server can take advantage of are **remote direct memory access (RDMA)** and **single-root input/output virtualization (SR-IOV)**.

These technologies are becoming increasingly common, but they are currently only available on higher-end adapters. *Chapter 6, Network Traffic Shaping and Performance Enhancements*, is devoted to these and other advanced networking technologies.

Adapter teaming

Windows Server 2012 introduced the ability to form teams of network adapters natively within the operating system. In previous Windows versions, teaming required specific support from hardware manufacturers. It was usually not possible to create a single team across adapters of different hardware revisions or from different manufacturers. The quality of teaming could vary significantly from one driver set to the next. As a result, teams sometimes caused more problems than they solved. Microsoft official policy has always been to support Windows networking only when no third-party teaming solution is present.

With built-in support for adapter teaming, many new possibilities are available for Hyper-V Server cluster nodes. These will be discussed in great detail in later chapters. What is important to know now is that the technology is available and directly supported by Microsoft. One major misconception about this technology deals with bandwidth aggregation.

If you or other interested parties have particular expectations of this feature, you may benefit from reading ahead through *Chapter 5, Network Design*. In simple terms, the primary benefits of adapter teaming are load balancing and failover. Teaming also paves the way for converged fabric, which is also explained in *Chapter 5, Network Design*.

Active Directory

Microsoft Failover Clustering requires the presence of an **Active Directory** domain. The foundational reason is that the nodes of a cluster need to be able to trust that the other member computers are who they say they are, and the definitive tool that Microsoft technology relies on to make that determination is Active Directory. A Microsoft Failover Cluster also creates an Active Directory computer object that represents the entire cluster to other computers and some services. This object isn't quite as meaningful for a cluster of Hyper-V Server machines as it is for other clustered services, such as Microsoft SQL Server, but the object must exist. Other supporting technologies, such as Cluster Shared Volumes and SMB 3.0 shares that host virtual machines, are also dependent on Active Directory.

The requirement for Active Directory needs to be made obvious prior to the Design phase, as it may come as a surprise to some. Hyper-V Server itself does not require a domain, and as such it is not uncommon to find organizations that configure stand-alone Hyper-V Server hosts in workgroup mode to host publicly-accessible services in an untrusted perimeter or isolation network. This can be achieved through the natural isolation of virtual machines provided by Hyper-V Server and a better understanding of the virtual switch.

Virtualized domain controllers

Virtualizing domain controllers is an issue that is not without controversy. There are some very important pros and cons involved. Windows Server 2012 eliminated the more serious problems and planned placement of virtualized domain controllers can address most of the rest. It is not necessary that any decisions about this subject be made at this point of design; in fact, unless you don't have a domain environment yet, it can wait until after the virtualization project is complete. However, it should be brought up early on, so you may wish to make yourself aware of the challenges now. This topic will be fully explored in *Chapter 9, Special Cases*.

Supporting software

A Microsoft Hyper-V Server and a Microsoft Failover Cluster can both be managed using tools built into Windows Server and freely downloadable for Windows 8/8.1. However, there are many other applications available that go beyond what the basic tools can offer. You should begin looking into these products early on to determine what their feature sets are and if those features are of sufficient value to your organization to justify the added expenditure.

Management tools

Multiple tools exist that can aid you in maintaining and manipulating Hyper-V Server and Failover Clustering. The Remote Server Administration Tools, which are part of the previously mentioned tools built into Windows Server and downloadable for Windows 8/8.1, include Hyper-V Manager and Failover Cluster Manager. There are also a plethora of PowerShell commands available for managing these technologies. It is entirely possible to manage all aspects of even a large Hyper-V Server cluster using only these tools. However, the larger your cluster or the less time you have available, the more likely it is that you'll want to employ more powerful software assistants.

Foremost among these tools is **Microsoft System Center Virtual Machine Manager (SCVMM)**. This tool adds a number of capabilities, especially if it is used in conjunction with the larger System Center family of products. Be aware that you must be using at least Service Pack 1 of the 2012 release of this product in order to manage a Hyper-V Server 2012 system and at least version 2012 R2 in order to manage Hyper-V Server 2012 R2.

Third-party management products exist for Hyper-V Server and the market continues to grow. Take some time to learn about them, and if possible, test them out.

To aid you in defining your criteria, there are some commonly-asked-for features that the free Hyper-V Manager and Failover Cluster Manager tools don't provide:

- Conversion of physical machines to virtual machines (often called *P2V*)
- Templates—stored copies of virtual machines that serve as basic pre-built images that can be deployed as needed
- Cloning of virtual machines
- Automated balancing of virtual machines across nodes
- Centralized repositories for CD and DVD image files that can be attached to virtual machines on any node on-demand

- "Self-service" capabilities in which non-administrators can deploy their own virtual machines as needed

- Extensions to the Hyper-V virtual switch

You don't necessarily need all of these features, nor is it imperative that a single product provide all of them. What's important is identifying the features that are meaningful to your organization, what package(s) provide those features, and, if necessary, what you are willing to pay for them.

Backup

Backup is a critical component of any major infrastructure deployment. Unfortunately, it is often not considered until a late stage of virtualization projects. Virtualization adds options that aren't available in physical deployment. Clustered virtual machines add challenges that aren't present in other implementations.

The topic of backup will be more thoroughly examined in *Chapter 12*, *Backup and Disaster Recovery*, but the basic discussion about it can't wait. Begin collecting the names of applications that are candidates. Windows Server, including Hyper-V Server, includes Windows Server Backup. This tool can be made to work with a cluster, but it is generally insufficient for all but the smallest deployments. Ensure that the products you select for consideration are certified for the backup method you intend to perform. If your plan will be to back up some or all virtual machines from within the hypervisor, your backup application will need to provide specific support for Hyper-V Server in a Microsoft Failover Clustering Environment.

Training

Depending upon the size of your deployment and your staff, you may need to consider seeking out training resources for your systems administrator(s). Hyper-V Server and Failover Clustering are not particularly difficult to use after a successful implementation, but the initial learning curve can be fairly steep. It is entirely possible to learn them both through a strictly hands-on approach with books such as this one. Microsoft provides a great deal of free introductory material through the Microsoft Virtual Academy at `http://www.microsoft virtualacademy.com` and in-depth documentation on TechNet at `http://technet.microsoft.com`. However, some of your staff may require formal classroom training or other methods of knowledge acquisition.

A sample Hyper-V Cluster planning document

To help you get started, the following is a sample document for a fictional company called *Techstra*. Techstra is a medium-sized company that provides technical training on a wide array of subjects. Due to inefficiencies in resource allocation and the hardware lifecycle, their Director of Operations, who also holds the role of Chief Technology Officer, has decided to pilot a program in which a single cluster of computers running Hyper-V Server will host a variety of virtual machines. Traditionally, Techstra has grouped its computer resources by the roles that they provide, but the vision for this project is that a single large cluster will eventually run all of Techstra's server systems. There is also some talk about adding in desktop systems and creating a virtual desktop infrastructure, but there are no firm plans.

Techstra is not large enough to have dedicated technology project managers, but it is large enough to handle a project of this magnitude in-house. With the preceding information in hand, a senior systems administrator has been tasked with performing the necessary research and drawing up project documentation for review. What follows is an excerpt from such a document.

Sample project title – Techstra Hyper-V Cluster Project

Sample project overview: Techstra is faced with the challenges of managing a multitude of hardware platforms that are not consistently synchronized, maintained, utilized, or retired. To address these problems, Microsoft Hyper-V Server and Microsoft Failover Clustering will be implemented. Microsoft Hyper-V Server is a virtualization platform that allows for multiple operating systems to run on a single computer system inside virtual machines. Microsoft Failover Clustering will be used to group several physical computer systems running Microsoft Hyper-V Server together to provide redundancy and resource distribution for these virtual machines.

Key personnel for this project are the Information Technology Department Manager, Senior Systems Administrator, and Senior Network Administrator.

Personnel to keep updated on project progress are the Director of Operations, Education Department Manager, Internet Presence Department Manager, and Marketing Department Manager.

Sample project – purposes

The specific purposes of this project are as follows:

- Hardware consolidation
- Hardware lifecycle management
- Isolation of test and training systems
- Rapid turnover for training systems
- Provisioning of systems by the training department without involving systems administrative staff
- Embodiment of corporate *We Use What We Teach* philosophy
- Migration path for a number of physical servers that are reaching end-of-life
- Longevity protection for two line-of-business applications that cannot be upgraded or replaced and that require operating systems that are no longer being sold

Sample project – goals

The goals for this project are as follows:

- Deployment of three physical hosts running Hyper-V Server
- Deployment of one internally-redundant SAN device for high-performance workloads
- Deployment of two general-purpose server-class computers running Windows Server 2012 with a file share for workloads with low performance needs but high capacity requirements
- Conversion of seven physical server deployments to the virtual environment
- Expansion of existing System Center 2012 deployment to include Virtual Machine Manager
- Systems administrators trained on Hyper-V Server, Hyper-V Manager, Failover Cluster Manager, and System Center Virtual Machine Manager
- Virtual machines backed up in accordance with corporate data protection and retention policy

Sample project – success metrics (subsection of goals)

For this project to be considered successfully completed, all of the following conditions must be demonstrably satisfied:

- All virtual machines expected to provide services to other computers must be available and reachable outside of planned downtime windows
- On initial deployment, the cluster will be operating at no more than 70 percent of the resource capacity of two nodes under probable demand conditions
- The Hyper-V Server cluster must be able to survive the complete failure of any one node
- All cluster nodes can communicate with each other on all designated paths.
- The cluster can survive the failure of any single physical networking component
- Virtual machines that were running on a failed or isolated node must be available within 10 minutes
- All high availability virtual machines can be successfully Live Migrated from any host to any other host
- If any node is manually shut down or restarted, its high availability virtual machines are gracefully moved to other nodes
- All cluster nodes are being patched according to the corporate standard
- All virtual machines are being backed up according to the corporate standard
- Backups of virtual machines can be successfully restored
- Systems administrators responsible for supporting the Hyper-V Server cluster demonstrate reasonable competence and comprehension with its components according to their level, as follows:
    - Help desk personnel can identify a failover event
    - Help desk personnel can identify a failed node
    - Help desk personnel can make reasonable predictions of service restoration for virtual machines on failed nodes
    - Junior systems administrators can satisfy all expectations of help desk personnel
    - Junior systems administrators can deploy new virtual machines from templates
    - Junior systems administrators can verify proper operation of and correct minor issues within patching systems

- ° Junior systems administrators can verify proper operation of and correct minor issues within backup systems

- ° Junior systems administrators demonstrate an understanding of resource allocation and load balancing including CPU, memory, and hard disk space

- ° Junior systems administrators understand the monitoring systems and are familiar with the procedures for event handling

- ° Senior systems administrators can satisfy all expectations of help desk personnel and junior systems administrators

- ° Senior systems administrators can make changes to the infrastructure

- ° Senior systems administrators can restore virtual machines

- ° Senior systems administrators can add, remove, and replace cluster nodes

- Non-IT staff that have been granted the ability to provision their own virtual machines are demonstrably able to do so

Review the sample project

Take some time to review the sample project and compare it to the stated parameters in its introduction and with the guidance provided earlier in the chapter. Take notice both of what is there and what isn't there.

The *Success Metrics* portion is easily the longest section, and in an actual project would be much longer. It is intentionally quite specific in nature. Filling this portion with seemingly minute details can help ensure that no stone is left unturned and that no eventuality is unplanned for. If this section is properly laid out and all of its conditions met, you are virtually guaranteed a successful deployment free of surprises.

Even though the introductory material discussed virtual desktops, there is no mention of it in the Goals or Purposes sections. While not directly stated, it is inferred that VDI is a nice-to-have feature, not a primary driver. This would be a prime example of an opportunity to set limits on the scope of the project. As you can see, each item in the project goals translates directly to a large number of success metrics, so there is a definite benefit in restricting how much you take on. In this case, the director that initiated the project has indicated that this is a pilot, which implies that it is expected that if the deployment is successful, it will be expanded at a later date. The fictitious systems administrator tasked with writing this document has elected to try to hold off on a VDI implementation for a later expansion project.

Even though the formal document skips over VDI, the project notes should contain reference to it. The director did indicate his desire to have a single large cluster to handle anything that the company chooses to virtualize. If there are any special requirements of a VDI deployment that the initial hardware cannot satisfy, then it may be difficult to meet the director's desire for a single cluster. The decision will need to be made to expend resources to ensure that the initial hardware can handle any load that would ever be expected of it or to assess the feasibility of a single cluster versus two (or more) and against the usage of a single cluster augmented by one or more standalone Hyper-V Server systems. One way to bring this into the formal document would be to introduce it as a "Desirable" goal.

As it stands, this project document would be considered to be in draft form. The author was able to make some practical decisions regarding its contents and layout, but encountered at least one decision point that will need to be handled at a higher level and/or by group discussion. This should only be considered a beginning point for the planning phase, not the end.

Once these initial portions of the plan have been approved, the next step is to outline the remaining phases and the timelines they will be completed in. Those are procedural processes whose execution will depend upon your organization's operations.

Summary

Microsoft Hyper-V Server and Microsoft Failover Clustering are two powerful technologies that, when combined, provide great opportunities to protect your computing workloads and to more fully exploit your hardware resources. These technologies encompass a large number of concepts with an attendant terminology bank. Mastery of these concepts and terminology are critical to properly utilizing the technology.

Another vital component of a successful deployment is planning. A document that codifies the constituent steps of the project is a simple way to guide its progress and keep it on target. The success of a project can almost always be measured by the quality of the planning that went into it.

To understand a Hyper-V Server cluster and to properly plan to deploy one, you must possess an awareness of the components and resources that it will require.

Once you have successfully defined the parameters of your project, you are ready to move on to designing a cluster that fulfills them. This will be the focus of the next chapter. If you are building a project document, it is not necessary — in fact, it is not recommended — that you finalize the goals and purposes portions prior to moving on to design. These sections should be fairly firm at this point, but you should also allow for situations that you encounter during design to influence these earlier parts.

2
Cluster Design and Planning

A Microsoft Hyper-V Server cluster involves many components. Designing such a cluster requires you to understand how those components operate, what they need, and how they will interact. This chapter will extend beyond the basic introductory material of *Chapter 1, Hyper-V Cluster Orientation*, and take a closer look at the technologies and what you will need to implement them.

By the end of this chapter, we will have covered:

- Determining requirements of existing physical systems that will be moved into the virtual environment
- Designing a Hyper-V Server cluster with sufficient capacity for CPU, disk, network, and memory resources
- Planning for shared storage devices for the cluster
- Planning networking for the cluster
- Licensing considerations in virtualization and cluster environments
- Deciding between 2012 and 2012 R2
- Planning for physical placement of cluster-related equipment
- The security considerations and options for a Hyper-V Server cluster

Starting the design phase

If you are following a project document as recommended in *Chapter 1, Hyper-V Cluster Orientation*, then you should have completed the first part of the planning phase by defining your purposes and goals. The design phase is the second portion of planning in which you architect a solution to achieve those goals. In this phase, you will specify the hardware to acquire and their necessary configurations. You will begin by understanding what is necessary to run Hyper-V Server in a cluster and then size it to meet your specific needs.

Planning for existing systems

If you will be moving existing software loads into your new Hyper-V Server cluster, you'll need to determine what sort of resources they'll need to have access to. If you followed the earlier chapter, you've already determined which workloads cannot be virtualized. If not, make that determination before you start gathering metrics.

Deciding how you will virtualize physical systems

There are two basic approaches to moving physical systems into a Hyper-V Server cluster. The first is to perform a **physical-to-virtual** (**P2V**) conversion. The P2V process is a direct transfer of an operating system environment installed directly on hardware that copies it into a virtual equivalent. Aside from the *hardware* components, the server and installed applications do not change. The second approach is to create an empty virtual operating system environment and migrate applications and data.

Both P2V and migration approaches have their merits and drawbacks. P2V has a much higher failure rate but the process is usually straightforward. Microsoft does not provide any free method to perform a complete P2V function. It is available in System Center Virtual Machine Manager 2012 but has been removed in R2. You can use Disk2Vhd, part of Microsoft's Sysinternals suite, to create a VHD from the disks of a physical system, although it has a number of limitations. You can then create a new VM and attach the VHD. You can find this tool at `http://www.sysinternals.com`. Note that P2V conversions may have operating system and application licensing implications.

Migration is usually more involved but results in a clean system. The basic process is to build a completely new virtual machine or copy from an empty template. Applications are migrated according to their manufacturer's instructions. You can contact any relevant software or systems support teams for assistance.

This book will not directly cover either approach, as its focus is on the operation of Hyper-V Server in a cluster.

Determining requirements for existing systems

For many software applications and servers, you can work with the vendor to come up with a configuration for virtual operating systems that will handle the load. Unfortunately, few environments are that simple. It is highly likely that at least a few systems are handling multiple applications simultaneously. Other systems may host applications that have been designed in-house and as such have no formal requirement lists. It is tempting to simply duplicate the parameters of existing deployments into virtual counterparts. This will certainly address the issue, but because it is common to over-provision standalone systems, it is almost as certain to waste resources. Since it is fairly trivial to add power to a virtualized operating system, it is best to size individual virtual machines to their anticipated load. Build your hosts to match those expectations with some extra capacity.

There are two basic approaches to sizing virtualization hosts for existing physical workloads. The first, and easiest, is to use the Microsoft Assessment and Planning Toolkit. This is a largely automated system that measures your existing workload and then compares it to a defined hardware set. The second method, which requires more effort on your part but provides more detailed information, uses Performance Monitor to gather usage statistics. Either choice has its own benefits and drawbacks, so you may select a hybrid approach.

Microsoft Assessment and Planning Toolkit

The **Microsoft Assessment and Planning Toolkit (MAP)** is a free solution accelerator that is intended to aid you in planning for several scenarios. Two of these are server virtualization and desktop virtualization.

The toolkit is an installable application. It is periodically updated, so the best place to look for installation requirements and downloads is on its primary TechNet page: `http://aka.ms/map`. The tool will run on a single computer and remotely scan all computers that you ask it to. It will store its results in a database; if you don't indicate otherwise, it will create a local instance of Microsoft SQL Server 2008 Express for the purpose. For ease of use and to ensure that the toolkit itself does not interfere with results, it is recommended that you run it from a management workstation and allow it to create the local database.

Not urgent to remove, but this was mentioned in the previous paragraph. The following instructions and images were taken from Version 8.5. If you are using a later version, don't worry. The tool is well-designed and you should have little trouble finding what you need. If you are using an older version, it may not support current products, so you are encouraged to update prior to continuing.

To use MAP to prepare physical machines for deployment as Hyper-V Server guests:

1. Download and run the installation package. If any prerequisites are missing, the installer will stop and provide links. You'll need to meet those prerequisites and then restart the installer.

2. On the tool's first run, it will ask you to create a database or connect to an existing one, as shown in the following screenshot. Data that is collected about your environment will be stored in this database and can be referred to or extended at any time. While not covered in this book, the tool can be used for other purposes besides physical-to-virtual planning, so you may wish to use a generic database name. Upon giving your database a name and optionally a description, click on **OK**.

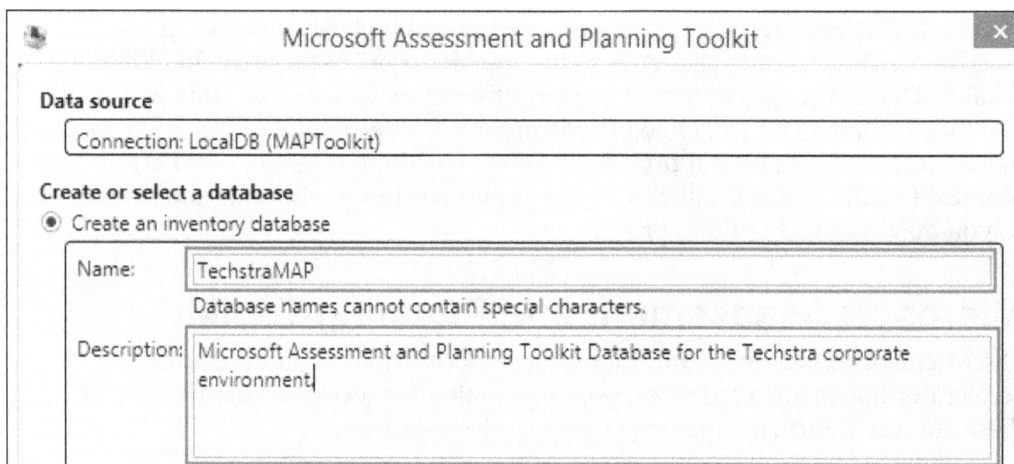

3. After the database has been created (or populated if you connected to an existing one), you will be left at the primary screen. Feel free to explore the application as much as you wish. This book only discusses server virtualization, so when you are ready to proceed, switch to that tab. The **Server Virtualization** tab is partially shown in the following screenshot:

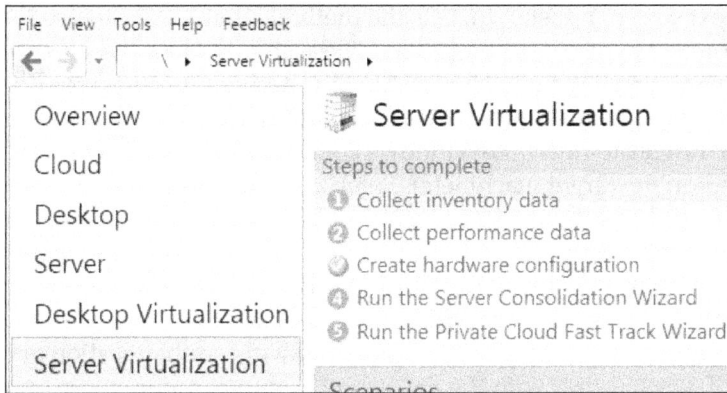

4. There are five possible steps to perform. You're likely to only run four; you probably won't need both steps **4** and **5**. Begin by clicking on **1 Collect inventory data**.

5. The inventory screen, partially shown in the following screenshot (the missing portion includes only the **Previous**, **Next**, **Cancel**, and **Finish** buttons), displays all possible inventory scenarios for the application. For the purposes of server virtualization, the first three are the only ones that will be used in this process, although you can include any in your inventory that you wish. Once you have made your selections, click on **Next**.

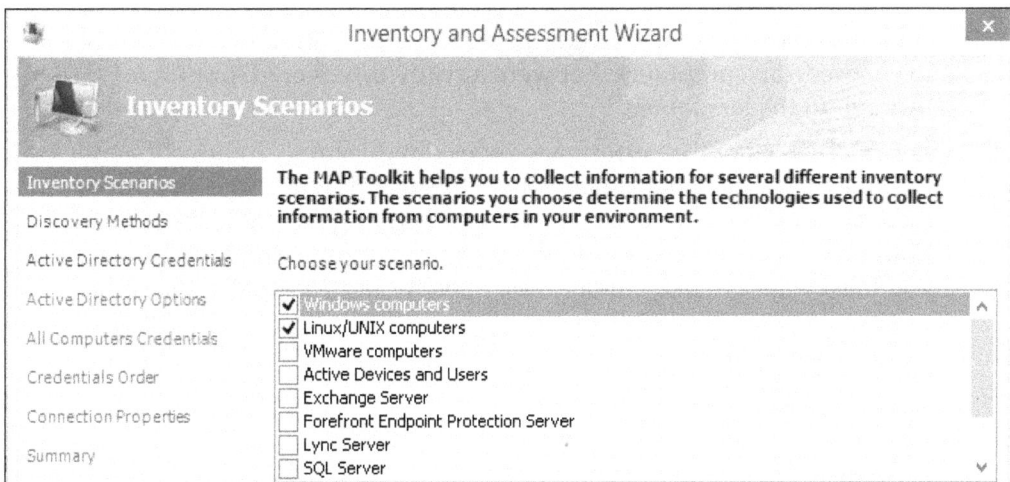

6. The next screen, not shown, lists the methods that MAP can use to discover and connect to network computers. These should be fairly self-explanatory. In general, you'll want to choose **AD DS (Active Directory)** for domain computers, **Windows protocols** for non-domain-joined Windows computers, and **IP ranges** to find non-Windows computers. Firewalls will need to be opened on the target machine(s). Refer to the help files if you need further assistance. The subsequent screens will ask you for the necessary information to satisfy the discovery methods that you chose. Windows targets will use the credentials you specify for WMI. Linux and UNIX targets will use the credentials you specify for SSH. Ensure that an SSH server is available on those units and that they only require password authentication and do not use SSL keys; confer with the SSL server documentation in use on your distribution for more information. Upon clicking on **Finish**, the discovery will run.

7. Once the inventory process has completed, close that window to return to the main screen, which should still be on the Server Virtualization tab. Click on **2 Collect Performance Data**.

8. This screen, also not shown, asks you to choose whether to run performance metrics for Windows machines, Linux machines, or both. You'll also need to select the amount of time for the performance trace to run. The longer the gatherers are allowed to run, the more thorough the results will be. It is recommended that you allow them to run for a week or two over a time when standard workloads will run and at least one expected heavy workload will occur. The following screens will look similar to those from the inventory screen, although now you'll be able to choose from computers that were already discovered. Continue through to the last screen.

9. The final screen of the performance scan should simply indicate that it is running on the designated machines. However, it will also notify you if there are any problems connecting to or operating on any of the targets. You can close this window and the scan will continue running. However, you must leave the main application open for the duration of the scan.

10. Once the scan completes, you can run through **3 Create Hardware Configuration**, where you can edit or define the hardware that you'll be running your comparison against. You can choose to edit or create single hosts or *infrastructures*, which adds in shared storage. The problem with the infrastructure option is that you must set a minimum of four hosts. If you'll be creating a two-node cluster, do not select infrastructure; a failover event will reduce your cluster to one operative node, so you need to ensure that a single node can handle your projected workload.

11. When prepared, click on **4 Run the Server Consolidation Wizard**. On the first screen, select the option for **Windows Server 2012 Hyper-V** and click on **Next**. You can edit hardware on the next screen much like under option three.

12. After the hardware screens, you'll be presented with the **Utilization Settings** page, shown in the following screenshot. Select your target utilization percentages; they default to 100%, but you'll want to reduce them at least to a percentage that will allow for one or more host failures, especially if you intend to add virtual machines later.

Server Virtualization and Consolidation Wizard

Utilization Settings

Virtualization Technology

Hardware Configuration

Utilization Settings

Choose Computers

Computer List

Summary

Specify the utilization settings to use when consolidating.

This defines a ceiling on resources of the infrastructure or the host in which the virtual machines will be placed. Defining a reasonable ceiling limit on the resources allows for periodic spikes in performance.

Processor	80	(50 - 100) %
Memory	80	(50 - 100) %
Storage Capacity	80	(50 - 100) %
Storage IOPS	60	(50 - 100) %
Network Throughput	60	(50 - 100) %

13. On the **Computer List** screen, as seen in the following screenshot, you'll be given a choice between selecting computers from a previous scan or importing from a file. Accept the default choice and continue to the next screen. Notice here that the tool can identify some special load types. Choose the computers that you want to include in the plan and click on **Next**.

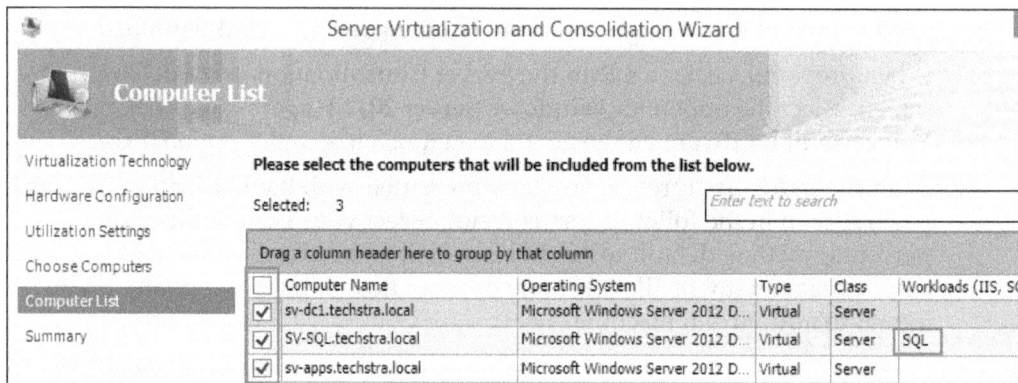

14. The assessment will run. Click on the **Close** button when it completes. You will be returned to the main window. Underneath the **Scenarios** section, shown as follows, will be listed the number of hosts you'll need to handle the indicated workload with the hardware that you've specified.

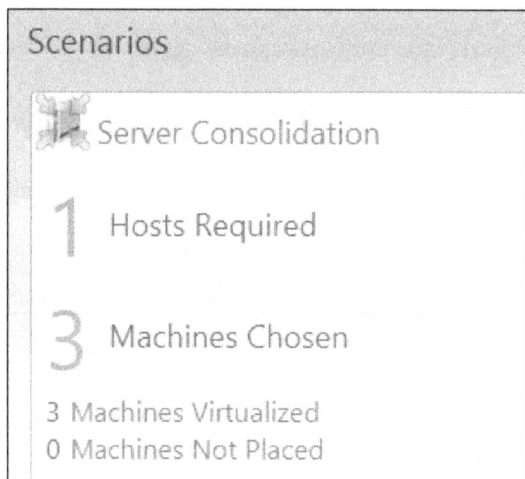

15. If you click on the panel, you'll be taken to a screen with more details about the plan. Underneath the synopsis is a **Host Summary** section that will show you the projected utilization percentages. An example image is shown as follows:

Host Summary							
Host Name	CPU Utilization(%)	Memory Utilization(...	IOPS	Disk Utilization(GB)	Network Throughp...	Virtual Machines Ho...	
Host1	5.08	3.139	5	49.52	0.00	3	

Performance Monitor

The most comprehensive way to plan for the existing physical loads is to track their performance in Performance Monitor. If you're not familiar with this tool, turn to the chapter on performance monitoring for usage instructions. As you would with MAP, use a fairly idle computer to collect performance metrics from the systems you plan to virtualize and have it track all systems for a representative amount of time. One to two weeks usually provides a fairly accurate performance picture. Unlike MAP, Performance Monitor only works on Windows systems. Third-party monitoring tools are also available if Performance Monitor cannot provide the results you need.

The Performance Monitor metrics that are of most value are as follows:

- Memory: Available Mbytes
- Memory: Pages / sec
- Network interface: Bytes total / sec
- Physical disk: % Disk Time
- Physical disk: Avg Disk Queue Length
- Physical disk: Disk Bytes / sec
- Physical disk: Disk Transfers/sec
- Processor: % Processor Time
- Server work queues: Active Threads

The above metrics were taken from a Windows Server 2012 computer; other Windows versions may be somewhat different, but they will all have similar objects. Also, there may be value in getting separate read and write measurements from disk objects and separate send and receive measurements from network objects. This is because there are ways to balance disk and network configurations that favor one over the other. Balance is usually preferred in a virtualization environment due to load variety, but if your workloads seem to favor a particular direction, you may choose to architect to accommodate that.

Of course, these metrics are generic in nature. If you anticipate a certain need that these metrics won't capture, feel free to design any tracking method that monitors the objects you are interested in. For instance, if you are considering the migration of a specific application and not its entire server, you can set monitors on that application's activity. Additionally, applications can create and register their own counters that Performance Monitor can track. Active Directory and Exchange Server are among these.

General approaches to reading the metrics

What you're mostly interested in is how the machines behave on average. Peak activity periods will come and go, but unless they are sustained you may not want to consider them too strongly. For instance, if a CPU spikes to 100% for three or four seconds ten times a day and is otherwise idle, there is no need to consider that a heavy load. If it hovers above 80% for an hour, that is probably substantial.

If there are periods of high activity, ensure that you understand what they are before adjusting your plan to accommodate them. As an example, you may find regular intervals of very high disk activity. If you simply size a disk subsystem to handle the load, you might find that you have spent extra money on a high-powered SAN just to speed up backups that occur when no one is using the system anyway.

Also, remember that your cluster will be a shared resource environment. If you determine that twenty separate systems need a combined 2,000 disk transfers per second on average but did not note that their peak workloads never occur simultaneously, you may inadvertently oversize your system.

Memory measurements

Your primary goal with memory metrics is to determine how much memory to allocate to a system once it is virtualized. The easiest way seems to be to compare how much physical memory it has to how much physical memory it uses. However, this simple metric may hide a memory starvation issue. If the *Pages/sec* metric is high and available memory is low, the machine may not have enough physical memory. You could also track for page file usage, but unfortunately this isn't a great metric for determining just how much extra memory the system needs. If possible, try to resolve this prior to virtualization. If it is not possible, make a note that this load will probably benefit from additional memory once virtualized.

Conversely, if available memory is high and remains high, the system has more memory than it needs to perform its role. You may consider reducing the memory assigned to it once it is virtualized. *Chapter 7, Memory Planning and Management,* contains many additional details about memory, including how to use Hyper-V Server's **Dynamic Memory** feature for workloads with varying demands.

Network measurements

These are fairly straightforward and easy to understand. Systems with high networking utilization need to be carefully considered as they may not make the best candidates for virtualization. Hyper-V Server 2012 can employ quality of service controls to keep them from choking out other systems, but they may be best left on their own systems. However, if you have one high utilization system among many low utilization systems, teaming with a system with ten-gigabit or greater will probably be sufficient. Also, keep in mind that you are likely to encounter systems with 100 Mb adapters and possibly even 10 Mb adapters. Their usage will change once placed on a gigabit-capable system.

Disk measurements

Disk space consumption is usually the largest concern, but you won't use Performance Monitor for that. The next things you'll want to determine are how much data your disks are moving and how many read/write requests they are performing. These two metrics are not necessarily tied together; it is certainly possible to have a high number of read or write requests that move very little data.

If disk activity seems very high, first ensure that it is not due to memory paging. Heavy paging loads place the burden on the disk.

% Disk Time isn't normally useful by itself. If it is a very low number, then you probably don't need to spend a lot of time digging into the other metrics. The *Avg Disk Queue Length* metric tells you if your disk system is able to keep up with the load. Usually, if it is consistently above two, there is a problem that needs to be addressed; in many cases, it is actually a sign of insufficient memory. The remaining two, *Disk Bytes / sec* and *Disk Transfers / sec*, tell you how much data is being moved and how many moves are occurring, respectively. The latter is a rough estimate of **input/output per second (IOPS)**.

Translating disk numbers from disparate systems into a single set of numbers to size shared storage is extremely difficult. Disk activity usually occurs in spikes, and it is very rare for multiple systems to spike simultaneously. Do not simply add up all the transfers per second and bytes per second and attempt to purchase a system that meets it; such a system may be prohibitively expensive and it will almost always be idle. If you are considering a SAN, many vendors have tools that can help you size for this purpose. Be aware that even the best of those tools are factoring in some guesses.

Processor measurements

The processor measurements are more straightforward but potentially misleading. Sustained high CPU time is what you want to watch for. A high load does not indicate that assigning additional virtual CPUs will be beneficial, but it does indicate that a virtualized instance will probably consume a noticeable amount of CPU time. A high number of active threads may indicate that the system may benefit from more vCPUs when virtualized. Not all applications benefit from having multiple virtual CPUs available; some perform best with only one. You may need to consult with your application vendor's support team or with other organizations who use the product to learn how any given software will behave.

Some applications lean the other way, benefiting not only from additional vCPUs, but from Hyper-V's *NUMA*-awareness to keep a virtual machine's memory near the physical CPUs that are accessing it. NUMA will be explained in *Chapter 7, Memory Planning and Management*.

Host computer components

The next concern is designing and sizing the host computers that will run Hyper-V Server. You now have some idea of the load your virtual machines will need, so you need to understand what the requirements are to fit those needs.

Hyper-V Server requirements

The hypervisor itself doesn't require much in terms of hardware. It shares an official requirements list with the full Windows Server 2012 product, which is as follows:

- 64-bit CPU (x64, not Intel Itanium) running at a minimum of 1.4 GHz
- 512 megabytes of main system RAM
- 32 gigabytes of available hard drive space

Hyper-V's requirements extend beyond these to the following:

- The CPU's options for hardware-assisted virtualization support must be enabled in the BIOS
- CPU support for Data Execution Prevention must be enabled in the BIOS (NX on AMD chips, XD on Intel chips)

While not required for the Server edition of Hyper-V unless you intend to use RemoteFX, **second-level address translation (SLAT)** can greatly enhance the performance of memory-intensive virtualized workloads. The various features of RemoteFX have required and recommended features of their own (one of which is SLAT), so if VDI is part of your plan, ensure that the hardware you purchase supports those.

These are the minimum requirements to install Hyper-V Server. If you use only these minimum requirements, you will not have enough resources to be able to virtualize any load. The following sections will discuss how you can appropriately size your hardware.

CPU

There is no one-to-one matching of the **virtual CPUs (vCPUs)** inside virtual machines to the physical CPUs of the hosts. When a processing thread is created inside a virtual machine, Hyper-V Server sends it to the next open CPU core, usually without any concern over which actual CPU it is sent to. The number of vCPUs assigned to a virtual machine limit how many active processing threads it can have at any given time, not which physical CPUs it has access to. This means that there's no simple way to map existing CPU requirements in a physical system to what it will need when moved to a virtual environment. A concept diagram follows:

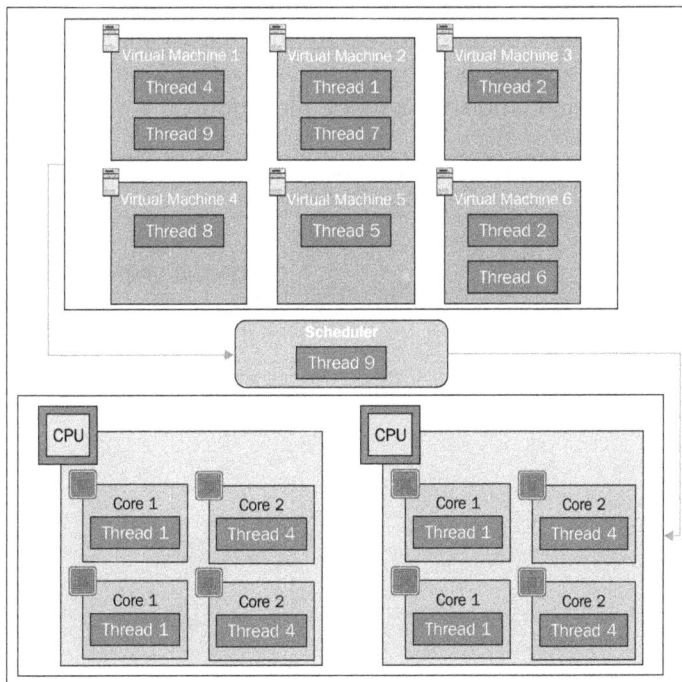

In the previous diagram, threads are numbered in the order in which they were started. Note that the image shows a simplified view of what actually occurs in order to help you to understand the concept. Actual thread scheduling is somewhat more complicated than the indicated round-robin style.

Microsoft indicates that a single physical core can support eight vCPUs for legacy operating systems and twelve for Windows Server 2008 R2 and later server operating systems or Windows 7 and later desktop operating systems. However, the actual supportable load is primarily determined by how much CPU processing time a virtual machine calls upon multiplied by the number of threads it activates. Make sure that the CPUs you select for your hosts can support the load you will be placing upon them. If you're uncertain on how to proceed, core count is usually more important than core speed in a virtualization environment. Since you're building a cluster, adding hosts may be preferable to choosing more expensive systems with more CPU sockets or cores. If you will be using virtual machines with many vCPUs, it is recommended that you read *Chapter 7, Memory Planning and Management,* so you understand NUMA before sizing your host.

Memory

Memory is not a scheduled, shared resource like CPUs. Whatever memory Hyper-V Server assigns to a virtual machine at any given time is completely dedicated to that machine until Hyper-V Server takes it away. Dynamic Memory can be employed in some cases to allow virtual machines to request and release memory to the hypervisor as their needs change. This does not change the non-shared nature of memory. The following image is a visualization of memory allocation:

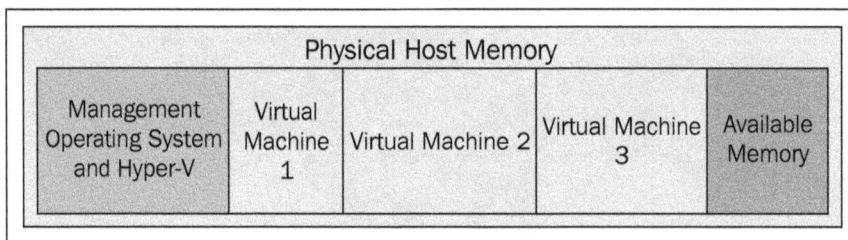

Physical Host Memory				
Management Operating System and Hyper-V	Virtual Machine 1	Virtual Machine 2	Virtual Machine 3	Available Memory

As with CPU, you may reach a point where it makes more sense to scale out than to attempt to increase the amount of physical memory in a single host computer. Another option is to plan to reduce the amount of memory allocated to virtual machines. In many cases, the amount of memory installed in single-use physical computers is more, sometimes dramatically more, than is actually necessary. Because it's rather simple to allocate more physical memory to a virtual machine, you can plan to start small and add additional RAM if virtual machines appear to need it.

As you size your physical RAM to the anticipated load, remember that Windows, like other modern operating systems, can work with less physical RAM than is actually needed. If a virtual machine doesn't have enough RAM, it will begin the process of *paging*—using the hard drive as a stand-in for memory. Some paging is expected and is almost unavoidable, but enough of it will cause a noticeable drag on system performance. Also, even if a guest has sufficient RAM for all services, its operating system will try to maintain a comfortable amount of free RAM and may initiate paging when it is not strictly necessary. Since access to disk is, like CPU, a resource that must be scheduled among virtual machines, heavy disk access is something to be avoided when possible. Take care in the way that you allocate memory.

One thing about Hyper-V Server that distinguishes it from other hypervisors is that, with the exception of guest startup, it never pages the memory assigned to a virtual machine. Any paging involving a guest is initiated and controlled by that guest and utilizes a page file created and managed by that guest. The management operating system will provide paging for its own processes as any other operating system would. The following image shows how page files are placed for the hypervisor and its guests:

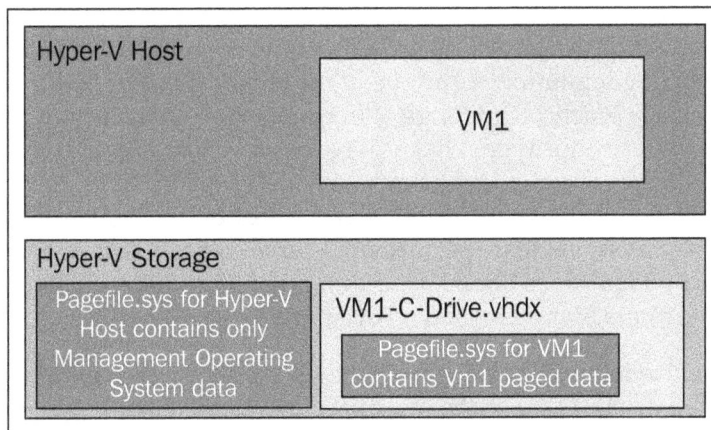

[Hyper-V Server does not control or provide paging for virtual machines.   ]

The management operating system will function well down to about 512 megabytes of available RAM if it provides no other service than Hyper-V Server. It is recommended to leave one gigabyte or more for the management operating system. This number increases as the number of virtual machines increases. Refer to *Chapter 7, Memory Planning and Management,* for a more thorough discussion on precise memory allocation.

Host networking

Networking will be more fully examined in the next section. Please review that before completing your hardware specifications for host computers. Members of Hyper-V Server clusters typically have substantially greater networking requirements than other Windows Server deployment types.

Host storage

In a cluster environment, the storage that you'll spend the most time on will be the shared storage, not the host storage. However, host storage must still be planned for because that is the location that Hyper-V Server will run from. You have two options. One is to use internal hard drives. The other is to use a USB flash drive. Either option is perfectly viable for a basic installation. The farther you intend to deviate from a basic installation, the more sense it makes to utilize traditional internal drives.

The two primary reasons to use USB flash drives are expense and ease of system replacement. A flash drive needs to have at least thirty-two gigabytes of capacity in order to satisfy the minimum requirement for Hyper-V Server 2012. The cost for a drive of that size is practically negligible in comparison to the rest of the hardware required for a project of this type. They can be kept in quantities and rapidly duplicated for easy replacement in the event of a failure. However, the most current systems commonly available both in terms of the host bus and in flash drives are still USB 2.0. They have adequate performance for a Hyper-V Server system that will store its virtual machines elsewhere, but if you will require anything else to be installed on the system, then they may prove to be insufficient.

If you choose to use internal disks, you have a choice between traditional spinning disks and solid-state storage. For the most part, the management operating system and hypervisor will not benefit substantially from the speed offered by a solid-state system, so spinning disks is the most common option. It is recommended that you configure these drives in a mirror (RAID 1).

Even though Hyper-V Server requires little in the way of configuration and can be replaced fairly quickly, this is a very simple way to implement basic redundancy and fault tolerance with a minimal investment. Also, you may choose to run some software inside the management operating system and you may even find cause to place some virtual machines on internal storage. Each additional burden you place on the management operating system beyond hypervisor installation increases the benefits you can gain from using spinning disks and building in a failsafe.

Management operating system

Even though you've already decided on Hyper-V Server for your hypervisor, there is more than one way to gain access to its technologies. The two major options you have are to use Hyper-V Server 2012 or Windows Server 2012 with Hyper-V as a role. In all cases, Hyper-V is the hypervisor. You are deciding what to use as the *management operating system*. That term will be explored in more detail in the next chapter.

Hyper-V Server

Microsoft makes Hyper-V Server freely available as a standalone product in the form of Hyper-V Server 2012 or Hyper-V Server 2012 R2.

Pros of using Hyper-V Server are as follows:

- No licensing costs for the hypervisor or management operating system
- Security from reduced surface area
- Stability from reduced surface area
- Reduced contention for resources
- Fewer patches

Cons of using Hyper-V Server are as follows:

- No official GUI is available; no local Windows desktop
- Greater difficulty due to lack of familiarity
- Less support from third-party vendors
- Some software cannot be installed
- Minimal set of Windows roles and features available

One of the biggest draws to using a standalone deployment of Hyper-V Server is the lack of a licensing cost. Anyone is free to download, install, and use Hyper-V Server on any hardware that supports it. The application is irrelevant; it can be used in home networks and in Fortune 500 datacenters.

Hyper-V Server does include Windows Server as its management operating system. A potential drawback is that it is a severely pared-down image. Any role or feature not necessary for successful operation of Hyper-V Server has been removed. The upside is that the overall surface area for malicious attacks or unintended software failures is significantly reduced. The downside is that the Windows desktop interface that most Windows administrators are accustomed to is unavailable, and some excluded roles or features may be desirable.

Windows Server

Microsoft's full-featured, general-purpose server product includes Hyper-V Server as an installable role.

Pros of using Windows Server are as follows:

- Familiar Windows graphical interface is available; can be added or removed as desired (requires a reboot)
- Greater support from third-party vendors
- Easier to install and manipulate applications (no role beyond Hyper-V or application not necessary to support Hyper-V is recommended)

Cons of using Windows Server are as follows:

- The management operating system requires a full Windows Server license
- Greater security risk from larger surface area
- Greater stability risk from larger surface area
- More contention for resources from installed roles, features, and applications
- Familiarity lures novice administrators into a false sense of security
- More patches

Running Hyper-V as a role inside Windows Server is a popular option. The ease of use and familiarity of the Windows desktop interface can ease administrators into the new territory of Hyper-V and Failover Clustering. Application and third-party vendor support for Windows with a desktop interface is much broader. However, comfort comes at a cost. New administrators might be more inclined to take risks in a GUI environment; since a single Hyper-V system might be hosting any number of critical guests, casual tinkering could have drastic effects. The complete Windows installation is also larger, resulting in a greater attack surface for malicious users, more components that could break, and a higher likelihood that systems will need to be rebooted for patching.

Deciding on a management operating system

There is no universal factor to help you decide between installing Hyper-V Server or Windows Server. Examine the pros and cons list of each method and determine what fits your situation best. Take some time to really think them through; reasons that seem obvious at first sometimes collapse under closer inspection. For instance:

- An organization with a very high security environment doesn't necessarily need to strip all the way down to Hyper-V Server. Such an organization probably goes to great lengths to isolate critical systems such that there is no meaningful difference between a GUI and non-GUI installation from a security perspective.

- The Windows Server GUI may seem easier at first glance, but many common operations will require command-line and PowerShell interactions to complete.

- Administrators are commonly surprised by the number of familiar tools that are available within the standalone Hyper-V Server. Most applications that run on the Windows desktop will run just as well without it.

- A functioning cluster node doesn't need direct interaction. It is easier to manage all nodes simultaneously from a central system. This makes the presence or absence of a GUI somewhat trivial in the long run.

- If you are leaning toward Windows Server but see the appeal of a GUI-less system, it is possible to convert between Core, Minimal Interface, and full GUI modes with only a reboot. This is not possible with Hyper-V Server.

- If you will be running Windows Server as a guest operating system, you will be required to purchase a license that will automatically be applicable to the management operating system. If you will not be running any Windows Server 2012 guests, then Hyper-V Server 2012 may be the better choice for a management operating system. The reasons will be discussed in the next section.

- It's true that Hyper-V Server requires fewer patches, but it only takes one that requires a reboot to cause an interruption. With the introduction of Cluster-Aware Updating in the 2012 products, the visible-service impact of rebooting for patches is virtually eliminated.

Along with these important considerations, there is one that should not factor meaningfully into the decision: do not be concerned with using Windows Server Standard Edition versus Datacenter Edition as the management operating system. The two are technologically identical. The sole difference is related to licensing rights for guest machines. This will be explored in the Licensing section later in this chapter.

Deciding between Hyper-V Server 2012 and 2012 R2

The additional features and capabilities of R2 are certainly impressive. Alone, they would make the decision almost trivial — R2 is the superior product. However, such a choice should not be made on capability alone. New operating systems tend to require several months to shake out their most egregious bugs, and Windows Server 2012 was no exception. If you are starting your journey to virtualization soon after the release of R2, it may be wise to start with 2012 and wait. If you have chosen to install Windows Server and run Hyper-V as a role, licensing is another consideration. While the licensing model is effectively the same for both versions, R2 is a new operating system, not a free upgrade or Service Pack. If you own licenses for 2012 without Software Assurance, the switch to R2 is a new purchase.

The TechNet library contains quick lists of the new features of Hyper-V and failover clustering in the R2 series. They are viewable at `http://technet.microsoft.com/en-us/library/dn282278.aspx` and `http://technet.microsoft.com/en-us/library/dn265972.aspx`, respectively. This book will cover most of the new features, specifically excepting those that have no relation to a cluster, such as enhanced session mode, online export and resizing of virtual hard disks, and automatic virtual machine activation. The referenced pages include information on all of these features.

If you start with 2012 with the intent to move to R2, be aware that there is no direct upgrade path for a cluster. You can build a completely new cluster and use the Cluster Migration Wizard or you can split one or more nodes from the existing cluster, upgrade them to R2, and place them in a new cluster. Due to a new feature in R2, you'll be able to use Live Migration to relocate virtual machines from your old cluster to the new one. Once all the virtual machines have been removed from the old cluster, it can be destroyed. Its nodes can then be upgraded to R2 and joined to the new cluster. To ease the transition, it is recommended that you place all guests on SMB 3.0 shares, even if it is only temporarily. Multiple clusters can access the same share location, but not the same CSV or cluster disk. While this book will not provide direct steps on this scenario, it will teach you enough that you'll be able to perform this task.

Networking

Networking in a Hyper-V Server cluster can be very confusing for newcomers. A clustered Hyper-V Server host requires a large number of distinct network connections in comparison to most other computing system deployments. The traffic types were covered in *Chapter 1, Hyper-V Cluster Orientation*. For review, they are given as follows:

- Management
- Live Migration

- Cluster and Cluster Shared Volumes
- Virtual machine
- Storage (unless using direct-attached)

The recommended setup is to use at least a one-gigabit adapter for each of the above. If you won't be using Cluster Shared Volumes, then you can skip having a dedicated adapter for cluster communications. The pathways to iSCSI, SMB 3.0, and Fibre Channel benefit from the redundancy of multiple adapters, and most storage can leverage **multi-path I/O (MPIO)** to aggregate bandwidth. Be aware that it is common to overestimate the amount of bandwidth that storage systems actually require. Keep this in mind if you are considering using more than two adapters per host for storage.

An important new feature in Windows Server 2012 and Hyper-V Server 2012 is native teaming. What this gives you in a Hyper-V Server cluster environment is the ability to create a *converged fabric*. With this technology, multiple physical adapters are placed into a single large team and the various networking roles are then run on that one team. In the past, you might have teamed two physical adapters and assigned management traffic to them, then teamed two others and those set aside for Live Migration traffic, and so forth. The problem with that method was that every role required two adapters and they were mostly idle. With converged fabric, you no longer need to dedicate a unique failover adapter for each individual role. This has the benefit of providing improved redundancy and load-balancing using a lower number of adapters. Teaming and converged fabric will receive much more thorough coverage in the networking chapter.

If you will be using ten-gigabit adapters, the recommendation is to use at least two. One can provide adequate bandwidth for most scenarios. Two provides for load-balancing and redundancy. As with gigabit adapters, these can be placed in a converged fabric so that all communication types can share and be balanced across these two adapters. Note that even though it is possible to create a converged fabric that mixes one-gigabit and ten-gigabit adapters, it is not recommended. You won't be able to meaningfully control how traffic is shaped across the physical adapters so that the ten-gigabit adapters have priority.

As you build your cluster, you'll notice that switch port connections add up quickly. Ensure that you have sufficient switching hardware to handle it all. If you will be employing teaming, consider your options carefully. If you connect all the adapters for a single host to a single switch, you have more options for link-aggregation technologies, but you are also introducing a potential single-point of failure. You may choose to address this by distributing the connections for each host across multiple switches and setting switch-independent teaming modes, or you can connect each host to its own switch to maximize aggregation possibilities and plan for a switch failure to cause complete isolation of a single host.

Isolating iSCSI onto its own network is always recommended. Using dedicated physical adapters and switches results in the best performance and security. If dedicated switches are not feasible, the next best option is to segregate the traffic onto iSCSI-specific VLANs. It is possible to include your iSCSI connections in your converged fabric, but overall this is less efficient than using MPIO.

As mentioned in the previous chapter, you'll need to define subnets for the Live Migration network, cluster/CSV network(s), and storage network(s). They will need to be separate from the subnet the management adapter is part of. The management adapter can be in the same network you use for other servers. You may also consider the usage of **virtual LANs (VLANs)**. All of the networking components in Hyper-V Server 2012 and Windows Server 2012 can work with the 802.1q standard for VLAN tagging. If you do not have a working knowledge of subnetting or VLAN technologies, work with your networking team or spend time learning about them before finalizing the networking portion of planning.

Advanced networking hardware

Most organizations will find that standard gigabit will suit their needs perfectly. Most of the rest will get the extra bit they need from ten-gigabit hardware. For a few, even that isn't enough. It can't be stressed enough that networking is one of the places where system designers commonly over-architect in anticipation of loads they won't actually have. Of course, some actually will need more. There are two types of solutions for those environments.

If speed is an issue that ten-gigabit Ethernet can't solve for you, there are faster technologies available. A few manufacturers provide forty-gigabit and higher solutions today, and 100-gigabit solutions are on the way. Some have been released with support for and demonstrated to work with Hyper-V Server. For these solutions, it is recommended that you work with a vendor that has expertise with such hardware.

If speed itself isn't as much of a concern as overall networking efficiency, hardware that is capable of **data center bridging** (DCB) can provide an answer. The Ethernet specification does not require the prevention of data being lost. If a system's input buffer overflows, it is allowed to silently drop any following data that won't fit. Unfortunately, this can include waypoints in the communication chain, such as switches and routers, as well as endpoints. The onus is upon higher level systems to detect these conditions and correct them if necessary. TCP, for instance, was designed specifically to overcome the inherent unreliability of complicated interconnects. Some endpoints don't anticipate this sort of loss and struggle on congested networks. A common example is **Fibre Channel over Ethernet** (FCoE).

Fibre Channel does not share Ethernet's tolerance for data loss, so mixing the two can cause problems in connected storage systems. **Data center bridging** is a group of IEEE standards that addresses these and other issues by shifting transmission reliability to the hardware. Hyper-V Server 2012 and Windows Server 2012 have specific support and capabilities to work with hardware that implements these standards. Methods of working with these technologies will be explored in further networking chapters; for now, be aware that these options are available to you if you determine that they are a necessity for your environment.

Shared storage

To provide high availability for virtual machines, shared storage is absolutely essential. Shared storage can be directly attached to your Hyper-V Server hosts or can communicate with them over a TCP/IP network, **Fibre Channel** (**FC**) interconnects, or other networks. You may utilize dedicated devices or general purpose servers to fulfill this requirement.

Storage area network devices

Storage area network (**SAN**) devices are considered mid-end to high-end storage components. While the term has broad and sometimes inconsistent applications in the realm of interconnected shared storage devices, it is most commonly used to refer to a singular self-contained unit. A SAN contains a bank of hard drives that can be accessed by multiple hosts. What defines a unit as a SAN is that it presents its storage at the block level, just the way that internal storage would. SAN storage devices have sophisticated capabilities beyond simply providing disk storage and I/O. Exact features will vary among vendors and models. Some features that are of interest in a Hyper-V Server deployment are given as follows:

- **Offloaded data transfer (ODX)**

  In a traditional file copy, the operating system reads in all data and copies it back to the disk. Hyper-V Server and Windows Server can instruct SANs that support ODX to perform these transfers without needing to send anything through the operating system.

- **Internal redundancy**

  In addition to the redundancy afforded by particular configurations of the internal hard drives, SANs typically also provide other redundancies such as multiple power supplies, multiple network attachments, and hard drive controllers. It is possible to have a SAN that has no single point of failure except the device itself.

- **Hardware-assisted VSS snapshots**

  Your virtual machines will be created on NTFS volumes that live on the SAN. Backing up those virtual machines will cause a VSS snapshot to be taken by the management operating system. If your SAN supports it and provides a **device-specific module (DSM)**, the operating can instruct it to handle the snapshot process.

- **Device snapshots, cloning, and so on**

  SANs usually have a number of ways to manipulate and protect data that don't involve any operating system input. Many grant you the ability to perform tasks such as creating snapshots and clones of SAN volumes.

- **Data deduplication**

  Some SANs have the ability to ensure they store only one copy of a unique block of data. For instance, the files that make up a Windows Server 2012 installation are identical across different virtual machines. A system with active deduplication stores only one copy of the individual blocks that make up these files. Be advised that the trade-off for the reclaimed storage space is a higher drain on computing and memory usage in the SAN. For some systems, this may have a noticeable impact on the way that virtual machines perform. Use deduplication with caution.

- **Drive type and size mixing**

  Some SANs will mix solid-state drives with spinning disks. This allows you to have the combined benefits of the speed of solid-state with the high capacity of spinning drives. Also, some SANs allow you to create different RAID volumes within the same system.

- **Intelligent data placement**

  Some SANs have the ability to track data usage and then automatically move frequently accessed data to faster drives while moving untouched data to slower drives.

- **Device grouping**

  A distinguishing characteristic of SANs is that they have some methodology to facilitate storage expansion. Some allow you to add drives to an existing device. Some grow by attaching more drive storage bays to an existing base unit. Some are self-contained, but can network with other SANs of the same or a similar model to provide a larger unified logical space.

- **Replication**

  Many SAN devices have built-in capability to replicate to other SAN devices. High-end units can even do this in real-time and thereby provide redundancy across SAN devices. Such technology is a requirement for multi-site clusters in which virtual machines are expected to continue operating even if a site is lost.

- **Thin-provisioning**

  Thin-provisioning is a common term in virtualization that refers to the ability to request a certain amount of a resource but only receive it on an as-needed basis. In the case of drive space on a SAN, you can thin-provision 100 GB of space and the SAN will only provide you with a few megabytes to start off with. As the system attempts to place more data within this thin-provisioned space, the SAN automatically grows the allocated storage up to the 100 GB maximum.

When considering SAN devices, ensure that the vendor has rated it to work in a multi-host Hyper-V environment. If the vendor does not specifically mention Hyper-V Server, check that the device supports SCSI-3 Persistent Reservations. In Hyper-V Server and Windows Server, each node will require the ability to register a persistent reservation or you will be unable to use Cluster Shared Volumes on the device. It is possible to use Hyper-V virtual machines without CSVs, but you will not be able to create more than one highly available virtual machine on any given **logical unit number (LUN)** — the term for logical drives created on a SAN.

Network-attached storage devices

Network-attached storage (**NAS**) devices are less expensive alternatives to SAN devices. The lower price is usually attended by a smaller feature set. The primary difference between these and SAN systems is that NAS devices typically do not provide block-level access. Instead, they provide network access to a formatted volume for the purpose of sharing files. Some NAS devices emulate block access, but this is commonly accomplished by abstracting space that is actually stored inside a file on the NAS device. Another notable difference is that NAS devices do not typically have the grouping capability of SANs, so their expandability is limited to the empty drive bays of a single chassis. Of course you can employ more NAS devices, so this may not be a meaningful limitation.

If you choose a NAS, it must be able to emulate block access (usually by acting as an iSCSI target) or expose SMB Version 3.0 shares, and it must support simultaneous connections from multiple hosts. If it emulates block access as an iSCSI target, it must support SCSI-3 persistent reservations.

General purpose computers

With special software, you can convert any general purpose computer into a SAN. Microsoft began providing iSCSI Target Software natively with Windows Server 2012. As an added bonus, Windows Server 2012 introduced the capability to cluster this resource so that two Windows Server systems can expose redundant iSCSI connections to the same storage. A number of third parties also provide iSCSI target software. Some Linux distributions can provide this capability natively or through third-party packages. With any of these, you can set aside hard drive space on the system and make it available to your Hyper-V Servers.

Another option is a Virtual SAN Appliance. This is a self-contained software application that runs as a virtual machine and exposes a section of the host's drive space as SAN storage. The benefit of VSAs is that most of them can be used on multiple physical computers to create a redundant storage cluster. Most freely-available iSCSI software targets do not have this capability.

With Windows Server 2012, you also have the option to create SMB 3.0 shares to host virtual machines. Also new in Server 2012 is the ability to cluster the file server role so that you can make the data on these SMB 3.0 shares continuously available in much the same way you are using clustering to make virtual machines highly available. With this capability, you can convert a computer into a NAS device capable of running virtual machines and you can even cluster it to provide redundant NAS services.

Shared storage performance characteristics

Based on the performance metrics you pulled from the existing systems and information provided by software vendors on new workloads, you hopefully have a general idea of what sort of performance your shared storage will need to provide. SAN manufacturers will be happy to share the capabilities of their equipment with you. If you are employing lower-end NAS devices or general purpose computer systems, you may need to calculate these on your own. *Chapter 4, Storage Design*, contains a deep dive into disk performance. You may want to familiarize yourself with its contents prior to deciding on a storage solution.

Designing shared storage

As a general rule, SANs provide the fastest and most reliable storage, then NAS devices, and finally general purpose computers. Cost is usually an accurate indicator of any given solution's capabilities and reliability. The art and science of maximizing the potential of your shared storage is covered in much more detail in *Chapter 4, Storage Design*.

However, you should be able to make an acquisition decision with only a general overview of what capabilities a device provides compared to your organization's needs and expectations.

Besides consulting with vendors and checking official lists of supported devices, consider investigating Internet forums and user groups. Sometimes, a device is certified for Hyper-V Server clusters but users have not been impressed with their capabilities.

Software licensing

Virtualization and clustering introduce potentially complex licensing considerations. The first issue you'll deal with is how to license your guest operating systems. Next, you'll consider the applications that will run on them.

Windows Server and guest virtualization rights

Microsoft has dramatically simplified their licensing scheme beginning with Windows Server 2012. Two of the editions, Standard and Datacenter, include *guest virtualization rights* with each license sold. Standard edition provides for two guests while Datacenter allows an unlimited number of guests. It is important to understand how these work as licensing may influence the number of physical hosts that you purchase.

The terms that Microsoft uses in its licensing documentation to distinguish the operating system that is installed directly on hardware from virtualized guest operating systems are **Physical Operating System Environment** (OSE) and **Virtual OSE**, respectively. These terms are rarely used in other contexts. When you purchase Windows Server 2012 Standard or Datacenter licenses, they grant you the right to run one physical OSE on up to two physical processors on the same motherboard. You may then run as many virtual OSEs on those licensed processors as your license allows.

The obvious question in a Hyper-V Server cluster arrangement is: how does this affect migration technologies? The only thing that matters is that the physical processor(s) that a virtual OSE is running on is/are licensed. To make it easy, start by thinking about Essentials edition, which has no virtualization rights whatsoever. If you will run one virtual OSE of Windows Server 2012 Essentials in a cluster of three hosts, that instance can only be migrated to hosts whose processors have been licensed for Essentials. In all likelihood, this means three Essentials licenses.

The reason for this is that all Windows Server licenses are *assigned* to one or two CPUs and both must be on the same motherboard. If you need another set of CPUs to have that license (perhaps because you need to Live Migrate a virtual OSE to them), then you must re-assign the license to them. This act is considered a *transfer*. For any given Windows Server license, this can only occur once every 90 days. For some Microsoft products, this 90 day period can be waived within a server farm, but not for Windows Server on your own systems.

[Windows Server 2012/R2 licenses are *always* assigned to a specific piece of hardware, *never* to a virtual machine.   ]

The virtualization rights provided by the Standard and Datacenter editions effectively create licensed slots on the CPUs that virtual OSEs can freely move in and out of. The licenses themselves are fixed. There are some things to keep in mind about virtualization rights, and these are given as follows:

- You are also granted *Downgrade Rights*, so the virtual OSEs granted by virtualization guest rights can be any version of Windows Server that is still in its support lifecycle.

- Similar to Downgrade Rights, you also have *Down-Edition Rights*. Virtual OSEs can be the same edition as the physical OSE license or below.

- The terms of OEM licenses vary; consult with your hardware vendor. All OEM licenses are locked to one piece of hardware and cannot be transferred under any circumstances. In general, they will provide the same virtualization guest rights as other license types and virtual OSEs can be moved through them in the same fashion.

- Virtualization rights apply no matter what physical OSE or hypervisor you are using, even if that hypervisor isn't a Microsoft product at all. Your only concern is that you have purchased sufficient virtualization rights to cover all of your virtual OSEs.

- Multiple licenses can be assigned to the same CPU set. If you need to run six Windows Server virtual OSEs on a dual-CPU system, assign three Windows Server Standard licenses to it.

- Licenses cannot be split. Both of the CPUs covered under a single license must exist in the same host. If you have two hosts with only one CPU apiece, you must still purchase two licenses. Likewise, if you only buy one Standard edition license, make a cluster of two physical computers and install Hyper-V Server on both of them, then place a virtual machine running Windows Server on each one of those hosts, one of those virtual machines is out of licensing compliance.

- The host operating system must always be properly licensed. For Hyper-V Server, this is not a concern unless the system has been configured in such a way that it is providing services other than Hyper-V. For any Windows Server installation, always ensure you are in compliance.

- If a host is running Windows Server Standard edition and all virtualization rights from assigned Standard edition licenses are in use, the physical OSE cannot provide any services other than Hyper-V.

- When a virtual OSE moves from one host to another, the license key does not matter. What is important is that the destination host has sufficient available virtualization rights.

- The "sweet spot" where Datacenter edition makes more sense than Standard edition is around 11 guests on a single dual-CPU host—at the published rates. Your costs may be different.

- Hyper-V Replica target virtual machines must be licensed as though they were active, running, and distinct virtual machines.

Virtualization rights are perhaps best understood through illustration. The following diagrams show some possible scenarios. All assume two-socket hosts; for a four-socket host, simply double the licensing requirements. Our first example, shown as follows, is a three-node cluster with four guests:

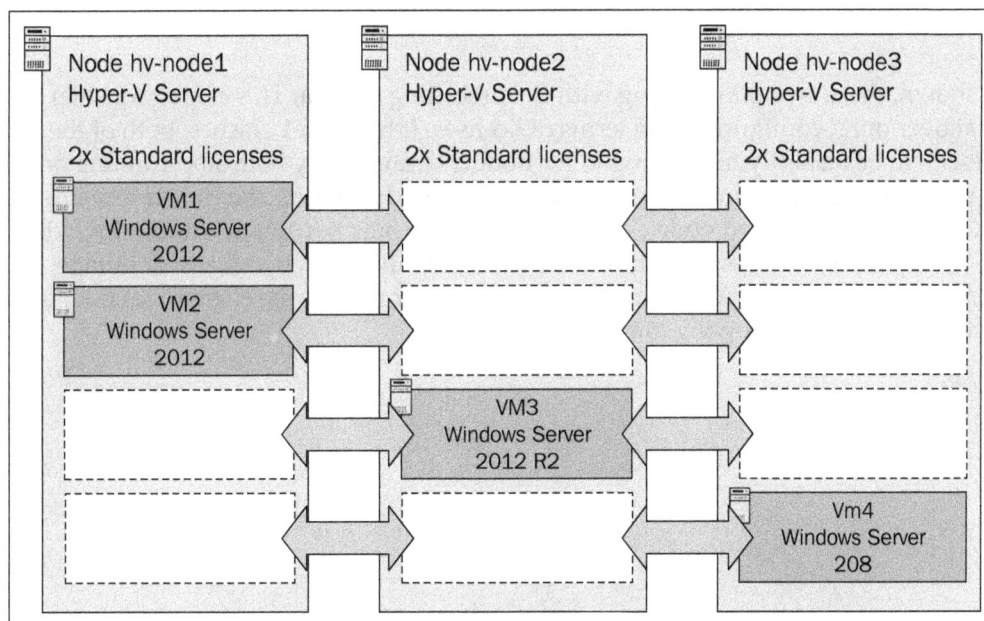

That cluster is composed of three hosts with four virtual machines. Each host has been assigned two Standard edition licenses which grant a total of four virtual OSE licenses. One license per host would only allow for two virtual OSEs. In that case, the architect might choose to redesign the hosts such that the cluster only uses two hosts, which would eliminate the need for two of the Standard edition licenses.

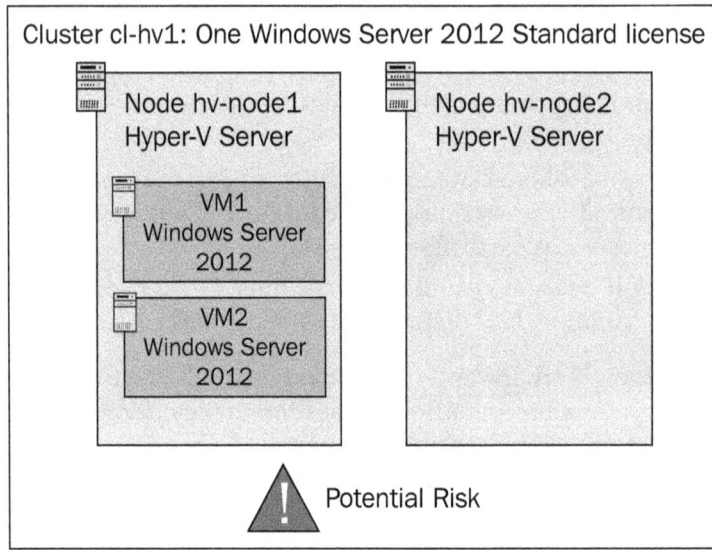

As shown, there is nothing wrong with the preceding system. This can be considered a "failover only" configuration in terms of licenses. If **hv-node1** crashes, both of the guests will be instantly transferred to **hv-node2**. Because they both stop running on **hv-node1** at the same time before either is started on **hv-node2**, the cluster remains in compliance. The failed node can be replaced with new hardware without invoking the 90-day clause. However, if the failure isn't permanent, such as a power outage, the 90-day rule applies. Also, if a Live Migration ever occurs, the cluster will not be in compliance. The following image shows this:

Cluster cl-hv1: One Windows Server 2012 Standard license

Node hv-node1
Hyper-V Server

VM1
Windows Server
2012

Node hv-node2
Hyper-V Server

VM2
Windows Server
2003 R2

Out of license compliance

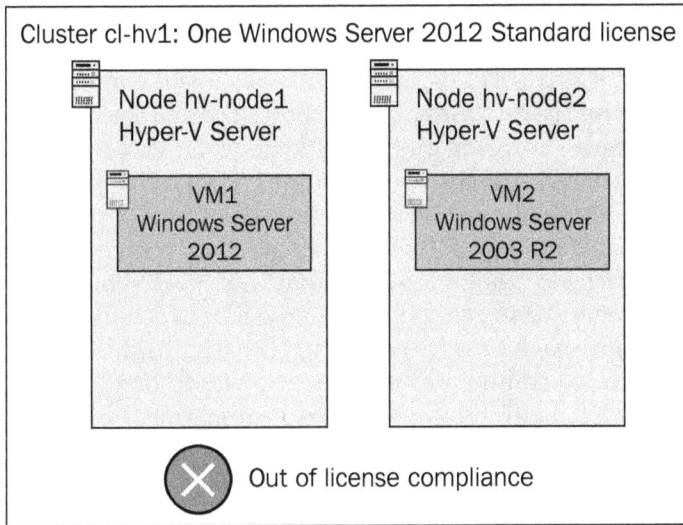

This configuration is out of compliance. There are two guest licenses, but they are connected to a single physical processor license which cannot be split across hosts. This cluster can be made compliant through the purchase of a single Windows Server 2012 Standard edition license. Trying to Live Migrate both of the systems at once does not avoid the licensing issue because they will not stop running on the source system at exactly the same time.

The next scenario involves two nodes with only one guest, shown as follows:

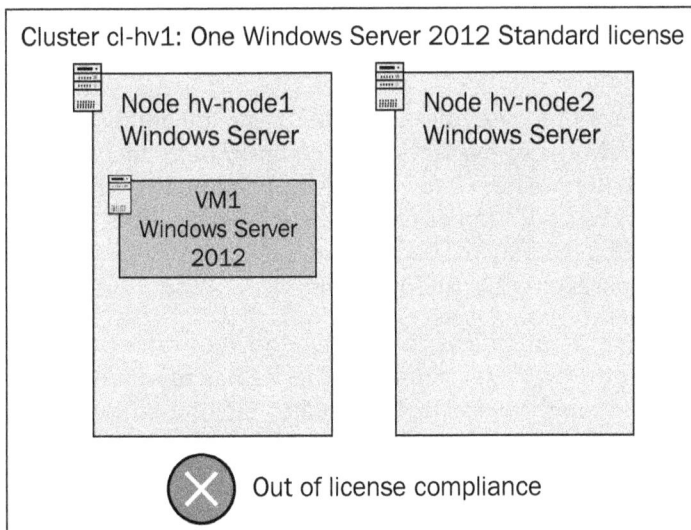

Cluster cl-hv1: One Windows Server 2012 Standard license

Node hv-node1
Windows Server

VM1
Windows Server
2012

Node hv-node2
Windows Server

Out of license compliance

This configuration is a little confusing. There is only one physically-bound license but two hosts, both of which are running a copy of Windows Server. However, **node hv-node2** isn't running any services, and as this is a cluster configuration, it could be considered an *active/passive cluster*. In this configuration, some Microsoft server applications only require licensing on the active node. However, this licensing type does not include operating systems, and **hv-node2** has a full copy of Windows Server installed. Therefore, it must be fully licensed. Another option would be to build this cluster using Hyper-V Server 2012 as the management operating system instead of Windows Server. That would eliminate the need to buy a second Windows Server license. However, **VM1** could only be moved between the nodes once every 90 days. That is because each time it is moved, a license transfer event would need to occur. The recommended solution for this scenario would be to have one Windows Server license for each host. If it doesn't mess up pagination, I would recommend a paragraph break here as we are moving to a new topic. The final example involves Hyper-V Replica and is shown in the following image:

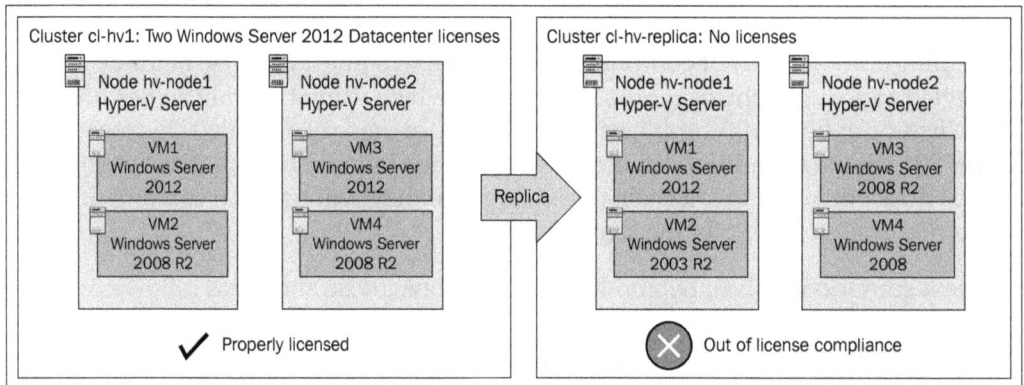

This is a possible disaster recovery design. In this case, the build assumes that if cluster **cl-hv1** fails entirely, VMs on **cl-hv-replica** can be brought up in its place and the two Datacenter licenses will transfer. Unfortunately, this is not a valid assumption. Virtual machines serving as Hyper-V Replica targets must be licensed as though they were actively running virtual machines. The recommended solution in this case will be to purchase enough licenses to cover all four hosts.

Even though licensing is much less complicated in Windows Server 2012 than it was in previous Windows Server versions, and R2 has retained that simplicity, it can still be very confusing. Microsoft only makes major changes to their licensing scheme in conjunction with major new product releases, but their master Product Use Rights document is updated quarterly. You can review it at the following location: http://www.microsoft.com/licensing/about-licensing/product-licensing.aspx.

A simpler document with examples is available at `http://www.microsoft.com/licensing/about-licensing/briefs/virtual-licensing.aspx`.

The licensing discussion as presented in this book should be used as nothing more than a basic guideline to help you conceptualize licensing needs. You are always strongly encouraged to work with Microsoft or a licensing reseller to determine your exact needs. If you would like help from a Microsoft licensing expert, they provide telephone-based assistance (`http://support.microsoft.com/kb/141850`). Any authorized Microsoft license reseller should have a licensing expert available for consultation, and many will often provide licensing consultation at no charge.

Software Assurance

Software Assurance grants additional benefits, such as the ability to maintain a replica copy without a full license. Consult with a licensing expert for more information.

Client access licenses

Hyper-V Server only provides services to its virtual machines, so it requires no client access licenses of any kind. Windows Server 2012 running Hyper-V as a role and providing no other services also does not require client access licenses. The virtual OSEs and applications as well as the services they provide must be appropriately licensed. As a general rule, client access licenses have no different requirements for a server in a virtual instance than for a server in a physical instance. Consult with your software vendors to determine if they have any special client licensing requirements when the server is provided by a virtual OSE.

Other software licenses

Two other types of software need to be considered. The first is software that will run on management operating systems. As a rule, you shouldn't install anything within a management operating system that isn't absolutely required to be there. This will generally include things such as management tools and backup software agents. These types of applications will typically be licensed per node. Software that provides other services, especially to computers besides virtual OSEs, can cause violations of the licensing agreements for your physical OSEs. If your license is for Windows Server 2012 Standard edition and all virtualization guest rights are consumed, it is a violation of the licensing agreement to provide any services to other computers or users. There is no concern if the software is solely for the purpose of managing, monitoring, or providing services to the management operating system or its virtual machines.

The second type is software that will run on the guest machines. Hopefully, these will all be licensed to the virtual machine and there will be no issues. However, there are a few vendors that bind their software to physical hardware. Ensure you check with each vendor for software you intend to place in a cluster to ensure that you remain in licensing compliance.

Hyper-V and cluster-related software planning

Deploying Hyper-V Server and Failover Clustering to provide services for your virtual machines is only one piece of the overall puzzle. The hypervisor and cluster will also need to be monitored and maintained. Applications used for these purposes need to be included and accounted for in your planning.

Remote software applications

It is common for maintenance and monitoring applications to run on remote systems. In this case, *remote* may not be an entirely accurate descriptor. It is not unheard of for some of these tools to be installed on highly available guests within the cluster. Regardless of where they actually live, these applications will interact with your cluster and its nodes using remote techniques. This may involve providing TCP/IP connectivity, manipulating firewall ports, setting user and group permissions, and installing agents.

Truly remote applications, such as RemoteApps and software intended to run in a VDI scenario, may have particular licensing requirements of their own. Always check with your application vendor to ensure you will be in compliance.

Local software applications

Installing software on a server running Hyper-V is discouraged. Local software competes with the virtual machines for host resources, adds to the attack surface, and provides another potential source of faults that could crash the host—and all its guests. However, it's sometimes unavoidable, and in some smaller environments, may be desirable despite the risks.

If you will be installing software locally, ensure that you plan appropriately for its expected resource consumption. So as not to cause contention in a cluster environment, local applications should be placed on local storage. As with any other software, make sure that you are compliant with its licensing agreement. Locally installed applications and the reason for their usage should be clearly specified in your planning document.

Blade hardware

Blade systems are an acceptable choice for separated virtualization systems, but they provide something of a mixed bag. The primary issue is that they tend to not have many physical network adapters. Another is that they have a lower upper limit on the amount of installable RAM and on the speed and power of their CPUs. This presents a problem for virtual machine density. The cost of an individual blade is lower than an individual rack-mount or free-standing system, but the blade chassis and the cumulative effects of higher licensing to make up for reduced guest density may cause the costs to tilt your planning away from a blade system.

Physical placement

All of this equipment is going to need a final home. If you're transitioning from a physical deployment to a Hyper-V Server cluster, the net space usage may actually decline. However, there is an interim period in which you'll need to have both. If you're adding switches, you'll need space for those as well. The extra wiring will need to be routed and managed.

Security is another concern. Theft and direct access by malicious individuals need to be prevented. Physical security is just as important as digital security.

Security

With Hyper-V providing a core infrastructure role, security is of vital concern. The simplest approach is to simply add the systems into your domain and keep the default security. Access to the management operating system and hypervisor are restricted to the local administrator account and members of the Domain Admins group. New in the 2012 series of server products is a local Hyper-V Administrators group. Members of this group are allowed to manage everything related to Hyper-V on that particular host but they are not managers of the host computer, and membership in that group doesn't grant access anywhere else in the domain.

Domain separation

Some administrators choose to place Hyper-V hosts outside of the domain for a variety of reasons. For single hosts, a *workgroup* configuration is sometimes chosen. Systems running Hyper-V are simply never joined to the domain, therefore a compromised Hyper-V Server system theoretically does not place the domain at any risk. Whether or not this is an effective strategy is simply not relevant when it comes to a cluster. A computer that is not an Active Directory member cannot participate in a Microsoft Failover Cluster. If it is imperative to move the Hyper-V hosts outside of the primary domain, the next best option is to create another domain. This domain can be a new forest. It can be a subdomain of your existing domain. Either way, it sets up a very effective security boundary that separates your Hyper-V hosts from your other systems. A concept diagram is shown as follows:

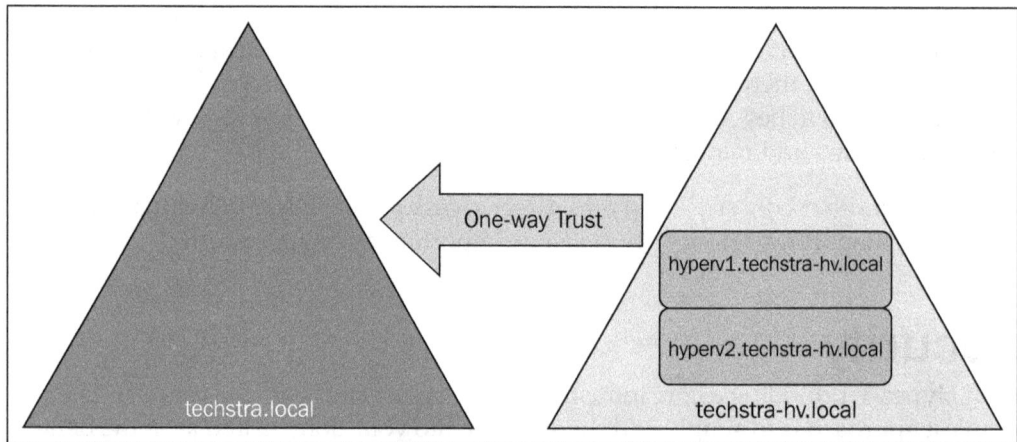

These Hyper-V Server hosts have been placed into a completely separate forest from the primary domain. This creates a completely disconnected domain system. An alternative would be to use a subdomain. In that configuration, universal groups would be able to cross the domain boundaries a little more easily, although a trust relationship would still be required for meaningful management. Making the trust one-way prevents accounts in the trusting domain from accessing resources in the trusted domain. So, in the above diagram, members of Domain Admins in **techstra-hv.local** would not have any rights or permissions in **techstra.local**. It would be possible for members of the Domain Admins group in **techstra.local** to access resources in **techstra-hv.local**, but only if they have been explicitly granted permissions.

A complete discussion of Active Directory domains and trusts exceeds the scope of this book.

Misconfiguration of a trust can reduce security, which is clearly worse than not using a trust at all. If you are interested in forming a solution similar to the above, please consult with an Active Directory expert. Keep in mind that every domain needs at least one domain controller. A single domain controller cannot host more than one domain.

Hyper-V isolation

Hyper-V Server itself provides a significant level of isolation for the virtual machines. Interactions between the host and guest are limited to what is provided by the Hyper-V Integration Services, if installed. For the most part, data transactions are limited to exchanges of key-value pairs. If a compromised virtual machine were able to interact with the host, it would do so through the Hyper-V Virtual Machine Management service. This service runs under the Local System on the Hyper-V host, which by default has no permissions anywhere else in the domain.

Network isolation

In conjunction with the built-in isolation of the hypervisor, virtual machines can be effectively walled off using networking equipment. The Hyper-V virtual switch that your virtual machines connect through has the same isolation capabilities as a standard network switch. The following diagram illustrates one way this could be put into practice:

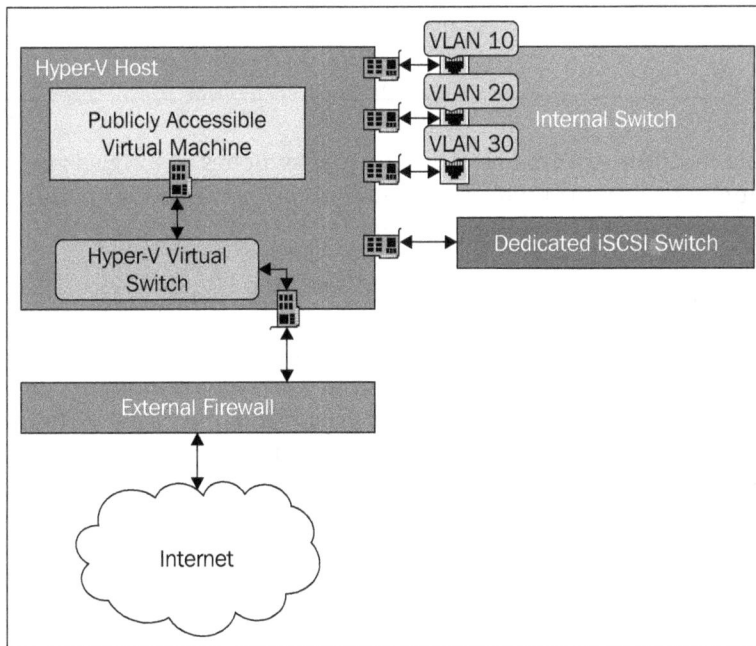

In this scenario, the **Hyper-V Virtual Switch** is assigned to a physical adapter that connects directly to an Internet firewall. Incoming connections connect directly to that virtual switch and any virtual adapters assigned to it. Other physical adapters are attached to an internal switch that has assigned their traffic into VLANs. An adapter intended to carry iSCSI traffic is connected to a switch that has been set aside for that purpose.

It's not required that you connect all virtual machines to the same virtual switch. You don't even need to connect all the adapters in any given virtual machine to the same virtual switch.

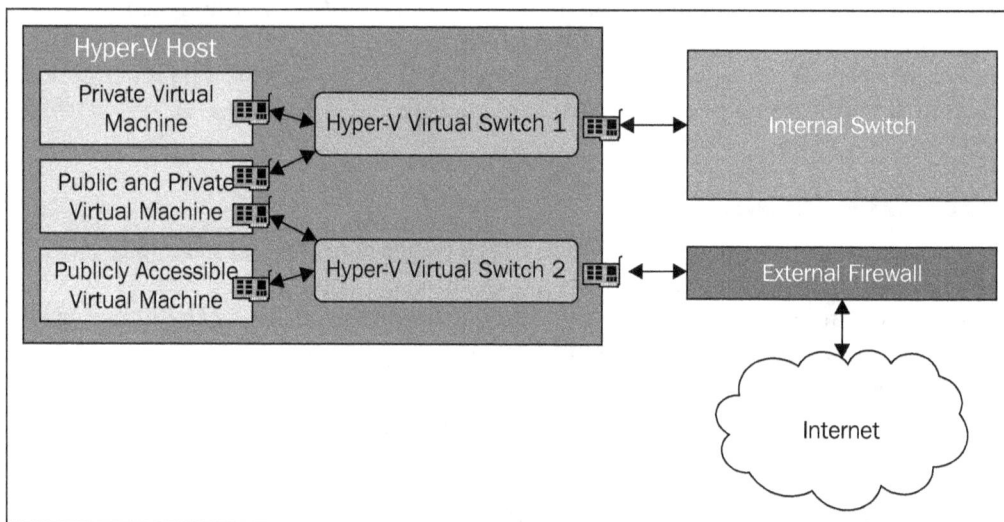

You can create multiple external Hyper-V virtual switches as long as you have the physical adapters to support them. They can then be connected into your networking hardware to suit your security requirements.

Not all the concepts around isolation, security, and the Hyper-V virtual switches are presented here, so don't worry if you don't completely understand these diagrams and scenarios. They will be much more thoroughly examined in further chapters on networking. As you design your hosts and network environment, you only need to understand that if you wish to perform physical isolation of the virtual network adapters, you'll need to assign physical adapters in the host for this purpose. If you intend to use those adapters in a team environment for redundancy and load-balancing, you'll need to provide sufficient physical adapters to satisfy that need.

Complete the planning phase

Before permanently moving on from this chapter, wrap up the planning phase. This involves reviewing the purposes, goals, and design portions. Make sure that they are all completely aligned; the purposes must clearly detail a vision for the completed project, the goals must clearly detail the way that the purposes will be fulfilled, and the design must clearly detail the way that technology will implement the goals. Once these three conditions have been satisfied, the planning portion of the master project document should be locked down and no further changes are allowed.

When planning is complete, gather vendor quotes and start acquiring the equipment, software, and licensing that make up your design.

Sample project – planning and design

After much research and several meetings, Techstra's administrator in charge of designing the project has made changes to the goals section and has laid out a design section that details the software and physical components to be purchased with the idea to scale out later as necessary. Because the MAP scan revealed that a single host can handle the projected load and the cost of licensing a three node cluster turned out to be prohibitive, the hardware design has been reduced accordingly. Previous sections were adjusted to match. The next section shows the results of the hardware plan. Once this section is complete, the entire planning portions are reviewed and finalized.

Sample project – hardware

In this project, we have the following hardware components:

Hosts (2):

- Microsoft Windows Server 2012 (Standard Edition, 2 licenses per host)
- Dual eight-core CPUs
- 64 GB RAM
- 2 x 300 GB mirrored internal 7.2k hard drives
- 5 x 1 GbE network adapters

Network Attached Storage: general-purpose computer:

- Windows Server 2012 with iSCSI target
- One dual-core CPU
- 8 GB RAM

- 6 x 300 GB 10k hard drives in RAID-5 array
- 3 x 1 GbE network adapters

Switching hardware:

- 2 x 24-port layer-2 switches

Summary

Planning to move existing physical systems into a Hyper-V Server cluster is a process that takes time and consideration. You should now have the ability to carry out this assessment with confidence that you will be purchasing sufficiently powerful equipment. You should also be able to project load needs for new software installations.

Once the basic assessment is complete, the next step is thinking through all the necessary hardware components. You now have the basic knowledge needed to carefully weigh the various options available to you. You are also now aware of the physical placement needs for the extra hardware of a cluster.

You have learned how to plan for the fundamental security design of a Hyper-V Server cluster. You can make an informed decision between leaving the system in your existing domain, branching out into a subdomain, or separating into an entirely new forest.

At this point, you are ready to end the planning phase and move forward into the initial setup phase. Start your ordering! In the next chapter, you'll become acquainted with the tools that you'll use to build and manage your cluster. Along the way, you'll put your knowledge to use by actually creating the cluster in its initial deployment.

3
Constructing a Hyper-V Server Cluster

A cluster of Hyper-V Servers is made up of numerous parts. There is the hypervisor itself, the Windows Server installation serving as the management operating system, and the Failover Clustering component. Microsoft provides a plethora of tools to manage all of these. One of the best ways to become oriented to these tools is through the construction of your cluster. The purpose of this chapter is to show you how to build the cluster you've designed. Along the way, you'll become familiarized with some of the management applications you'll be using to maintain your systems.

This chapter will cover:

- Acquiring and installing the management tools
- Performing initial node configuration
- Connecting your nodes into a cluster

Documenting the initial setup phase

It's vitally important to keep track of the activities you carry out during the initial build of your environment. The purpose of this documentation is to ensure that you can quickly duplicate your work if you need to rebuild or expand your cluster at some point in the future. Things that seem obvious or memorable now will be easily overlooked in six months. At first, the document doesn't need to be formal. A simple pen and paper notepad might be all you need. You'll want to pay special attention to any steps that are particular to your equipment and environment. You'll also want to take note of BIOS, firmware, and driver versions that you use.

Build steps not covered in this book

Before diving into the tools, you need to prepare your equipment. Most of these steps will be specific to the hardware that you have chosen to use, so this book can only provide extremely generic directions. It also does not cover the installation of Windows Server or Hyper-V Server, mostly because the installation process itself has no real options to set. Perform these tasks, following your hardware vendor's instructions where applicable:

- Configure your switching hardware:
    - Set up VLANs
    - Assign switch ports to VLANs or trunks
    - Enable jumbo frames if you will be using iSCSI and your storage vendor supports it
- Configure your shared storage system; create LUNs (iSCSI and Fibre Channel) or shares (SMB 3.0 systems)
- Set the BIOS options for your hosts:
    - Enable hardware virtualization assistance: VT-x for Intel CPUs and AMD-V for AMD CPUs.
    - Enable data execution prevention: XD for Intel CPUs and NX for AMD CPUs.
    - Enable EPT for Intel CPUs and NPT or RVI for AMD CPUs. These are second-level address translation (SLAT) settings. It is required for many RemoteFX features; it is otherwise optional but provides significant performance benefits.
    - Disable any hardware trusted execution modules.
    - Disable C1E power states.
- Install Windows Server or Hyper-V Server on the hosts
- Install hardware drivers as necessary or desired

There may be other steps not mentioned here that are specific to your environment, such as setting up routing for your Ethernet environment or attaching Fibre Channel interconnects.

Auxiliary built-in tools

A number of smaller tools exist that you won't use often but will likely have need of while assembling your cluster. Some tools do not exist in both installation types, but all that are available in a non-GUI environment are also available in the GUI. All of these are included automatically, so no downloads or configuration steps are required. These tools are listed as follows:

Control Panel or Administrative Tools icon (in GUI installations of Windows only)	Command-line invocation (in all installations)
Date and Time (in Control Panel)	`timedate.cpl`
Disk Management (in Computer Management in Administrative Tools)	`diskpart.exe`
iSCSI Initiator (in Administrative Tools)	`iscsicpl.exe`
Registry Editor	`regedit.exe`
System Information	`systeminfo.exe`

These extra tools are generic Windows tools, so they will not be thoroughly explained in this book, although you will see some of them appear in examples.

If you are deploying without a GUI, one tool that you may select to use is the text-based Server Configuration tool. This is available on all Hyper-V Server and Windows Server installations, although it is of most use in non-GUI environments. Unless configured otherwise, this tool starts automatically on each login to the console of a non-GUI system. It can be manually started by entering `sconfig.cmd` at an elevated prompt. The following is a screenshot of this tool:

This chapter will focus on demonstrating the GUI and PowerShell methods of configuring these and other settings. The Server Configuration tool is certainly useful when you don't have access to a GUI, but it cannot be scripted. Feel free to use any combination of approaches that suits your needs and comfort level.

Acquiring and enabling the GUI tools

The GUI tools are categorized under **Remote Server Administration Tools (RSAT)**. They can also be used to manage roles and features on a local system. All of these tools require Windows 8/8.1 or Windows Server 2012/R2. Tools in newer operating systems can manage the earlier Hyper-V Server. Older tools can manage newer systems, but not the newer features. The tools are included automatically in the server operating systems, but you will need to download them from Microsoft for Windows 8 or 8.1.

Windows 8 Remote Server Administration Tools download link:

`http://www.microsoft.com/en-us/download/details.aspx?id=28972`

Windows 8.1 Remote Server Administration Tools download link:

`http://www.microsoft.com/en-us/download/details.aspx?id=39296`

If you are running 32-bit Windows 8, use the download whose filename ends in `-x86.msu`. Get the download ending in `-x64.msu` for a 64-bit edition. Run the `.MSU` package and allow it to complete before continuing.

Enabling the tools on Windows 8/8.1 from the GUI

After you've downloaded and installed the RSAT package, the individual tools are available to be enabled. Follow the following steps to activate the individual tools:

1. Open the Control Panel by bringing up the Charms bar from the top-right corner of the screen (hover over **Settings** and click on **Control Panel**).

2. Click on **Programs** (use **Category View**) or **Programs and Features** (use **Icon View**).

3. Click on **Turn Windows features on or off**, which is in the top-center of the right-hand pane in Category View and in the middle of the left pane in Icon View.

4. In the **Windows Features** dialog that appears, start with the Hyper-V section. Expand it and check **Hyper-V Management Tools**. Leave **Hyper-V Platform** unchecked unless you wish to install Client Hyper-V to run on the Windows 8 computer. The dialog should appear as shown in the following screenshot:

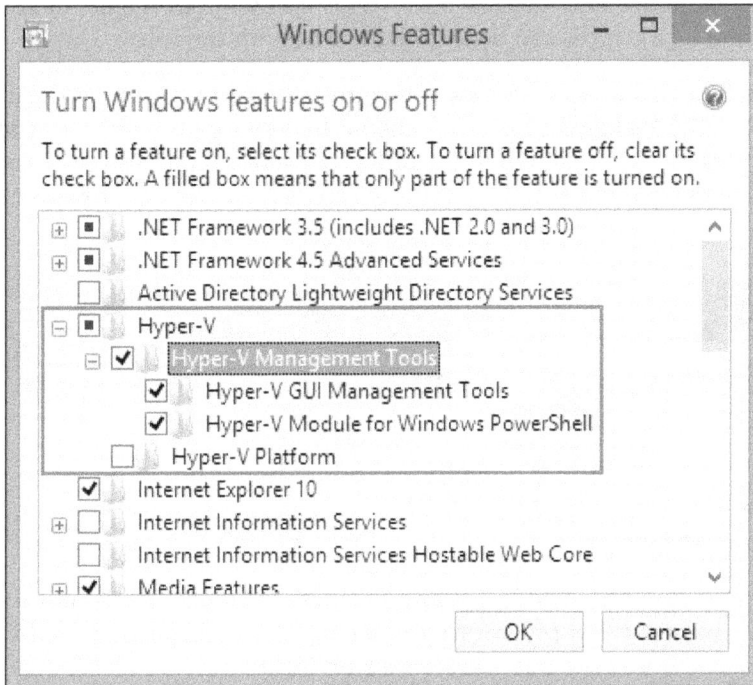

5. Scroll down to **Remote Server Administration Tools** and expand it. There are three portions here: **Feature Administration Tools**, **Role Administration Tools**, and **Server Manager**. To enable the tools described in this chapter, check **Server Manager**, **Failover Clustering Tools** (under **Features**), and **NIC Teaming Tools** (under **Features**).

6. Click on **OK**. Once the installation completes, you can access the new applets under **Administrative Tools**. Open the Start screen, right-click anywhere, and choose **All Apps** in the bottom screen (in Windows 8.1, you only need to click on the down arrow in the circle near the bottom of the Start screen). **Administrative Tools** will appear under the **Apps** heading.

Enabling the tools on Windows Server 2012/R2 in the GUI

The process for Windows Server is very similar to that for desktop Windows. The following steps are unnecessary on systems that will participate in your Hyper-V cluster as the tools can be installed along with the roles:

1. From Server Manager, you can start from the second item on the dashboard or from the Manage drop-down menu. In either place, click on **Add Roles or Features**. Both are shown in the following screenshot. You can also start from the Control Panel using the first three steps from the Windows 8 instructions:

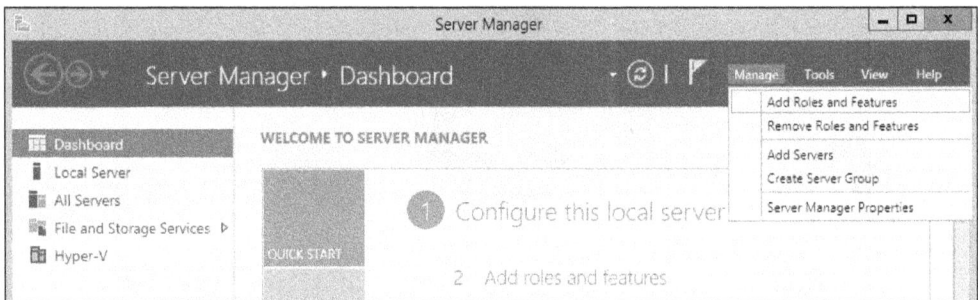

2. This will open the **Add Roles and Features Wizard**. The default first page of this wizard is simply informational and has a **Skip this page by default** checkbox. If you see this screen, click on **Next**.

3. The second screen asks for the installation type. Accept the default of **Role-based or feature-based installation** and click on **Next**.

4. The third screen has you select the server that you wish to install features to. This can be any Windows or Hyper-V Server of the same version that has been added to this console or it can be a .VHD or .VHDX file that contains an offline installation of Windows Server. If you haven't added any other servers to this Server Manager console, the only available option will be the current server. Select it and click on **Next**.

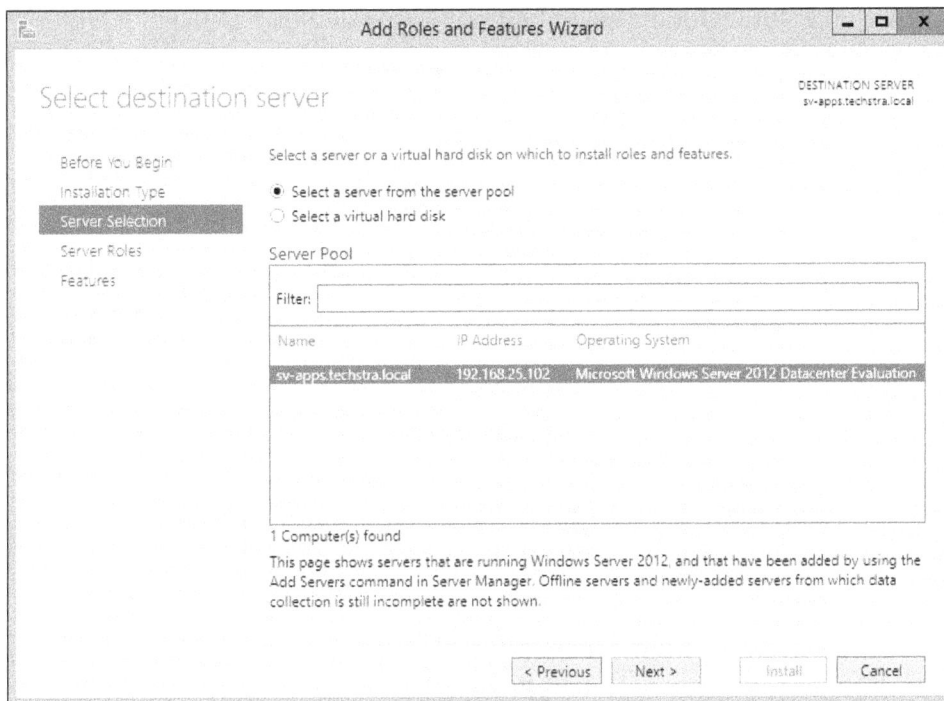

5. The fourth screen is for the selection of server roles. For this particular operation on you are not selecting any roles, so click, **Next**.

6. The fifth screen is for feature installation. Scroll down to **Remote Server Administration Tools** and expand it. Expand **Feature Administration Tools**. Select the box for **Failover Clustering Tools**. This will automatically select the sub-items **Failover Cluster Management Tools** and **Failover Cluster Module for Windows PowerShell**. The other two items contain deprecated executables used to manage clusters. Their usage will not be covered in this book. Expand **Role Administration Tools** and select **Hyper-V Management Tools**.

This will automatically select both sub-items as shown in the
following screenshot:

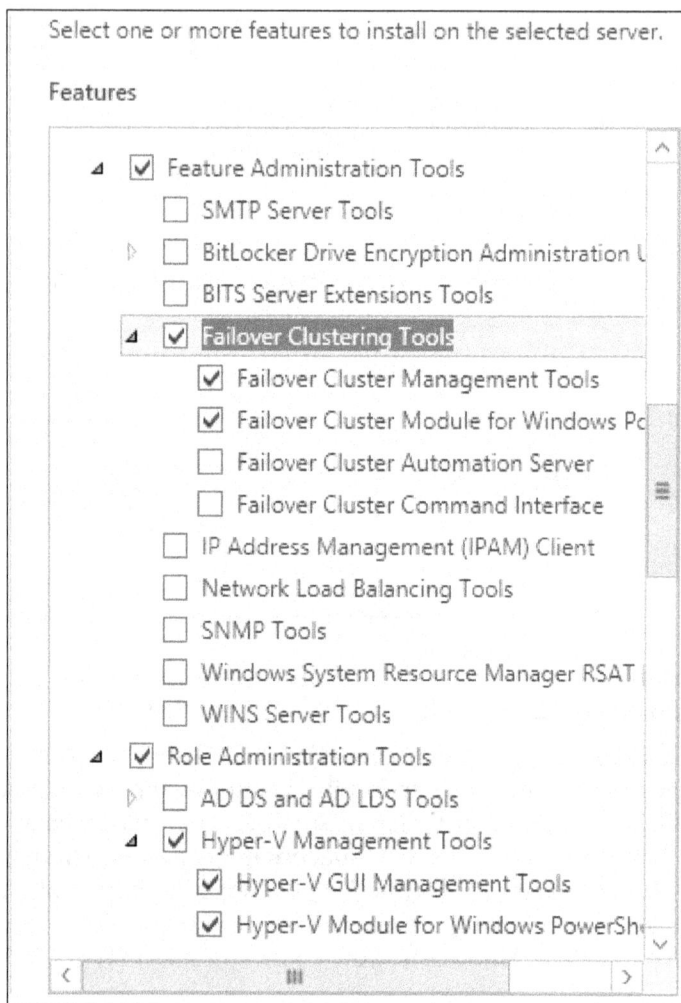

Select one or more features to install on the selected server.

Features

◢ ☑ Feature Administration Tools
  ☐ SMTP Server Tools
  ▷ ☐ BitLocker Drive Encryption Administration L
  ☐ BITS Server Extensions Tools
  ◢ ☑ Failover Clustering Tools
    ☑ Failover Cluster Management Tools
    ☑ Failover Cluster Module for Windows Pc
    ☐ Failover Cluster Automation Server
    ☐ Failover Cluster Command Interface
  ☐ IP Address Management (IPAM) Client
  ☐ Network Load Balancing Tools
  ☐ SNMP Tools
  ☐ Windows System Resource Manager RSAT
  ☐ WINS Server Tools
◢ ☑ Role Administration Tools
  ▷ ☐ AD DS and AD LDS Tools
  ◢ ☑ Hyper-V Management Tools
    ☑ Hyper-V GUI Management Tools
    ☑ Hyper-V Module for Windows PowerSh

7. The next screen is a summary of the items you selected. Review it for
   accuracy and click on **Install**. When the installation completes, close
   the wizard. The tools are now available under **Administrative Tools**.

Enabling the tools using PowerShell

The tools are very easy to enable using the PowerShell console. On Windows Server 2012 and Hyper-V Server 2012, issue the following command at an elevated PowerShell prompt (if you're not certain how to elevate a PowerShell prompt, this will be explained later in the PowerShell section):

```
Install-WindowsFeature -Name RSAT-Clustering, RSAT-Hyper-V-Tools
```

> **Downloading the example code**
>
> You can download the example code files for all Packt books you have purchased from your account at http://www.packtpub.com. If you purchased this book elsewhere, you can visit http://www.packtpub.com/support and register to have the files e-mailed directly to you.

For Hyper-V Server and Windows Server installations in Core mode, the preceding command only enables the PowerShell modules. If you want to add in the deprecated cluster commands, you can append the -IncludeAllSubFeature switch (2012 only).

On Windows 8/8.1, you first need to have downloaded and installed the RSAT package. See the first paragraph of this section for details. Once you have this installed, run the following command at an elevated PowerShell prompt:

```
Enable-WindowsOptionalFeature -Online -FeatureName Microsoft-Hyper-
V-Tools-All, RemoteServerAdministrationTools-Features-Clustering,
RemoteServerAdministrationTools-ServerManager
```

Configuring nodes

To begin configuring a node, it's helpful to have first documented how you expect the node to be configured. Most importantly, you'll need to have decided what the computer name will be and what IP addresses it will have. If you will be employing NIC teaming, that should be clearly documented. Connections to physical switch ports should be documented and the physical switch should be prepared. Unless you intend to place all physical NICs into a single team, you may choose to connect them later so that you can match the logical adapters that Windows sees to the physical adapters.

You can configure a node through the GUI or through command-line and PowerShell prompts. If desired, you can even mix GUI and shell methods. Unless your node is running a version of Windows Server with a GUI, you'll have to run these visual tools from a remote system. To do that, the node will need to be attached to the network and have its security properly adjusted. For non-GUI installations, it is highly recommended that you use PowerShell for initial setup.

Initial node configuration using GUI tools

When your freshly installed server boots, you will be presented with Server Manager. Begin on the **Local Server** tab. The initial steps are standard operations that would be performed on any Windows Server installation. The options of primary interest are indicated in the following screenshot:

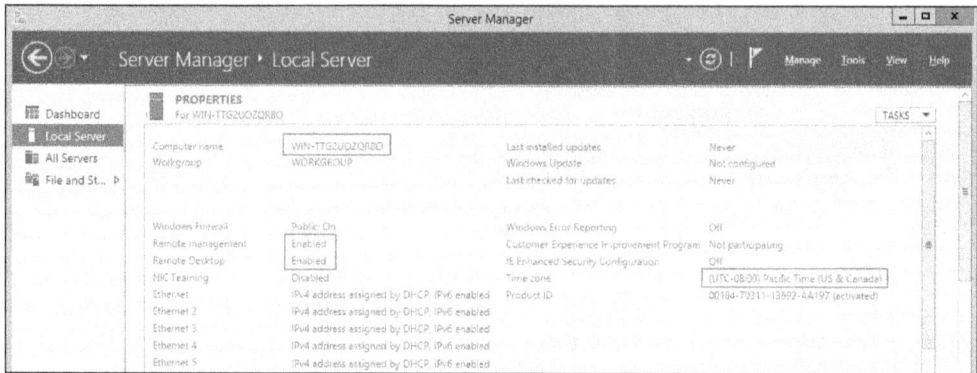

Click on the blue text on each item to be taken to the window where the option can be changed. Be aware that renaming the system will require a reboot. Renaming can be delayed until the end of these steps and done at the same time as the domain join, if desired. The examples in this book use the naming convention as used by the fictional Techstra company from *Chapter 1*, *Hyper-V Cluster Orientation*, so further screenshots in this section will show it with a name of **sv-hyperv1**.

Using the GUI to configure networking

The natural sequence is to configure networking immediately after the preliminary setup. If you are planning to use virtual network adapters in the management operating system and you want those to be in the initial configuration (for example, if you are planning to use a virtual adapter for the management role), then skip forward to role installation and return after the Hyper-V role has been enabled. The virtual switch and virtual adapters are not available until that has been completed.

Renaming network adapters

First, identify the physical network adapters. On the **Local Server** tab in **Server Manager** (shown previously), click on the blue text after any of the network adapters to be taken to the network adapter configuration screen. Ensure you use consistent names for your adapters so that they are easily identifiable. Preferably, use a name that allows you to determine which physical adapter it represents. The simplest way to determine this is to either unplug the physical cable or disable its switch port in the switch's interface. Conversely, you can start with all adapters unplugged and connect them one at a time while you rename the adapters. The following screenshot shows an adapter being renamed:

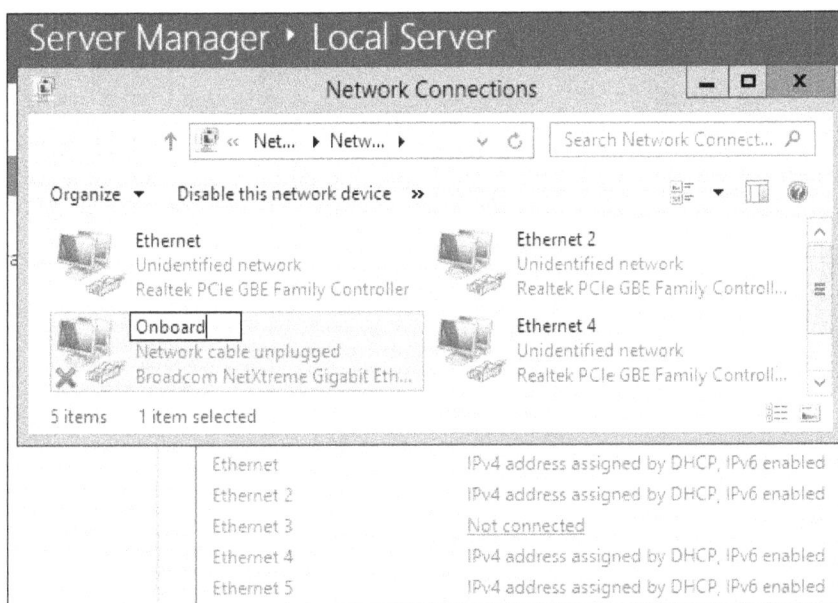

You can rename an adapter by highlighting it and pressing *F2* or by right-clicking and choosing **Rename**.

> It is highly likely that you will be typing these names in PowerShell commands, so it is recommended that you use a convention with short and memorable names.

In the R2 series of products renaming the adapters may be unnecessary due to a new feature called **Consistent Device Naming (CDN)**. If Windows is able to determine names from compliant hardware, it will automatically use them. They will show up with designators such as **NIC 1** and **SLOT 5**.

Creating network teams

Next, you'll want to create any teams that you intend to use. On the **Local Server** screen in **Server Manager**, click on **Disabled** next to **NIC Teaming**. You'll be presented with the **Nic Teaming** window. Click on the **Tasks** drop-down list in the **Teams** section and click on **New Team**. The following screenshot shows this:

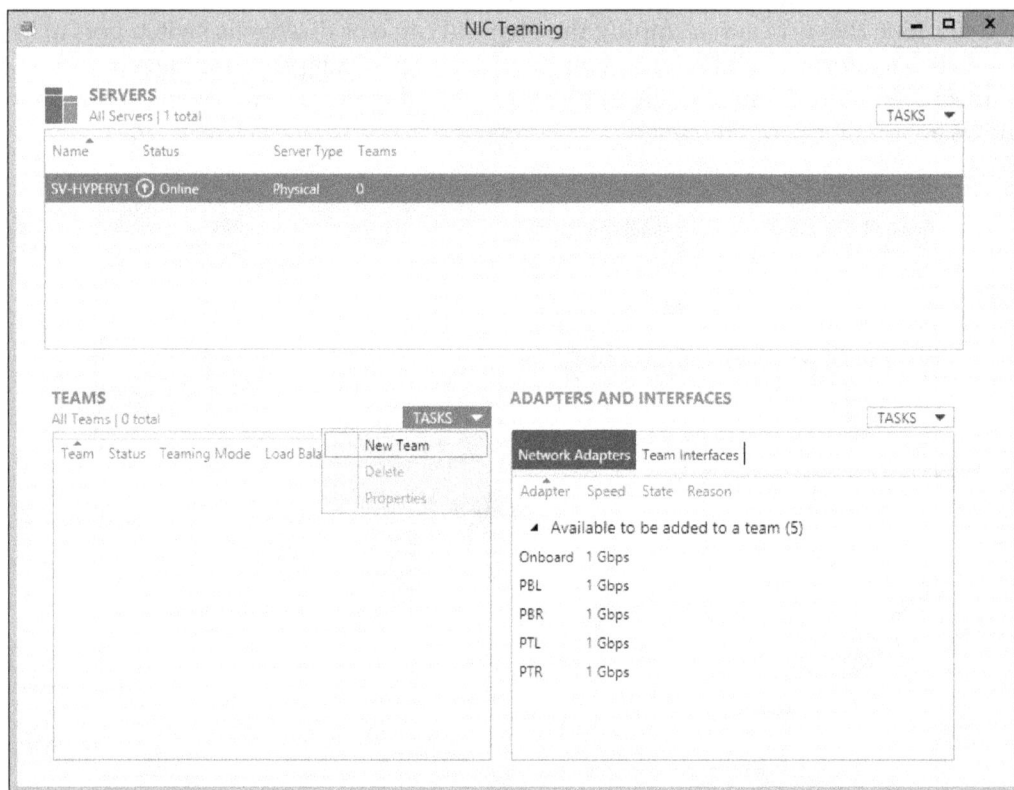

In the screen that appears, first give the team a name. If you are teaming adapters for a specific purpose, such as Live Migration, name the team accordingly. If you are teaming for *converged fabric* (this concept is explained in detail in *Chapter 5, Network Design*), use a generic name. Next, check the adapters that will be used in this particular team. Finally, click on the drop-down list for **Additional properties** and set these items accordingly. If you're not certain what to choose, pick the Switch Independent teaming mode, as the other two require special settings on your switch. Clicking on the link after **Primary team interface** allows you to set the traffic on the new logical adapter so that it is tagged for a specific VLAN. Unless you have a specific need of this, it is recommended that you leave it in the default VLAN.

If you want the team to participate in a specific VLAN, it is preferred to use your switch's interface to place the switch ports in a native VLAN instead of tagging in the operating system. VLAN tagging at the team level is strongly discouraged if the team will host a Hyper-V virtual switch.

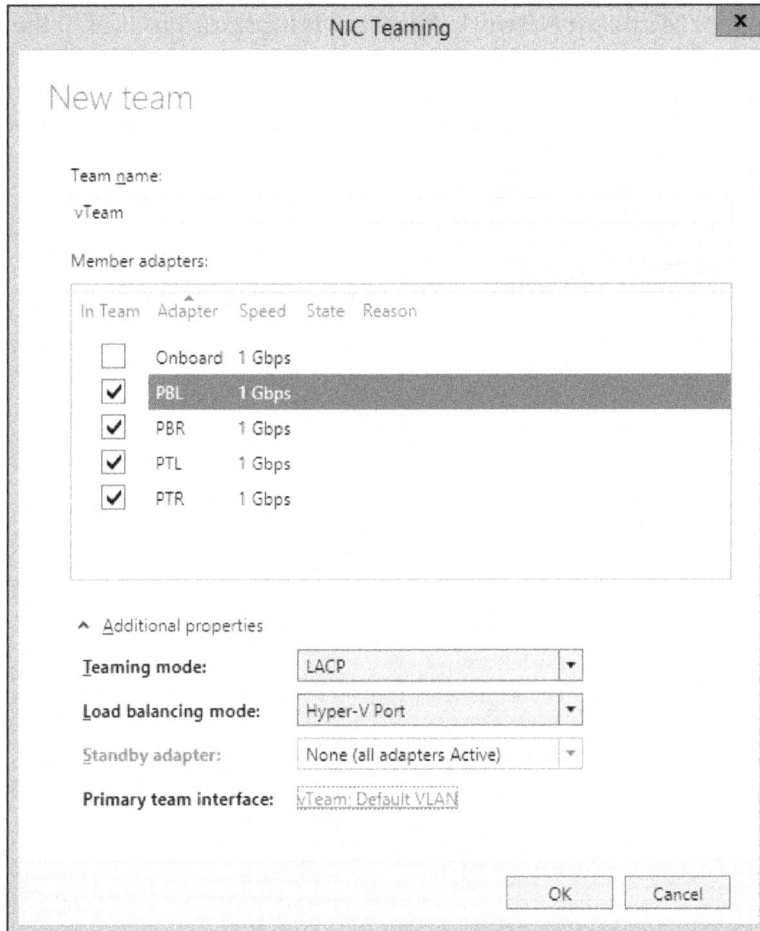

Once the team is created, it will appear in the previously empty boxes in the NIC Teaming window. You can double-click on these new objects to make any necessary changes. After creating or making changes to an LACP team, it is normal for it to show LACP negotiation errors for a short time after creation. If these don't disappear after a few minutes, check your physical switch configuration. Not all switches support all possible LACP methods. As with converged fabric, the teaming mode and load-balancing modes are explained in greater detail in *Chapter 5, Network Design*. They can be modified later, so don't worry too much about making an incorrect decision.

The creation of a team also makes a new logical adapter to represent it. This is now visible in Server Manager (after it refreshes) while the physical adapters that comprise it are now hidden. If you access the **Network Connections** screen, it will appear there as well, and you can configure it like any other adapter. Notice that the member physical adapters are still visible in **Network Connections** but are now unbound from everything except **Microsoft Network Adapter Multiplexor Protocol**. If the team will be used for a single purpose, you'll make any necessary changes (like IP addresses and DNS server entries) on the new logical adapter. If you'll be using the team to host a Hyper-V virtual switch included as a converged fabric, don't assign IP information.

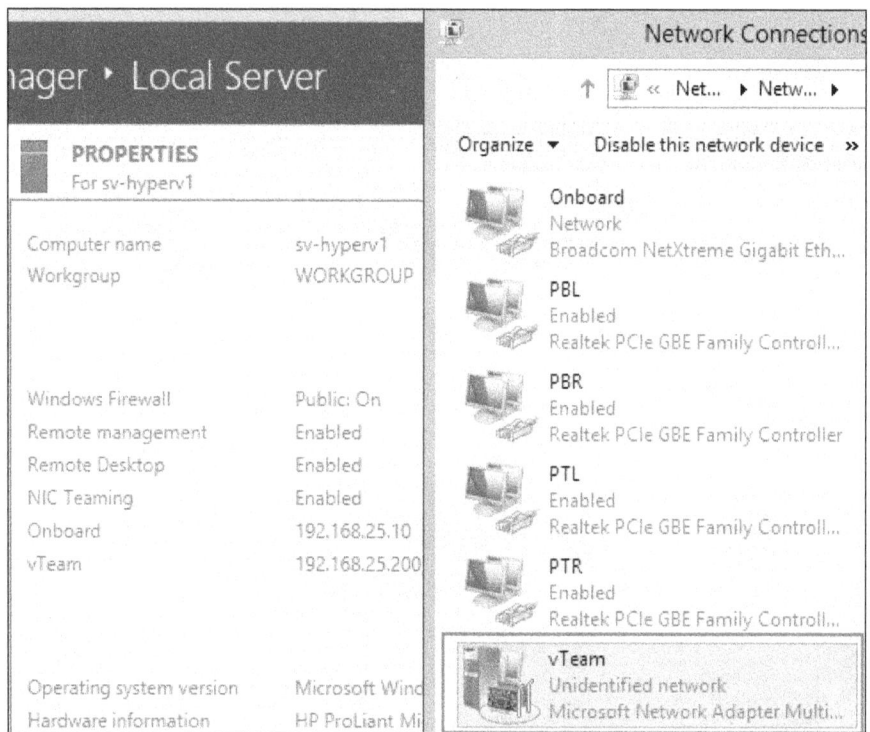

Enable roles and features

After the above options have been set, configure the system's roles. In Server Manager, you can click on **Manage** and then **Add Roles and Features** or you can click on **2 Add roles and features** from the dashboard. Screenshots are included previously in the section on adding the management tools to a Windows Server installation. This time, you'll want to select **Hyper-V** on the roles page and **Failover Clustering** on the features page. If you haven't already installed the related management tools, you will be prompted upon choosing the role or feature.

When installing Hyper-V as a role in this fashion, additional screens are added to the wizard. The first is simply informational. The next allows you to create a Hyper-V virtual switch. It is highly recommended that you create the switch later. If you create it now, you will not be able to set SR-IOV or the QoS method. The switch must be destroyed and recreated to set either. If you choose to create the switch now, you must ensure that you do not select a physical adapter that is part of a team. Instead, pick the logical adapter that represents the team as shown in the following screenshot:

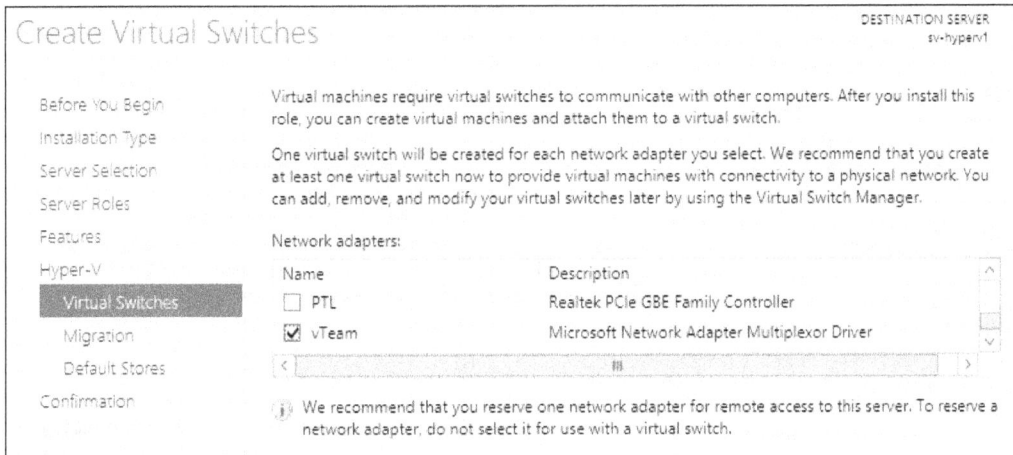

The next screen is for non-cluster Live Migrations. Since you will be creating a cluster, you can simply skip past this screen. However, cluster members can still perform Shared Nothing Live Migrations to each other and to any other Hyper-V Server hosts in this or a domain with a proper trust configuration, so you may elect to set these options now. Of course, they can also be set later, so there is no wrong way to configure this screen.

The third and final new screen will involve storage of virtual machines. Ideally you'd like to give these targets a shared location. However, this node doesn't yet know about those locations. They can be changed later by accessing the **Hyper-V Settings** screen of the node in Hyper-V Manager. Proceed through the rest of the wizard.

When the installation completes, you'll need to reboot the server. You can do this by switching to the **All Servers** tab, right-clicking on the server, choosing **Shut Down Local Server**, setting the options accordingly, and clicking on **OK**.

> The server will automatically restart two times after enabling the Hyper-V role.

If you chose to create a switch during the Hyper-V role installation, the management operating system will now have a virtual adapter on that switch which has any of the IP settings that were set on the adapter you assigned for the switch. If you don't want this adapter, the later sections of this chapter on Hyper-V Manager and PowerShell will show you how to remove it.

Creating or modifying a virtual switch

Before you can create a virtual switch, you'll need to know the **Description** of the network adapter you'll create it on. Open **Network Connections**. Each adapter will have a description field which is light gray in color in the default view. It will contain the hardware label, and if there are multiple adapters of the same manufacturer and type, a number. Since this is a long name, you can move the mouse cursor over each adapter to show the tooltip with the full name. You can also switch the view to **Details** mode. Refer to the screenshot in the previous section, *Renaming network adapters*, for examples.

Open **Hyper-V Manager**. Highlight the node in the left pane. Right-click on it and choose **Virtual Switch Manager**. Alternately, click on the link with the same name in the right pane. **New virtual switch** should already be highlighted. Ensure that **External Switch** is highlighted in the right pane and click on **Create Virtual Switch**. The following screenshot shows the resulting dialog with the information filled in:

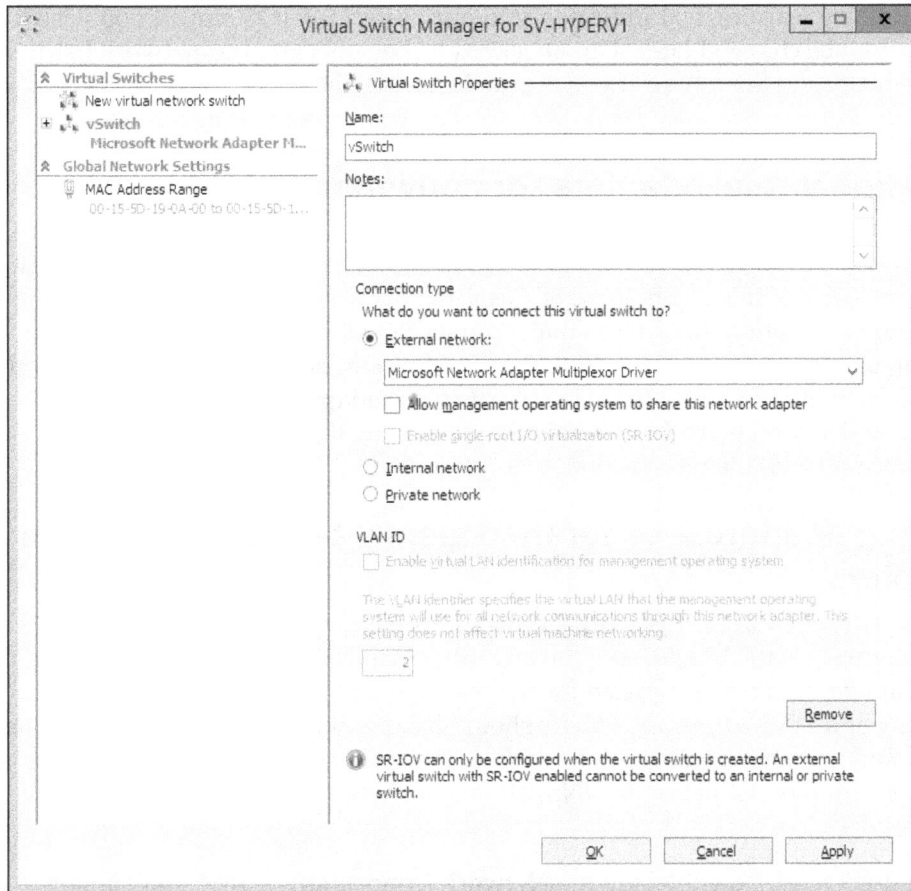

You need to provide a name for the switch, which is vSwitch in this scenario. Under **External Network**, you must select the **Description** of the adapter you want to create the switch on. In this case, the **Microsoft Network Adapter Multiplexor Driver** is the description of the teamed adapter that was created in the preceding steps.

If you click on the checkbox to **Allow management operating system to share this network adapter**, a new virtual adapter will be automatically created and assigned to the management operating system. All settings from the selected adapter will be transferred to this new virtual adapter. The selected adapter will be transformed into a switch and will no longer have any TCP/IP settings of its own. You do not need to select this option now; it can be selected at any time. You can also use PowerShell to add virtual adapters (shown in the PowerShell portion of this chapter). They will be discussed in *Chapter 5, Network Design*.

As the dialog warning text indicates, you must select **SR-IOV** now if you wish to use it. It cannot be changed later. This checkbox has no effect if your network hardware does not support SR-IOV or if you create the switch on a team. SR-IOV is given in detail in *Chapter 6, Network Traffic Shaping and Performance Enhancements*.

Creating virtual adapters for converged fabric

This part is optional, and you will only need to follow it if you intend to use *converged fabric*. Please review *Chapter 2, Cluster Design and Planning*, if you need an explanation of this technology, or *Chapter 5, Network Design*, if you need more in-depth information. In order to make converged fabric work, you must create virtual adapters that are assigned to the management operating system. Currently, there is no method within the GUI to create these adapters. Please refer to the PowerShell section given later in this chapter, create the necessary adapters, and continue with the next section.

Setting IP addresses for management operating system adapters

This is performed in the **Network Connections** window, and the process is the same as configuring static IP addresses on any other Windows installation. However, only the adapter you have designated for the management role should have assigned gateway and DNS addresses. Others should have only an IP address and a subnet mask. Furthermore, all adapters aside from the management adapter should be excluded from participating in DNS. More explanations will be provided in *Chapter 5, Network Design*.

If you don't recall how to get to the **Network Connections** screen, look under the **Rename Network Adapters** section. Right-click on an adapter and click on **Properties**. Double-click on the **Internet Protocol (TCP/IP)** with the version in use on your network (typically version four). Enter the IP address on the first page. To disable the registration of an adapter in DNS, click on the **Advanced** button, switch to the DNS tab, clear the checkbox titled **Register this connection's addresses in DNS**, and click on **OK** all the way back to the **Network Connections** window.

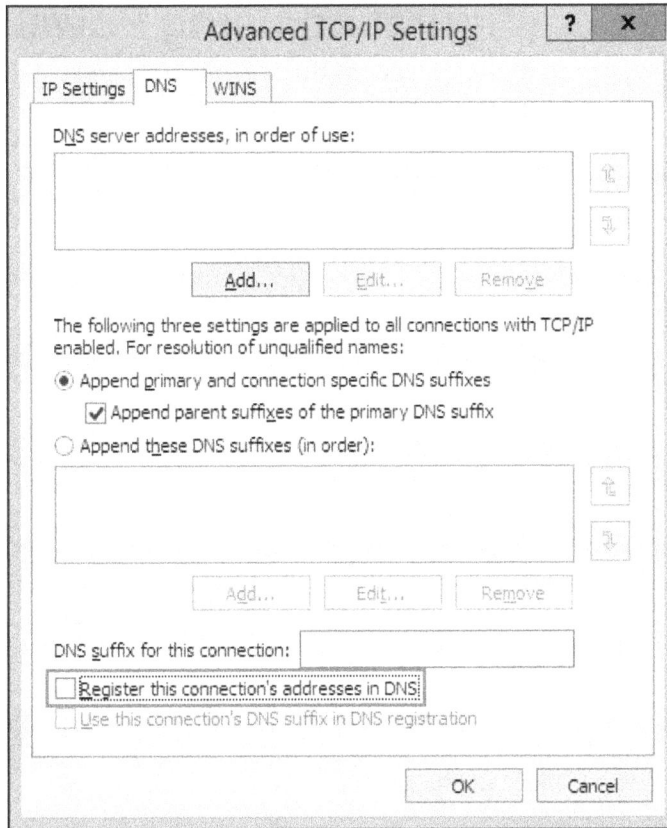

The management network and the Live Migration network must have their own IP addresses. It is recommended but no longer required that you have a network dedicated to the cluster communications role as well. These IP addresses must be in separate subnets. These IPs must also be on distinct physical or logical (team or virtual) adapters. Additionally, if your connection to shared storage is over an IP network, you will need at least one address and adapter for that, also in a separate subnet.

Joining the computer to the domain

Joining the management operating system to the domain is performed just like any other Windows Server installation. You can start on the **Local Server** page in **Server Manager** and click on the workgroup name to get started. If you didn't rename the system at the beginning of these steps, don't forget to do so.

Initial node configuration using PowerShell

All of the same steps used in the GUI configuration method can be performed at a PowerShell prompt, as can some that cannot be performed in the GUI. Not all possible options for each command will be shown here. The entire PowerShell library is available on Microsoft's TechNet site.

For Windows 8 and Windows Server 2012, use the following URL:

```
http://technet.microsoft.com/en-us/library/hh801904.aspx
```

For Windows 8.1 and Windows Server 2012 R2, use the following URL:

```
http://technet.microsoft.com/library/dn249523.aspx
```

Unless otherwise specified, all commands are entered using a PowerShell prompt running with administrative credentials. This is the default mode for Hyper-V Server and Windows Server in Core mode. To access PowerShell in either of these installations, just type powershell at any command prompt and press *Enter*. For a GUI installation of Windows Server, you must be running at an elevated prompt. To initiate that, right-click on the PowerShell icon and click on **Run as administrator**.

> Type logoff at the command prompt to end your session. If you accidentally close all command prompt windows, press *CTRL + ALT + DEL* (*CTRL + ALT + END* in an RDP session) and click on **Task Manager**. Click on **File**, then **New Task (Run)**. Type CMD in the **Open** field and press **OK**.

Remember that PowerShell is a complete *shell*, just like the existing command line. It has its own rules for handling input and parameters. So, even though you can call on the same commands from PowerShell that you can from a command line, they may not always behave the way that you expect them to. Familiar DOS commands, such as dir, may behave differently than expected as they are actually aliases for PowerShell cmdlets.

If you are completely new to PowerShell, you can still use these directions. Newcomers are encouraged to become acquainted with PowerShell first. You can begin on the related TechNet page: http://technet.microsoft.com/en-us/library/bb978526.aspx. To maximize clarity for those unfamiliar with PowerShell, the commands in this book will avoid positional parameters and shortened aliases with the exception of ft and fl (aliases for Format-Table and Format-List, respectively).

Any time you need to restart the computer from PowerShell, issue the `Restart-Computer` command. This executes instantly without confirmation.

Basic configuration

You can use the aforementioned `timedate.cpl` file at any prompt to change the system time and time zone. You can also use the `Set-Date` cmdlet to set the time, but there is no native PowerShell command to set the time zone. Your domain may issue a time zone and clock corrections through group policy, so you may elect to skip this portion. The command will look as follows:

```
tzutil /s "Central Standard Time"

Set-Date 1:40pm
```

At a regular command line or in PowerShell, you can enter `tzutil /?` for more information on using this built-in utility. The `Set-Date` cmdlet can be much more involved than is shown. Refer to the online help for more information.

You can rename the computer with the `Rename-Computer` PowerShell cmdlet:

```
Rename-Computer -ComputerName . -NewName sv-hyperv2
```

In the preceding command, the period after the `ComputerName` parameter indicates *this computer*. You will receive a message in yellow text indicating that you must reboot in order for the name change to take effect. You can choose to reboot now or wait until a later point. The computer name is unimportant until you join a domain.

Enable roles and features

The complete cmdlet for setting all necessary roles and features is shown in the following command:

```
Add-WindowsFeature -Name Hyper-V, Failover-Clustering, RSAT-Clustering, RSAT-Hyper-V-Tools
```

If you are running Hyper-V Server, the Hyper-V role is already enabled, but there is no harm in naming a role or feature that is already installed. Adding the tools is recommended but optional since their functions can be performed remotely. You could use the `IncludeManagementTools` parameter to automatically install RSAT tools for indicated roles instead of specifying the tool names, although unlike the shown command, it will not install tools for roles that are already enabled.

Once the roles and features are enabled, a table will be displayed showing the outcome. If a reboot is required, this will be indicated in the **Restart Needed** column. If a reboot is necessary and you intend to use converged fabric, you will need to reboot before continuing. Otherwise, you may skip the creation of the virtual switch and return to that after completing the remaining configuration steps and rebooting the host.

> The server will reboot two times while enabling the Hyper-V role.

Using PowerShell to configure networking

Windows Server 2012 introduced many new PowerShell cmdlets for network adapter management. They replace most of the functionality of the deprecated NETSH.EXE tool.

Rename network adapters

Renaming network adapters in PowerShell is simple, and is shown as follows:

```
Rename-NetAdapter -Name "Ethernet 2" -NewName "Onboard 1"
```

You'll need to determine how Windows matches its adapters to the physical hardware. The easiest way to do this is to unplug all adapters except one or plug in all except one. The following command will show you which adapters are connected:

```
Get-NetAdapter | Where-Object "Status" -eq "Up" | fl Name
```

If you wish to see adapters that aren't plugged in, change Up to Disconnected. You can use the pipeline to automatically submit an adapter for renaming:

```
Get-NetAdapter | Where-Object "Status" -eq "Disconnected" |
Rename-NetAdapter -NewName "Onboard 2"
```

If you use the pipeline in a way that attempts to rename more than one adapter, only the first will actually get the new name. The rest will generate errors.

> Network adapters can also be manipulated by using their interface indexes and descriptions using the InterfaceIndex and InterfaceDescription parameters.

Converged fabric

The next two sections will explain how to create the teams and switches that make up a **converged fabric**. If you prefer, there is a script that can automatically place all available physical adapters into a converged fabric for you. It is available from the TechNet gallery at `http://gallery.technet.microsoft.com/scriptcenter/Create-ConvergedNetwork-2c98bc37`. Converged fabric is explained in *Chapter 5, Network Design*, so read through that if you need more information.

Creating network teams

Creating teams in PowerShell is a quick and simple process. You need to know which adapters you want in the team, what mode you want the team to use (Switch Independent, Static, or LACP), and the load balancing algorithm (Hyper-V ports, transport ports, IP address hash, or MAC address hash—R2 introduces Dynamic). You'll notice that there are more load balancing options available through PowerShell than there are in the GUI. The different options are covered in *Chapter 5, Network Design*. To create a team, use the following command:

```
New-NetLbfoTeam -Name "ManagementTeam" -TeamMembers "Onboard 1",
"Onboard 2" -TeamNicName "Management" -TeamingMode SwitchIndependent
-LoadBalancingAlgorithm TransportPorts
```

Remember that when you are entering parameters that have predefined options, such as `TeamingMode` and `LoadBalancingAlgorithm`, you can use *TAB* to cycle through their options.

The name you provide for the `TeamNicName` parameter will become the name for the logical adapter that represents the team. Choose a name that is short enough that it won't be burdensome to type into further PowerShell commands but which clearly indicates what function the team serves. If you do not provide this parameter, the logical adapter name will be identical to the team name.

This sample creates a team on two adapters, presumably for management, and leaves other physical adapters available for other purposes such as other teams. The examples throughout this book combine available adapters into a single team called `vTeam`.

Create a virtual switch

Unlike the GUI role wizard, adding the Hyper-V role by PowerShell does not automatically create a virtual switch.

[System Center Virtual Machine Manager sees these as *standard switches*. You must use SCVMM to create *logical switches* with complete SCVMM functionality.]

The following command will create an external virtual switch that can be used for both converging management operating system roles and hosting virtual adapters for virtual machines:

```
New-VMSwitch -Name "vSwitch" -AllowManagementOS $false -NetAdapterName
"vTeam" -EnableIov $false -MinimumBandwidthMode Weight
```

[The `SR-IOV` and `MinimumBandwidthMode` parameters are completely optional, but they cannot be changed after the switch is created. All other options can be changed later. *Chapter 5, Network Design*, and *Chapter 6, Network Traffic Shaping and Performance Enhancements*, cover these settings.]

The shown command creates a virtual switch and assigns it to an adapter with the name `vTeam`. Assigning a virtual switch to an adapter automatically makes it an *external switch*. You can create one external switch per adapter. That adapter can be physical or a logical adapter that represents a team. You cannot create a switch on a virtual adapter. When an adapter is assigned to a virtual switch, it can serve no other purpose. Switch types and details will be explored in *Chapter 5, Network Design*.

Setting the `AllowManagementOS` parameter to `false` prevents the command from automatically creating a virtual adapter. It does not block them from being added manually, as will be shown in the next section. If you omit this parameter or set it to `true`, a virtual adapter will be created that has the same name as the virtual switch. The IP settings that were assigned to the physical or logical adapter will be transferred to this new virtual adapter.

[All cluster nodes must use the same names for virtual switches to ensure that virtual machines attached to them can move between nodes.]

Create virtual adapters

The only way to create virtual adapters for the management operating system is to use PowerShell. The command structure is very simple:

```
Add-VMNetworkAdapter -ManagementOS -SwitchName "vSwitch" -Name
"Management"
```

The `ManagementOS` parameter is a *toggle*; if not included, the system assumes you are trying to operate on a virtual adapter assigned to a virtual machine and will prompt you to provide the VM's name. This toggle appears in all virtual adapter PowerShell commands.

Virtual adapters in the management operating system live a dual life. For PowerShell commands and operations that are related specifically to virtual adapters, they are referred to by the name that you provided in the creation command. For general network adapter commands and applications, they are called `vEthernet` (the name used in the command). So, the preceding command would create an adapter named `vEthernet` (Management).

> Only use `Rename-VMNetAdapter` to rename virtual adapters. It overrides any changes made using `Rename-NetAdapter` or from the GUI.

Assigning virtual adapters to VLANs

With the requirement that cluster nodes use separate subnets for their various roles, you may choose to place them in separate VLANs as well. If you are employing virtual adapters on converged fabric for these roles, the virtual switch will need to handle the VLAN tagging for those adapters. Set VLANs on your virtual adapters with the following command:

```
Set-VMNetworkAdapterVlan –ManagementOS -VMNetworkAdapterName "Management"
-Access -VlanId 10
```

Setting IP addresses for management operating system adapters

The PowerShell command for IP address assignment is very straightforward. Only assign a gateway to the management adapter. Except for geographically distributed clusters, adapters for other cluster roles do not need, and do not benefit from, the ability to route. For those adapters, use the following:

```
New-NetIPAddress –InterfaceAlias "ClustComm" -IPAddress 192.168.30.10
-PrefixLength 24
```

The `PrefixLength` parameter refers to the subnet mask. This is given in CIDR notation; if you are unfamiliar with CIDR, consult with a networking expert or resource.

For the management adapter, which does need to be able to route, there is only one additional parameter, shown in the following code:

```
New-NetIPAddress -InterfaceAlias "vEthernet (Management)" -IPAddress
192.168.10.10 -PrefixLength 24 -DefaultGateway 192.168.10.1
```

There are a number of PowerShell commands that include the noun `NetRoute` for manipulation of gateway addresses. This topic is beyond the scope of this book.

In order to resolve the names of other computers and to register its own name, your system will need to know the addresses of DNS servers in your domain. Assign these addresses only to your management adapter:

```
Set-DNSClientServerAddress -InterfaceAlias "vEthernet (Management)"
-ServerAddresses 192.168.1.20, 192.168.1.21
```

You do not want the other adapters to register their addresses with a DNS server as this can cause problems for other systems that try to communicate with the management operating system. Run the following command on those adapters:

```
Set-DnsClient -InterfaceAlias "vEthernet (LiveMigration)"
-RegisterThisConnectionsAddress $false
```

Join the computer to the domain

The final major configuration change to be made during initial setup is to join the management operating system to your domain. This is a process that requires two PowerShell commands. The first sets up a PowerShell variable that holds the credentials that are used to join the domain. It is possible to completely script this. In this example, you will use a command that generates a pop-up box where you can type in the account information to join the domain. Remember to enter your credentials in `DOMAIN\Account` or `account@domain` format:

```
$JoinCredential = Get-Credential
```

```
Add-Computer -ComputerName . -Credential $JoinCredential -DomainName
"Techstra.local"
```

Optional node configuration steps

You have completed the required steps for initial node configuration. After the system is joined to the domain and you have rebooted, perform any other steps that are particular to your standard process for domain member servers. Run Windows Update (use option 6 in `sconfig.cmd` on non-GUI installations). Install any monitoring agents or other such software. If you will be using iSCSI or Fibre to connect to storage, perform the preliminary connection steps as indicated by the storage manufacturer's instructions.

You may also choose to configure remote access settings on your cluster nodes. The most useful is Remote Desktop, but it is also possible to open up access for other tools as well. Because your nodes are part of Active Directory and you will presumably want to apply all settings equally, it is highly recommended that you use **Group Policy** to control these settings instead of manually applying them on each node. If you wish to enable Remote Desktop manually, it is enabled in the GUI as in all versions of Windows: on the **Remote** tab in Computer properties. It can also be set from option 7 in `sconfig.cmd` (other remote access can be enabled using option 4). You can also enable Remote Desktop from the command prompt with the following command:

```
cscript %windir%\System32\Scregedit.wsf /ar 0
```

Prepare other nodes

Run the same procedures as above on all other computers you intend to add into your cluster. If you documented the steps that you followed, this should require very little time. If you used PowerShell, consider placing the commands into a configurable script. Also, System Center Virtual Machine Manager grants the ability to remotely deploy predefined Hyper-V systems.

> It is possible to use Sysprep on a Hyper-V server system. However, many of the more involved settings, such as adapter names and network teams, are not retained, so Sysprep is usually not of much value.

Building the cluster

Once you have at least one node ready to go, it's time to build the cluster. As with node configuration, it can be performed from the GUI or from PowerShell.

Cluster validation

Microsoft provides a cluster validation wizard to scan your systems and determine if they are suitable to be joined in a cluster. The tool is generic in nature, meaning that it is for validating all possible cluster types, not just Hyper-V Server clusters. The purpose and nuances of this tool are discussed in *Chapter 10, Maintaining and Monitoring a Hyper-V Server Cluster*. Validation is an important step, so do not skip it.

Running cluster validation in the GUI

If you're not certain that your equipment and configuration are cluster-ready, the GUI method of validation is preferred so that you can see the results instantly in an easy-to-read format. The tool to use is **Failover Cluster Manager**, which, assuming you followed the instructions from the first part of this chapter, is accessible from **Administrative Tools**. The validation wizard can be run from any domain member. It can be run using the following steps:

1. Start the wizard by right-clicking on **Failover Cluster Manager** at the top of the left pane and clicking on **Validate Configuration...** or by clicking on the link with the same name in the center pane. Both are shown in the following screenshot (R2 appears slightly different):

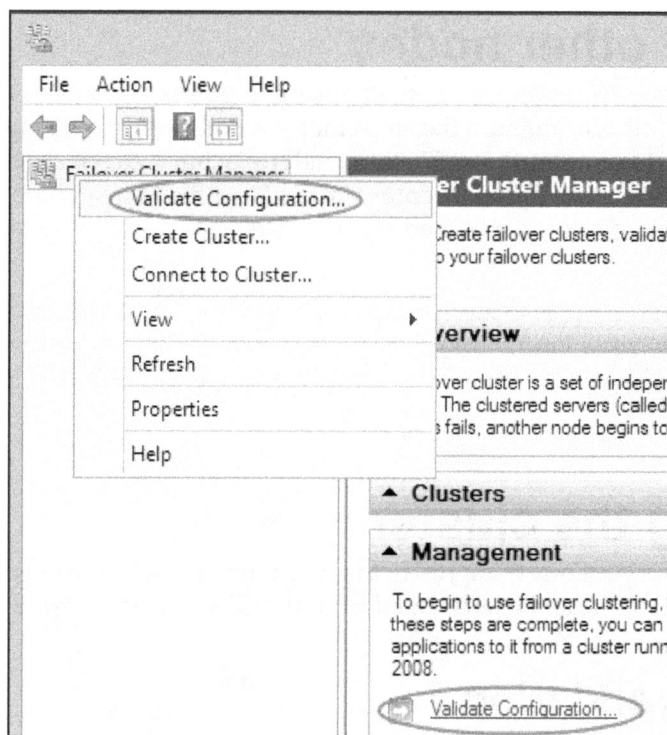

2. The first screen, unless you've previously instructed it not to appear, is simply informational. Click on **Next**.

3. Enter the names of the servers to be added into the cluster. You can type them in and click on **Add** or you can click on **Browse** to locate them in the directory. You only need the short name; once it verifies the server, it will automatically populate the **Selected servers** box with its fully-qualified domain name. It is quite common for the retrieved names to appear with different casing. This is purely cosmetic. Click on **Next** once you have selected all desired servers. This is shown in the following screenshot:

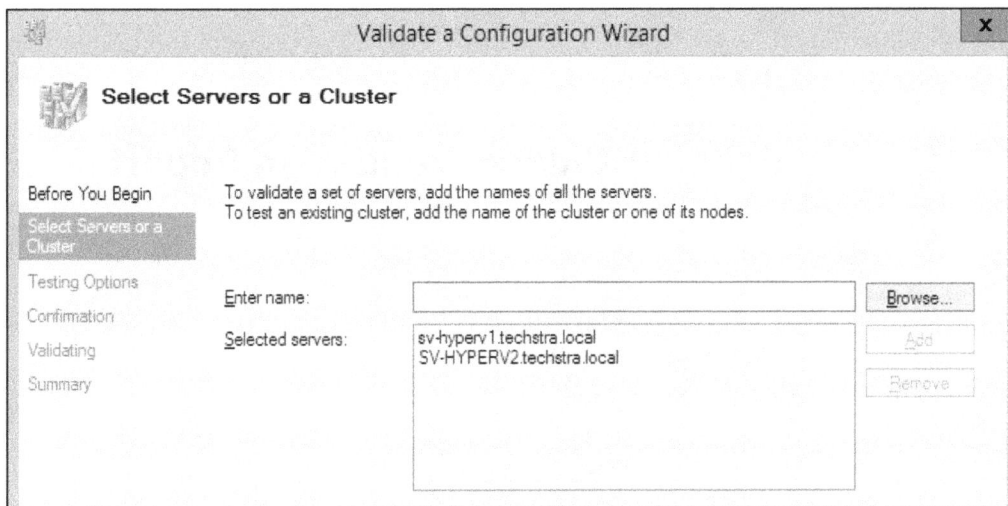

4. On the **Testing Options** screen, your choices are between running all tests or only a subset. Because this cluster is not yet active, it is better to run all tests and expect some warnings and errors than it is to try to exclude tests that you know will not pass. If you are running on an active cluster, you may wish to skip storage tests as I/O is interrupted during a full test. Choose your options and click on **Next** until you reach the confirmation screen.

5. The confirmation page lists the items you have chosen. Review them and click on **Next** to begin the tests or **Back** to make changes. The tests will take a few minutes to run. If you have many LUNs to validate, they will add to the required time.

6. Once completed, you'll be automatically brought to the summary page. Click on **View Report** to see the results. You can also click on **Finish** and view the reports later. This final screen is shown below:

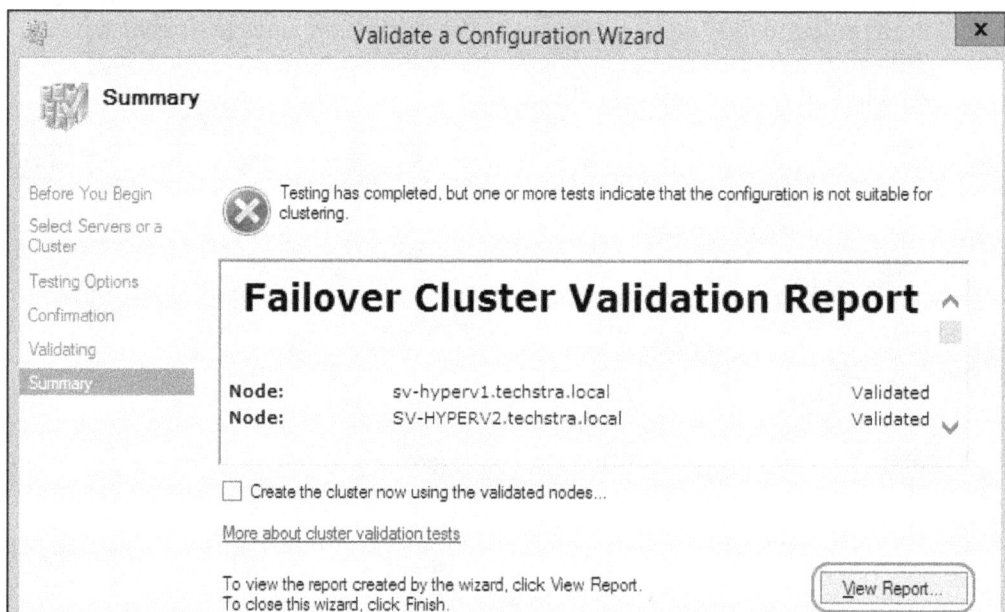

For help analyzing the results, read the first section of *Chapter 10, Maintaining and Monitoring a Hyper-V Server Cluster*.

Using PowerShell for cluster validation

As with the GUI version, the PowerShell validation can be run from any domain member that has the tool installed. The basic format of the command is extremely simple:

```
Test-Cluster sv-hyperv1, svhyperv2
```

There is some output from this that indicates whether a particular test passed or not, but details are stored in a cluster report file. The location and name of that file are given at the end of the validation process.

```
PS C:\Users\administrator.TECHSTRA> Test-Cluster -Node sv-hyperv1, sv-hyperv2
WARNING: Storage - Validate Disk Access Latency: The test reported some warnings..
WARNING: Storage - Validate Microsoft MPIO-based disks: The test reported some warnings..
WARNING: Storage - Validate SCSI device Vital Product Data (VPD): The test reported some warnings..
WARNING: Storage - Validate SCSI-3 Persistent Reservation: The test reported some warnings..
WARNING: Storage - Validate Storage Spaces Persistent Reservation: The test reported some warnings..
WARNING: Storage - Validate Disk Arbitration: The test reported some warnings..
WARNING: Storage - Validate Multiple Arbitration: The test reported some warnings..
WARNING: Storage - Validate Disk Failover: The test reported some warnings..
WARNING: Storage - Validate File System: The test reported some warnings..
WARNING: Storage - Validate Simultaneous Failover: The test reported some warnings..
WARNING: System Configuration - Validate Operating System Installation Option: The test reported failure..
WARNING: System Configuration - Validate Software Update Levels: The test reported some warnings..
WARNING: Network - Validate IP Configuration: The test reported some warnings..
WARNING:
Test Result:
HadFailures, ClusterConditionallyApproved
Testing has completed, but one or more tests indicate that the configuration is not suitable for clustering.
Test report file path: C:\Users\administrator.TECHSTRA\AppData\Local\Temp\2\Validation Report 2013.04.06 At
18.49.30.xml.mht

Mode            LastWriteTime     Length Name
----            -------------     ------ ----
-a---      4/6/2013   6:51 PM     420149 Validation Report 2013.04.06 At 18.49.30.xml.mht
```

There are a number of options you can submit to change the way that the validation process runs. Refer to *Chapter 10, Maintaining and Monitoring a Hyper-V Server Cluster*, for ways to modify the tests and read the results.

Cluster creation

Once you have cleared up any issues that the validation wizard identified, you are ready to create your cluster.

Creating a cluster using the GUI

You may have noticed that the last page in the validation wizard includes a checkbox to **Create the cluster now using the validated nodes…**. If you still have that available, checking that and clicking on **Finish** will start the cluster creation wizard. If you do not, then the **Create Cluster** menu items are in the same locations where you found the **Validate Configuration** items.

The first few screens that you see in the creation wizard will depend upon how you started the wizard. First, there is a welcome screen with information. If you started the wizard directly instead of from the end of the validation wizard, you'll have to select the nodes to add and you will be given an opportunity to perform a validation. If you choose to do so, it will switch to the validation wizard.

After the validation page or step, you will be on the **Access Point for Administering the Cluster** page. This is asking for two pieces of information. The first is the **Cluster Name**; this is the name of an Active Directory computer object that will represent the entire cluster. The second part is an IP address that will be assigned to the cluster name. The wizard will have preselected any network(s) with a gateway. If you have followed the guidance of this chapter, only the designated management network will be an option. Assign a unique IP to this cluster network. This will become the IP address that represents the entire cluster. It is relatively unimportant for a cluster of Hyper-V Server computers, but it is required. This is shown in the following screenshot:

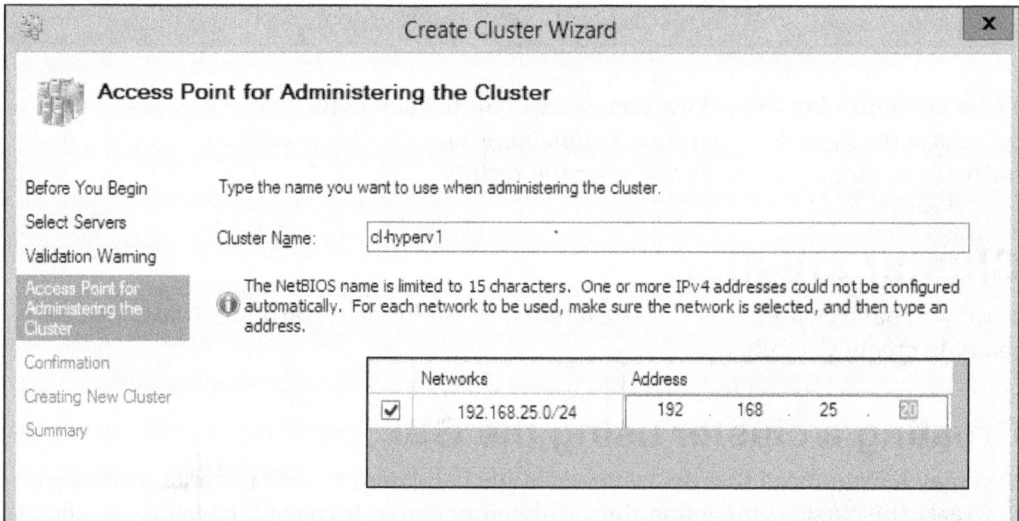

The next screen is, as its name implies, primarily for confirmation. However, it also includes a checkbox to **Add all eligible storage to the cluster**. If checked, any iSCSI, Fibre, or direct-attached storage that has been formatted with NTFS and is visible to all nodes will be placed into the **Available Storage** for the cluster. If you are running an even number of nodes, one of these will be automatically selected for quorum.

After clicking on **Next** on the confirmation screen, the cluster is created. If you have an even number of nodes and did not attach a formatted LUN to all nodes, you'll receive a warning indicating that quorum is not properly configured.

Creating a cluster using PowerShell

Using PowerShell to assemble the nodes into a cluster is very straightforward:

```
New-Cluster -Name cl-hyperv1 -Node sv-hyperv1, sv-hyperv2 -StaticAddress
192.168.25.20 -NoStorage
```

The `Name` parameter will become an Active Directory computer object that represents the entire cluster. The `StaticAddress` parameter creates an IP address for the cluster. The `NoStorage` toggle parameter has the same effect as leaving the **Add all eligible storage to the cluster** checkbox empty in the GUI wizard; any common storage is left unconfigured. If this toggle is not used, any storage that is visible to all nodes will be placed in the **Available Storage** pool, and if you have an even number of nodes, one of the storage targets will be automatically selected as the quorum witness.

Handling cluster creation errors

It is extremely rare for a cluster that passed preliminary validation to fail to create. The wizard can usually manage to successfully create something of a cluster even when the validation tests fail. Failure is so rare that when it does happen, the creation tool does not handle it well. In addition to addressing the problem that prevented cluster creation, you'll need to perform a bit of manual clean-up before you can attempt to create the cluster again. Use the following command:

```
Clear-ClusterNode -Name sv-hyperv1, sv-hyperv2
```

Because your cluster wasn't fully created to begin with, it is probable that this cmdlet will produce one or more errors. However, the clean-up process usually completes despite these messages.

Cluster post-creation steps

Congratulations! You have successfully created a functional failover cluster! However, it's going to need storage and will benefit from some tweaking.

Prepare storage

This chapter only discusses using storage that is already connected and recognized by the hosts. *Chapter 4, Storage Design*, will look closer at the tools used to connect to storage, but your hardware manufacturer is the best source for directions specific to their equipment.

Once all of your nodes have established a basic connection to storage, the next step is to get it into a usable condition. You can use the venerable Disk Management MMC snap-in, `diskpart.exe`, or PowerShell for this.

Server Manager can be run locally from each server, but you can also add others to the Server Manager console on one unit and manage them all at once. The following screenshot assumes you have connected to all of your nodes from a single Server Manager console.

In Server Manager, navigate to **File and Storage Services** in the left pane then click on **Disks** underneath **Volumes** in the center pane. You should be presented with a window similar to the following screenshot:

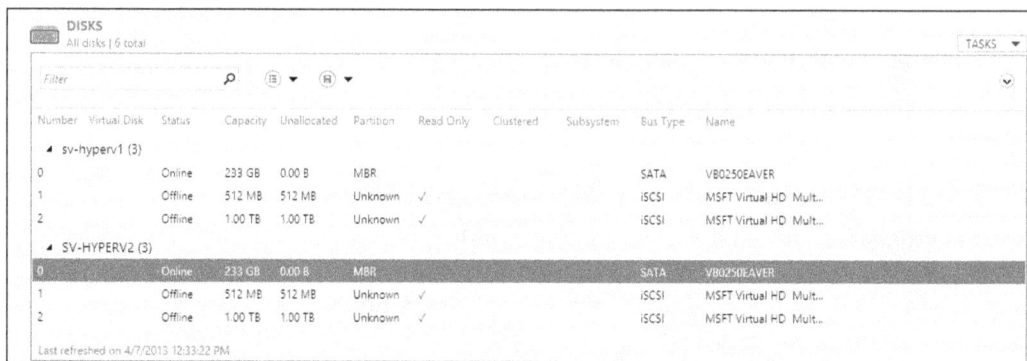

If you don't see the disks that you expect, click on **Tasks** in the top-right corner then **Rescan Storage**. The disks from the preceding screenshot represent raw disk space exposed on an iSCSI target. Notice that the iSCSI disks are visible to both nodes, but offline. All nodes must be connected to each disk you wish to use:

1. Pick any node; it does not matter which. Right-click on a disk you wish to add to the cluster and click on **Bring Online**. You will receive a warning that data loss may occur if the disk is already connected to another server. The warning is valid; you should not be operating on disks that are already in use. Click **Yes** to bring it online.

2. The status will change to **Online**, but will be otherwise unchanged. You can optionally *initialize* the disk, which creates the basic data structure on the disk that allows it to be used and places an identifying signature on it. However, you can also skip straight to clicking on the **New Volume** option on the right-click menu as that will automatically initialize the disk for you.

> Server Manager only initializes disks as *GPT*. For the purposes of a Hyper-V Server cluster, there is no harm in this. If you have need of the *MBR* standard, you will need to use Disk Management or `diskpart.exe` to initialize the disk.

3. Clicking on **New Volume** starts a wizard. The first screen is only informational. The second allows you to select the server and disk to work with; since you started from the right-click menu on a specific disk, this should already be populated as desired. Verify and click on **Next**.

4. If you didn't already initialize the disk, you'll be presented with a dialog box informing you that initialization will proceed. Click on **OK**. The wizard will ask for the size of the volume, defaulting to a size that consumes all space. Click on **Next**.

5. The next screen asks for a drive letter, path, or none of the above. If you intend to use this disk as a *Cluster Shared Volume*, it doesn't really matter what you select as all identifiers will be removed. For other uses, such as quorum, set a drive letter. Make your selections and click on **Next**.

6. The **File System Settings** page asks for format, cluster size, and a volume name. The format must be NTFS for use in a Hyper-V Server 2012 cluster as a quorum or CSV. ReFS can be used to hold virtual machines in R2. The default allocation selection should be acceptable; only override if your storage vendor indicates you should. If you wish to identify the disk by name in disk management tools, use a meaningful name; once added to a cluster, the name is not easily changed. Click on **Next**. Verify your settings and click on **Create**.

7. *Do* repeat for other disks. Do *not* repeat for the same disk(s) on other nodes! Only bring any given disk online on one server!

`diskpart.exe` can be used in place of the above. Such usage is beyond the scope of this book. PowerShell can also be used, but it can be somewhat tricky because the results aren't quite as easy to understand.

`Get-Disk` by itself will show all connected disks that the system knows about. It may not be as obvious which disks are which, however. You can also use `Get-Disk | fl *` to see much more information. Disks marked as Offline may be disks that you can't access online or they may be disks that are currently attached to other nodes, so be vigilant. Disks with a **Partition Style** of **RAW** have not been initialized and are usually safe to add. If you are uncertain, remember that Disk Management, Server Manager, Failover Cluster Manager, and so on can be used to connect to remote systems, so you are not required to use PowerShell even for systems without a GUI.

Using the output of `Get-Disk`, you only need the disk number and a single cmdlet to bring it online and initialize it:

```
Initialize-Disk -Number 4
```

Then, create a volume and format it:

```
New-Partition -DiskNumber 4 -UseMaximumSize -DriveLetter N
Format-Volume -DriveLetter N
```

Be aware that both `New-Partition` and `Format-Volume` have other parameters. Use `Get-Help` to view them.

Add prepared storage

Now that the storage is prepared, use Failover Cluster Manager to add it to your cluster. This is shown in the following steps:

1. If your cluster doesn't come up automatically, use the **Connect to Cluster...** option on the right-click menu of the **Failover Cluster Manager** item in the left pane. There is also a link in the center pane. Enter the cluster's name or the name of any of its nodes.

2. Expand **Storage** then right-click on **Disks** and choose **Add Disk** as shown in the following screenshot:

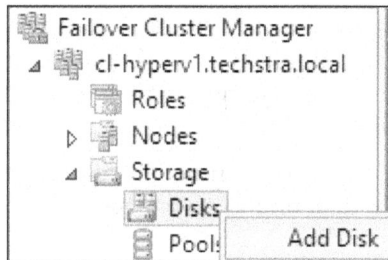

3. You will be presented with all of the disks that are visible to all nodes. They will be identifiable by the disk number and the node that currently has them set to online. Check the disks you want to use and click on **OK**.

You can rename a cluster disk by right-clicking on it and accessing its **Properties** screen. You can convert a simple cluster disk to a CSV by choosing **Add to Cluster Shared Volumes** on the same right-click menu. Do not convert a disk you intend to use for quorum to a CSV.

The preceding steps can be duplicated in PowerShell. Determine available disks with `Get-AvailableClusterDisk`, which needs no parameters for basic operation. Its output can then be sent through `Add-ClusterDisk` using the pipeline as shown in the following command:

```
Get-AvailableDisk | Add-ClusterDisk
```

For advanced options that allow you to add only a subset of disks, you can modify parameters on `Get-AvailableDisk`. Run `Get-Help Add-ClusterDisk -Examples` for examples, or view Microsoft's online TechNet information at:

```
http://technet.microsoft.com/en-us/library/hh847309.aspx
```

Configure quorum

You do not need to set any quorum settings on a cluster that has an odd number of nodes. A simple majority of running nodes is sufficient to establish quorum. A cluster with an even number of nodes requires a tie-breaker. The preferred way is to use a LUN on shared storage set aside specially for quorum purposes. That LUN must be formatted with NTFS. It will require very little space, but it is recommended that you use a LUN that is 512 MB as that is the minimum optimal size for an NTFS partition. You also have the option to point to a simple file share. The only requirement for that file share is that it exists on an NTFS partition.

The following options are a basic configuration. For more information and advanced steps, refer to *Chapter 11, High Availability*. To configure quorum, follow the given steps:

1. Right-click on the cluster's name in Failover Cluster Manager, go to **More Actions**, and click on **Configure Cluster Quorum Settings....** This will open the quorum wizard.

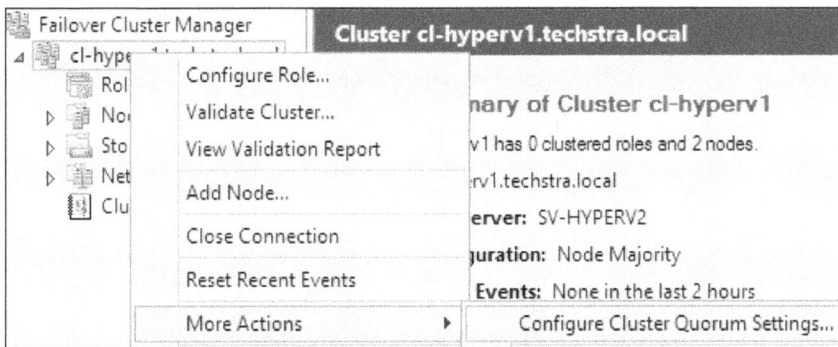

2. Click on **Next** on the first informational screen. If you have only one disk in cluster storage, you can accept **Use typical settings**. If you have more, choose **Add or change the quorum witness** and click on **Next**.

3. Unless the wizard recommends not configuring a witness, choose one of the top two options. The first, **Disk Witness**, uses a disk that you've added to cluster disks. The second, **File Share Witness**, uses a file share. This file share should not be on any of the cluster's nodes.

4. The remaining screens will depend on what you selected in Step 3. You'll either need to select one of the cluster disks (disk witness) or enter the UNC to a file share (file share witness). Proceed through to the end of the wizard.

To set the quorum with PowerShell, use the `Set-ClusterQuorum` cmdlet.

For a disk witness, use the following command:

```
Set-ClusterQuorum -NodeAndDiskMajority "Quorum Disk"
```

You can use `Get-ClusterDisk` to view the disks available for quorum. You cannot use the pipeline to apply it to the set cmdlet.

Set a file share witness using the following command:

```
Set-ClusterQuorum -NodeAndFileShareMajority "\\sv-shares\Quorum"
```

Configure networks

The final steps are to set cluster networks as desired. Expand the **Networks** node in Failover Cluster Manager and you will see all the networks the cluster has identified. To perform all the necessary steps, right-click on one and click on **Properties**. You'll be presented with the following screen:

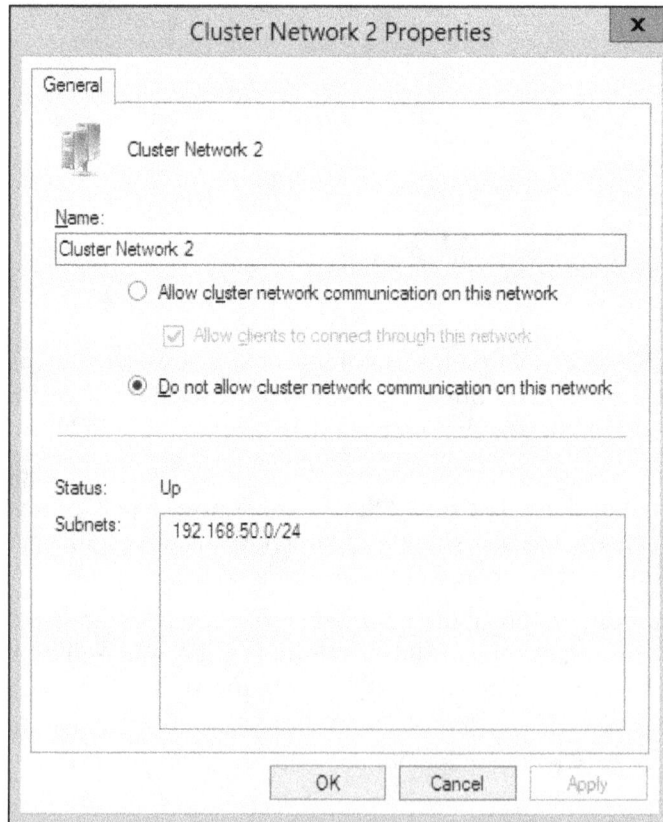

You'll probably want to start by renaming the network to something humanly-identifiable. Just change the **Name** field. The IP addresses shown in the **Subnets** section should help you identify which network you are looking at. Set the options as follows:

- Set the management network to **Allow cluster network communication on this network** and **Allow clients to connect through this network**.
- Set Live Migration and cluster communications networks (including CSV) to **Allow cluster network communications on this network**. Leave **Allow clients to connect through this network** unchecked.
- All networks used for storage communications or non-cluster traffic should be set to **Do not allow cluster communication on this network**. If the cluster creation wizard detected an iSCSI connection on any network, it would have already set this option for you.

There are no direct PowerShell equivalents to the above. You can use the dot operator with the Get-ClusterNetwork cmdlet to change items as follows:

```
(Get-ClusterNetwork -Name "Cluster Network 1").Name = "LiveMigration"
```

However, changing the network usage requires metric modifications. It's not terribly difficult, but it's not intuitive and is much more error-prone than using the GUI. This topic will be revisited in *Chapter 5, Network Design*.

Set Live Migration network preferences

The final network modification to make is to select which networks you wish to allow for Live Migrations in your cluster and how they should be prioritized. Right-click on the **Networks** node in Failover Cluster Manager and click on **Live Migration Settings**. A sample configuration of this dialog is shown in the following screenshot:

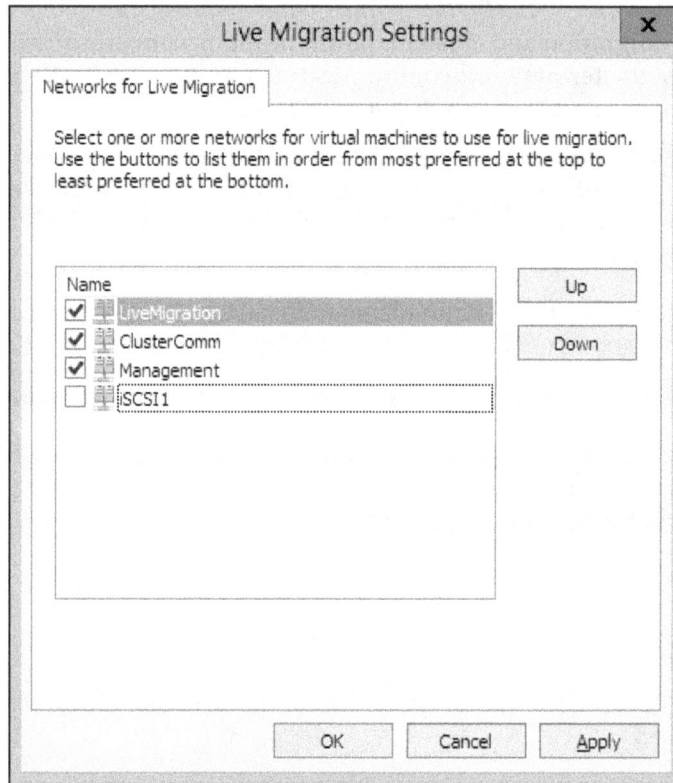

Obviously, this dialog is much easier to navigate if you have renamed the cluster networks. Use the **Up** and **Down** buttons to prioritize the networks to use. Uncheck boxes that you don't want Live Migration traffic on. Settings on this screen only apply to Live Migrations in the cluster. Adjusting Live Migration settings for communication with non-cluster nodes is controlled in Hyper-V Manager.

> In 2012, Live Migration will only use one network per host pair regardless of how many Live Migrations are checked on this screen. R2 removes this restriction, but both honor priority. If the highest-priority network is not available, it will then attempt to use the next in the list.

Summary

In this chapter, you learned how to obtain and activate the tools for Hyper-V Server and cluster management. You learned how to configure those nodes to run Hyper-V Server and participate in a failover cluster. You were also shown the steps necessary to perform basic cluster configuration.

At this stage, you should now have a cluster that is fully prepared to accept and manage virtual machines. For your planning document, you have nearly completed the initial deployment phase. There's still a lot to do to really get the most out of your system, though. The remaining chapters of this book will help you to enable its potential.

4

Storage Design

No other facet of a Hyper-V Server failover cluster has as many possibilities and variations as shared storage. The hardware options alone seem nearly limitless. Once you've settled on a hardware platform, you'll find that it has its own plethora of configurations. Unfortunately, there is no single right way to set up your storage. You can, however, make well-informed decisions that will result in a storage solution that meets the needs of your deployment.

Storage design and maintenance should be considered an ongoing endeavor, not something to be deployed and forgotten. You can connect Hyper-V Server hosts and clusters to multiple storage points, and Storage Live Migration allows you to relocate virtual machines from one storage location to another without interrupting operations. This allows you to dynamically adapt to changing needs and to relocate under- or over-provisioned loads to more suitable hardware.

The purpose of this chapter is to provide you with the necessary information to aid you in proper storage design, and show you how to implement it. This chapter will cover :

- Traditional storage options
- What SMB 3.0 shares can offer to your cluster
- Planning for the capacity needs of your cluster
- Planning fault tolerance for your storage
- Designing your storage for performance
- How to work with your virtual machines' storage

This chapter will approach these topics from basics to details. First, you will learn about drive technologies, and then you will learn various ways to arrange drives for redundancy and performance. Next, you will be introduced to ways to connect to storage, and finally, you will examine the methods of using storage for virtual machines.

Early storage planning

As you begin to consider the storage you're going to use, establish your priorities first. The four primary components you must balance are financial cost, speed, reliability, and capacity. Cost is typically the overarching control, and you can expect it to rise with increases in any of the other three. You may find that you need to sacrifice in one area or another to stay below your cost, so ensure that you have an established and agreed-upon prioritization of these elements.

To reliably support Cluster Shared Volumes, a storage device must support SCSI-3 **persistent reservations.** Persistent reservations are a finite resource; a device's limit is usually unpublished, and it is often lower than you might expect it to be. Fortunately, Hyper-V Server 2012 requires fewer persistent reservations than what 2008 R2 did. If your storage vendor has certified their products for Hyper-V Server 2012 in a multi-host environment, that usually indicates that they support persistent reservations. It is recommended that you have this verified in writing prior to making a purchase decision.

Another newly emerging option in storage devices is the ability to host share points that natively support Microsoft's SMB 3.0 protocol. An SMB 3.0 share point does not require the usage of CSVs, so there is no need for persistent reservations. Of course, general purpose computers running Windows Server 2012 can also host these share points, meaning that you may choose to forgo specialized hardware altogether.

Along with basic SMB 3.0 shares, there are a number of other possibilities with general purpose computers. Microsoft has enhanced its software iSCSI target and added it to the built-in options for Windows Server 2012 and R2. It has all the features necessary for hosting storage for a Hyper-V Server. Additionally, the new Scale-Out File Server and Storage Spaces features can be used for Hyper-V Server storage. All of these features can be hosted in a Microsoft Failover Cluster to provide a measure of redundancy.

Microsoft is not the only vendor providing software-based storage solutions. Other operating systems also have the ability to host iSCSI target software. Some software vendors have developed specialized *virtual SAN appliance* software, which is a virtual machine that presents its storage with many of the advanced features of a physical SAN.

Typically, dedicated storage hardware will have better performance and more options than a software solution. As hardware vendors have much more control over the entire contents of the provided solution, their employees and resellers can generally be of greater assistance to help you with capacity planning.

Since a software-based solution can use almost any type of hardware, more of the burden will be upon you, as the purchaser, to determine what sort of performance to expect from any given configuration.

Remember that you're not required to make a single decision. A Hyper-V Server cluster can connect to multiple shared storage systems. You can place a virtual machine with a high-demand SQL workload on a large FC array, while your archive-only image-retrieval virtual machines run from a stand-alone software-based iSCSI system.

Physical storage characteristics

A critical portion of your planning needs to focus on the design of the disk systems that will contain your virtual machines. The first thing you'll need are the IOPS projections you took from your work, as outlined in *Chapter 2, Cluster Design and Planning*. The second thing is the approximate amount of disk space that will be required. If you'll be using a dedicated storage device that employs iSCSI or Fibre Channel, it's recommended that you work with your hardware vendor's experts.

There are many resources available on physical storage. The author of this book has written a series of blogs posts devoted to the subject, starting with `http://www.altaro.com/hyper-v/storage-and-hyper-v-part-1-fundamentals`. This book will include only a basic introduction of the concepts to help you get started.

Physical disks

The most basic building block of your storage system will be the physical disks. Your choices are between spinning disks and **solid-state disks (SSD)**. Spinning disks are less expensive and have higher capacities. SSDs are faster but have shorter lifespans. You can purchase *hybrid* systems that use both types. The important terms to know when conversing about physical drives are IOPS and *sustained transfer rates*. You've already been introduced to IOPS; higher is better. The sustained transfer rate indicates the lowest speed at which the drive can reliably move data. Hard drives do have a cache that allows them to move frequently accessed data at a speed above the sustained rate.

Drive bus

Disks connect to their controllers using a bus. The three types in use today are: **IDE (integrated drive electronics)**, which is usually implemented with **SATA (serial advanced technology attachment)** disks, SCSI (**small systems computer interface**), and **FC (Fibre Channel)**. IDE/SATA is the slowest and least expensive and is usually found in laptops, desktops, and lower-end server storage systems. SCSI is faster and more common in server-class storage systems. In current hardware, SCSI is usually found as **SAS** (serial-attached SCSI), which has replaced older parallel SCSI. Fibre Channel is less common as a disk bus since it is no longer substantially faster or more reliable than SAS, but is still noticeably more expensive.

Traditional RAID

Spinning disks have moving parts, which means they are relatively slow and susceptible to failure. To combat both issues, server-class storage is commonly configured in a **RAID (redundant array of inexpensive/independent disks)** variant. There are a quite a few possibilities for RAID, but only a few are common for server-class systems. The following list briefly details the important differences:

- **RAID-1**: Also known as a mirror, it reads and writes identical data on two disks. If one fails, the other is used transparently. If both are working, read operations can be taken from both simultaneously and independently. Writes happen on both at once, but because it is the same data, only at the speed of a single drive. RAID-1 requires exactly two disks.

- **RAID-10**: Known as a stripe of mirrors. Drives are paired into mirrors like a RAID-1. Data is then *striped* across these mirror sets. The stripe allows for I/O to be distributed across the sets, resulting in very fast read/write operations. RAID-10 requires a minimum of four disks and must use an even number. Half of the total disk space is used for mirrored data.

- **RAID-5**: This is a *parity* RAID. Most of the data is live, but a portion equivalent to the size of one of the disks in the array is a calculation of the live data. If a disk is lost, the calculated parity can be used to determine what data it held and the array can continue to operate in *degraded* mode. The parity calculation causes a performance penalty on writes that makes it slower than an equivalently sized RAID-10. Reads are not impacted. Due to the characteristics of disk media, there are risks associated with using RAID-5 with very large disks. Your hardware vendor will be able to guide you on the proper use of RAID-5 with their systems. RAID-5 is appropriate when read operations are more common than writes and utilization of space is more important than raw performance. In RAID-5, space available for data is equal to the total number of disks minus one.

- **RAID-6**: This is another parity RAID. It uses the equivalent of two disks for parity with a more complicated calculation method. Like RAID-5, there is a penalty on writes for parity calculation. It has somewhat better safeguards against data corruption than RAID-5 does, but it is also risky to use with very large disks. As with RAID-5, your vendor will be the authority on how to implement RAID-6 safely. RAID-6 is used when space is more important than raw performance but RAID-5's protections are considered insufficient.

Storage Spaces

A new introduction with Windows Server 2012 (and Windows 8) is **Storage Spaces**. While it does not have the capabilities of mid-level or high-end SANs, it provides a large number of storage capabilities at a very low cost.

> Storage Spaces is available on desktop operating systems, but desktop-based storage is not appropriate for use with your Hyper-V Server cluster.

Storage Spaces require a Windows Server 2012 or R2 installation. You instruct the operating system to create a *pool* from available physical storage, and then configure *spaces* — virtual disks — in the pool. The physical disks should be directly-attached and can be SATA or SAS. USB 3 is also supported, but not recommended for a server deployment. Drives can be internal to the computer or inside an attached **JBOD (just a bunch of disks)** enclosure. Using disks that are in a hardware RAID of any type is not supported. The Storage Spaces filter can detect most hardware RAIDs, so do not attempt to fool it.

The Storage Spaces filter does not offer any traditional RAID configurations, but it does have protection schemes of its own that are conceptually similar. Additionally, Storage Spaces can be clustered. Once a Storage Space has been designed, its pools are presented to other systems as an empty storage field. It can even be used as a basis for other storage techniques. For example, you can use two Windows Server systems to create a Scale-Out File Server that provides redundant connectivity to a Storage Space. Storage Spaces can also host CSVs and SMB 3.0 shares.

A new feature of Storage Spaces in Windows Server 2012 R2 is *automatic tiered storage*. This allows you to mix SSDs and spinning disks in the same pool. A Storage Spaces watches how data is utilized and automatically moves more heavily accessed data to faster SSD, while relocating data that has been used less frequently to slower spinning disks.

The major benefit of Storage Spaces it that it brings shared storage to organizations that cannot afford more full-featured SANs. Learn more about Storage Spaces at http://technet.microsoft.com/en-us/library/hh831739.aspx.

Shared storage connectivity

The final consideration for storage is what method you'll use to connect to it. The top-tier choice is Fibre Channel. It's the most expensive but also the most reliable. Fibre Channel has its own protocol, conveniently called **Fibre Channel Protocol (FCP)**, which is lossless and therefore does not have the overhead of iSCSI. Fibre Channel requires special switching hardware, cables, and **host bus adapters (HBA)**. It can be converted to run over TCP/IP networks if necessary. FC is available in 2, 4, 8, and 16 gigabit per second speeds.

iSCSI is another common option. This is a protocol that encapsulates SCSI commands for transmission over a standard TCP/IP network. iSCSI can run on a standard computer system, such as Windows Server 2012 or R2. It utilizes common Ethernet cables, hardware, and switching devices. Its speed is dependent upon the capabilities of the Ethernet hardware used. As it uses TCP/IP, it does have more overhead than FC. As previously mentioned, Microsoft supplies an iSCSI target with Windows Server. Read about it and all its capabilities on its TechNet page: http://technet.microsoft.com/en-us/library/hh848272.aspx.

An emerging connection choice is **server message block (SMB)**; a protocol designed by Microsoft. In earlier versions, its primary application was for simple file sharing. SMB 3.0, introduced with Windows Server 2012, is capable of serving real-time storage needs. Its features include multi-channel, which allows it to automatically employ multiple network cards and paths to aggregate transfer bandwidth. If you use hardware capable of **remote direct memory access (RDMA)**, SMB 3.0 transfers are significantly accelerated by employing **SMB Direct**. As Microsoft publishes the specifics of SMB, other vendors are able to integrate it into their products. Hardware devices are available that provide SMB 3.0-based storage.

SMB 3.0 will be discussed further throughout the course of this book. You can also learn more about it on its TechNet page: http://technet.microsoft.com/en-us/library/hh831795.aspx. Microsoft publishes a blog that contains updates, sample deployments, and detailed technical information: http://smb3.info.

Hyper-V Server storage space utilization

Hyper-V itself is not concerned with drive technologies or connection methods. All it expects is one or more locations to place virtual machine files. Deployment planning will include understanding how Hyper-V Server uses storage.

Management operating system

The files for Hyper-V Server and its management operating system require 32 GB for a supported configuration, although by default, it will use less than half of that. It is recommended that this be placed on some form of internal storage, although Hyper-V Server can be booted in any fashion that Windows Server supports, including across a network. Files that make up the management operating system will be almost exclusively read, and most intensively during boot cycles. During normal operations, these files are very nearly idle. Therefore, there is no need to design storage for Hyper-V Server and its management operating system to provide high performance.

Earlier versions of Windows and Hyper-V Server would create page files that aligned with the size of physical RAM. Since a system designed for Hyper-V Server commonly has large amounts of RAM, this led to some inordinately sized page files. Hyper-V Server does not use this page file for guests, so the drive space was largely wasted. In Hyper-V Server 2012 and R2, default page file allocation is far more sensible and usually does not require tuning. Typically, the automatically sized page file will be at or below two gigabytes. If you use other applications in the management operating system, the file may be automatically grown to accommodate usage. Under normal conditions, the management operating system's page file will see very little usage, so tuning it is unnecessary.

BIN files

Hyper-V Server can place a virtual machine into a *saved state*. In this condition, a virtual machine is not running, but all of its memory and disk contents, active threads, and pending operations are stored in files. The BIN file contains the contents of memory of a saved virtual machine. If a virtual machine's Automatic Stop Action is set to **Save the virtual machine's** state, as shown in the following screenshot, the BIN file is always present and is equivalent to the virtual machine's allocated RAM. The file is pre-allocated to ensure that state saves will occur as quickly as possible and to prevent the space from being inadvertently consumed by other activities:

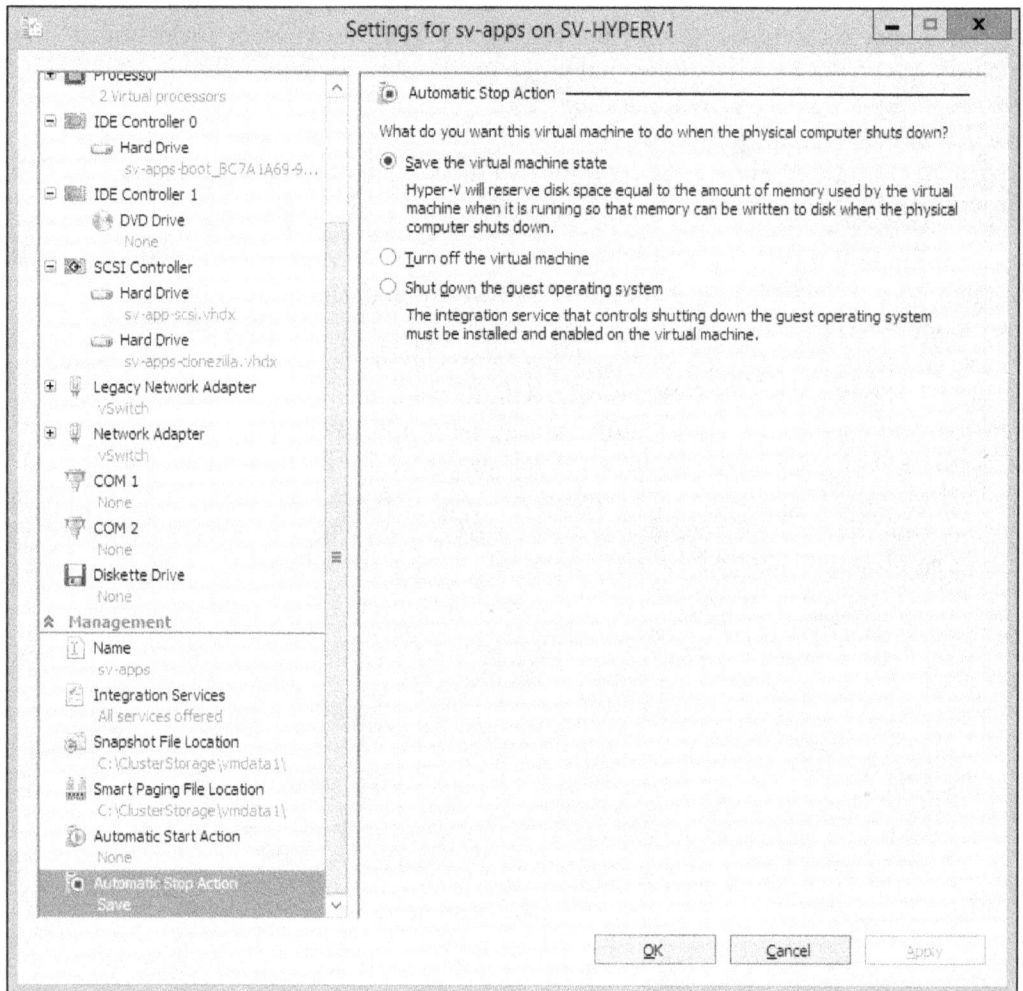

The preceding dialog is accessible for a clustered virtual machine by opening its Settings dialog in Failover Cluster Manager, and for a non-clustered machine, by opening its Settings dialog in Hyper-V Manager.

VSV files

A VSV file is related to BIN files in that they also contain information for a saved virtual machine. The VSV contains the state of all the virtual machine's hardware. This file will only be a few megabytes in size.

XML files

Hyper-V Server tracks the active and snapshot configuration of a virtual machine through XML files. These are normal XML files and viewing them in a standard XML viewing application is completely harmless. However, it is highly recommended that you do not perform any modifications of these XML files as it is far easier to render a virtual machine completely useless than it is to make any useful modifications by hand. Use the dedicated Hyper-V management tools instead. These files will rarely exceed 100 kilobytes in size. One will exist for the virtual machine and one per snapshot.

SLP files

Virtual machines often require a lot more RAM to start than they do to operate. One method Hyper-V Server 2012 and later uses to accommodate this is a short-term second-level paging strategy called **Smart Paging**. Under a very specific set of circumstances (which will be covered in-depth in *Chapter 7, Memory Planning and Management*), Hyper-V will handle page operations for virtual machines. When a smart paging event occurs, Hyper-V Server will create one or more SLP files that are cumulatively equivalent in size to the virtual machine's **Startup RAM** value. These will be deleted as soon as the virtual machine no longer needs them. If you will be employing Dynamic Memory, it is a good idea to spare enough storage to contain SLP files for all virtual machines that enable it.

VFD files

A VFD file is a virtual floppy disk image. Hyper-V Manager can create these files and attach them to the virtual floppy drive, a virtual machine, where they can be used just like a standard floppy disk.

VHD and VHDX files

VHD and VHDX files represent the *hard drives* that your virtual machines use for their data storage. Of all Hyper-V-related files, these will consume the most storage and make the best use of high performance arrays. These are the Hyper-V files you will spend the most time planning for and manipulating.

IDE and SCSI virtual controllers

Like any computer, your virtual machine will communicate with its storage through a drive controller. Of course, in a guest machine, these controllers are virtual. In terms of performance, there is no discernible difference. There are some usage differences. For guests in Hyper-V Server 2012, the SCSI controller requires a driver that does not load until the guest has begun much of its boot cycle. This means that a guest will be unable to boot if its boot VHD[x] is connected to the virtual SCSI controller. Also, due to driver load processing, the guest will not be able to use a page file placed in a VHD[x] attached to the virtual SCSI controller. In Hyper-V Server 2012 R2, you have the ability to create *Generation 2* virtual machines that do not have legacy components like the IDE controller. These machines do not have any such limitations, but they do require a guest operating system of Windows Server 2012 or later.

VHD versus VHDX

VHD is the first generation of Microsoft virtual hard disk files. It supports fixed, dynamic, and differencing types (discussed in the next section). It has an upper size limit of 2 terabytes. VHDX increases this limit to 64 terabytes and adds protection against data loss in the event of power failure. The only drawback to VHDX is that it cannot be mounted in operating systems prior to Windows/Hyper-V Server 2012 and Windows 8. It is possible to convert a VHDX file to VHD and vice-versa, so it is recommended that VHDX be the default choice in all 2012 deployments.

It is also possible to create VHDX files that use a 4,096 byte *sector* to align with the new physical drives. As there is no physical sector involved, there is no performance loss by employing the standard 512 byte format. Also, the virtual IDE controller does not support VHDX files with 4,096 bytes; only the SCSI virtual controller does. The real benefits of VHDX files with 4,096 byte sectors will only be realized with extremely large virtual disk files that are connecting to the virtual SCSI chain.

VHD and VHDX types

Virtual disk files are available in three primary types: fixed, dynamic, and differencing. The type that you choose will vary between workloads. A single virtual machine may use more than one type of drive. The following text will only mention VHD, although all information is applicable to both VHD and VHDX.

Fixed

Fixed is also the traditional name for non-removable storage, usually spinning hard disk drives. In the case of VHD files, it refers to a virtual hard disk that has a specific, constant size. When you create a fixed VHD, you indicate what its size is (such as 120 GB). A 120 GB VHD file is created immediately. Of the three VHD file types, this provides the fastest performance. In fact, the performance of a fixed VHD in comparison to raw storage on the exact same system is so close that there is no practical reason to choose raw storage.

Despite its name, it is possible to add space to a fixed VHD file. Turn the virtual machine off (not necessary for virtual SCSI disks in R2), use Hyper-V Manager for a non-clustered virtual machine or Failover Cluster Manager for a clustered machine, open its Settings dialog, and click on the **Edit** button on the fixed drive you wish to expand. This can also be done using the `Resize-VHD` PowerShell cmdlet.

Dynamic

When talking about VHD files, dynamic means *dynamically expanding*. This, and other similar operations are known as **thin-provisioning**. Thin-provisioning is when you define a resource to be of a certain maximum capacity, but the actual physical backing for that capacity is only provided as needed. When created, a dynamic VHDX file is only a few megabytes in size. As data is written to it, Hyper-V Server expands the file to accommodate the newly requested space, up to the maximum specified size.

There is a very real danger when using dynamic VHDX in that it is possible to allocate more space than actually exists. As an example, you can create 30 Windows Server virtual machines on a 1 terabyte LUN, each with a 40 gigabyte dynamic VHDX. Since Windows Server typically uses less than 20 gigabytes for itself, this is theoretically safe. However, the maximum size you've allocated for the VHDX files alone is 1.2 terabytes, which does not include space needed for the other supporting files. As long as this situation is monitored, it may not ever present a problem. In the event that all space on a volume is consumed, Hyper-V will pause all the virtual machines unless space is freed.

Differencing

Differencing disks are created in two ways. One is as an AVHD (or AVHDX) file. This disk is automatically created when a virtual machine is snapshotted (a checkpoint in R2), hence the leading *A*. The second type is when you manually instruct Hyper-V to create a differencing disk. In both cases, there is a parent disk that the differencing disk is attached to. As its name implies, the differencing disk tracks differences from the parent disk. For a snapshot/checkpoint, this means that if the snapshot is discarded, Hyper-V Server can just go back to using the parent disk file and it will be exactly as it was when the snapshot was taken. For manually created differencing disks, this allows you to use a single base file to build multiple virtual machines.

The mechanics of a differencing disk are actually very simple. Whenever a virtual machine performs a write operation that adds or makes changes to disk data, that information is placed into the differencing disk. When the virtual machine needs to read data, the differencing disk is checked to see if it has a newer version, and if not, the read occurs from the parent disk. In this usage, performance is usually not heavily impacted. However, it is possible to chain differencing disks, and performance suffers as the chain length increases.

Differencing in relation to fixed and dynamic is not a *versus* type of scenario. A differencing disk can be attached to any type. Differencing disks should primarily be used as temporary measures, such as snapshots/checkpoints, and testing virtual machines. They have the dynamic growth behavior of a dynamic disk but no upper limit on size. Since they track all changes, it is entirely possible for a dynamic disk to exceed the size of a parent. Unchecked usage of differencing disks can quickly lead to paused virtual machines. If this occurs, all virtual machines with files in that location will be paused.

> Never manually manipulate any virtual disk file that is part of a differencing chain in any way. This can cause permanent data loss. Clicking the **Inspect** button on a VHD in Hyper-V Manager or Failover Cluster Manager will open a dialog that shows if a disk is differencing, and if so, what its parent is.

Fixed versus dynamic disks

A very controversial subject is the debate between using fixed and dynamic disks. There really is no single "best answer" that will fit every solution. Due to this, your best approach is to learn all of the concerns and considerations and decide how they fit your environment and deployment needs. Some of these concerns are listed as follows:

- **Write Performance:** When a dynamic VHD file is instructed to write data beyond its current size, it must first expand its size by a certain number of blocks. This operation does take time, and in some loads it might be measurable. However, once the file is expanded, it does not dynamically shrink. Therefore, write operations that don't cause the VHD file to expand don't need any more time than they do for a fixed VHD.

- **Read Performance:** Read performance between the two types is functionally identical.

- **Fragmentation:** Hyper-V Server uses the file system to store VHD files the same way that any other process on a Windows system stores its data. When a fixed VHDX is created, it will be laid down on the disk as contiguously as possible, given current fragmentation levels. The placement of its blocks will never change unless a defragmentation pass is run. With dynamic VHD the odds of fragmentation are higher, and can be much higher if the systems perform many expanding writes. Fragmentation will be revisited in the performance section.

- **Space Allocation:** If you use only fixed VHD files, there is never really a concern of over-allocation. You'll know at creation time if you haven't got enough space. Dynamic VHD files need to be monitored to ensure that they don't overrun the available storage. With such monitoring, VHD growth is a containable risk. Leverage it to put more physical disk space to use without wasting gigabytes of space on fixed VHD files that will remain partially empty.

It is always safe to use fixed VHDX files and this is a common recommendation. Some usages demand it; for instance, you should always use a fixed VHDX for all SQL loads except the very lightest. Other usages are not as suited to the fixed format, such as system volumes for virtual machines that don't change often and/or store data on completely different VHDX files. It is perfectly acceptable to attach both types to the same virtual machine, so you could create a SQL virtual machine with a dynamic C: drive and attach fixed VHDX files to hold SQL data and logs.

> Whether you choose to employ dynamic/differencing disks or not, it is a best practice to always monitor storage locations of virtual machines for low space conditions.

Pass-through disks

Pass-through disks require no particular planning for storage because the entirety of a pass-through disk is connected directly to a virtual machine and holds nothing other than the data that the guest places on it.

Other storage usage considerations

In addition to the space that Hyper-V Server and its virtual machines use, other processes will need space. Chief among these are backup applications. If you will be using an application that interfaces with Hyper-V itself to backup guests, it will need to be VSS-aware. VSS works by making snapshots of volumes (not entirely dissimilar to Hyper-V's snapshot/checkpoint process), and allocates empty storage blocks for its work. The amount of space that VSS actually requires will vary based on the workload and the amount of time it takes for the backup operation to process, but it is a good idea to maintain at least twenty percent of a volume's space for VSS operations. In the case of the typical Hyper-V Server cluster deployment, this twenty percent will apply to CSVs and SMB 3.0 shares.

If you will be installing other applications alongside the hypervisor (hopefully only for the purposes of system management!), these will have their own storage requirements that must be accounted for.

Hyper-V Server storage performance

In most cases, storage performance will primarily be a concern for the VHDX files. Most other operations are occasional and short-lived.

The simplest (and most common) recommendation is to always use fixed VHDX files on RAID-10 systems. If you can afford it, this will certainly result in the best performance. However, a better recommendation is to understand the sort of performance that your Hyper-V Server cluster will require and ensure that your storage can provide at least that amount. *Chapter 2*, *Cluster Design and Planning*, covered using the MAP tool to assess your existing environment. If you explore other areas, it can also help you plan to deploy other Microsoft applications. So, if your measured and projected workload will need no more than a few hundred IOPS, there is little sense in building an oversized system to deliver thousands.

Pass-through disks

A technology that was widely used in older Hyper-V Server versions, but is rapidly falling out of favor, is the pass-through disk. This is a storage LUN or physical disk that is presented directly to a guest without any virtualization layer or VHDX abstraction. In previous versions, the performance difference between pass-through disks and fixed VHDX disks was noticeable, although very slim. In Hyper-V Server 2012, pass-through disks are usually not any faster, and when they are, it is difficult to actually measure the difference.

The lone advantage that pass-through disks offer is that they can be expanded without taking the guest machine offline. This advantage can be completely negated through careful provisioning. R2 can resize SCSI disks while online, so that final benefit is lost. The drawbacks are that a pass-through disk is not portable, a guest using it cannot be moved by Shared Nothing Live Migration, hypervisor-based backup applications must pause the guest to back it up, and snapshots are completely unaware of the pass-through disk and its contents. It is recommended that pass-through disks not be used.

Expansion

If you decide later that you need more disk performance than you initially counted on, it is possible to expand storage. One method is by scaling up. RAID-5 and RAID-6 arrays can usually be expanded online, and just by adding a disk. RAID-10 arrays must be expanded two disks at a time. The Storage Spaces filter has its own methods for expansion. Expanding existing arrays onto new disks requires a rebuild operation of some sort. That takes time and requires a fair bit of disk activity that will usually impact operational performance. Also, you may not have any more drive bays to fill. In these cases, it may be preferable to expand by scaling out.

Scaling out storage is performed by adding new storage locations. In some configurations, you might add new disks to an existing storage chassis and create a new array alongside existing ones. In other configurations, you will acquire entirely new storage devices. This is usually the more expensive approach, but it doesn't place your existing data in any danger. You can use the new storage only as targets for new virtual machines, or you can employ Storage Live Migration to relocate existing machines to it.

Fragmentation

Fragmentation was briefly covered in the discussion around fixed versus dynamic disks, but it is a topic that deserves further inspection. File *fragmentation* occurs when portions of a file are stored in non-contiguous locations on a disk. It is really only a concern on single, slow disks, like those found in end-user computer systems, and then only if the application requires high performance disks or is sensitive to disk latencies. With fast disks in multi-spindle arrays, the effects of fragmentation often fade away in the regular latencies of spinning hard disks. In very high-load read/write operations, such as SQL servers, it is sometimes possible to measure the impact of fragmentation. In the majority of scenarios, negative performance from fragmentation cannot even be detected without running a drive benchmark tool.

Running a defragmentation process in a Hyper-V Server cluster is not recommended for the following three reasons:

- It is unlikely to result in noticeably improved performance:

  this is really the chief reason. Defragmentation takes a long time, it adds a lot of wear and tear to your disks, and usually doesn't result in a meaningful improvement.

- You can use Storage Live Migration instead:

  defragmenting a storage location with virtual machine files requires that you take the virtual machines offline for the duration of the operation, and as previously stated, that operation can take a very long time. Set up an empty LUN and use Storage Live Migration to move the machines to it one at a time. Assuming the LUN was created in contiguous empty space, the virtual machines' files will be written contiguously as they move to the new storage. If the new LUN isn't as fast as the old one, you can just move them right back. This way, you don't incur the downtime and you have smooth and high-performing high-capacity reads and writes instead of the choppy block-by-block read/write operations of a defragment process.

- Your storage device may not like it:

  defragmentation of SSDs is a good way to send them to an early grave with absolutely no performance improvement. It can also be a bad idea on some medium-end and high-end spinning disk systems. The storage industry is well-aware of the performance problems inherent to spinning disk systems and are constantly devising new ways to combat them. One is by *intelligent data placement*. Storage Spaces in R2 and some SANs can monitor the data and dynamically relocate heavily accessed blocks to the fastest locations on disk. A defragmentation process completely invalidates all of the measurement metrics it uses and can cause your relatively unused data to wind up on high-speed storage.

Fragmentation and dynamic VHDX performance

As mentioned in the preceding section, fragmentation is one of the most contentious topics in discussions regarding dynamic VHDX files. Fragmentation does cause a performance hit and for some workloads it can be meaningful, however, it must be treated realistically.

First, remember that dynamic VHDX files do not become retroactively fragmented. Consider the installation of a new virtual machine. You set its C: drive as a dynamically expanding disk and then install Windows to it. It will almost immediately balloon to around 20 gigabytes in size, and that 20 gigabytes of consumed space will be no more fragmented than a fixed VHDX would have been. Dynamic VHDX files do not dynamically shrink, so all of those blocks will stay exactly where they are unless someone intentionally runs a defragment tool or uses Storage Live Migration to move them.

Think of this in the context of patching a new system. After deploying the new virtual machine, you run Windows Update on it. This process downloads a relatively large quantity of data and then patches the system. The fear is that this causes the VHD to become fragmented, negatively affecting performance. The following diagram illustrates how this actually looks. The top line is a representation of the newly patched system in a VHD. The bottom line represents the same guest in a fixed VHD:

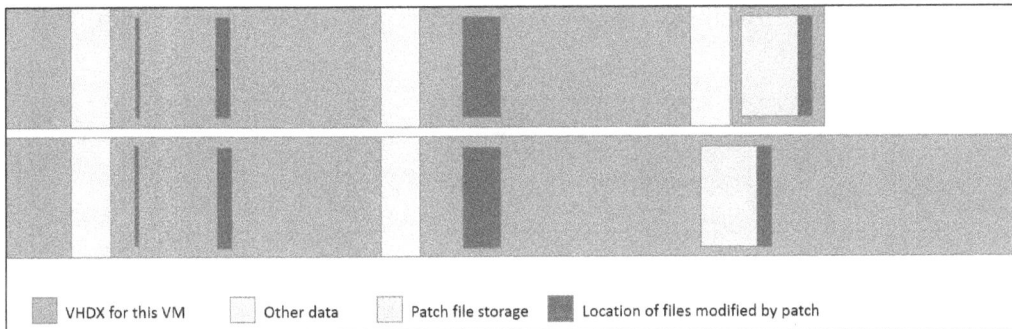

At deployment time, both disks are created to fill in any existing spaces left by previous disk operations. When the dynamic disk was patched, it caused a growth spot that was separated from the main disk by some previous existing data; this, of course, was not necessary for the fixed disk because it had already allocated that space. However, the patch data was placed contiguously in this case. In both of the patches, some patch files were placed optimally and others were placed at the end of the data volumes inside their respective types. An in-guest defragmentation cycle might arrange the files more appropriately, but the dynamic VHDX did not become significantly more fragmented than the fixed VHDX.

Working with storage

Now that you have seen the technical details of storage, it's time to become familiar with the actual operations involved with manipulating your storage.

> If your storage device manufacturer included specific instructions to connect to and work with their equipment, their instructions take precedence over anything in this chapter.

Connecting to iSCSI storage

The directions here will be for connecting to standardized iSCSI targets without a specific interface, such as the Microsoft iSCSI Software Target. The simplest way to connect to iSCSI storage is with the built-in GUI application, which is available on all levels of Windows Server and Hyper-V Server 2012. From a command or PowerShell prompt, run `iscsicpl.exe`. For a GUI installation, you can find the iSCSI Initiator under Administrative Tools. On first run, you will be greeted with the following dialog:

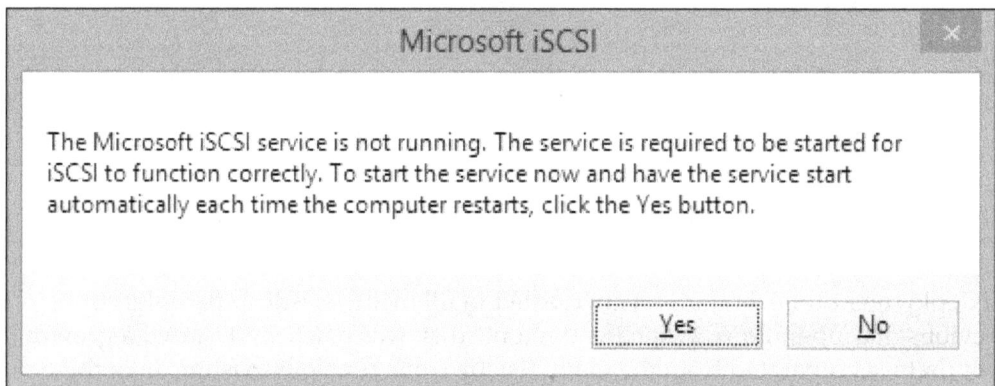

Microsoft iSCSI

The Microsoft iSCSI service is not running. The service is required to be started for iSCSI to function correctly. To start the service now and have the service start automatically each time the computer restarts, click the Yes button.

Yes   No

Click on **Yes** to continue. You will be presented with the following dialog box:

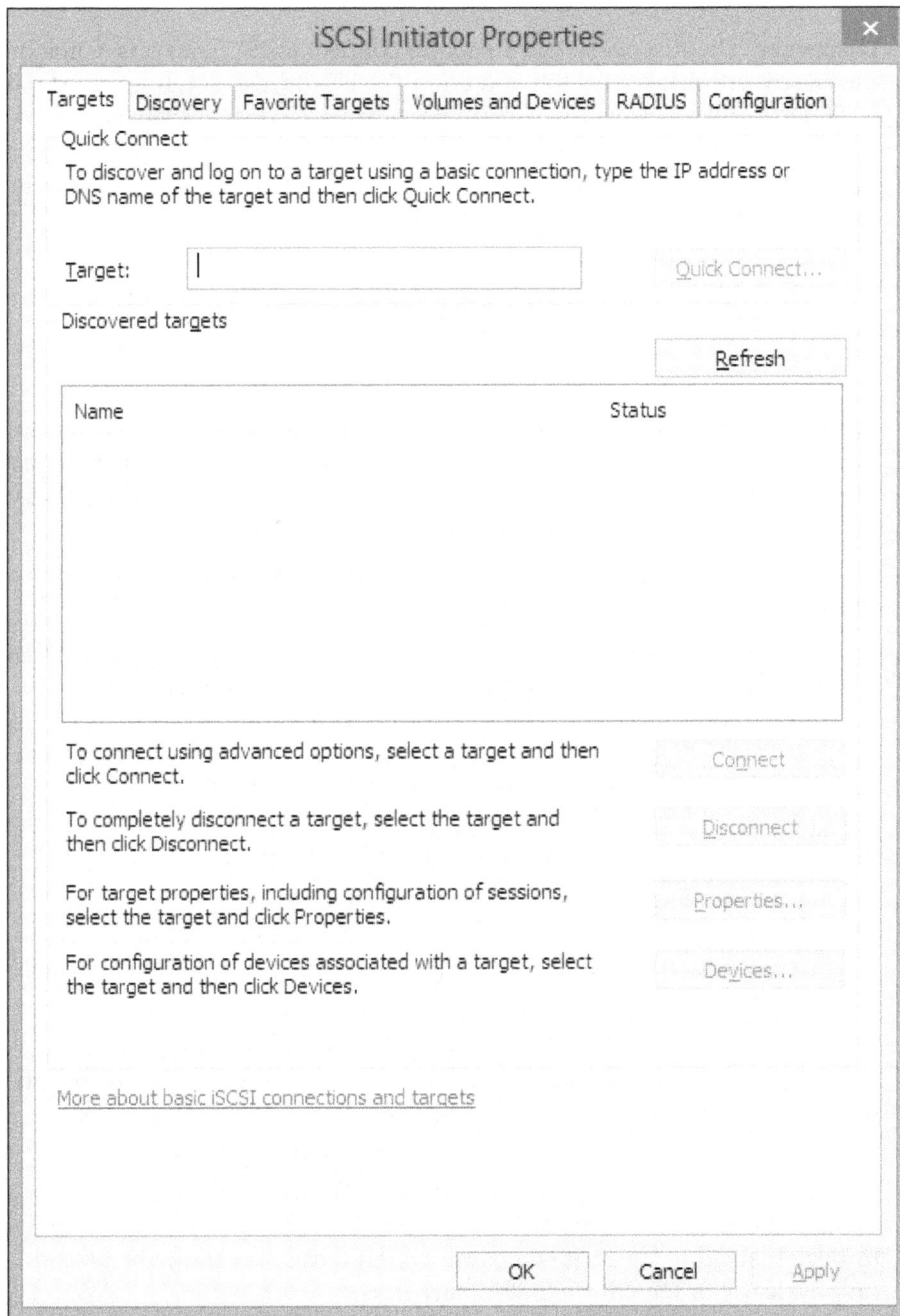

The default **Targets** tab displays all discovered LUNs and their status. This is the page you will generally spend the most time on. Let's discuss the other tabs first.

- **Discovery**: The discovery tab is used to connect to iSCSI targets. Click on the **Discover Portal...** button and enter the IP address or name (short name or FQDN) of the target. The default port for iSCSI traffic, **3260**, is pre-filled, but you can change this if your iSCSI target portal operates on a different port. If the portal requires a login, click the **Advanced...** button and enter the necessary login information in the corresponding fields.

> iSNS deployments are not common. If your hardware requires this, instructions will be included with that equipment.

- **Favorite Targets**: This tab shows connections that this system will attempt to restore each time the Microsoft iSCSI Initiator Service is started, usually at reboot. If you choose to permanently disconnect a target, ensure that you remove it from the **Favorite Targets** list.

- **Volumes and Devices**: For a Hyper-V Server deployment, you can ignore this tab.

- **RADIUS**: RADIUS is a standard authentication function that some iSCSI targets employ. This involves using a third-party authentication server, must like Active Directory. The Microsoft iSCSI Target Software does not support RADIUS authentication. If your storage target does, you can set up a RADIUS server on Windows Server using the built-in Network Policy Server. Refer to the following TechNet article for more information: `http://technet.microsoft.com/en-us/library/cc755248.aspx`.

- **Configuration**: In general, you should ignore the **Configuration** tab. It allows you to change the initiator name, which, by default, is based on the computer name and is therefore guaranteed to be unique within a Windows Active Directory domain.

- If your target uses mutual CHAP authentication (which means that your initiator must sign on to the target, and then the initiator must also authenticate to your initiator), the shared secret is entered on this tab.

- Usage of IPSec on an iSCSI link is discouraged unless it is specifically required to meet a high-security demand. IPSec adds considerable overhead to TCP communications and you will most likely notice the impact. Instead of IPSec, it is recommended that iSCSI traffic be placed on physically or logically isolated networks.

The **Report** button generates a text-file dump of the active and saved connections on the system.

The basic process for connecting to an iSCSI LUN is as follows:

1. For a target without security and on the default `3260` port, enter the target's IP or name (short name or FQDN) in the **Quick Connect** field on the **Targets** tab. Otherwise, use the **Discovery** tab as outlined above.

2. When discovery completes, all LUNs on that portal made visible to this initiator will appear as **Inactive** on the **Targets** tab.

3. You can quickly connect to a LUN by highlighting it and pressing **Connect**. If you wish to manually set individual connections, you can highlight and click on **Properties**, then use the **Add** button to add individual sessions. With either method, you are presented with the following dialog:

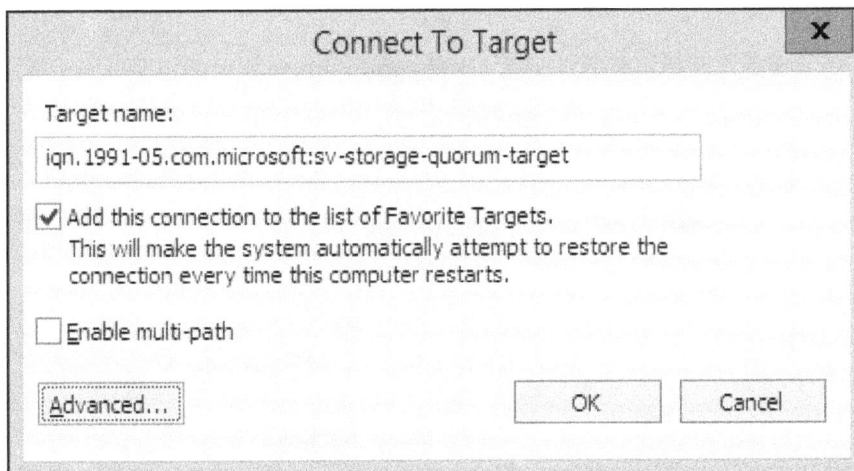

- ○ The checkbox to **Add this connection...** will place the LUN on the Favorite Target list so that it is reconnected at each restart.

- ○ The **Enable multi-path** checkbox allows MPIO for this target. Ensure that your target supports MPIO before using. If this is the first connection to this target, additional steps may be necessary to fully enable MPIO. These will be covered in the Enabling and using Multi-path IO section.

- If your target doesn't do well at automatically selecting the proper IP channels to use or if you need to login to the LUN, click on the **Advanced...** button. This is the same basic screen as seen when connecting to a target portal. You can specify which source and destination IP to use for a single connection and enter CHAP security. It is possible for a LUN to use different security than its portal.

Upon connecting to the LUN, it will show up in disk management much like a local disk.

Connections can also be made using PowerShell commands. These aren't as difficult as using the command-line version of the iSCSI initiator (`iscsicli.exe`), but they can quickly become complicated if you need to perform advanced authentication. Since `iscsicpl.exe` is available on all Windows and Hyper-V Server platforms, it is recommended that you save the PowerShell commands for scripting purposes.

To connect to a portal (for discovery), use the following command:

```
New-IscsiTargetPortal -TargetPortalAddress 192.168.50.100
```

If you'd like to specify initiator addresses to make multipath discovery easier:

```
New-IscsiTargetPortal -TargetPortalAddress 192.168.50.100
-InitiatorPortalAddress 192.168.50.10
```

Of course, you can also use names instead of IP addresses. Other parameters that may be necessary for authentication are `AuthenticationType`, `ChapUsername`, `ChapSecret`, `IsHeaderDigest`, and `IsDataDigest`.

The `Connect-IscsiTarget` cmdlet is used to connect to LUNs. You can pipe in the output from `Get-IscsiTarget` if you wish:

```
Get-IscsiTarget | Connect-IscsiTarget
```

Alternatively, you can connect using the parameters `NodeAddress`, `TargetPortalAddress`, and `TargetPortalNumber`. You can specify the source initiator with `InitiatorPortalAddress`. In the previous command, `Connect-IscsiTarget` uses the same security parameters as `New-IscsiTargetPortal`.

All documentation for the various 2012 PowerShell iSCSI initiator cmdlets is available on TechNet: http://technet.microsoft.com/en-us/library/hh826099%28v=wps.620%29.aspx. R2 documentation is available at http://technet.microsoft.com/en-us/library/hh826099%28v=wps.630%29.aspx.

Connecting to Fibre Channel storage

As FC storage requires special drivers and special software, your manufacturer should have included directions for connectivity. You can optionally use *Storage Manager for SANs*, which is a feature that can be installed on Windows Server 2012 and R2. It won't have all the features of the software specific to your device. See the following TechNet article for more information: `http://technet.microsoft.com/en-us/library/cc753405.aspx`.

Connecting to SMB 3.0 shares

SMB 3.0 shares are by far the easiest; there is no connection routine. When designing a virtual machine and/or its storage, simply enter the share name for the location. Use the format `\\SERVER\SHARE_NAME`.

Enabling and using Multipath IO

Multipath IO (MPIO) is only needed for iSCSI and FC targets. SMB 3.0 will automatically use multi-channel if multiple paths are detected and available. To use MPIO, you must first install the feature. You can perform this by using the **Add Roles and Features** wizard and selecting **Multipath I/O** on the **Features** screen as shown in the following screenshot:

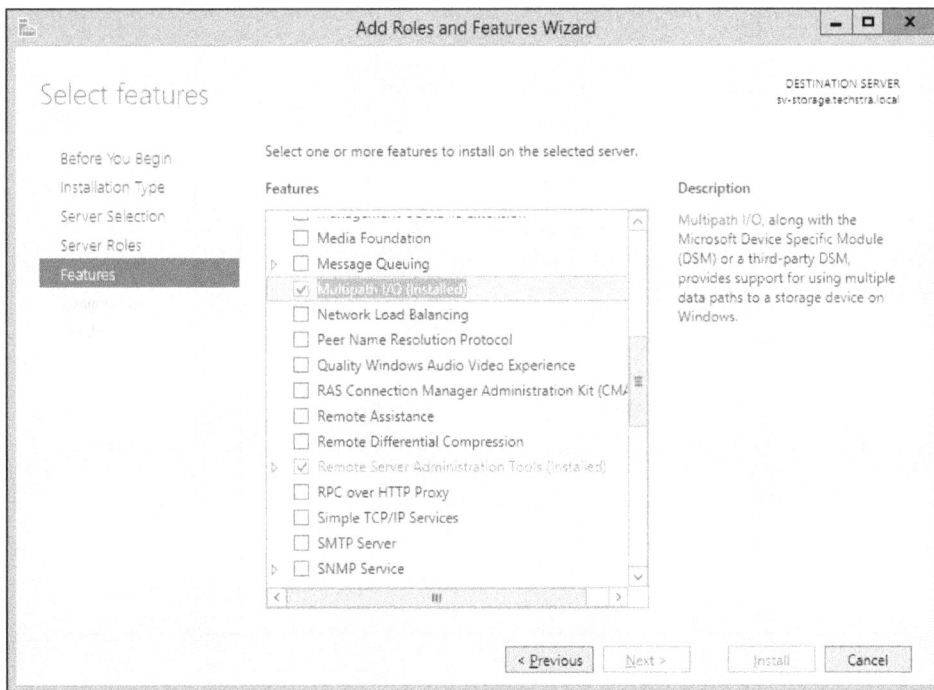

You can also enable it with PowerShell:

```
Install-WindowsFeature -Name Multipath-IO
```

After it's enabled, you'll need to turn it on for specific targets. Run `mpiocpl.exe` from a command or PowerShell prompt, or in **Administrative Tools**, double-click the MPIO icon. The **Vendor 8Product 16** entry is simply a placeholder and doesn't do anything, so ignore it. If it is the only item that is displayed on the first tab, then your system is not MPIO-enabled for any other targets. Switch to the **Discover Multi-Paths** tab. If neither of the check boxes are available, then your system does not detect any MPIO-capable devices. You may need to install a manufacturer-specific DSM (instructions should be provided by the manufacturer). If either check box is enabled, check it and click on **OK**. After a reboot, MPIO is enabled and functional. You can return to the iSCSI Initiator applet (`iscsicpl.exe`) to check for multi-path sessions, (click on **Properties** on a LUN, as shown in the following screenshot), or to create additional sessions (The **Add** button is on that same window):

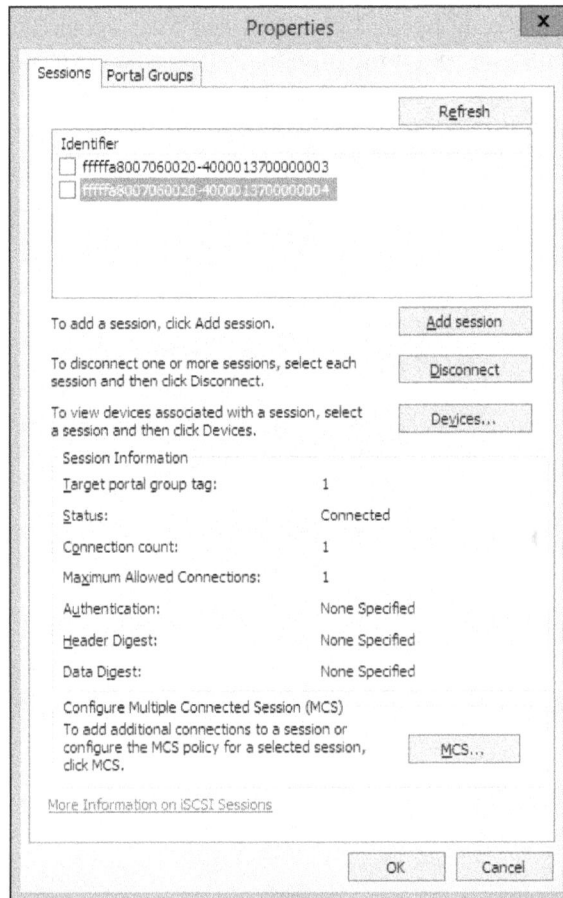

Depending on your connection method, you will either see multiple sessions in the **Identifier** box (most common), or the **Connection Count** and **Maximum Allowed Connections** field will have numbers higher than one.

You can use the **Devices...** button on the previous screen to access and change the MPIO policies for the LUN.

There are a number of available PowerShell cmdlets for working with MPIO. The most useful of these is `Set-MSDSMGlobalDefaultLoadBalancePolicy`, which sets the default method of load balancing on MPIO connections:

```
Set-MSDSMGlobalDefaultLoadBalancePolicy -Policy LQD
```

In this command-line, `LQD` indicates Least Queue Depth, which means that traffic will favor the path that currently has the fewest pending I/O operations. You can cycle through the options by pressing the *Tab* key immediately after typing in the `Policy` parameter and pressing the *spacebar* key. Other options are Fail Over Only (`FOO`), Round Robin (`RR`), Least Blocks (`LB`), and `None`.

View documentation for this and other 2012 MPIO-related cmdlets at:

`http://technet.microsoft.com/en-us/library/hh826113%28v=wps.620%29.aspx`

The cmdlets have not changed for R2, but the URL is:

`http://technet.microsoft.com/en-us/library/hh826113%28v=wps.630%29.aspx`

Managing disks

You can still work with disks using the Disk Management snap-in which is part of Computer Management. However, Windows Server 2012 adds new power to Server Manager for disk management. These are available under the **File and Storage Services** tab. Click on **Disks** under **Volumes** to get started. You can refer to the *Prepare Storage* section at the end of *Chapter 3, Constructing a Hyper-V Server Cluster*, for a walk-through of using Server Manager and PowerShell to bring new storage online. Don't forget that you'll need to establish a connection to the disk from all cluster nodes before you can use it as cluster storage!

To be used, disks must be formatted. Quorum disks must always be NTFS. Hyper-V Server 2012 requires that its virtual machines be placed on NTFS. Hyper-V Server 2012 R2 allows its virtual machines to be placed on the ReFS file system as long as it is hosted by Windows Server 2012 R2. You can learn about ReFS from the TechNet site:

`http://technet.microsoft.com/en-us/library/hh831724.aspx`

Once a disk is added to each node, you must then make it available for cluster use. In Failover Cluster Manager, navigate to the **Storage** node. Expand it and click on the **Disks** node. Click on **Add Disk** in the right pane. All available disks will appear. Check the boxes for any that you wish to add and click on **OK**. Once added, you can right-click on any of them and click **Properties**, where you can rename them to be more user-friendly.

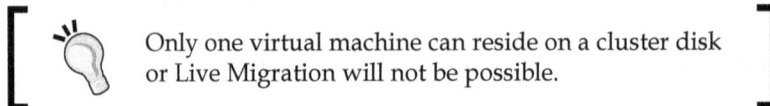

> Only one virtual machine can reside on a cluster disk or Live Migration will not be possible.

The benefit of cluster disks is that they don't require Persistent Reservations.

Cluster Shared Volumes

Access the **Disks** sub-node of the **Storage** node. Right-click on any cluster disk (except any quorum disk witness), and choose **Add to Cluster Shared Volumes** to convert it to a CSV. This is unnecessary for virtual machine storage on SMB 3.0 shares.

Finding and renaming Cluster Shared Volumes

You can rename the cluster's representation of the CSV right inside **Failover Cluster Manager**. Open its Properties dialog and change the name there. However, adding a CSV creates a *symbolic link* in the NTFS folder structure and while its name will also be **Volume1**, it will be separate from the name in Failover Cluster Manager. Even though these are symbolic links and not actual folders, they can be renamed using standard Windows and command-line tools for renaming folders. You can locate the volume in Windows Explorer under C:\ClusterStorage from any node in the cluster. You can rename a folder from a command or PowerShell prompt using the following command:

```
ren C:\ClusterStorage\Volume1 VMData1
```

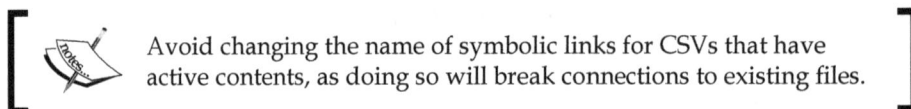

> Avoid changing the name of symbolic links for CSVs that have active contents, as doing so will break connections to existing files.

CSV cache

The CSV cache feature was introduced the 2012 product series. This cache is a portion of system memory set aside on each node that caches that node's CSV reads (not writes). To use it, you must first enable it. For 2012 (not R2), on any node, run the following cmdlet:

```
Get-ClusterSharedVolume -Name "VMData1" | Set-ClusterParameter
CsvEnableBlockCache 1
```

You can omit the Name parameter to set all simultaneously. If you later decide that you want to disable it, run the same cmdlet with a 0.

In R2, the cache is already enabled. If you wish to modify it, replace CsvEnableBlockCache with EnableBlockCache.

Once the feature is enabled, set the amount of memory to be used for block cache. You can use any amount you like, but 512 megabytes is recommended. On any 2012 (not R2) node:

```
(Get-Cluster).SharedVolumeBlockCacheSizeInMB = 512
```

This setting can also be disabled by re-entering the cmdlet with a 0.

For R2, replace SharedVolumeBlockCacheSizeInMB with BlockCacheSize.

Reboot the hosts after making these changes.

> Remember that this cache is taken from the host's main memory, making it inaccessible for use by virtual machines.

Placing virtual machines on storage

The final task you need to learn is placing virtual machines on storage. This is done at creation time and when moving a virtual machine. By default, Hyper-V will try to place virtual machines on internal storage at a local location that is not cluster-accessible. You can override this on each usage, or you can modify the default settings. In Hyper-V Manager, right-click on a node and choose **Hyper-V Settings...**. The first two tabs, **Virtual Hard Disks** and **Virtual Machines**, hold the default locations. The other location are as follows:

- For CSVs, target locations will be C:\ClusterStorage\CSVName
- For non-CSV cluster disks, indicate the drive letter
- For SMB 3.0 shares, enter the UNC

It is critical that all of a virtual machine's storage files be placed on shared storage, or Live Migration and other cluster operations will fail. If you need to relocate them, right-click on any virtual machine in Failover Cluster Manager, go to **Move**, and click on **Virtual Machine Storage**. The resultant dialog box (as shown in the following screenshot), will show you where each item resides and allows you to select a location to move them to. You can also manually enter a UNC with the **Add Share** button:

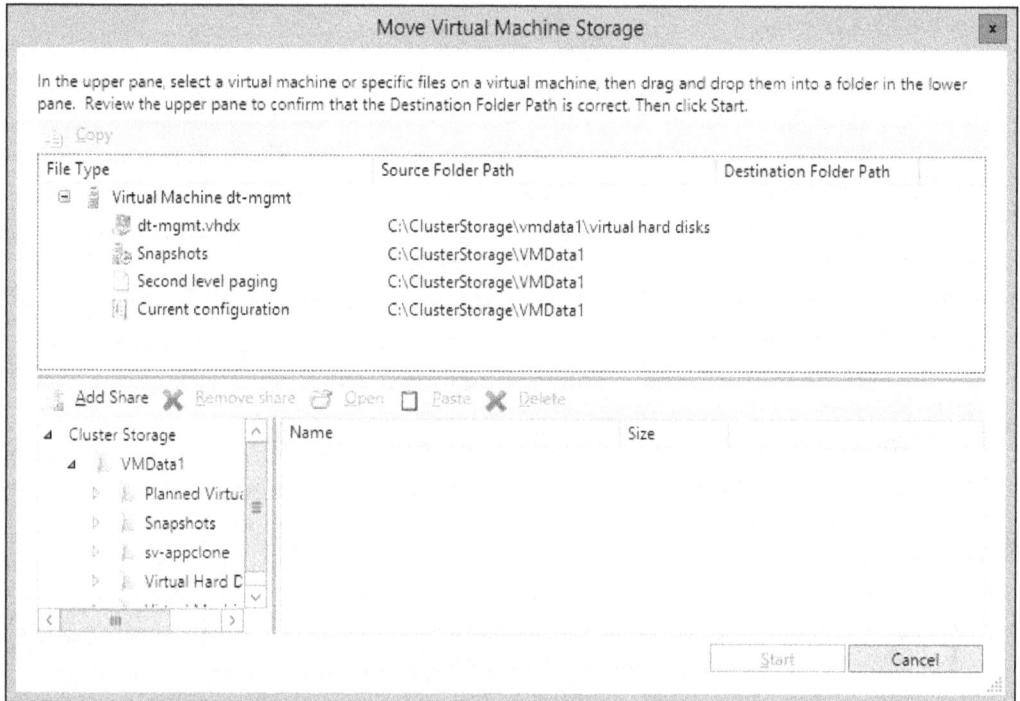

The command `Move-VMStorage` is the equivalent PowerShell cmdlet to this screenshot, shown as follows:

```
Move-VMStorage -Name "sv-apps" -IncludeStorage -DestinationStoragePath
"C:\ClusterStorage\VMData1"
```

This command usage moves all data to the same location. Using other parameters, you can direct where components are placed. Use `Get-Help Move-VMStorage -Examples` and review Example 2.

You can also place and create VHDX files from a virtual machine's property sheet in Failover Cluster Manager, but you can't move an existing one there. The `New-VHD` PowerShell cmdlet is used to create these files independently of a virtual machine.

It is certainly possible to split a virtual machine's data and configuration across different storage targets. This adds a complexity that is difficult to track and maintain. It adds additional points of failure, as the guest will stop if it loses access to storage. If possible, place the virtual machine in a location with sufficient capacity and performance for the machine's toughest workload.

Storage deduplication

A feature that is gaining increased interest and attention is storage deduplication. Virtual machines usually have a substantial amount of data in common with other virtual machines, such as operating system files. Rather than keep each individual file in a separate location, a deduplication system will save one copy of any given data block. If that same data block is needed anywhere else, only a reference to the original block is saved. This can substantially reduce the amount of disk space needed. However, it can increase the amount of processing power needed to store and especially to retrieve data.

Some high-end storage devices have their own deduplication methods. Microsoft does not provide direct support for any of these, but they will not prevent you from using them. If any issues appear to be related to vendor deduplication, they may ask you to turn it off or refer you to the hardware vendor for support.

Deduplication was introduced as a native feature of the files services offered by Windows Server 2012. However, it is not supported on CSVs at all, nor is it supported to run any part of a virtual machine from a Windows Server 2012 deduplicated volume.

The rules are changed somewhat for R2. Microsoft will support **VDI (virtual desktop infrastructure)** deployments on Windows Server 2012 R2 deduplicated storage. Other uses are technically supported, but not recommended as the performance impact is very difficult to predict. You can read more about this on the following Microsoft blog entry: `http://blogs.technet.com/b/filecab/archive/2013/07/31/extending-data-deduplication-to-new-workloads-in-windows-server-2012-r2.aspx`.

Storage QoS (2012 R2 Only)

Hyper-V Server R2 adds Storage **QoS (Quality of Service)**. With this feature, you can ensure that any given virtual hard drive does not exceed a certain number of IOPS. This can help you to ensure that no I/O-hungry virtual machine can drown out the others. There is also a minimum option available, although unlike the maximum, this is nothing more than a point at which an alert is set. Hyper-V cannot guarantee this minimum.

To set these limits in the GUI, open the **Settings** dialog for a virtual machine in Hyper-V Manager or Failover Cluster Manager. In the left pane, expand the virtual hard drive you wish to modify and click **Advanced Features**. In the right pane, set the desired minimum and maximums. This dialog with sample settings is shown in the following screenshot:

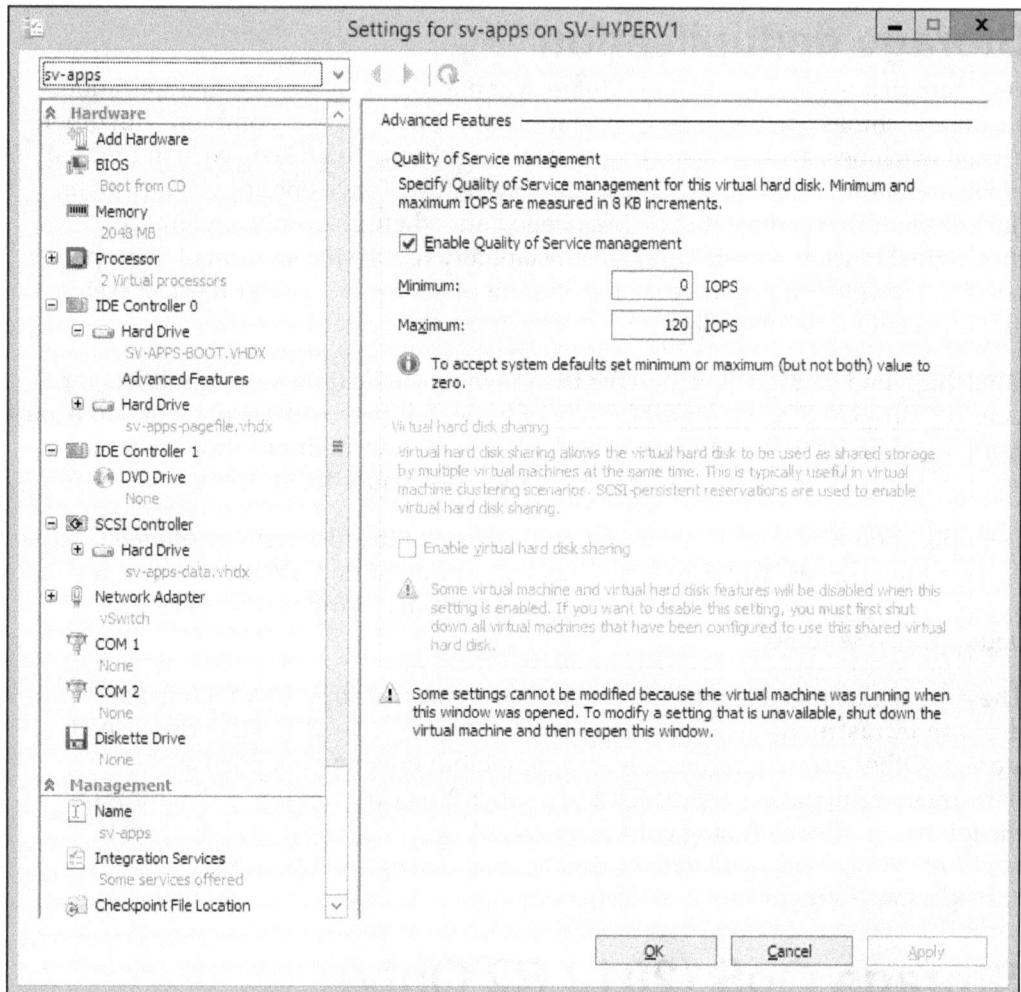

The **measured in 8KB increments** means that I/O chunks will be rounded up to the nearest 8KB and each 8KB block will be treated as a single I/O. So, a 3KB I/O action will be treated as one I/O and a 37KB I/O action will be treated as 5 I/Os. Using zeros in either field means that Hyper-V will set no limit for it.

Enhanced features

A feature introduced in Windows Server 2012 allows it to use **TRIM** (for IDE disks) and **UNMAP** (for SCSI disks). These commands allow the operating system to notify the disk which blocks it is no longer using, rather than perform a direct delete operation. TRIM or UNMAP work automatically if the hardware supports them and cannot be disabled. They will most commonly be found on SSDs and SAN systems.

Hyper-V can also use TRIM or UNMAP to optimize space usage for dynamic VHDX files and pass-through disks, but not VHD files. A benefit for VHDX files is that they will only consume the amount of physical space they are actually using, even if those of the fixed format type. When placed on a *thin-provisioned* LUN (iSCSI/Fibre Channel disk space that is only allocated space as needed, similar to a dynamic VHD file), these VHDX files will not require the LUN to grow beyond actual storage used.

TRIM or UNMAP are triggered automatically when data inside a dynamic VHDX file is deleted, including during defragment processes. It can be triggered for any virtual disk when the file is *compacted*. This process reclaims empty blocks from deleted files inside the virtual disk. Compact is initiated by clicking on the **Edit** button on the virtual disk's tab in the **Settings** dialog for the virtual machine, or it can be initiated via PowerShell using the following command:

```
Optimize-VHD -Path "\\sv-storage\Virtual Machines\Virtual Hard Disks\SV-
APPS-BOOT.VHDX"
```

The storage doesn't need to support TRIM or UNMAP for the compact and optimization process to work. The features just decrease the amount of time required. Without the optimization process, VHDX files on TRIM or UNMAP-capable storage will report that they are using more space than they actually are.

Another new feature is **off-loaded data transfer** (**ODX**). Ordinarily, copying a file from one location to another requires that its contents be read into memory and then sent back to the storage. With ODX, Windows Server can instruct the storage to perform the copy on its own. This feature is automatically enabled, but will only work on storage devices that support it—usually SANs. Unfortunately, not all implementations of ODX are stable. If you find that you are having troubles with storage and cannot determine the issue, try disabling ODX. You can read more about this feature and the methods to enable and disable it on TechNet:

```
http://technet.microsoft.com/en-us/library/jj200627.aspx
```

Summary

In this chapter, you took an in-depth look at hard drives and how they can be arranged and presented to a Hyper-V Server cluster. You learned how to compare hard drive performance metrics, RAID array capabilities, and connection technologies. You were shown how to set reasonable expectations of performance and design a sensible storage environment for your cluster.

You also learned how to connect to and manipulate your shared storage. You also learned how to place virtual machines on your shared storage.

In the next chapter, we will shift gears entirely and explore the world of Hyper-V Server networking in a cluster environment.

5
Network Design

Networking for a Hyper-V Server cluster doesn't have the same dizzying array of options as shared storage, but it's still one of the most confusing challenges newcomers will face. As with shared storage, there is no single right way to design networking for your cluster. Also, if you're not accustomed to setting up network configurations more complicated than one IP address per machine, there are many concepts to learn.

In this chapter, we will cover:

- The operation of the Hyper-V virtual switch
- Assigning virtual adapters to VLANs
- Understanding networking concepts for Hyper-V in a Failover Cluster
- Configuring the networking options offered in Hyper-V Server 2012 R2
- Planning your physical networking layout
- How to design impacts load-balancing, bandwidth, and fault tolerance
- Details of the native adapter teaming functions
- Creating a converged fabric
- Setting the Windows Firewall for a clustered Hyper-V Server

Each Hyper-V and cluster networking concept will be introduced and its challenges thoroughly discussed. Once these are fully explored, the converged fabric feature and how it can provide solutions to some challenges will be covered.

The Hyper-V virtual switch

Hyper-V provides a virtual switch as an available resource for its virtual machines. As shipped, it provides some smart layer-2 capabilities. It is also possible for third parties to create software solutions that add capabilities with the extensibility feature of the switch.

A Hyper-V switch can be created in one of the following modes:

- Private
- Internal
- External

A private virtual switch allows communications between guests on a single Hyper-V host. The management operating system cannot participate and there is no direct functionality that allows traffic on this switch to interact with any other network, including a physical wired network. An internal virtual switch is much like the private virtual switch with the sole exception of allowing the management operating system to participate. It also does not provide any capability to communicate with any other network. An external virtual switch is tied to a physical adapter on the host and provides a communication path with the connected physical network.

To use a virtual switch, a virtual adapter is created on a virtual machine or the management operating system. That adapter is then connected to the desired switch. The following illustration shows the logical process involving all three switch types:

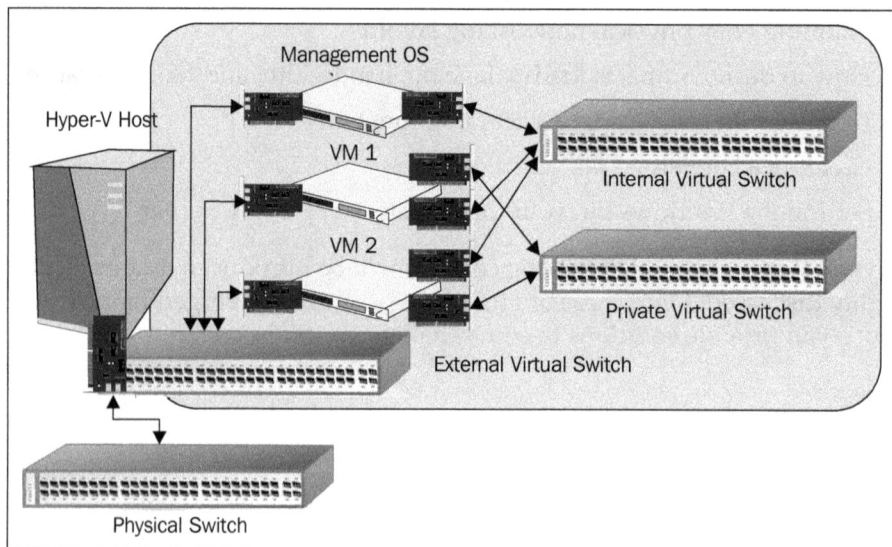

Just as with a physical deployment, virtual adapters are connected to virtual switches in a one-to-one pairing. So, to connect a virtual machine to more than one switch, it must have more than one adapter. As the image suggests, the only virtual switch type that provides for any interaction with a physical network is the **External Virtual Switch**.

When an external virtual switch is created, it is assigned to a physical or a teamed adapter through the management operating system. For the duration that it hosts a virtual switch, that adapter does not, and cannot, serve any other purpose. If you check the properties of an adapter hosting a virtual switch, you will see that it is unbound from all protocols and services with the exception of the **Hyper-V Extensible Virtual Switch**. Teamed adapters will also be bound to the **Microsoft Load Balancing/Failover Provider**.

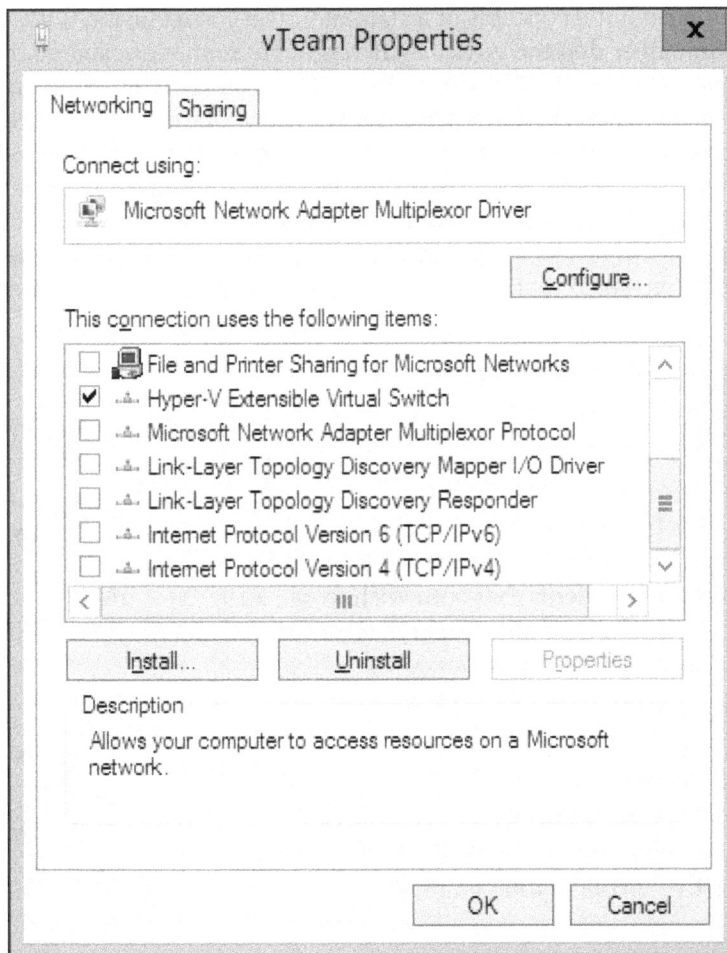

The system will generally prevent attempts to add any other services or protocols to the adapter being used as the virtual switch. Do not attempt to modify or override this behavior.

With the virtual switch bound to it, the management operating system can no longer directly use it to communicate with the physical network. Now the management operating system can have its own virtual adapters that allow it to communicate through the virtual switch, just like a virtual machine. Previous versions of Hyper-V allowed the creation of a single virtual adapter by checking the **Allow management operating system to share this network adapter** checkbox on the properties for the virtual switch. As discussed in *Chapter 3, Constructing a Hyper-V Server Cluster*, the 2012 version still has that checkbox, but it can now have multiple adapters on the same virtual switch.

As you transition from the concepts of a standalone host to a cluster, it is vitally important to remember that the virtual switch is not a clustered resource. The clustering service is unaware of the virtual switch's existence, cannot manage it, and, other than mismatched switch names, cannot warn you of inconsistent virtual switch configurations between different hosts. Virtual machines that move from one host to another in a cluster expect to find virtual switches with the same names as those on its source host or they will be unable to connect virtual adapters. You will receive errors if you attempt to Live Migrate a virtual machine to a mismatched host or attempt to start a virtual machine on a host that does not have the expected virtual switches.

Network virtualization

The 2012 products introduced the concept of network virtualization to Hyper-V. Do not confuse this with the virtual switch. The most common example of a virtual network is an instance of an IP subnet that exists solely within the context of Hyper-V. The purpose of such a network is usually isolation from other similar networks. The most common application is in cloud hosting environments. For instance, a cloud provider may have two clients that both wish to use a `192.168.20.0/24` subnet. Ordinarily, this would not be possible in the same environment without collision. By virtualizing the networks, both can co-exist.

One issue with the 2012 implementation was that it did not provide any native way for these networks to communicate with other networks. Other solutions such as a software router inside a virtual machine (such as the router provided by Network Policy and Access Services built-in to Windows Server or the new Windows Server Gateway feature of 2012 R2) or a hardware router were necessary. 2012 R2 introduces a native virtualization gateway.

However, full utilization of the capabilities of network virtualization in either 2012 or 2012 R2 require a matching installation of System Center Virtual Machine Manager. Microsoft has provided some fairly thorough documentation on the concepts, scenarios, and requirements to work with network virtualization. The launch page for the documentation is available at the following TechNet site: `http://technet.microsoft.com/en-us/library/jj134230.aspx`.

Redundancy and load balancing for the virtual switch

This is only applicable to the external switch type and involves physical adapters. Because an external switch must be bound to a single adapter, all virtual adapters connected to the switch share that single adapter. Although the actual networking needs of most common virtualized workloads are not large enough for this to be a meaningful problem, it can present a bottleneck. The hypervisor will manage networking resources so that no single virtual adapter monopolizes the adapter, but it is possible for the line to become cramped. While you shouldn't make any untested assumptions about how your virtual machines will use bandwidth, there are some things whose loads are often dramatically overestimated. These are as follows:

- **Mail Servers**: Except in large organizations, mail servers do not typically demand high quantities of bandwidth. Most organizations place limits on how large an attachment can be and on how many recipients a single e-mail can be sent to. E-mail sent to or received from mailboxes outside the organization must route across the organization's Internet connection, which has available bandwidth that is typically a small fraction of LAN speeds. Depending on your mail server architecture, e-mail that travels internally is usually not sent instantly across the network to all recipients. Instead, the mail server delivers it to mailboxes stored locally where the users will retrieve it at their leisure. Even in organizations that generate enough e-mail traffic that bandwidth needs are a concern, the load is usually well-distributed across multiple servers. Proper architecture would demand that if virtualized, these servers should be distributed across multiple Hyper-V hosts, which will generally prevent any single host from requiring high bandwidth.

- **SQL Servers**: A design goal of most SQL implementations is to ensure that most data processing occurs on the server and involves the network and remote clients as little as possible. Do not assume that even a busy SQL server will generate high bandwidth needs.

- **File Servers**: Most of the data stored on the average corporate file server is relatively dormant. It is uncommon for users to place consistently high bandwidth demands on a file server.

- **Print Servers**: Even very high demand print servers hosting hundreds or even a few thousand print queues do not use substantial amounts of bandwidth. This is primarily because no physical print device can produce printed material nearly as quickly as the network can deliver the data. Also, even large print jobs are measured in hundreds of megabytes and are transferred in seconds even over a network with contention.

In all cases, you should rely on data retrieved from your initial performance measurements as explained in *Chapter 2, Cluster Design and Planning*, and monitoring as discussed in *Chapter 8, Performance Testing and Load Balancing*, as a guideline for anticipating the network needs of your cluster.

Because the virtual machines have their own virtual adapters with their own MAC addresses and because they will be opening multiple distinct networking channels, placing the virtual switch on a teamed adapter presents the possibility of distributing the load simultaneously across physical member adapters. With the typically low bandwidth needs of most guest systems, this is likely to be underwhelming.

Even if there isn't enough load on a virtual switch to have a measurable need for high bandwidth, fault-tolerance and redundancy is always desirable. In versions prior to 2008 R2, there was no Microsoft-supported solution. In 2012 and later, native operating system teaming can be used in two ways to provide redundancy and load-balancing for an external virtual switch. The first is to create a team of physical adapters and create the virtual switch on the team. The second is to create multiple external switches using multiple physical adapters, create multiple virtual adapters inside virtual machines, and use teaming inside the guest operating system. The former method is by far the easier approach and will instantly provide redundancy for all virtual machines on the virtual switch. The second method can only be implemented in Windows Server 2012 and other guests that natively support teaming of virtual adapters. The reason that you might consider this method is that network teaming at the host level disables some features, notably **single-root I/O virtualization (SR-IOV)**. This will be explored further in *Chapter 6, Network Traffic Shaping and Performance Enhancements*.

Assign virtual adapters to VLANs

One of the layer-2 features provided by Hyper-V virtual switches is 802.1q VLAN tagging. A **VLAN (Virtual Local Area Network)** is a network concept in which smart switches logically separate network traffic based on a numeric entry in the packet. In a simple network, individual switch ports are assigned to specific VLANs, and they can only communicate directly with other switch ports in the same VLAN. Because these are assigned to individual packets, VLAN 7 on one switch is VLAN 7 on all other switches (subject to proper switch configuration, of course).

In Hyper-V, there isn't as much distinction between a switch port and a virtual adapter, so the commands assign the VLAN to the adapter and not to the switch port. To set the VLAN for a virtual machine, access the virtual machine's property sheet in Hyper-V Manager or Failover Cluster Manager. Each virtual machine's network adapter has an **Enable virtual LAN identification** checkbox that, when checked, allows you to enter the VLAN number into a textbox. For the management operating system, if it only has one virtual adapter on the virtual switch, you can adjust its VLAN in the Virtual Switch Manager inside Hyper-V Manager (right-click on the host to access it).

You can also set these from PowerShell. If your management operating system has multiple virtual adapters on the same virtual switch, PowerShell is your only option:

```
Set-VMNetworkAdapterVlan -VMNetworkAdapter "Management" -Access -VlanID 5
-ManagementOS
```

For adapters in virtual machines, omit the `ManagementOS` parameter and specify the VM's name:

```
Set-VMNetworkAdapterVlan -VM "sv-dc1" -VMNetworkAdapter "Network Adapter"
-Access -VlanID 7
```

Hyper-V Server networking in a cluster

Failover clustering has its own networking needs, and the expansion of Hyper-V across separate nodes adds to its networking requirements as well. When a group of computers are clustered together, the clustering service will identify all the adapters on each node and select a single adapter per subnet from each node to represent that node. Each unique subnet is set up as a cluster network. When the status of an adapter changes, such as having its cable unplugged, being disabled, or undergoing an IP address change, or if an adapter is added, the cluster immediately re-evaluates the status of any related cluster network.

The cluster distinguishes networks by their subnets. Each IP address in a given subnet indicates presence in that subnet. The clustering service will only allow a single IP from each node to participate in a single subnet.

Cluster networks can be seen in Failover Cluster Manager under the **Networks** node in the tree in the left pane. They can be seen in PowerShell by using the `Get-ClusterNetwork` cmdlet. Usage of these tools and manipulation of these networks will be explored a bit later in this chapter. First, we will examine the roles that the various cluster networks will play. There are three of these roles.

Management

The Management role is all the traffic that is meant specifically for the management operating system. This is analogous to the typical network connection on traditional non-hypervisor, non-clustered Windows computers. It is required on any networked computer, and it is only specially named in this context to distinguish it from the other network traffic types. This is the connection that is registered in DNS. As a result, it handles all inbound connections to the host name, such as RDP and management console sessions. Outbound requests, such as Windows Update and over-the-network backups from the hypervisor, are also considered management traffic.

The cluster-specific part that the management role plays is that it hosts the **cluster name object (CNO)**. This is a computer object created in Active Directory which represents the entire cluster. It has its own IP address and is registered in DNS. At any given time, one node owns the CNO and, as a result, also holds the CNO's IP address. The adapter chosen to host the management role will also host the CNO.

You can view information about the CNO on the cluster's home page in Failover Cluster Manager. Simply click on the cluster name in the tree on the left. The basic information is at the very top of the screen while more detailed information, such as the IP address, is under the **Cluster Core Resources** section at the bottom of the window. The following screenshot is from Windows Server 2012; R2 looks slightly different:

Failover Cluster Manager
⊿ cl-hyperv1.techstra.local
    Roles
  ▷ Nodes
  ▷ Storage
  ▷ Networks
    Cluster Events

Cluster cl-hyperv1.techstra.local

Summary of Cluster cl-hyperv1

cl-hyperv1 has 3 clustered roles and 2 nodes.

Name: cl-hyperv1.techstra.local

Current Host Server: sv-hyperv1

Quorum Configuration: Node and Disk Majority (Quorum)

Recent Cluster Events: None in the last 24 hours

▼ **Configure**

▼ **Navigate**

▲ **Cluster Core Resources**

Name
  Cluster Name
⊟ Name: cl-hyperv1
    IP Address: 192.168.25.20

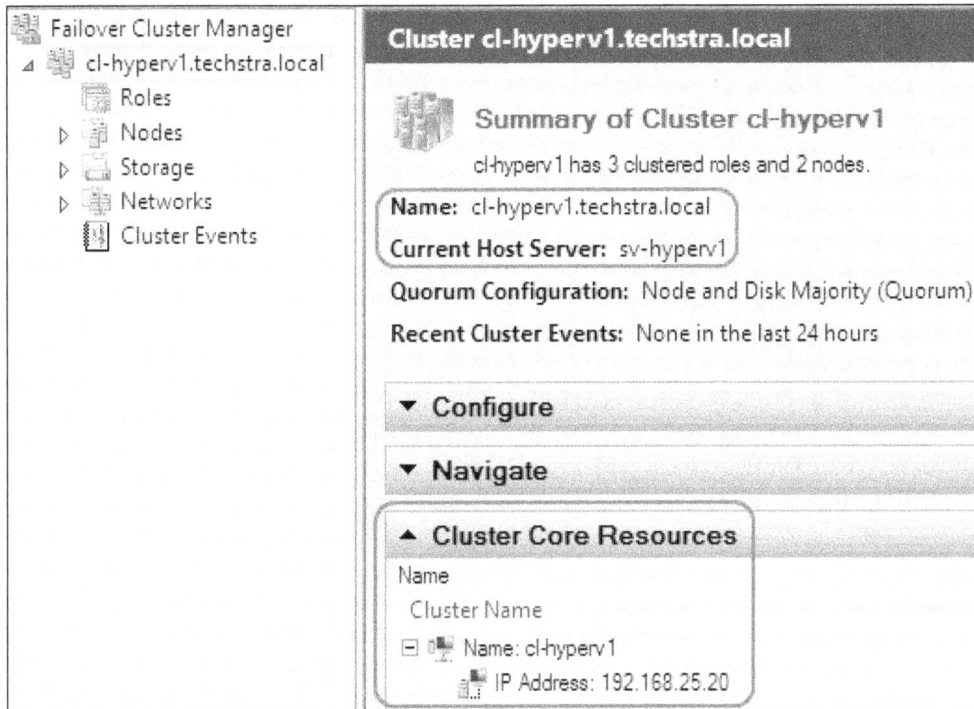

In the **Cluster Core Resources** section, you can double-click on the cluster name or right-click on it and left-click on **Properties** to access its properties sheet. Here, you can rename the cluster object, find further details on its status, and configure its failover policies. You can do the same on the IP address field, which allows you to change the CNO address if the need or desire arises. These changes will require the resource to be briefly taken offline. This will not impact running virtual machines.

To locate the CNO in PowerShell, run the following:

```
Get-ClusterResource -Name "Cluster Name" | Format-List *
```

If you'd like to see details about the cluster IP address, substitute "IP Address" for "Cluster Name" in the Name parameter. Oddly enough, this will show all details about the cluster IP address except what the address actually is. This is because the IP, and related information, is a cluster parameter. To see these parameters, pipe the resource to the Get-ClusterParameter cmdlet:

```
Get-ClusterResource -Name "Cluster IP Address" | Get-ResourceParameter
```

Most of the settings retrieved by this command cannot be modified. However, the IP can be changed with the `Set-ClusterParameter` cmdlet:

```
Get-ClusterResource -Name "Cluster IP Address" | Set-ClusterParameter
-Name Address -Value 192.168.25.19
```

You will receive a yellow message stating that the resource will need to be taken offline and brought back online. This will not impact your virtual machines, but unlike the GUI method, the PowerShell cmdlet will not automatically perform this reset for you. First, stop the resource:

```
Stop-ClusterResource -Name "Cluster IP Address"
```

You aren't notified of this, but when the IP address resource is stopped, the name resource is also stopped. You can start both of them separately, starting with the IP address resource, or you can simply start the name resource which will bring them both online together:

```
Start-ClusterResource -Name "Cluster Name"
```

Ordinarily, there is no need to manage the CNO or cluster IP address. If the owning node fails or is shut down, the cluster will automatically relocate the resources to another node. They can be moved manually using the GUI or PowerShell. In Failover Cluster Manager, right-click on the cluster's name in the tree, navigate to **More Actions | Move Core Cluster Resources**, and then click on **Best Possible Node** to have the clustering service automatically choose a node or click on **Select Node...** to choose one yourself.

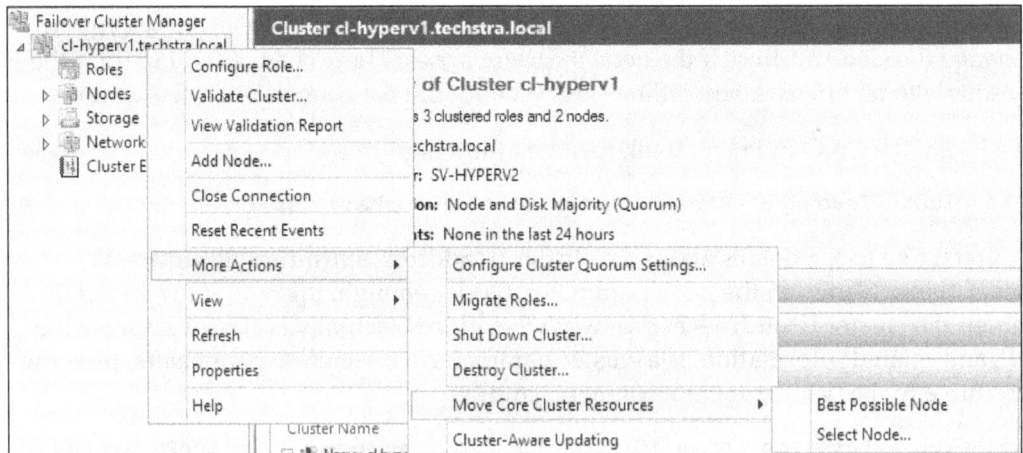

In PowerShell, issue the following cmdlet:

```
Move-ClusterGroup -Name "Cluster Group" -Node sv-hyperv2
```

If you omit the `Node` parameter, the clustering service will decide which node to place the resources on.

> If your cluster is using a cluster disk for quorum, it will be moved with the cluster name and cluster IP address resources.

Redundancy and load balancing for management traffic

Management traffic typically benefits very little from the load-balancing feature of adapter teaming, but it is worth considering the need to use teaming for redundancy. If you have a limited number of physical adapters and your hosts have a built-in out-of-band management system by the hardware vendor, you may consider using only one adapter for this load or even folding it in with one or more other roles on the same physical adapter or team.

Cluster communications

This cluster network role is common in all Microsoft Failover Clusters. Ordinarily, it is a very lightly utilized network, but it is very important. Every second, each node will attempt to communicate with all other nodes in a process called the heartbeat. If a node is unable to contact enough other nodes to maintain quorum, it will shut itself down.

Changes made to the cluster are shared among the nodes using this network. The shared information can be seen on any node by looking in `C:\Windows\Cluster` and in the registry under `HKEY_LOCAL_MACHINE\Cluster`.

If you are using **Cluster Shared Volumes** (**CSV**), they will also make use of this network. In normal operations, they will exchange metadata about files on the CSV. Metadata is essentially all information about a file except for its contents, such as ownership, open and closed status, and security. Since a Hyper-V Server cluster is unlikely to have a large number of files on its CSVs (in comparison to a file server, which might have hundreds of thousands or even millions of files), this metadata traffic is typically negligible.

CSVs do have a unique ability that can cause this traffic to spike. If a node loses its direct connectivity to a CSV, I/O for any virtual machines it owns which are running from that CSV is redirected across the cluster communications network. The I/O is handled by a coordinator node, which is simply the node that owns the CSV. Traffic across the cluster communications network can become very heavy if the virtual machines on that node are placing high I/O demands on the storage. This is called **Redirected Access Mode**.

In previous versions, Redirected Access Mode was a fairly common occurrence. When the contents of a CSV were backed up, there was no coordination of the **Volume Shadow Copy Service** (**VSS**) across the nodes, so CSVs were placed into Redirected Access Mode during each backup. In 2012 and later, CSV has been updated so that it can coordinate VSS operations in a way that no longer requires Redirected Access Mode. Realistically, only loss of connectivity to storage will trigger it in current versions.

Redundancy and load balancing for cluster communications

In 2012 and R2, cluster communications and CSV traffic will automatically leverage SMB 3.0 multi-channel. In the event that Redirected Access Mode is activated, all cluster networks that are enabled for cluster traffic will be used to carry this traffic. As you may recall from *Chapter 3, Constructing a Hyper-V Server Cluster*, this setting is modified on the properties sheet for the network in Failover Cluster Manager:

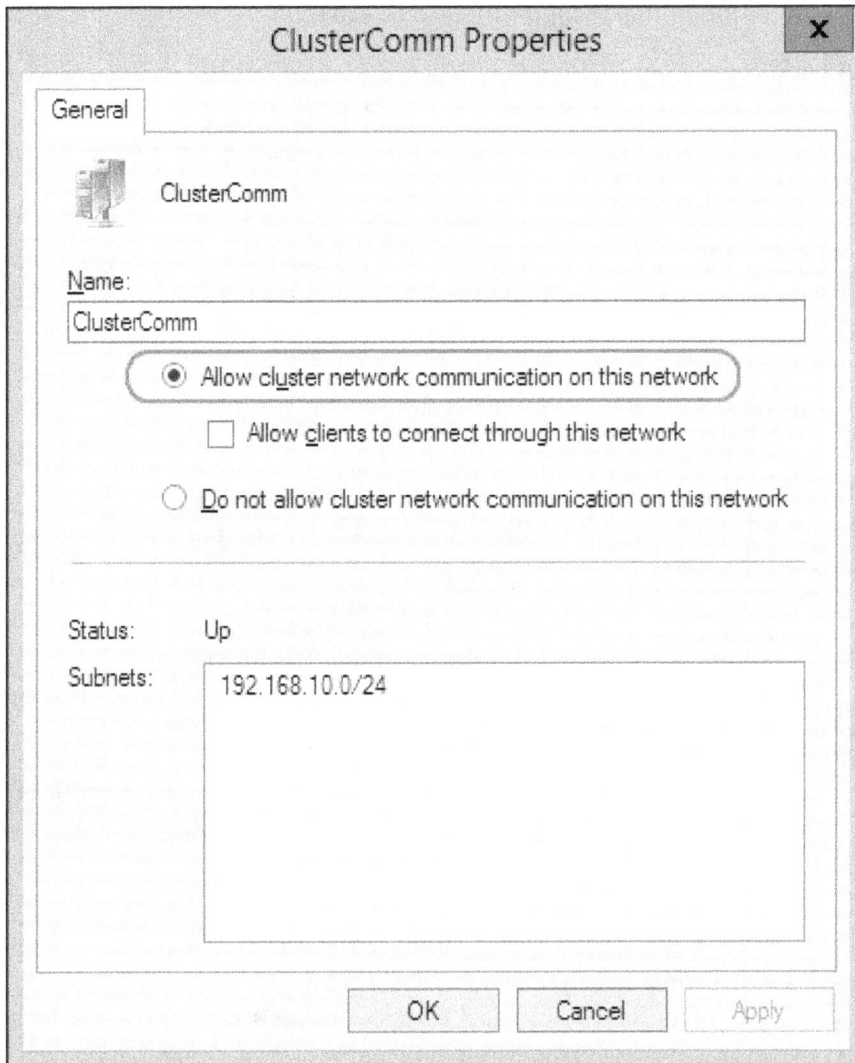

Any network with this option set is eligible for cluster communications. Of course, it can also be set using PowerShell. If you want to modify the cluster preferences for cluster communication, PowerShell is the only way. All of these functions employ the `Get-Cluster-Network` cmdlet.

To see how your networks are currently being utilized, run the following:

```
Get-ClusterNetwork | Format-Table Name, Role, AutoMetric, Metric
```

The Role column is a numeric value between 0 and 3:

- A **0** indicates a network that is excluded from all cluster communications. This is the preferred setting for iSCSI connections.

- A **1** indicates a network that can be used for cluster communications but does not accept incoming requests from non-clustered machines (such as RDP connections). This is the preferred setting for cluster communications networks and the Live Migration network.

- A **3** represents a network that is enabled for cluster communications and allows incoming connections. This is the required setting for the management network.

- A **2** is not a valid option and the system will reject any attempt to set a role number to this value.

The `AutoMetric` column simply indicates if the network's metric has been manually set or if the cluster determined the metric. If you manually set the metric, this will automatically change to `false`. If you set it to `true`, it will override any manual settings.

The `Metric` column indicates how the cluster prioritizes the networks for cluster communications. The automatically assigned metrics have specific numbering schemes that are based on the role type of the network. Networks with a role of zero begin numbering at 79840, although the number is largely irrelevant since they are excluded from cluster communications. Networks with a role of three begin at 70384, incremented by one for each additional network in this category. Networks with a role of one begin numbering at 39840.

When the cluster service needs to send cluster or CSV communications, it starts with the network with the lowest metric. If that network is unavailable or if cluster communications are already in process and it determines that multichannel is appropriate, it will work its way upward by network metric. So, to manually set the preferred network(s) for cluster communications, you need to modify the metric. To do this, you simply need to choose numbers below the base default of `39840`. It can be any number you like. Unfortunately, there is no `Set-ClusterNetwork` cmdlet; you use `Get-ClusterNetwork` and adjust in a somewhat non-intuitive fashion:

```
(Get-ClusterNetwork -Name "ClusterComm").Metric = 500
```

If you run the `Get-ClusterNetwork` command, you'll see that `AutoMetric` has changed to `False`. If you want to return to an automatically assigned metric, simply set `AutoMetric` to `True`:

```
(Get-ClusterNetwork -Name "ClusterComm").AutoMetric = $true
```

If you want to adjust the network role using PowerShell, it's the same pattern:

```
(Get-ClusterNetwork -Name "ClusterComm").Role = 1
```

If you choose to assign multiple networks for cluster communications, simply use the metric to ensure they are chosen ahead of all others. The following screenshot shows a system in which two networks have been intended for cluster communications and their `AutoMetric` has been set to ensure they are given preference over the Live Migration network, which is also a role one network:

```
PS C:\> (Get-ClusterNetwork -Name "ClusterComm").Metric = 500
PS C:\> (Get-ClusterNetwork -Name "ClusterComm2").Metric = 501
PS C:\> Get-ClusterNetwork | ft Name, Role, AutoMetric, Metric

Name                           Role        AutoMetric              Metric
----                           ----        ----------              ------
ClusterComm                       1        False                      500
ClusterComm2                      1        False                      501
iSCSI1                            0        True                     79840
LiveMigration                     1        True                     39840
Management                        3        True                     70384
```

> The virtual switch does not appear in any cluster network list because it does not have any IP protocols associated with it.

SMB multichannel configuration

As you design cluster networks, remember that SMB multichannel in a cluster will attempt to use one physical channel per unique subnet. So, if you have one virtual adapter designated for cluster traffic and it is assigned to a virtual switch that is on a team of four physical adapters, only one adapter will be used. If you set up a second virtual adapter for cluster communications, then it will use up to two physical paths. Of course, you can use separate physical adapters as well. Remember to place each additional adapter per host in its own subnet and match them to the additional adapters in the other hosts or they will not be used.

You can see how SMB multichannel is being used in real-time with the following cmdlet:

```
Get-SmbMultichannelConnection
```

Since cluster communications are usually idle, the output of this command may show nothing or very little most of the time.

If you want to restrict SMB multichannel to specific adapters, perhaps to prevent it from crowding your management adapter, use the following cmdlet:

```
New-SmbMultichannelConstraint -ServerName "sv-hyperv2" -InterfaceAlias
"vEthernet (ClusterComm)", "vEthernet (ClusterComm2)"
```

In the previous command, the `ServerName` parameter refers to the target server, meaning that the server you run the cmdlet on will only use the two indicated adapters for SMB multichannel while communicating with the node or computer called `"sv-hyperv2"`. Be judicious about using this cmdlet with the R2 series, as Live Migration can now use SMB, and therefore multichannel, as well.

These are only basic ways to work with SMB 3.0 multichannel, but they should be sufficient for working with inter-node communications. However, you can find a wealth of information about the subject on its official TechNet page at `http://technet.microsoft.com/en-us/library/hh831795.aspx` and on the Microsoft-run blog at `http://smb3.info`.

Live Migration

Live Migration is a Hyper-V Server technology that allows a virtual machine to be moved from one computer running Hyper-V Server to another without perceptible downtime for the virtual machine or connected clients. In a cluster, this is performed by transmitting the contents of the virtual machine's memory, its active processing threads, and the active configuration data for the machine across a cluster network to another node. The storage for a clustered virtual machine is in a shared location, so it is not part of this transfer. Live Migration traffic is defined by the Hyper-V application, not by Microsoft Failover Clustering, so the clustering service is not really aware of it specifically. The Failover Cluster Manager tool has been programmed with some extensions to help you to utilize and manage Live Migration. During a Live Migration, the cluster network carrying its traffic will usually become saturated unless it can transmit data more quickly than the source or destination host can copy memory. When no Live Migration is in progress, this role is idle.

Redundancy and load balancing for Live Migration traffic

Live Migration in 2012 is a standard TCP communication stream, so it does not benefit from any of the acceleration technologies of SMB 3.0 or MPIO. Hyper-V Server 2012 adds the capability to Live Migrate more than one virtual machine at a time; however, this still uses only one TCP stream between any two hosts.

This means that teaming and converged fabrics will not accelerate migrations in a host pair and that no matter how many networks are available, only one will be used for Live Migration.

> The default number of Live Migrations that can be carried out simultaneously is two. This number can be changed on the Hyper-V Settings dialog for a host in Hyper-V Manager. If more Live Migrations are initiated than can be performed at once, the remainder is queued.

In 2012 R2, Live Migration behavior is changed. You have three choices: you can leave it in the original TCP mode, you can have it compress the data but still use only one TCP channel, or you can have it use SMB. If SMB is enabled, then it will automatically use multichannel if possible.

First, for either version, you must indicate which networks you will allow cluster Live Migration traffic on. Access the Failover Cluster Manager, expand the cluster if necessary, right-click on the **Networks** node, and click on **Live Migration Settings...**. You will be presented with a screen similar to the following:

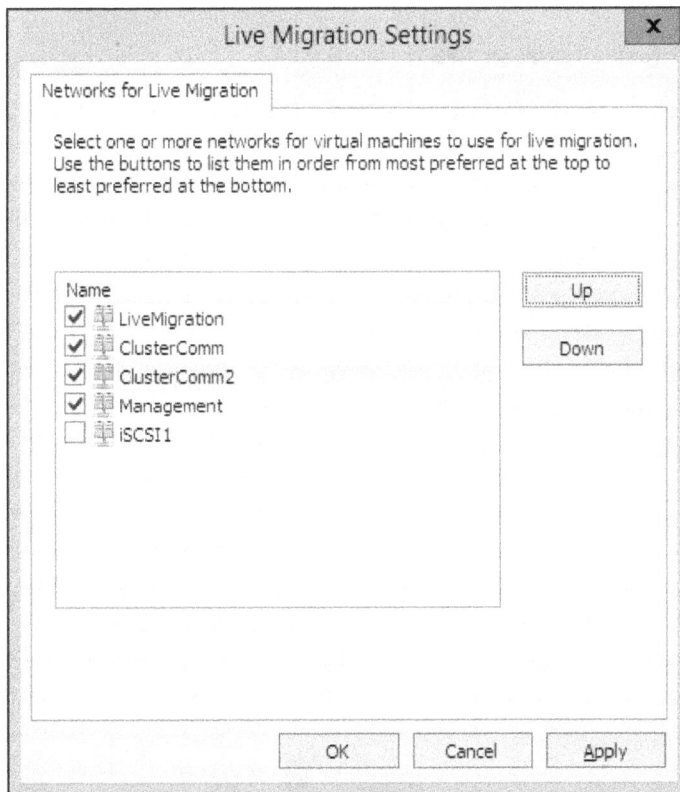

Highlight any of the items and use the **Up** and **Down** buttons to arrange them in the priority you want them used for Live Migration. Unchecking a network will prevent it from being used for Live Migration traffic. Live Migration will attempt to use the first checked network; if it is unavailable, it will switch to the second and continue until it exhausts all checked networks. In R2, if you have selected the SMB option and no constraints prevent it, all checked networks will be used.

There are no native PowerShell commands to change this setting. The PowerShell settings related to Live Migration can only be used for Shared Nothing Live Migration, which is a Live Migration that moves between two non-clustered hosts that do not have access to shared storage.

It is possible to modify these settings by using the registry. Navigate to HKEY_LOCAL_ MACHINE\Cluster\ResourceTypes\Virtual Machine\Parameters. Here, you will find two keys, MigrationNetworkOrder and MigrationExcludeNetworks. These are String keys, which mean they hold a single line of printable characters. That single line is a semicolon-separated list of networks represented by their unique identifier. Those network IDs can be seen a few keys up at HKEY_LOCAL_MACHINE\ Cluster\Networks. They can also be retrieved using the Id property of the Get-ClusterNetwork cmdlet:

```
Get-ClusterNetwork | Format-Table Name, Id
```

Since the IDs are easy to retrieve and there are PowerShell commands to manipulate the registry, it is possible to use PowerShell to manipulate these networks. The following listing is a sample PowerShell script that will change the networks listed in the previous screenshot so that they are in the order of the screenshot, but both the "iSCSI1" and "Management" networks are excluded from Live Migration:

```
## Set-ClusterLiveMigrationNetworks.ps1
##
## Assigns priorities to cluster networks to use in Live Migration and
## excludes networks that should not be used in Live Migration.

# Make hash tables to store the network IDs
$NetworksToInclude = @()
$NetworksToExclude = @()

# Store the registry keys in variables (to make the script more
legible and easier to maintain)
$RegistryLocation = "HKLM:\Cluster\ResourceTypes\Virtual Machine\
Parameters"
```

```
# Make a table of the network IDs to include IN ORDER
$NetworksToInclude += (Get-ClusterNetwork -Name "LiveMigration").Id
$NetworksToInclude += (Get-ClusterNetwork -Name "ClusterComm").Id
$NetworksToInclude += (Get-ClusterNetwork -Name "ClusterComm2").Id

# Make a table of the network IDs to exclude. Order is not important.
$NetworksToExclude += (Get-ClusterNetwork -Name "Management").Id
$NetworksToExclude += (Get-ClusterNetwork -Name "iSCSI1").Id

# Turn the hash tables into semicolon separated strings, as that is
what needs to be in the registry.
$NetworksToIncludeString = [String]::Join(";", $NetworksToInclude)
$NetworksToExcludeString = [String]::Join(";", $NetworksToExclude)

# Insert the strings into the registry
Set-ItemProperty -Path $RegistryLocation -Name "MigrationNetworkOrder"
-Value $NetworksToIncludeString
Set-ItemProperty -Path $RegistryLocation -Name
"MigrationExcludeNetworks" -Value $NetworksToExcludeString
```

The previous listing was designed for ease of reading. It could be expanded to prompt the user for dynamic selection. Also, it's not necessary to use more than one entry for either of the networks. You can use a hash table with only one entry, or you can skip the hash table and Join together, and just insert the ID directly.

Setting the Live Migration mode in 2012 R2

To set the Live Migration mode in R2, open Hyper-V Manager. Right-click on a host and click on **Hyper-V Settings**. Expand Live Migrations and click on **Advanced Features**. If you choose **TCP/IP**, the traditional single path per host pair is used. Compression will cause the virtual machine's memory to be compressed and sent over a single TCP/IP connection per host pair. SMB will encapsulate the uncompressed contents of the virtual machine's memory and make it accessible to any SMB-acceleration features available, such as multichannel and RDMA. Multichannel was previously discussed in the Cluster Communications section; RDMA will be covered in *Chapter 6, Network Traffic Shaping and Performance Enhancements*.

A screenshot of the configuration screen is shown next:

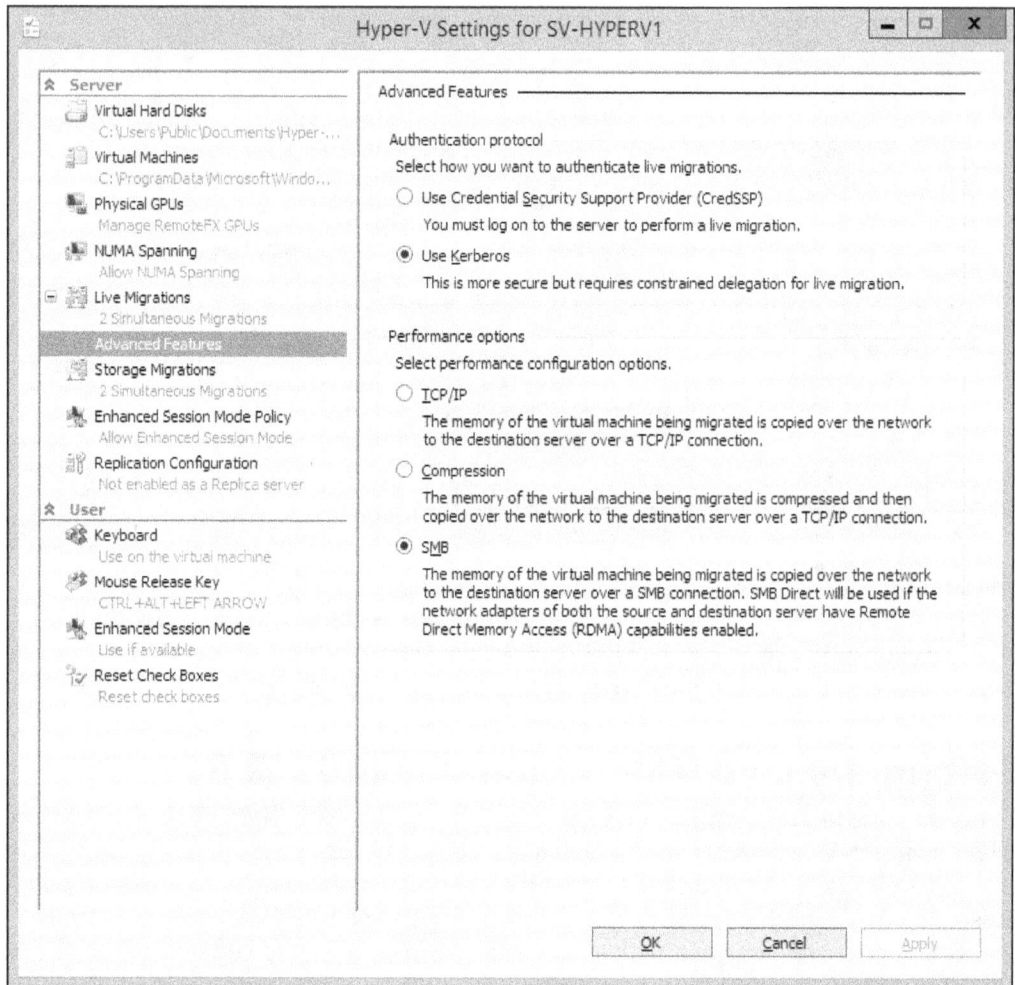

The **TCP/IP** option is preferred if you want to control how Live Migrations occur and you have limited resources. This will prevent Live Migration from interfering with other operations. Use **Compression** if you have excess CPU resources available but lean network resources. If multichannel and other network technologies are available, **SMB** is the preferred choice as it is comparatively light on CPU.

Storage connectivity

Connections to storage are not cluster-controlled networks; in fact, you should specifically disallow cluster communications on those networks. They must be accounted for as you design your cluster's networking, however. TCP/IP storage connections are something of a special consideration as you may wish to completely isolate them from other types. The basic concepts around connections to storage were covered in *Chapter 4, Storage Design*. To recap, teaming is not appropriate for iSCSI or SMB 3.0 storage. MPIO should be used when multiple dedicated adapters are available for connections to iSCSI. SMB 3.0 connections can be left for multichannel to automatically determine the optimal connections to use, or you can also manually specify which adapters to use.

For optimal performance of the network connection to storage, the key is usually latency, which is the amount of time it takes for a network packet to travel from source to destination. The principal design consideration to keep latency to a minimum is to ensure that all storage traffic stays on the same subnet. This eliminates the need for a router hop that automatically adds some delay to the transmission. Latency can be further augmented by keeping all other traffic types off of the subnet(s) used for storage. This is because services running on general-purpose adapters will need to make broadcasts across the entire subnet for various reasons, and these broadcasts need to be processed by all adapters on that subnet. Any time your storage adapters spend working with broadcast traffic is time they cannot spend working with storage data. Finally, keep the number of physical devices involved to a minimum; if possible, use direct connections or a single switch between hosts and shared storage.

For bandwidth, ensure you first know the actual data rate of your storage system and then get an estimate for how much it is actually likely to move using the tools discussed in *Chapter 2, Cluster Design and Planning*. There is no value in designing network connectivity with capacity to exceed a speed beyond reasonable peak and expansion estimates. Overestimates for this traffic are quite common. For example, 50 virtual machines of mixed loads can often be served quite well using two MPIO-enabled 1GbE connections.

The virtual switch in a cluster

It is vital to remember that the virtual switch is not a cluster-controlled resource. Because the switch itself has no protocols bound, the cluster does not, and cannot recognize it as being a network resource. All virtual switches on all hosts are known only to their owning hosts. In order for a virtual machine to migrate freely between nodes, the switches that its virtual adapters connect to must be able to find a switch with exactly the same name and exactly the same parameters on each node. Otherwise, Live Migrations will fail and Quick Migrations will result in virtual machines that won't start. The cluster itself cannot, and will not, police these switch names to ensure consistency (although the Cluster Validation Wizard will warn you about it).

Adapter teaming

In previous versions, many administrators chose to use teaming software provided by network adapter manufacturers. Individual roles would be placed on their own network teams. This presented three problems.

First, Microsoft does not directly support third-party teaming solutions; if a problem arose that appeared to be network-related, you would be asked to break any manufacturer teams for troubleshooting purposes. If breaking the team solved the problem, it was likely that you'd get no other answer, even if the actual problem was due to a misconfiguration and not any inherent flaw in teaming.

Second, a functional team could be inadvertently broken by a faulty driver upgrade. These problems don't always manifest in an easy-to-troubleshoot fashion, and other times they cause blue-screen loops that are difficult to correct.

The third problem is actually the worst of the three. Third-party teaming in Hyper-V Server 2008 R2 meant that a great many physical adapters were required to protect all the roles, yet most of those adapters were idle most of the time. This was a substantial amount of equipment to purchase and maintain, and it meant that a single host could completely consume a sixteen-port physical switch.

Hyper-V Server and Windows Server now support NIC teaming natively. A team can be created using the Server Manager GUI or the PowerShell New-NetLbfoTeam cmdlet as shown in *Chapter 3, Constructing a Hyper-V Server Cluster*. This alone can eliminate the first problem and dramatically reduces the risk of the second. You may certainly choose to use this traditional approach to teaming for NICs.

Also new beginning with Hyper-V Server 2012 is the concept of converged fabric, and this feature has the potential to dramatically change the way that you design your physical network. A converged fabric combines the native teaming function with the Hyper-V virtual switch to consolidate multiple roles onto a single team of adapters. Converged fabric will be discussed in the next section. For now, we will continue to examine teaming to gain a better understanding of the options.

Teaming fundamentals

The basic concept of teaming is simply to add redundancy and load-balancing by combining multiple physical adapters into a single logical entity. Windows Server and Hyper-V Server allow you to add up to 32 physical adapters into a single team. When the team is created, it will automatically have a logical adapter created inside the operating system (or management operating system, if Hyper-V is installed). This adapter represents the team and is the only adapter you should use or modify, although the member adapters will still be visible.

A network team can be used to host any single role, including a virtual switch. It's also possible to use a team to create a converged fabric that hosts multiple roles.

What the team does not do is provide simple bandwidth aggregation. It can load-balance traffic across the team so that the available bandwidth can be more efficiently utilized, but uneven performance is to be expected. When a single transmission is initiated, all of its packets will use only one physical link. Load-balancing occurs when another transmission is initiated that the team can distinguish from the first transmission. The ways it determines difference are its load-balancing algorithms.

Teaming modes

There are three teaming modes: Switch Independent, Static, and LACP. Setting the teaming mode can be done by accessing Server Manager and clicking on the Enabled or Disabled link next to NIC Teaming on the Local Server page. It can also be set or modified using the `TeamingMode` parameter of the `New-NetLbfoTeam` and `Set-NetLbfoTeam` cmdlets. The GUI dialog is shown next:

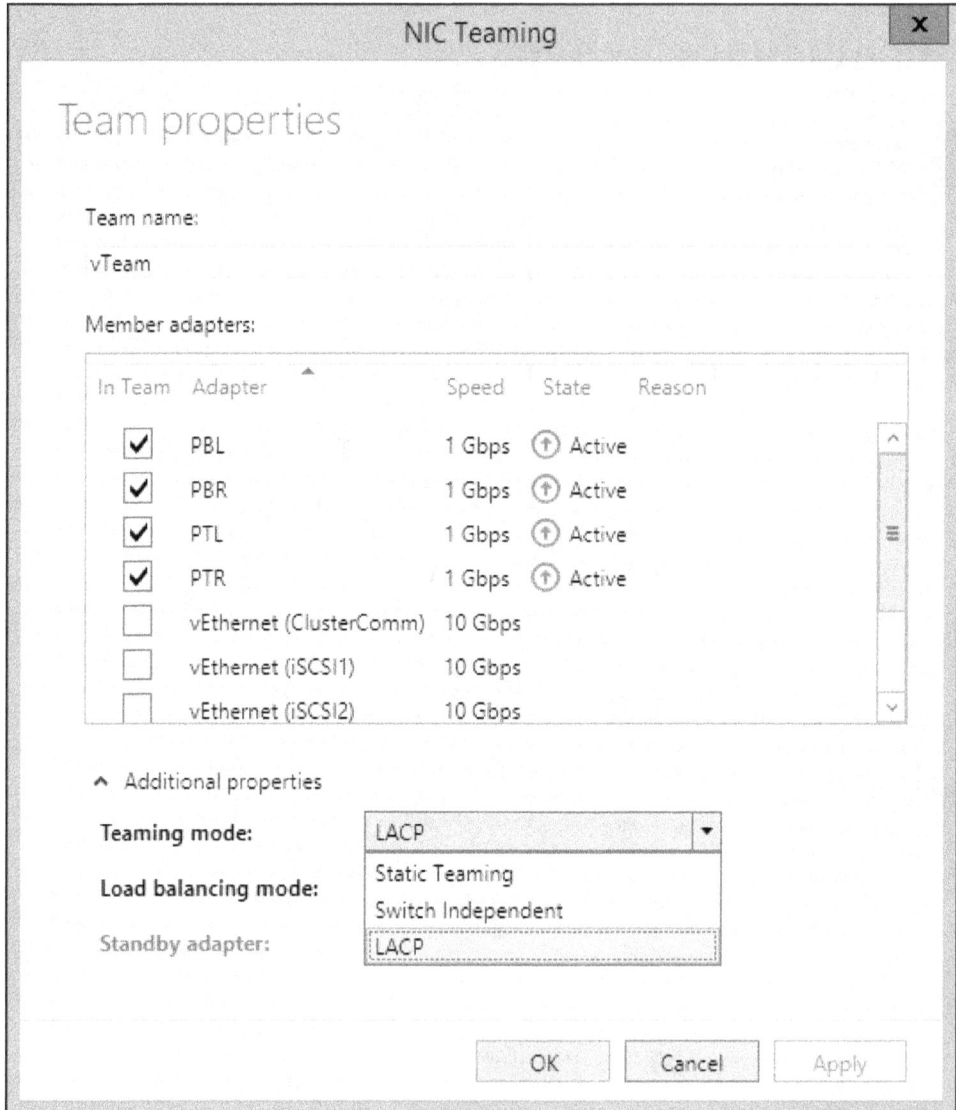

Switch Independent teaming

This is the simplest mode. It can be used with basic unmanaged physical switches. It can also be used to straddle a NIC team across more than one physical switch. Also, if desired, the Switch Independent mode allows for an active/passive configuration. If the team will not be hosting a virtual switch, then all connected physical switch ports can remain unconfigured or be set in regular switch port access mode. If you want traffic on the adapter to participate in a particular VLAN, it is best to configure this on the physical switch.

The drawback to the Switch Independent teaming mode is that it is the least efficient inbound load-balancing method. Outgoing traffic will be balanced as evenly as possible across the physical ports, but all inbound traffic will go through a single physical adapter. This is because networking hardware must register a MAC address to one and only one port. Since the physical switch(es) are completely unaware of the existence of the team, this must be a single physical switch port. Usually, this isn't a severe problem, especially since virtual adapters can be registered across different members when using the Hyper-V Port load-balancing algorithm, which will be discussed a bit later.

The Switch Independent mode is best used when physical redundancy is of prime importance and the roles assigned to the team will not benefit greatly from balancing inbound traffic across multiple adapters. Management, Live Migration in pre-2012 R2 deployments, and cluster communications all fall into this category in most installations.

Static teaming

Static teaming requires the cooperation of a connected physical switch. There is standardization (802.3ad), but not all manufacturers adhere closely to this. Switch vendors may opt to choose a unique name for their technology, but the most common label is **Link Aggregation Group (LAG)**. If you're unfamiliar with your switch's functions, you'll need to consult with your networking team or the hardware manufacturer for configuration steps and details.

In Static teaming, switches identify the team as a singular unit. MAC addresses register on the team and not an individual switch port. This overcomes the Switch Independent mode requirement for all inbound traffic to flow through a single adapter. The primary drawback to Static teaming is that it cannot be split across switches as the Switch Independent mode can. Some switches have the ability to be placed in a stacked configuration, in which they can operate as a single switch. Some stacked switches allow for individual LAGs to use ports across stack members, providing physical redundancy while retaining the benefits of a Static team.

LACP teaming

LACP stands for Link Aggregation Protocol. This is a standardized Ethernet protocol (802.1ax) that supersedes and enhances the Static team. When all is functioning, it provides the same benefits and suffers the same drawbacks as Static teaming. What it provides is an enhanced ability to detect problems in the interconnections. If either end of an LACP connection is misconfigured or there is any other problem on any part of the link, the endpoints will know to avoid the problematic connections.

> Contrary to a common misperception, LACP does not provide any enhancements for load-balancing or traffic aggregation that Static teaming does not.

Load balancing algorithms

The teaming modes create the links between devices. The load-balancing algorithm you select will guide the system in balancing outbound traffic across the member physical ports. Inbound load-balancing is handled by the switch. In the case of Switch Independent teaming, all inbound traffic flows through one port because the switch is not aware of the team. The new Dynamic load-balancing algorithm in R2 changes this behavior.

By default, only the Address Hash and Hyper-V Port options are shown in the GUI (R2 adds Dynamic). More granular options can be set using the `New-NetLbfoTeam` or `Set-NetLbfoTeam` cmdlets:

```
Set-NetLbfoTeam -Name Team1 -LoadBalancingAlgorithm IPAddresses
```

Any options that have been set in PowerShell will appear in the GUI. After entering the `LoadBalancingAlgorithm` parameter, you can use *TAB* to cycle through the available options.

Address Hash techniques

There are a total of three Address Hash modes. As explained above, the GUI only shows the generic Address Hash entry. With this option selected, Windows will select the most effective method and fall back through less efficient modes as necessary.

All of these methods work on the principle of leveraging a hash. A hash in this context is a singular representation of a group of data items. When determining what physical adapter to use in order to transmit outbound traffic, Windows builds a hash out of components of the traffic and then assigns all traffic that fits that hash to a particular adapter.

Transport Ports hash

The Transport Ports hash is the most comprehensive hashing method that Windows can use for load-balancing. This is also referred to as a four-tuple hash because it includes four components: the source IP address, the source TCP or UDP port, the destination IP address, and the destination TCP or UDP port. When this mode is enabled, all outbound packets that match on all four of these criteria will be assigned to a single adapter. Any packet with any differing component may be transmitted using a different adapter.

IP Addresses hash

The IP Addresses hash is a two-tuple hash and contains the source and destination IP addresses of a packet. Windows will fall back to this method for TCP/IP traffic that is neither TCP nor UDP in nature, such as ICMP, or when it does not have access to the port information, such as with IPSec communications. This method is not as efficient as Transport Ports balancing because all traffic from any one source to the same destination will always be on the same adapter. It is also possible to manually select this method using PowerShell as shown above. If manually selected, it will appear in the GUI selector as well.

MAC Addresses hash

The MAC Addresses hash is also a two-tuple hash and is roughly as efficient as the IP Addresses hash in most cases. However, a single MAC address can host multiple IP addresses, so this has the potential to be the least efficient method. Windows will fall back to this algorithm for traffic that is not IP-based, and, as with the other types, it can be manually selected.

Hyper-V Port balancing

The first thing that sets the Hyper-V Port balancing mode apart is that it's only useful when an external Hyper-V virtual switch is placed on the team. All the other methods can be used effectively even if Hyper-V is not installed. This technique assigns a Hyper-V virtual switch port directly to a physical adapter.

Dynamic (R2 only)

The reason that most aggregation methods do not split a single TCP stream is because of packet reordering. As communications are queued across the various team members, there is absolutely no way to know when a given adapter will be able to send any given transmission.

If a TCP stream were broken up, it is highly probable that its components would be sent out of order. While TCP/IP can handle this condition to a certain degree, it requires significant additional overhead, so it is usually more efficient to restrict one stream to a single adapter. By using an advanced technique that depends on a technology known as flowlets, TCP streams can be efficiently managed across multiple adapters. Therefore, the Dynamic mode can do a good job of efficiently distributing all outbound data evenly across constituent physical adapters.

The effects of teaming selections

The different options for teaming and address hashing can make the teaming possibilities look artificially complicated. In reality, there are only four basic ways to configure a team in 2012. Choose a Switch Independent or a Switch Dependent mode first and then choose a hashing algorithm or the Hyper-V Ports algorithm.

Switch Independent with hash

Using the Switch Independent mode with a hash is the least efficient method in terms of inbound traffic because all MAC addresses for virtual adapters will be registered on a single physical adapter. It works well for outbound traffic, however.

Switch Dependent (static or LACP) with hash

This is a very efficient mode of operation. The physical switch will balance traffic incoming to the host and Windows will balance outgoing traffic.

Switch Independent with Hyper-V Ports

In this mode, teaming will be able to register the independent virtual adapters to separate physical adapters, overcoming some of the limitations with the address hash. However, this does not truly load-balance the incoming traffic; it merely keeps all of it from coming across a single adapter. Outbound traffic is well-balanced across the virtual machines, but no virtual adapter will be able to use more than one physical port, even if its traffic presents unique hashes.

Switch Dependent (static or LACP) with Hyper-V Ports

With the switch balancing incoming traffic, this mode presents superior balancing of inbound traffic over the Switch Independent method. It has the same restriction of no virtual adapter being able to exceed the bandwidth of a single physical adapter.

Understanding the change brought by R2's Dynamic algorithm

The Switch Independent mode will benefit the most from R2's Dynamic load-balancing algorithm. With it enabled, even inbound traffic can be balanced. All other modes will see an improved utilization of hardware, although the differences will be most noticeable on networks that commonly have single-stream large transfers.

Effect of teaming on other technologies

There are a number of hardware-assisted technologies that are beneficial to networking operations. The number one thing to remember with all of these is that they are designed to overload network processing from the host's CPUs to the network adapter hardware in some fashion or another. If your hosts don't have meaningful levels of CPU contention, your gain from any of these technologies will be minimal. So, for a low or even moderately-loaded system, you may not get a substantial return on time invested in enabling, testing, and potentially troubleshooting these technologies.

The following list only explains how the enhanced technologies are affected by teaming. The technologies themselves will be explained and investigated in the next chapter:

- **Virtual Machine Queues (VMQ)** must register a queue for every virtual adapter on each physical adapter in the team. This can rapidly deplete the available queues. The exception is in Switch Independent mode. In that case, each virtual adapter will register a single queue on a single adapter. Virtual adapters are matched to physical adapters in a round-robin fashion.

- **SR-IOV** and **RDMA** are incompatible with any teaming method.

- **TCP Chimney** is no longer supported in 2012 and later. It will not be discussed in the next chapter. Refer to the following TechNet article for more information: `http://technet.microsoft.com/en-us/library/hh831568.aspx`.

- **802.1x authentication** is likely to cause service interruptions on a team and as such is not supported. This technology is mostly intended for wireless infrastructure and is generally inapplicable on server connections. The topic of 802.1x is outside the scope of this book.

- Virtual switch QoS should be set to the `Weight` method, not the `Absolute` method. The reason is that if an absolute minimum is set that is greater than the capacity of a single adapter and enough team members fail, that traffic could drown out all others.

- There are a number of other offloading technologies, such as IPSec, large send, and checksum offloads. If all adapters support these technologies, the team will support them as well. It should be noted that these technologies rarely offer significant improvements when they work, and some of them actually impair performance in some cases.

Practical teaming guidance

There is no single *correct* teaming and load-balancing method, nor are there any solid best practices to follow. The biggest choice to make initially is whether or not to use a Switch Dependent or Switch Independent teaming method, as that is the hardest to change later. The biggest draw to the Switch Independent method is its ability to connect to multiple physical switch devices to eliminate the risk of a single point of failure. With the Dynamic load-balancing algorithm of R2, the limitations of the Switch Independent mode are greatly lessened. There is also a valid philosophy of binding each host to its own physical switch so that a switch failure isolates the host, allowing Hyper-V Server and Failover Clustering's high availability design to handle the outage.

The load-balancing algorithm can be changed on-the-fly from Windows or Hyper-V, although there is some potential for dropped packets as the MAC addresses move across adapters. In most cases, everything will be finalized within the standard TCP retransmit window so most traffic will successfully recover. Of course, if your physical switch also needs to be reconfigured, the transition won't be as seamless.

Some points to help you in your decision are as follows:

- VMQ should be used whenever the hardware supports it, but it should be disabled in every case when it does not.

- Hyper-V Port load-balancing has greater effect as the ratio of virtual adapters to physical adapters rises. If the virtual-to-physical adapter ratio is near or below one, the hashing methods usually provide better overall performance.

- If the Hyper-V Ports load-balancing algorithm is used in conjunction with the Switch Independent teaming mode, the virtual switch can register the MAC addresses of virtual adapters on separate physical adapters to statically balance incoming traffic. With the Address Hash algorithm and the Switch Independent mode, all inbound traffic is on a single physical member.

- A single virtual adapter will not be able to exceed the speed of a single physical adapter when using Hyper-V Port load-balancing, but it may be able to when using hashing and will almost certainly be able to with Dynamic.

- Any given single traffic stream will not be able to exceed the speed of a single physical adapter in any mode except Dynamic.

- You can use teaming with SR-IOV by creating multiple external switches and teaming within the guests. However, you cannot team virtual adapters within the management operating system, so this will only work for guests. It also requires that you use guest operating systems that support teaming within Hyper-V. For Microsoft operating systems, this is only available in Windows Server 2012 and later.

Converged fabric

Converged fabric describes a network that combines multiple traffic types across the same hardware. A non-Hyper-V application of this term is an Ethernet switch that carries Fibre Channel traffic through media convertors.

For Hyper-V, a converged fabric is created when a single external virtual switch hosts multiple roles. In a traditional non-converged design, each role (management, cluster communications, Live Migration, virtual machine traffic, and storage communications) has dedicated adapters or even dedicated teams. This is still a perfectly valid and useful configuration, but it is highly wasteful of adapter capacity and functionality. By leveraging native adapter teaming, all of these roles can share physical adapters while exploiting the Hyper-V switch to keep the traffic properly segregated. You can augment your converged fabric by using QoS (a topic explained in *Chapter 6, Network Traffic Shaping and Performance Enhancements*) to shape traffic.

The following diagram compares the traditional teaming design to a potential converged fabric design:

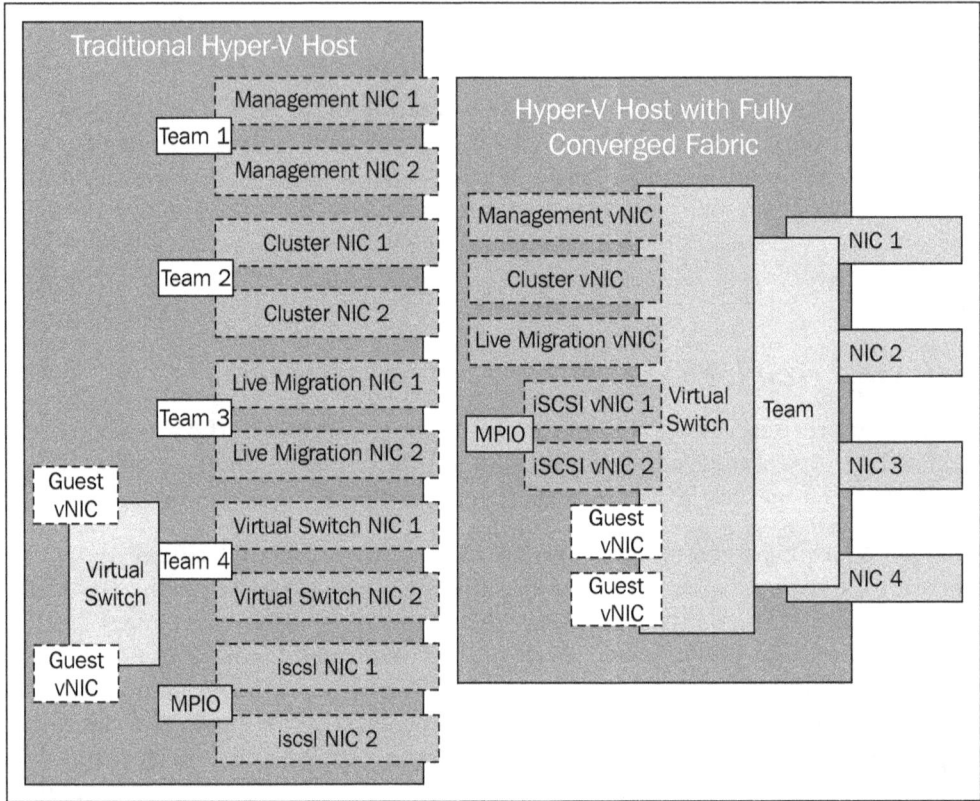

The previous diagram portrays a completely converged fabric in which all traffic and all roles run across a single team that includes four physical members. It hosts the same total number of roles as the traditional model, but with far fewer NICs. The diagram shows four physical adapters, but the number used is arbitrary. In this case, all roles are backed by up to four physical adapters; up to three adapters can fail and the system will maintain complete connectivity — albeit with constricted bandwidth. However, with teaming's load-balancing features, bandwidth utilization will be far superior to the traditional model. There is also substantially less concern about the costs of fully protecting all network roles. If you have 10GbE available or are considering it, converged fabric allows you to run all roles on a single adapter and provide redundancy to all roles using only two.

The best part about converged fabric is that if you've read through both *Chapter 3, Constructing a Hyper-V Server Cluster* and this chapter up to this point, you already know how to create and use a converged fabric. A quick review will suffice to round up all the preceding information. This assumes that you have four physical adapters and you've renamed them to NIC1, NIC2, NIC3, and NIC4.

```
# Create a team on the physical adapters.
New-NetLbfoTeam -Name "vSwitchTeam" -TeamMembers "NIC1", "NIC2",
"NIC3", "NIC4" -TeamingMode SwitchIndependent -LoadBalancingAlgorithm
HyperVPort


# Create a virtual switch and enable relative weight QoS. Do not
create a virtual adapter now.
New-VMSwitch -Name "vSwitch" -NetAdapterName "vSwitchTeam"
-MinimumBandwidthMode Weight -AllowManagementOS $false


# Create virtual adapters for all management operating system roles
Add-VMNetworkAdapter -Name "Management" -SwitchName "vSwitch"
-ManagementOS
Add-VMNetworkAdapter -Name "ClusterComm" -SwitchName "vSwitch"
-ManagementOS
Add-VMNetworkAdapter -Name "LiveMigration" -SwitchName "vSwitch"
-ManagementOS
Add-VMNetworkAdapter -Name "iSCSI1" -SwitchName "vSwitch"
-ManagementOS
Add-VMNetworkAdapter -Name "iSCSI2" -SwitchName "vSwitch"
-ManagementOS


# Assign virtual adapters to VLANs
Set-VMNetworkAdapterVlan -VMNetworkAdapter "Management" -Access
-VlanId 5 -ManagementOS
Set-VMNetworkAdapterVlan -VMNetworkAdapter "ClusterComm" -Access
-VlanId 10 -ManagementOS
Set-VMNetworkAdapterVlan -VMNetworkAdapter "LiveMigration" -Access
-VlanId 15 -ManagementOS
Set-VMNetworkAdapterVlan -VMNetworkAdapter "iSCSI1" -Access -VlanId 20
-ManagementOS
Set-VMNetworkAdapterVlan -VMNetworkAdapter "iSCSI2" -Access -VlanId 20
-ManagementOS
```

Practical converged fabric guidance

As with most other aspects of the new networking features in Hyper-V Server, there are no strict best practices around the design of converged fabric. Although the examples above show a fully converged fabric, there is absolutely nothing that requires this. Feel free to split out roles as desired. It is also perfectly acceptable to create multiple teams and even multiple external virtual switches to reach the desired configuration.

Most reasons to split roles will be related to storage connectivity. One practical reason is that not all networking features will bubble up through to the virtual adapters. As indicated earlier, teaming excludes some acceleration technologies. Virtual adapters cannot use RSS until 2012 R2, so using a virtual adapter to connect to SMB 3.0 storage may impair storage performance. Another reason to split roles is that in some environments, not all VLANs can be trunked to a single set of network ports. For instance, your iSCSI network may be physically isolated from all others. Using dedicated adapters will be your best option in that situation. Also, even though the team driver will distribute traffic across the physical members, there is no guarantee that your storage connections won't wind up sharing a physical adapter.

> It is acceptable to place iSCSI traffic on one or more virtual adapters that are part of a converged fabric, but it is not supported to use iSCSI directly on a team. Instead, use MPIO on multiple virtual adapters or on unteamed physical adapters. Instructions are given in *Chapter 3, Constructing a Hyper-V Server Cluster*.

Planning the physical layout

As you saw in the traditional layout explanation, in previous versions of Hyper-V, it was recommended that a minimum of one gigabit adapter be separately dedicated to management, cluster communications, and Live Migration for a total of three adapters. An external virtual switch for the virtual machines to communicate with the physical network required its own physical adapter. An iSCSI connection required at least one more dedicated adapter. There were recommendations to accommodate a lower number of adapters, but three gigabit adapters or one 10GbE with one 1GbE was the minimum supported configuration. Neither of these minimums accounted for storage connectivity or redundancy. With the 2012 series, the physical requirements are substantially more relaxed and there are more options. The traffic types themselves stay the same.

Your primary goal in designing the network layout for your Hyper-V Server cluster is to ensure that you provide sufficient bandwidth for all roles. The way that you meet that goal involves balancing redundancy, speed, and expense. The new teaming feature is likely to change the way that you think about your network design.

With the information provided in this chapter, you should be able to make an informed and reasoned decision on how to select and configure hardware to use for your cluster's networking needs. Unfortunately, there are no simple or universal answers. However, it is reasonable to assume that 3 to 4 gigabit adapters will acceptably cover the management, cluster communications, and Live Migration needs of most deployments while providing an acceptable level of automatic redundancy. Smaller deployments can probably fit all roles on four adapters.

If you will be using 10GbE or faster adapters, two is a logical minimum to ensure redundancy. More than two 10GbE or faster adapters in the same system is not likely to produce meaningful results in any but the most heavily network-dependent installations. Additional 10GbE adapters can aid SMB multichannel and, in R2, will have a positive impact on SMB-based Live Migration speeds. Remember that the hosts have an upper limit on how quickly they can process and move data to and from adapters, and this limit can be reached with only a few 10GbE adapters.

Make certain that you spend some time determining how you want to approach physical switch hardware. The first decision to make will be whether or not to use Switch Independent teaming mode. If you're not using VLANs, switch independence allows you to use less expensive unmanaged switches. Also, assuming that connectivity beyond the switches is also redundant, switch independence also allows a host to tolerate the loss of an entire switch without becoming isolated. The loss of a physical switch is a fairly uncommon occurrence, but it can also come in handy for things like scheduled switch maintenance. An alternate approach is to use a switch-dependent mode and leverage Hyper-V Server's high availability features to handle host isolation in the event of switch failure. No approach is perfectly correct; choose the option that best suits your organization's needs and comfort level.

One item not yet fully examined is Data Center Bridging, which will be more thoroughly covered in the next chapter. This is a hardware-controlled Quality of Service technology that requires hardware that can support DCB. This is not an inexpensive solution, so the decision to use it should be an informed one. If you're not yet certain, please read through the *Chapter 6, Network Traffic Shaping and Performance Enhancements* before finalizing your physical layout decision.

Firewall settings

The final major networking consideration for your Hyper-V Server hosts is the firewall configuration. Every organization adopts its own philosophy on computer-level firewall implementation, and the only true *best practice* in this regard is that you have taken reasonable steps to protect your systems. Firewall rules do add some processing overhead to the networking stack. Your organization's network protection needs may be better served by performing firewalling at the outer perimeter and perhaps at other junctures within your network. If your organization is smaller and cannot afford high-end firewalling hardware, it may make sense to leave the host firewall activated.

Whatever approach you choose to use, it is recommended that you use group policy to set firewall rules. For one thing, your hosts must be domain-joined just to participate in the cluster, which means they are already receiving at least some group policies. For another, this ensures a uniform application of rules from a single point of configuration.

When all features are installed, the default configuration of a Hyper-V Server in a Microsoft Failover Cluster results in an enabled firewall that needs no changes in order for the host to perform all required duties. All cluster roles will be able to communicate with each other and all nodes will be able to initiate connections to backend storage. You will be able to remotely manage your hosts using Server Manager, Hyper-V Manager, and Failover Cluster Manager. The Hyper-V virtual switch has no protocols bound to it, so virtual machine traffic passes in and out without being touched by the host's firewall.

The changes you might consider making are related to remote management. The default configuration does not allow inbound connections from Remote Desktop, PowerShell, and some common MMC consoles, such as those found in Computer Management.

> All remote management connections are made only to the IP address designated for the Management role.

Remote desktop

When a Hyper-V Server system is started, it automatically brings up the Server Configuration menu, which is a text-based script to help perform some common administrative functions. It can be accessed on a Windows Server system by running `sconfig.cmd`. Option 7 from the main menu of this tool will allow you to enable or disable Remote Desktop, including the firewall rules.

As in all recent Windows operating systems, the Computer Properties screen in the GUI also contains a **Remote desktop** link that does the same thing.

To enable Remote Desktop in Group Policy, use the **Group Policy Management Console** (**GPMC**), which is automatically enabled on all domain controllers and is an installable feature on non-domain controller servers and desktops. Its basic usage is general knowledge and will not be explained here. To enable Remote Desktop connections, navigate to **Computer Configuration** | **Policies** | **Administrative Templates** | **Windows Components** | **Remote Desktop Services** | **Connections** and enable **Allow users to connect remotely by using Remote Desktop Services**.

PowerShell

To enable remote PowerShell from the system to be controlled, simply run:

```
Enable-PSRemoting -Force
```

Or, in GPMC, navigate to **Computer Configuration** | **Policies** | **Administrative Templates** | **Windows Components** | **Windows Remote Management (WinRM)** | **WinRM Service**. Set **Allow remote server management through WinRM** to **Enabled**. Enter the management adapter's IP address in the **IPv4** field for the tightest restriction, or use an asterisk (*) to open it up on all adapters. See the Firewall rules section, next, to continue.

Firewall rules

In a GUI installation, you can simply use the Windows Firewall applet in Control Panel to set the local firewall.

To use GPMC to create a policy that you can apply to multiple systems, create a new policy or edit an existing one.

To simply disable the firewall, navigate to **Computer Configuration** | **Policies** | **Network** | **Network Connections** | **Windows Firewall** | **Domain Profile** and set **Windows Firewall: Protect all network connections** to **Disabled**. If you'd rather set exceptions, continue reading.

Navigate to **Computer Configuration** | **Policies** | **Windows Settings** | **Security Settings** | **Windows Firewall with Advanced Security** | **Windows Firewall with Advanced Security**. This tool works very much like the advanced settings in the Windows Firewall applet, so if you've used that, you should have little trouble here. Right-click on the **Inbound Rules** node and click on **New Rule...** to create rules.

For Remote Desktop, select the **Predefined** dot and **Remote Desktop** from the drop-down box on the first screen and continue through to the end. You may change other options along the way if desired.

For PowerShell sessions, follow the same process as for Remote Desktop, but select **Windows Remote Management** from the drop-down.

For other common connections, most are in the predefined drop-down, such as **Remote Service Management**. You may use the other options to set policies just as you would for a local firewall. Create as many rules as necessary to achieve the desired connectivity.

Summary

This chapter took a detailed look at the networking components of Hyper-V Server and how it interacts with Microsoft Failover Clustering. You learned the basic operation of the Hyper-V virtual switch. You saw how cluster networks are used to support and augment the high availability features of Hyper-V Server. The specifics of Windows Server 2012 native adapter teaming were also thoroughly examined.

After the basic concepts were introduced and explained, you learned how to put them all together to create converged fabric.

You were able to apply this knowledge to design a physical layout to satisfy the needs of your system.

The chapter ended with an explanation of configuring the Windows Firewall to allow remote access connections.

In the next chapter, we will look at methods to shape traffic to guarantee bandwidth where it is needed and ways to improve networking performance.

6

Network Traffic Shaping and Performance Enhancements

In addition to the new technologies that Windows Server 2012 offers for transmitting and receiving network traffic, there are also new ways to manage how that traffic flows. This chapter will also introduce you to several hardware-based features that your systems can exploit to govern and improve networking performance.

In this chapter, you will learn about the following topics:

- Windows Server Quality of Service
- Using Data Center Bridging for hardware Quality of Service
- Changing advanced settings on network adapters
- Configuring jumbo frames for increased throughput
- Network acceleration features such as VMQ, RSS, RDMA, and SR-IOV
- The potential for the Hyper-V switch

Windows Server Quality of Service

Quality of Service (QoS) is a generic term that covers a large number of ways to shape network traffic. The general aim of QoS is to prioritize specific classes or services. Usually, this means ensuring that one or more traffic types have a minimum amount of bandwidth, but it can also mean suspending other traffic types to ensure the lowest possible latency for a given data stream. **Voice over IP (VoIP)** is a very common application for QoS because it is highly intolerant of network latency.

The Windows operating system has offered policy-based QoS for some time. New in Windows Server 2012 and Hyper-V Server 2012 is the ability to set QoS within the context of the virtual switch. Another new introduction is Data Center Bridging, in which the physical switching hardware does most of the QoS work.

Policy-based QoS

Policy-based QoS is a Windows Server technology designed to handle all traffic types. The new PowerShell cmdlets used to configure policy-based QoS are available at `http://technet.microsoft.com/library/hh967469.aspx`. This is extremely granular in nature and as a result, is a powerful and precise tool. A Hyper-V host is usually not the best application for this technology, as Hyper-V will have the most control over traffic to and from the management operating system, which is unlikely to have much variance. It will not have any visibility into the traffic of the virtual machines, so it does not warrant the fine control offered by policy-based QoS. The new Data Center Bridging technology shares many cmdlets with policy-based QoS, as it is effectively a hardware-enforced implementation of that technology. As policy-based QoS is more appropriate to a discussion on Windows Server networking, it will not be examined in-depth in this book. However, the section on Data Center Bridging will examine many of its cmdlets, so that section may serve as an introduction to the concept.

> Using policy-based QoS to specify bandwidth minimums will have a detrimental effect on traffic crossing teamed adapters. This does not apply when the policy is enforced by Data Center Bridging capable hardware.

Policy-based QoS can be set using Group Policy rather than modifying each host individually. For a cluster where all nodes should use the same policies, this is the preferred method. In your Group Policy, navigate to **Computer Configuration | Policies | Windows Settings | Policy-based QoS**.

Hyper-V QoS

The new Hyper-V QoS capabilities aren't nearly as granular as policy-based QoS, but they are much more suited to a Hyper-V host. To use Hyper-V QoS, you must decide before you create the switch whether you will use absolute QoS values, or relative weighting. In the absolute method, you specify the minimum and/or maximum bandwidth a virtual adapter may use. In relative weighting, you assign each adapter a number between one and one hundred. Adapters with higher numbers will be given higher priority.

Hyper-V QoS is enabled by default on each new virtual switch. If you create a virtual switch with the default settings or by using the GUI, it will be set to absolute weight mode unless SR-IOV is also enabled, in which case the default mode will be `None`. This cannot be changed later. You can only enable the relative weight mode or disable QoS entirely when the switch is created, and only if it is created via PowerShell, as shown in the following code:

```
New-VMSwitch -Name vSwitch -NetAdapterName "Ethernet 5" -
MinimumBandwidthMode Weight
```

> At the time of writing this book, the official Microsoft documentation for the `New-VMSwitch` cmdlet indicates that `Weight` is the default mode for virtual switches that do not have SR-IOV enabled, which is not correct.

Bandwidth limits are set directly on the virtual adapter. For virtual adapters assigned to virtual machines, absolute weights can be set in Hyper-V Manager (or Failover Cluster Manager for clustered virtual machines), by accessing the virtual machine's property sheet and selecting the virtual adapter. This is shown in the following screenshot:

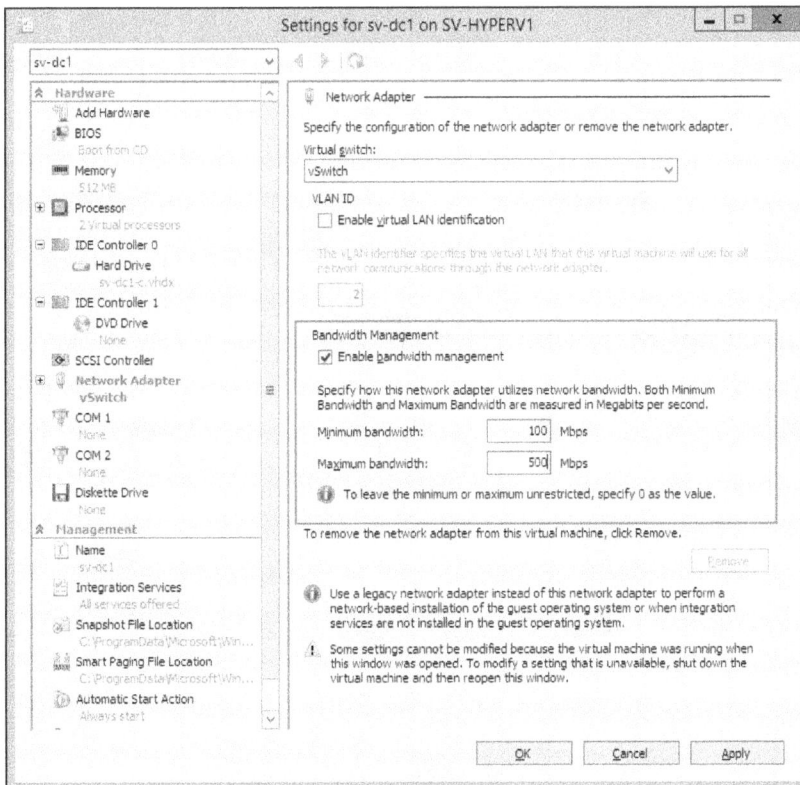

For virtual adapters assigned to the management operating system or to set relative weight on any virtual adapter, you must use PowerShell using the following command:

```
Set-VMNetworkAdapter -VMName "sv-dc1" -Name "Network Adapter"
MinimumBandwidthWeight 15

Set-VMNetworkAdapter -ManagementOS -Name "Management"
MinimumBandwidthWeight 10
```

Other available QoS parameters are `MinimumBandwidthAbsolute` and `MaximumBandwidth`. The two minimums cannot be used together. You cannot use a minimum weight setting for an adapter connected to a switch in absolute mode, nor can you apply a minimum absolute setting to an adapter connected to a switch in relative weight mode. The `MaximumBandwidth` is always in bits per second, and can be used on an adapter connected to a switch in either QoS mode. There are several things to note about these QoS settings:

- For absolute QoS, Microsoft's recommendation is that you use 100 megabits/s or higher minimums.

- The smallest number you can use for `MinimumBandwidthAbsolute` in the PowerShell cmdlet is 10000000 (10 Mbps). If you attempt to use a smaller number, the error message is not clear, for example: **A parameter that was not valid was passed to the operation**.

- The `MaximumBandwidth` parameter has no error checking of any kind except to ensure that you used a numeric value. The GUI will prevent you from setting a maximum that is lower than the minimum; PowerShell will not. The maximum setting takes precedence over the minimum. Therefore, if you set maximums, ensure that you use reasonably large numbers and that you remember that the number in PowerShell is always represented in bits per second.

- If a virtual machine has any adapters with QoS minimums set, it cannot be Live or Quick Migrated to a host whose virtual switch is not using the same QoS mode.

- If you create a virtual switch on an adapter team, it is recommended that you only use the relative weight QoS mode. If an adapter is added to or removed from the team, absolute numbers may result in sub-optimal or even non-functional configurations.

You can determine a switch's QoS mode with the following command:

```
(Get-VMSwitch -Name "vSwitch").BandwidthReservationMode
```

You can see its minimum absolute setting for the default pool with the following command:

`(Get-VMSwitch vSwitch).DefaultFlowMinimumBandwidthAbsolute`

Or, for a switch in relative weight mode:

`(Get-VMSwitch vSwitch).DefaultFlowMinimumBandwidthWeight`

These defaults can be overridden with the `Set-VMSwitch` cmdlet:

```
Set-VMSwitch -Name "vSwitch" -DefaultFlowMinimumBandwidthAbsolute
600000000
```

View the bandwidth settings for a management operating system's virtual adapter with the following command:

`(Get-VMNetworkAdapter -ManagementOS Name "Management").BandwidthSetting`

For a guest's adapter, use:

```
(Get-VMNetworkAdapter -VMName "sv-dc1" Name "Network Adapter").
BandwidthSetting
```

If you do not configure an adapter with a minimum setting, it will go into a default pool. All adapters in this pool share a single minimum; the minimum is not assigned to individual adapters. For switches in absolute QoS mode, the default minimum pool is 100 Mbps on a single physical adapter. If the switch is created on a team, the minimum is multiplied by the number of members. As an example, a team created across four adapters has a default minimum of 400 Mbps. For relative weight, the minimum pool always defaults to a weight of 1.

Data Center Bridging

Data Center Bridging (**DCB**) is an umbrella term that covers a group of networking standards that are cumulatively used to shape and control network communications in a mixed-traffic environment. Part of the initiative behind this technology is to provide lossless communications for fibre channel when it is converged into Ethernet fabric (commonly known as **Fibre Channel over Ethernet** (**FCoE**)). Another part is, of course, to aid in controlling quality of service across the data center. Where DCB differs from more traditional QoS, is that QoS is set on each individual computer, device, and/or switch; it is only responsible for traffic that it is currently handling. DCB is a cooperative effort that involves all of the hardware jointly.

Using DCB requires DCB-capable hardware. This applies to the physical adapters and to the physical switches that they connect to. If desired, QoS can be handled from within the physical switch fabric which leaves only a little to do on the Windows or Hyper-V side.

As with policy-based QoS, DCB is a generic Windows Server feature and is not particular to Hyper-V. Unlike the policy-based QoS described previously, DCB is a common implementation that extends beyond Microsoft operating systems. It is also a very large topic that requires expertise in networking to completely understand and deploy properly. What follows should be treated as an extremely basic tutorial on connecting a Windows or Hyper-V Server system into a DCB-enabled network.

First, you must install DCB. This can be done from the **Add Roles or Features** wizard in **Server Manager**, where it can be found as a line item on the **Features** tab. It can also be performed in PowerShell:

```
Add-WindowsFeature -Name DataCenterBridging
```

> DCB is solely manipulated using PowerShell. There is no GUI.

Once DCB is installed, if your physical adapters support DCB and the connected physical switch has DCB policies enabled and configured, you don't need to do anything else. The adapters will receive configuration information directly from the switch.

If you wish to override the default behavior and allow Windows to set local DCB policies, you must first disable automatic configuration (DCBX):

```
Set-NetQosDcbxSetting -Willing $false
```

You must then enable your physical adapter(s) to accept local DCB policies:

```
Set-NetAdapterQos -Name "Ethernet 7" -Enabled $true
```

Or:

```
Enable-NetAdapterQoS -Name "Ethernet 6"
```

> If enabling DCB returns an error, either the adapter does not support DCB or Windows cannot detect that it does. Updating the driver may correct this.

Repeat the previous actions for any other DCB-capable adapters. Once this has been completed, your host's adapter(s) will no longer accept DCB configuration commands from the connected switch. However, the switch may simply disable DCB for a connected system that doesn't accept DCB configurations, so there may be additional steps to take on the hardware in order for your host's settings to work.

Once the `Willing` flag has been disabled and your adapter(s) are enabled, you can begin defining how you want traffic to flow on your system. There are a number of methods to designate how traffic will be shaped. In all methods employing DCB, traffic flow is handled by 802.1p tags, so that will be examined first.

802.1p tagging

Under the 802.1p standard, an Ethernet frame can contain a three-bit tag specifically for QoS purposes. Three bits allow for eight numbers (zero through seven), therefore, you have access to up to eight different QoS traffic classes. They are prioritized in ascending order, with zero being the lowest and seven taking the highest precedence. A class is assigned bandwidth and latency settings and traffic is assigned to that class by type or by application. You must also enable flow control for that traffic class:

```
Enable-NetQosFlowControl -Priority 3
```

Or:

```
Set-NetQosFlowControl -Priority 3 -Enabled $true
```

> If flow settings are applied to a traffic class but flow control is not enabled for that class, the settings will be ignored.

You can use `Disable-NetQosFlowControl`, or `-Enabled $false`, with the `Set-NetQosFlowControl` cmdlet to reverse these settings.

Assigning applications and traffic types to QoS classes

To begin with, create a QoS policy. This uses the same `New-NetQoSPolicy` and `Set-NetQoSPolicy` cmdlets as software policy-based QoS. What's different is that the `Qos` class utilizes the `PriorityValue8021Action` parameter, which, as its name implies, assigns the policy to a specific 802.1p traffic class. Bandwidth rates are controlled on that class, not on the policy.

In contrast, a non-DCB system employing software policy-based QoS that cannot use the 802.1p tag would assign settings directly to the policy using the `MinBandwidthWeightAction` and `ThrottleRateActionBytesPerSecond` parameters of the aforementioned cmdlets. You also have access to the `DSCP` parameter. DSCP is an acronym for **Differentiated Service Code Point**, which is somewhat similar to DCB but is part of a TCP/IP header rather than the Ethernet frame, is specified by the application and not the network or operating system administrator, and doesn't require complete hardware cooperation to the same degree as DCB. These parameters are explained in Microsoft's documentation which was linked above in the policy-based QoS section. Using these parameters on a policy that is also DCB-controlled will have mixed results and is not recommended.

The following cmdlet will assign the Windows Server Backup application to traffic class 3:

```
New-NetQosPolicy -Name "Backup" -AppPathNameMatchCondition "C:\Windows\
system32\wbengine.exe" -PriorityValue8021Action 3
```

You can also designate traffic using TCP and/or UDP port information:

```
New-NetQosPolicy -Name "SSH" -IPPortMatchCondition 22
IPProtocolMatchCondition TCP -PriorityValue8021Action 4
```

In the previous cmdlet, you can also choose `None`, `UDP`, or `Both` for the protocol match. For some well-known protocols, the cmdlet accepts a number of predefined filters. Instead of using the `IPPortMatchCondition` and `IPProtocolMatchCondition`, you can enter `FCOE`, `ISCSI`, `LiveMigration`, `NetworkDirect`, `NFS`, or `SMB`. So, to create a policy for Live Migration, instead of designing a QoS policy for its TCP 6600 port, you can use the following:

```
New-NetQosPolicy -Name "Live Migration Policy" -LiveMigration
-PriorityValue8021Action 5
```

> The `LiveMigration` switch is inapplicable if Live Migration is set to SMB mode in R2. Set QoS for SMB traffic instead.

Additional parameters can be used to fine-tune QoS as desired, although these aren't typically as valuable in a Hyper-V Server. You can specify source and destination IP addresses, and the destination port. These and other parameters are shown in Microsoft's documentation for the `New-NetQosPolicy` cmdlet. Access the 2012 versions at `http://technet.microsoft.com/en-US/library/hh967468.aspx`. They are unchanged in 2012 R2, but the URL is: `http://technet.microsoft.com/en-us/library/hh967469%28v=wps.630%29.aspx`.

Policies can be listed with the `Get-NetQosPolicy` cmdlet, modified with `Set-NetQosPolicy`, and removed with `Remove-NetQosPolicy`.

> The same traffic class can be assigned in multiple policies.

Setting bandwidth on DCB QoS classes

Now that you have QoS policies created to assign traffic to classes, you can set aside bandwidth reservations for those classes, if desired. Remember that priority takes precedence over bandwidth minimums. To guarantee that the class that holds the Live Migration policy created previously will have access to at least twenty percent of the system's bandwidth: For instance:

```
Set-NetQosTrafficClass -Name "Live Migration Policy Class"
BandwidthPercentage 20 -Algorithm ETS
```

The only other option available for the `Algorithm` parameter is `Strict`. If your hardware supports **ETS (Enhanced Transmission Selection)**, it is probably the preferred choice. It ensures that classes with a higher priority do not completely drown out those with a lower priority.

> You are not required to place a bandwidth setting on a class. Priority sequence will still apply.

The default class

Any traffic that is not specifically placed into a QoS traffic class is assigned to the default class, which is priority 0. In a system with no policies, priority 0 contains all traffic and has access to all of the bandwidth. As you prioritize traffic and set bandwidth minimums, it is carved out of priority 0. Traffic classes and minimums that are removed are returned to the default class.

Changing advanced settings on network adapters

In the next several sections of this chapter, you will be introduced to a number of technologies that are designed to enhance the performance of network adapters. These features usually ship disabled, or tuned, for compatibility over performance. They are all found in the same locations and changed using the same methods; so rather than repeat the same instructions multiple times, each method will be shown here. We will use jumbo frames as the sample setting to be changed. Jumbo frames themselves will be discussed immediately after the examples.

Network adapter advanced settings can be changed in a local GUI (if one is available), through the registry, and by using PowerShell.

> Different vendors will use similar, but not necessarily identical names for some technologies.

Advanced adapter settings in the GUI

To modify the advanced settings in the GUI, your final destination is the advanced properties sheet of the physical adapter.

1. Right-click on the network adapter icon in the notification area of the taskbar and click on **Open Network and Sharing Center**, as shown in the following screenshot:

    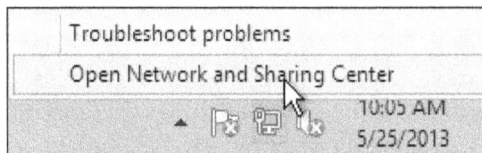

    Alternately, open **Control Panel** from the Start screen, open **Network and Internet**, then **Network and Sharing Center**. If you have set your Control Panel view to either of the icon modes instead of the default Category display mode, the **Network and Sharing Center** is at the top level.

2. In the left pane of the **Network and Sharing Center**, click on the **Change adapter settings** link. This will open a new window titled **Network Connections** that contains all network adapters.

3. Right-click on the adapter whose settings you wish to modify and click on **Properties**. Click on the **Configure...** button, as shown in the following screenshot:

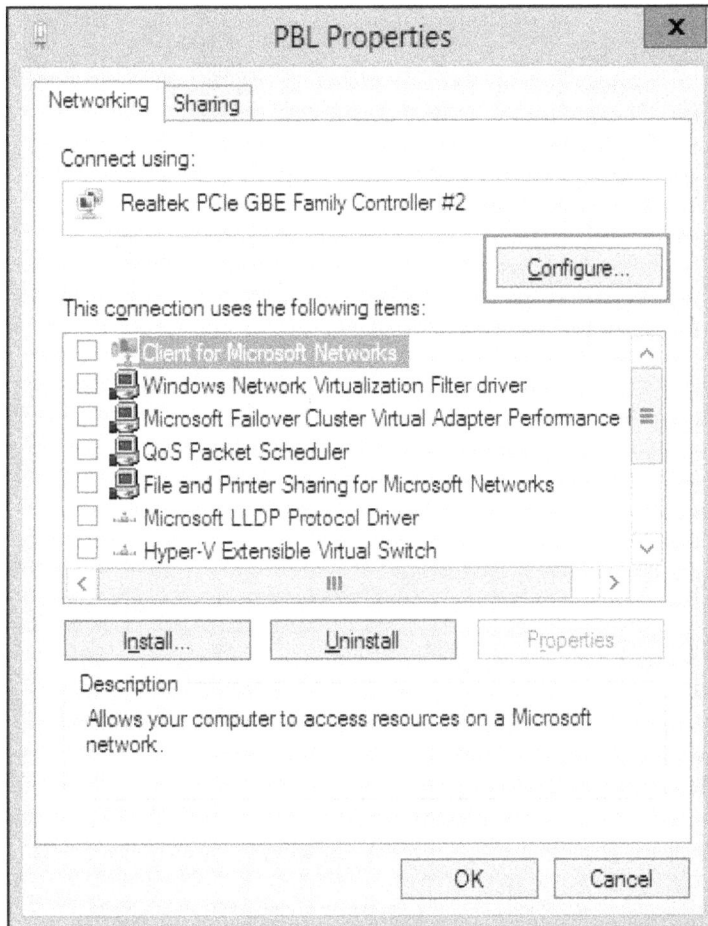

4. Select the **Advanced** tab. Underneath the **Property:** heading, you will find all of the advanced settings available on this adapter. To the right, under the **Value:** heading, there will be a drop-down box or a textbox where the selected setting can be changed. The following screenshot shows a sample **Jumbo Frame** option:

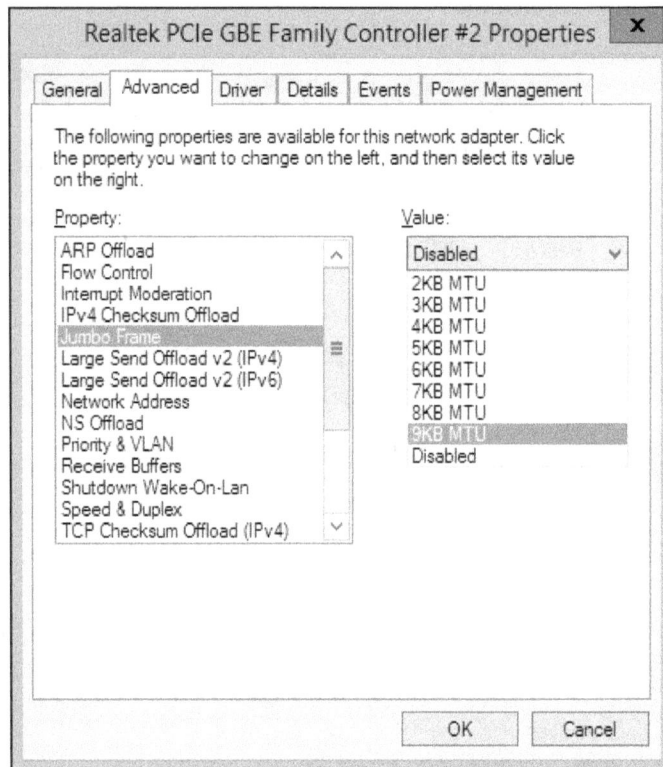

Normally, these settings will take effect immediately, once you've clicked on **OK** through all the dialogs. Using the right-click options on the adapter, using the **Disable** and **Enable** functions may be necessary, and in some cases a reboot will be required.

Advanced adapter settings in the registry

The properties dialog box shown in the previous sections is a view into a number of settings that are presented in the registry. It is possible to access the registry and methodically proceed through the adapters until you find the one that you're looking for, but you can save your time by determining the index of the adapter whose settings you wish to change prior to digging into the registry. The easiest way to find an adapter's index is using PowerShell, as follows:

```
Get-NetAdapter | Format-Table InterfaceIndex, Name, InterfaceDescription
-AutoSize
```

The **InterfaceIndex** field in the previous code contains the index.

Once you know the index, open the registry. You can simply type `regedit.exe` at a command or PowerShell prompt. In a GUI installation of Windows, open the Start screen and type in `regedit.exe` and press *Enter*. You can also press the Windows + *R* key together to access the **Run** window where you can enter `regedit.exe`.

Navigate to **HKEY_LOCAL_MACHINE | SYSTEM | CurrentControlSet | Control | Class | {4d36e972-e325-11ce-bfc1-08002be10318}**. Upon expanding this key, you will find a series of four-digit entries. Each of these numbers corresponds to an interface's index.

Click on the number of the adapter determined from the previous PowerShell command and look in the right pane. Key-value pairs whose names begin with an asterisk (*) are advanced settings. These keys are all free-form text fields, but most only have a few possible correct settings. To determine what those are, expand the **numeric** key for the adapter, then the **Ndi** key, and the **params** key. Find the key for the setting you wish to change and expand it. If that setting has a particular list of possibilities, you'll find an **enum** sub-key. Click on that and check the pane on the right for possibilities. The following screenshot shows the **enum** key for Jumbo Frames on adapter 13:

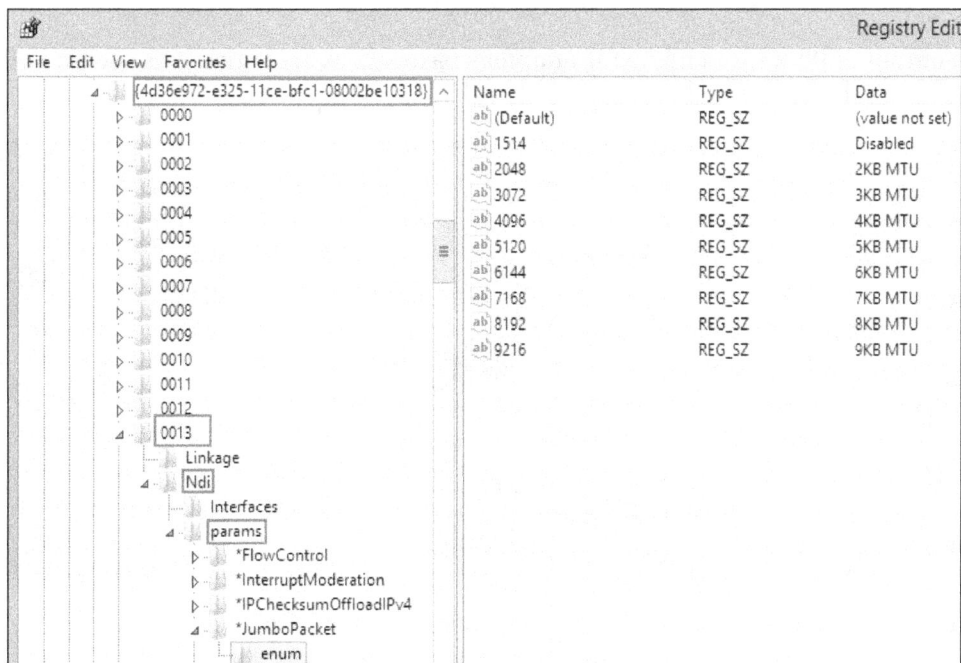

The **Name** portion of the key-value pair under the **enum** key is what is entered in the data portion of the key-value pair at the top of the adapter's key branch. The **Data** portion shows the text that is displayed in the dialog box in the GUI. So, using the system from the previous screenshot as an example, we learned that the number we need to know for adapter 13's nine-kilobyte jumbo frame setting is **9216**. With that number in hand, we would click the **0013** key, double-click on the *JumboPacket key-value pair, and type 9216 into the **Value data** field. Other adapters will use different numbers for the various settings, so it is important that you look for valid values prior to making changes.

In most cases, registry changes do not take effect automatically. Usually, disabling and then enabling the adapter will work. You can use the Disable-NetAdapter and Enable-NetAdapter cmdlets for this purpose. In some instances a restart of the computer will be necessary.

Advanced adapter settings in PowerShell

To see the possible entries for an adapter, use the Get-NetAdapterAdvancedProperty cmdlet. This can be used by itself:

```
Get-NetAdapterAdvancedProperty -Name "PTL"
```

It can also be used with the pipeline:

```
Get-NetAdapter -Name "PTL" | Get-NetAdapterAdvancedProperty
```

The output will look much like the adapter's base key in the registry, as shown in the following screenshot:

Name	DisplayName	DisplayValue	RegistryKeyword	RegistryValue
PTL	Flow Control	Rx & Tx Enabled	*FlowControl	{3}
PTL	Interrupt Moderation	Enabled	*InterruptModeration	{1}
PTL	IPv4 Checksum Offload	Rx & Tx Enabled	*IPChecksumOffloadIPv4	{3}
PTL	Jumbo Frame	Disabled	*JumboPacket	{1514}
PTL	Large Send Offload v2 (IPv4)	Enabled	*LsoV2IPv4	{1}
PTL	Large Send Offload v2 (IPv6)	Enabled	*LsoV2IPv6	{1}
PTL	ARP Offload	Enabled	*PMARPOffload	{1}
PTL	NS Offload	Enabled	*PMNSOffload	{1}
PTL	Priority & VLAN	Priority & VLAN Enabled	*PriorityVLANTag	{3}
PTL	Receive Buffers	512	*ReceiveBuffers	{512}
PTL	Speed & Duplex	Auto Negotiation	*SpeedDuplex	{0}
PTL	TCP Checksum Offload (IPv4)	Rx & Tx Enabled	*TCPChecksumOffloadIPv4	{3}
PTL	TCP Checksum Offload (IPv6)	Rx & Tx Enabled	*TCPChecksumOffloadIPv6	{3}
PTL	Transmit Buffers	128	*TransmitBuffers	{128}
PTL	UDP Checksum Offload (IPv4)	Rx & Tx Enabled	*UDPChecksumOffloadIPv4	{3}
PTL	UDP Checksum Offload (IPv6)	Rx & Tx Enabled	*UDPChecksumOffloadIPv6	{3}
PTL	Wake on Magic Packet	Enabled	*WakeOnMagicPacket	{1}
PTL	Wake on pattern match	Enabled	*WakeOnPattern	{1}
PTL	Network Address	--	NetworkAddress	{--}
PTL	Shutdown Wake-On-Lan	Enabled	S5WakeOnLan	{1}
PTL	WOL & Shutdown Link Speed	10 Mbps First	WolShutdownLinkSpeed	{0}

Making a change to a setting is done with the `Set-NetAdapterAdvancedSetting` cmdlet. The easiest way to do this is by using the pipeline. Use `Get-NetAdapterAdvancedSetting` to specify the adapter and the display name of the key-value pair to change, then use `Set-NetAdapterAdvancedSetting` to specify the registry value:

```
Get-NetAdapterAdvancedProperty -Name "PTL" -DisplayName "Jumbo Frame" |
Set-NetAdapterAdvancedProperty -RegistryValue 9216
```

You may also use the `RegistryKeyword` parameter instead of `DisplayName` in the `Get-NetAdapterAdvancedProperty` cmdlet, and you can use `DisplayValue` instead of `RegistryValue` in the `Set-NetAdapterAdvancedProperty` cmdlet.

Unfortunately, there is no direct way to determine the valid values for a setting by using PowerShell, as there is by examining the registry. If you attempt to use an invalid setting, the error message will show the values that it was expecting. For instance, attempting to set an incorrect value for jumbo frames on the previous adapter returns: **Set-NetAdapterAdvancedProperty : No matching keyword value found. The following are valid keyword values: 1514, 2048, 3072, 4096, 5120, 6144, 7168, 8192, 9216.**

Jumbo frames

As you are probably already aware, TCP/IP transmits data in chunks called **packets**. TCP/IP packets travel across Ethernet networks in containers called **frames**. These frames contain a few bytes that delineate the frame, and the contain source and destination MAC address. The rest is the payload, which is the data being carried by the frame. In the case of TCP/IP transmissions, the payload refers to the packet. A normal Ethernet payload is 1500 bytes in length or shorter. Anything longer is considered a jumbo frame. You will also occasionally see references to jumbo packet. The setting to limit payload sizes is called the **Maximum Transmission Unit (MTU)**. The exact numbers used will vary, sometimes because of rounding, sometimes because the entire frame is being referred to instead of just the payload. So, a standard frame could be indicated by 1500 or 1518. A jumbo frame comes in many varieties, but 9000, 9014, and 9216 are common.

The purpose of a jumbo frame is to increase transmission efficiency. The non-payload portion of the Ethernet frame and the packet header information in the TCP/IP payload are somewhat fixed in length, and always require about the same amount of time and effort to process regardless of the overall size of the packet. Allowing a single frame to carry a larger data segment increases the amount of data that can travel, without increasing processing requirements. The folllowing figure explains the concept in detail:

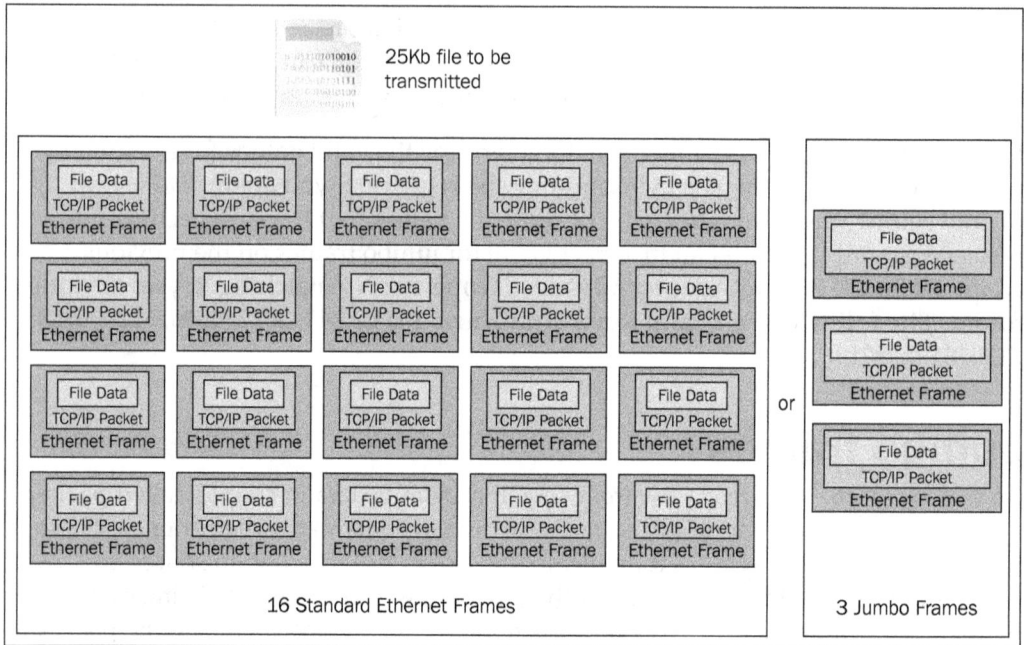

The drawback is that not all hardware supports jumbo frames, and not all hardware that supports it has it enabled. Frame sizes default to small numbers for a reason: it is easier for routing equipment on highly congested networks to handle large numbers of smaller packets through the use of various queuing and routing techniques. Occasional packet loss in these large networks is common and expected; the more data that a packet carries, the more that is lost when packets go astray. Of course, these issues are more prevalent in extremely large-scale networks, such as the Internet. They generally don't appear on internal networks with high-speed equipment.

Simply enabling jumbo frames blindly is not a good idea. If a jumbo frame arrives on a device that doesn't support jumbo frames, it will do one of the two things. If you're lucky, it will request the source device to fragment the frame and retransmit it. This requires more time and processing effort than simply not using jumbo frames. If you're not lucky, the device will simply drop incoming jumbo frames (such a device is called a **black hole router**). This is essentially a broken connection. Every single device from source to destination, and every switch or router in between must support jumbo frames, or these retransmissions and dropped data will occur.

Internal networks such as those used for cluster communications, SMB 3.0 traffic, and Live Migration are good candidates for jumbo frames. If you are using iSCSI and the storage vendor supports jumbo frames, you definitely want to enable jumbo frames for those connections. If your management network will connect to the Internet, it is a poor choice for jumbo frames.

Before enabling jumbo frames in Windows or Hyper-V Server, first ensure that your physical switch supports them and has the feature enabled. Next, ensure that your physical adapters support them.

Enable jumbo frames on your physical adapters first, following the instructions previously in one of the sections explaining how to change adapter advanced settings. The exact name of the technology and possible values will be different from manufacturer to manufacturer. Use the setting that is closest to 9000. If you are setting communications for a particular piece of hardware, the manufacturer may specify a different number.

> Ensure that you don't use a frame size larger than any equipment in the communications path can handle.

Virtual adapters also have this setting and do support jumbo frames. The **Display Name** is **Jumbo Packet**, the **Registry Keyword** is ***JumboPacket**, and the jumbo frame value is **9014**. Since all virtual adapters start with vEthernet, you can use one line to enable jumbo frames for all of them. The following usage illustrates how to use the **RegistryKeyword** parameter, but you're certainly free to use the same usage from the previous instructions:

```
Get-NetAdapterAdvancedProperty -Name "vethernet*" RegistryKeyword
*JumboPacket | Set-NetAdapterAdvancedProperty -RegistryValue 9014
```

> Do not set jumbo frames on adapters that will connect to the Internet.

In order for the virtual adapters to be able to pass jumbo frames, they must also be enabled on the virtual switch and on the physical adapter(s) that the virtual switch is bound to. The R2 products automatically enable this at the switch level, so no further configuration is required. Windows Server 2012 and Hyper-V Server 2012 will need additional work. Due to the way that the virtual switch is created, you will not be able to manipulate it through the GUI, and cmdlets such as `Get-NetAdapter` will behave inconsistently.

The only safe method to change jumbo frame settings on your virtual switch is through the registry. If you are working on Hyper-V Server 2012, the virtual switch is index 0008. If you are working on Windows Server 2012, the virtual switch index is 0024. These are the only locations you need to make the change, even if you have multiple switches on the same host. A computer restart will be required.

> It is not necessary, or possible, to set jumbo frames on the adapter that is created to represent a native adapter team.

One test for the proper configuration of jumbo frames is to use a ping with a custom data size. Of course, all firewalls must be open for ICMP traffic for this to work:

```
PING 192.168.50.100 -f -l 8972
```

The number `8972` in the previous command is the size of the packet to send. Any larger number will exceed the data portion of the standard jumbo frame. Any smaller number should go through without trouble. A successful test will result in four responses such as **Reply from 192.168.50.100: bytes=8972 time<1ms TTL=128**. If you receive no response, then some device along the way is acting as a black hole. Check that all adapters, switches, and devices in the communications path have jumbo frames enabled. System and switch restarts may be necessary. A response of **Packet needs to be fragmented but DF set** indicates that traffic could go through, but is encountering a device that does not—possibly cannot—support jumbo frames. The f parameter indicates to the ping command to not allow its test packets to be fragmented so that we can test packet sizes, but normal Ethernet traffic will not have this restriction. Jumbo packets sent across a network that is showing this message will be returned to the sender for fragmenting and retransmission. As with a black hole situation, check the devices. If you are unable to resolve the black hole or fragment-required situation, disable jumbo frames.

VMQ

VMQ (**Virtual Machine Queue**) allows traffic inbound to a particular virtual adapter to bypass much of the network processing stack of the management operating system. When a virtual adapter (legacy virtual adapters are not eligible) connects to the virtual switch, it will request a queue from the hardware adapter hosting that switch. If a queue is available, it will be assigned to that adapter. Traffic inbound to that virtual adapter will be marked by the hardware so that the management operating system will not need to inspect the packets to determine which virtual adapter it is intended for.

VMQ is a very useful technology and can have a measurably beneficial impact for virtual adapters in Hyper-V Server. Before you begin enabling it, ensure that your physical adapters actually support it. You'll also want to determine how many queues an adapter supports in order to prioritize virtual adapters that will have VMQ enabled.

To begin, enable VMQ on physical adapters that host virtual switches by using one of the previous methods for changing adapter advanced settings. The VMQ property typically shows up as **VMQ** or ***VMQ** in the registry and advanced settings displays. Intel adapters may show it as **VMDq**, which is their proprietary implementation of the technology. You can also use two cmdlets designed specifically for this purpose: `Enable-NetAdapterVmq`, and `Disable-NetAdapterVmq`. You can use the pipeline from a `Get-NetAdapter` cmdlet, or simply use the `Name` parameter with the adapter's name.

By default, virtual adapters have VMQ enabled, and no further steps are necessary if you're comfortable with this. When they connect to the virtual switch, whether by initial creation when their VM is turned on, or when it arrives by a migration, they will automatically attempt to have a queue created. Since queues are a first-come-first-served limited resource, you may choose to disable VMQ for adapters with lower inbound traffic volumes. This can be performed in the GUI (only for adapters connected to virtual machines), or with PowerShell.

To disable VMQ for a virtual adapter in the GUI, access its parent virtual machine's settings page in **Failover Cluster Manager** (or Hyper-V Manager if the VM isn't highly available). In the left pane of this window, click on the **+** next to the adapter that you wish to adjust, and then click on **Hardware Acceleration**. In the center pane, uncheck **Enable virtual machine queue**, as shown in the following screenshot:

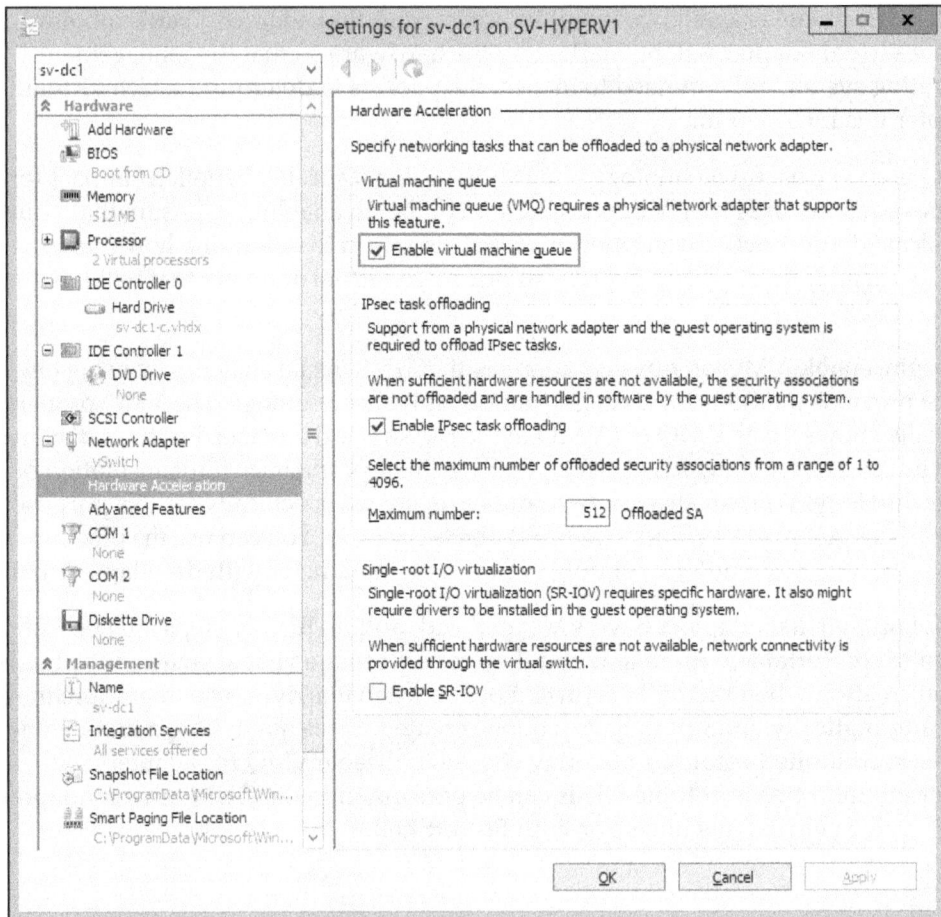

In PowerShell, there is no toggle. VMQ is disabled by setting the adapter's VMQ weight to zero.

To disable VMQ on a virtual adapter in the management operating system:

```
Set-VMNetworkAdapter -ManagementOS -Name ClusterComm -VmqWeight 0
```

To disable VMQ on a virtual adapter in a guest VM:

```
Set-VMNetworkAdapter -VMName "sv-dc1" -VmqWeight 0
```

The last cmdlet will set all adapters in the VM named `svdc1` to not use VMQ. You can use the `Name` parameter to specify an individual adapter. Since virtual machine adapters created through the GUI always have the name **Network Adapter**, you can narrow it down with the adapter's ID in `Get-VMNetworkAdapter`, and pipe it to the `Set-VMNetworkAdapter` cmdlet:

```
Get-VMNetworkAdapter -VMName "sv-dc1" | Where-Object Property "AdapterID"
eq -Value "d6320459-99be-4cb9-afce-42f9b3b7262f" | SetVMNetworkAdapter -
VmqWeight 0
```

The previous cmdlet is much longer than it needs to be so that it complies with this book's general philosophy of not hiding PowerShell operations behind aliases or positional parameters. If it it aids reading and/or comprehension, the `Where-Object` cmdlet portion can be reduced to the following: `where AdapterID -eq d6320459-99be-4cb9-afce-42f9b3b7262f`. Of course, you must substitute the displayed adapter ID with your own.

To re-enable VMQ on a virtual adapter, use the same cmdlets but set the `VmqWeight` parameter back to its default of 100.

> Lower values for `VmqWeight` are accepted, but the feature is poorly documented and testing has not revealed meaningful advantages.

VMQ and adapter teaming

VMQ works quite well with adapter teaming. In fact, if your team is in switch-independent mode, using VMQ will substantially increase performance. Without VMQ, all virtual adapters' MAC addresses are registered on the team's primary adapter for inbound traffic. With VMQ enabled, the MAC addresses are spread evenly across the team members. In switch-dependent modes, all MAC addresses are assigned to the combined channel, so queues must be created equally across all physical team members.

> The dynamic load-balancing algorithm, only available in 2012 R2, allows for traffic to be dispersed more evenly. Refer to *Chapter 5, Network Design* for details.

As you already know, a virtual adapter is created to represent the team at the same time that the team is created, and in turn, this is the adapter that the virtual switch is created on. This adapter has its own VMQ settings. If it detects that any member's adapter does not support VMQ, it should disable VMQ; in practice, this detection does not always work. If the team's adapter has VMQ enabled but any physical member cannot support VMQ, performance may be severely degraded. You can set VMQ on this adapter just as you would with a physical adapter.

The team adapter also has two other VMQ-related settings: **Virtual Machine Queues - Shared Memory** and **Virtual Machine Queues - VLAN Id Filtering**. The former setting leverages **Direct Memory Access** (**DMA**) to unload queues directly into the virtual machine's shared memory space. The latter allows the VMQ feature to process incoming packets using 802.1q VLAN tags, if present, in addition to the destination MAC address. Both of these features should be left enabled unless the underlying hardware does not support them specifically. If the hardware doesn't support VMQ at all, disabling VMQ by itself is sufficient to disable all three VMQ settings. If it is necessary to change either of these two special items, they are changed like any other adapter advanced setting.

VMQ interrupt coalescing

The downside to VMQ, is that every incoming packet that lands in a queue triggers a CPU interrupt. In a dense multi-processor system with high volumes of inbound traffic, the cost of handling interrupts can drastically reduce the efficiency of VMQ since its primary purpose is to reduce CPU load. To combat the effects of these interrupts, ensure that receive-side scaling is enabled and that the virtual adapters have access to only a subset of CPUs. This allows multiple packets to be handled with a single interrupt. The following section on RSS will guide you through making this change.

RSS

Receive-side scaling (**RSS**) support was introduced in Windows Server 2008. Without RSS, processing of all incoming network packets can only be handled by a single processor at any given time. RSS overcomes by allowing multiple processors to be involved. When a new inbound stream arrives on an adapter, a CPU is selected to process the operation using a mechanism that is very similar to the way that teaming selects a physical adapter for outbound communications. Any single incoming TCP stream will be processed by only one CPU; other streams may be distributed to other processors.

If you will be storing your Hyper-V virtual machines on SMB 3.0 shares, RSS is desirable, especially if you will be employing SMB multichannel. RSS can improve the throughput of SMB 3.0 communications by as much as 10 percent.

RSS is enabled globally by default and it is recommended that you leave it. To check the status of RSS, enter the following code at a PowerShell prompt:

```
Get-NetOffloadGlobalSetting
```

Check the output for the value of Receive-side scaling. Change it with:

```
Set-NetOffloadGlobalSetting -receiveSideScaling Enabled
```

To enable or disable RSS on an adapter, you can use any of the previous three methods. By default, it is already enabled on adapters that support it. You can also use the `Enable-NetAdapterRss` cmdlet.

vRSS (R2 only)

A new feature introduced in Hyper-V Server 2012 R2 is the ability for virtual machines to use RSS as well. This feature requires the hardware to support VMQ and it must be enabled as shown in the *VMQ* section. For vRSS to have any effect, the guest must have more than one virtual CPU assigned. Inside the guest, enable RSS as shown in the preceding RSS section, and read the following section to tune it.

Without vRSS, a virtual machine operates the same way as a physical machine does without RSS; one virtual CPU processes all inbound traffic. Even though the hypervisor may change which physical core a virtual CPU has access to from thread to thread, it will never have access to more than a single core at a time. vRSS allows it to distribute its inbound network traffic across virtual CPUs. The actual benefit of this feature depends on how much data the virtual machine transmits or receives.

RSS tuning

The `Set-NetAdapterRss` cmdlet is used to enable and tune RSS on a specific adapter. Enabling and disabling is performed with the `Enabled` parameter; disable with 0 or `$false`, and enable with 1 or `$true`.

Manual tuning of RSS is an involved process that, if performed incorrectly, can introduce problems that would not have been present if the system was allowed to perform automatic tuning. Furthermore, manual RSS tuning in a Hyper-V host is of limited value, especially in 2012.

The most common items you might wish to change control which processors an adapter can choose for packet processing. The first is `BaseProcessorNumber`, which selects its preferred CPU core. This is a simple number that starts at zero and ends at one below the number of cores available. So, in an eight-core system, valid values are 0 through 7 with each number representing one of the eight cores. The second parameter to change is `MaxProcessorNumber`, which is also a simple numeric field that specifies how many processors the adapter can use for RSS. When an adapter attempts to select a processor, it will only start with the indicated base processor, and for subsequent streams, it will only select processors in sequence from that base processor. So, if you set an adapter's base to processor 3 and specify a maximum of four processors, it will only use processors 3, 4, 5, and 6. You can use this fact to manually distribute adapters across CPUs and avoid overlaps that might cause detrimental performance. Usually, this tuning is of most value in systems with a very high core count, such as 32 and above.

> Related to these parameters are `BaseProcessGroup` and `MaxProcessorGroup`, which operate on NUMA nodes instead of individual processors. You can also restrict an adapter to a specific node with the `NumaNode` parameter. The subject of NUMA will be covered in more detail in *Chapter 7, Memory Planning and Management*.

You may establish a higher limit on the number of RSS queues an adapter can create by using the `NumberOfReceiveQueues` parameter. This value defaults to 2. Its upper limit is determined by the physical adapter's capabilities. Do not adjust this unless you have evidence from performance counters that the adapter is not fully utilizing its available CPUs to handle its inbound networking load.

You can review your RSS settings with the `Get-NetAdapterRss` cmdlet.

RDMA

Remote Direct Memory Access (RDMA) allows one computer to copy data directly to the memory of a remote computer across the network. This technology provides the foundation for other technologies to operate, and can provide substantial speed increases to data transfers. It requires hardware support, and at this time, most RDMA-capable networking equipment is in the higher-end range. Some of it requires that DCB be present and enabled. Be aware that placing RDMA-capable physical adapters into a team prevents utilization of RDMA.

RDMA is a foundational technology for SMB Direct, which is a new feature of SMB 3.0. It can greatly accelerate data transfers across SMB 3.0 shares, so where feasible, it is recommended for Hyper-V hosts that will store virtual machines on such shares. For R2 hosts, it will also greatly enhance Live Migration speeds when it is set to SMB mode (refer to the *Live Migration* section of *Chapter 5*, *Network Design*, for more information).

If your hardware supports it, RDMA is enabled by default. It can be enabled and disabled on an adapter using the methods presented earlier for changing advanced adapter settings. The `Enable-NetAdapterRdma` and `DisableNetAdapterRdma` cmdlets are also available. You can use the pipeline from a `Get-NetAdapter` cmdlet, or you can specify the adapter by name with the `Name` parameter. A `Set-NetAdapterRdma` cmdlet is also available; the only modification parameter it has is `Enabled`, which is a toggle between `0` and `1`, or `$true` and `$false`.

The subject of RDMA is fairly large and involved. If you will be using RDMA-capable hardware, you will most likely benefit from more research. Start with the Microsoft TechNet article on RDMA and SMB Direct: `http://technet.microsoft.com/en-us/library/jj134210.aspx`.

SR-IOV

Single-root I/O virtualization (SR-IOV) is a hardware-assisted feature that allows virtual machines to communicate directly with the physical hardware, bypassing the Hyper-V virtual switch and management operating system entirely. SR-IOV as a technology is by no means restricted to networking, but this is the only usage that will be covered in this book. As with RDMA, SR-IOV is typically only found on higher-end adapters, but it does not have any particular requirements otherwise.

An SR-IOV network adapter grants access to a **Physical Function** (**PF**) through a certain number of **Virtual Functions** (**VF**) that are made available for virtual adapters to use. These functions are a specific combination of hardware addresses and available function sets for utilizing a device. The PFs are how the hardware performs its duties while the VFs are how the PFs are made available to virtual adapters.

Remember from *Chapter 5*, *Network Design*, that a virtual switch must have SR-IOV enabled when it is first created or it will be unable to support SR-IOV. If you inadvertently created a switch without enabling SR-IOV, you'll need to destroy and recreate it.

As with VMQ, VFs are a scarce, precious resource. Individual virtual adapters can have SR-IOV enabled or disabled through the GUI and PowerShell. For the GUI, look on the virtual adapter's **Hardware Acceleration** sub-tab on the virtual machine's **Settings** window for the **Enable SR-IOV** checkbox (refer to the screenshot in the VMQ section of this chapter, as these settings are in the same location). SR-IOV is enabled or disabled through PowerShell using the `IovWeight` parameter of the `Set-VMNetworkAdapter` cmdlet, exactly as the `VmqWeight` parameter is used (0 for disabled, 100 for enabled):

```
Set-VMNetworkAdapter -ManagementOS -Name ClusterComm -IovWeight 0
```

There are two critical things to remember if you are considering using SR-IOV. First, SR-IOV is non-functional if its physical adapter is part of a team. The only way to provide physical network redundancy for guest virtual machines is to create multiple virtual adapters for each guest to be protected, and then team them inside the guest operating system. This requires a guest operating system that can support teaming, such as Windows 2012 or later. It also requires you to set the **Enable this network adapter to be part of a team in the guest operating system** option for the virtual adapter on the virtual machine's property sheet, as shown in the screenshot in the *Virtual adapter networking control* section later in this chapter. There is no way to team virtual adapters in the management operating system.

The second thing to remember is that no virtual switch extensions work when SR-IOV is enabled. The reason that these two features don't work is because almost all of the software networking stack in the hypervisor is bypassed in SR-IOV communications. Traffic travels directly between the virtual adapter and the virtual function. Extensions and teaming routines never have access to these communications.

SR-IOV tuning

There are two advanced options for tuning SR-IOV VFs. Few administrators will need to change these. Both are exposed as parameters on the `Set-VMNetworkAdapter` cmdlet.

The first parameter is `IovInterruptModeration`. After entering this parameter, you can use *Tab* to cycle through its options, which are Off, High, Low, Adaptive, and Default. These settings control how the VF handles hardware interrupts. Ordinarily, the VF will automatically adapt its interrupt-handling based on its traffic load. Do not modify this setting from its default without first identifying that you have a need to, and only do so after consulting with the device's manufacturer for an understanding of how their driver will react to the various options.

The second parameter is `IovQueuePairsRequested`. As in a physical machine, incoming network traffic raises interrupts. If your virtual machine has multiple vCPUs, each CPU will receive these interrupts. VFs allow for the virtual machine to leverage RSS to coalesce those interrupts, so that one interrupt can be raised for multiple packets. By default, the VF exposes a single system-to-VF queue pair. This parameter can be used to allow the virtual adapter to request more queues. In a physical system, the optimal number of queues is one per CPU, but the abstraction of CPU resources in a virtual machine reduces the benefits of such a configuration and the VF is free to ignore the request. It is recommended that you leave this parameter at its default of one unless guest networking performance is not operating as well as expected with SR-IOV enabled.

Other hardware-assisted offloading technologies

There are a number of other available technologies, but these provide fewer benefits in a Hyper-V environment and some have caused problems in some situations. Remember that manufacturers may use somewhat different names for these features. Furthermore, the technologies as presented are often broken down into sub-types on the actual adapters. For instance, an adapter may allow you to enable checksum offloading for TCP/IP Version 4 packets independently from TCP/IP Version 6 packets. The features that can be set using the previous instructions for changing advanced adapter settings are as follows:

- **Checksum Offload**: A simple data verification process called a checksum is computed on each packet. This setting offloads that process from the CPU to the network adapter, if it supports it. You can offload all traffic or choose between transmitted or received traffic only.

- **Large Send Offload (LSO)**: When data to be transmitted exceeds the maximum transmission unit size, the chore of breaking it into separate packets can be offloaded to the network adapter.

- **Encapsulated Packet Task Offload**: For some transmissions, one packet may be embedded in another. This setting allows the adapter to process the packet header for the encapsulated packet instead of passing it up to the operating system for extraction and processing.

- **IPSec offload**: IPSec is a security process that encrypts network packets. The encryption process can be offloaded to the network adapter. Encryption is a compute-intensive procedure under any situation, and offloading the task commonly results in severely degraded performance. Different adapters will have different offloading options.

- **Receive-Segment Coalescing (RSC)**: RSC groups multiple incoming packets into a single header for rapid processing. This technology is of the greatest benefit on high-load adapters, but those hosting virtual switches do not qualify. This feature will be automatically disabled on any adapter with a bound virtual switch. For other adapters, feel free to use this technology if it is available, but it is unlikely to have a significant effect on most Hyper-V hosts.

Many of these settings also have dedicated PowerShell cmdlets. Review 2012's list at `http://technet.microsoft.com/en-us/library/jj134956%28v=wps.620%29.aspx`. R2's cmdlets are viewable at `http://technet.microsoft.com/en-us/library/jj134956%28v=wps.630%29.aspx`.

Virtual adapter networking control

A few traffic control and shaping technologies are specific to virtual adapters, or are handled differently than on their physical counterparts. All of these settings are parameters of the `Set-VMNetworkAdapter` cmdlet.

IPSec offloading can also be enabled on individual virtual adapters. There is a checkbox in the GUI in the same location as the VMQ and SR-IOV settings (see the VMQ section for navigation instructions and a screenshot). It can be changed for any virtual adapter using the `IPsecOffloadMaximumSecurityAssociation` parameter of the `Set-VMNetworkAdapter` cmdlet.

Applications and guest operating systems have the ability to assign 802.1p tags to their traffic. You can instruct the host operating system to respect these tags with the `IeeePriorityTag` parameter. If it is set to On, tags will be allowed; if Off, they will be ignored. Tagged packets will be handled according to the system's QoS policies and/or DCB settings.

By setting the `DhcpGuard` parameter to On, a DHCP server on that virtual adapter will not be allowed to respond to incoming DHCP request packets. This allows you to prevent users who have autonomy over their own virtual machines from maliciously or accidentally configuring an unauthorized DHCP server. This parameter can also be set from within the virtual machine's settings window. Click the + next to the VM's network adapter, and click on **Advanced Features** to access the following screen:

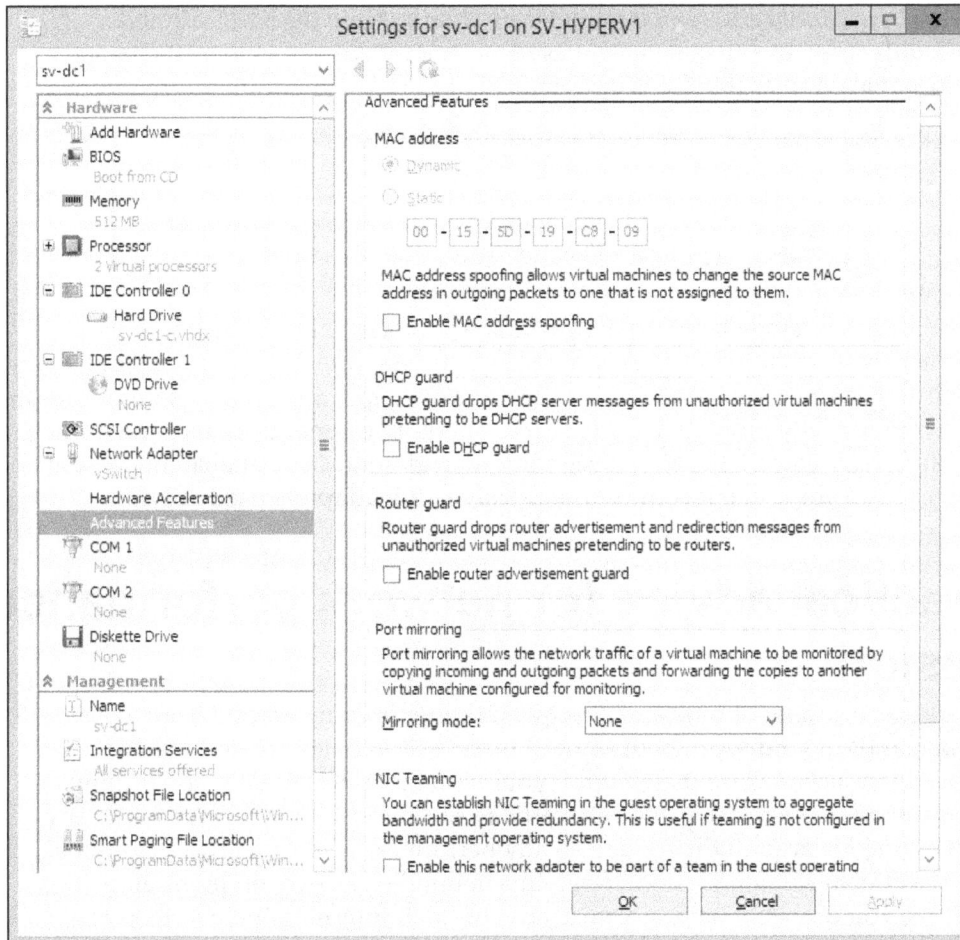

The `RouterGuard` parameter, which is also settable in the previous dialog location, prevents a software router listening on the virtual adapter from advertising itself on the network or sending redirection messages.

The `DynamicMacAddress` or `StaticMacAddress` parameters allow you to override or reset the automatically assigned MAC address for a virtual adapter. This can also be set in the preceding dialog location (the VM must be offline). This feature can be useful for testing purposes and deploying Microsoft **Network Load-balancing (NLB)**. NLB will be revisited in *Chapter 9*, *Special Cases*. It can also come in handy with software that requires a particular MAC address for licensing and with guest operating systems, such as Ubuntu Linux that may lose network connectivity during a Live Migration with dynamic MAC addresses.

Use the `DynamicMacAddress` parameter by itself to have the VM assigned a MAC address by the virtual switch; use `staticMacAddress` with a 12-character hexadecimal number (hyphens optional):

```
Set-VMNetworkAdapter -VMName "sv-dc1" StaticMacAddress 00155d194404
```

> MAC addresses must be unique across a network or collisions will occur.

`MacSpoofing` is a toggle parameter that allows the virtual machine to transmit Ethernet frames that indicate a source MAC address other than the address held by the virtual adapter. As with the MAC address override, this can be useful for testing, but it is potentially more dangerous. MAC spoofing essentially makes the traffic appear to have come from an entirely different adapter. Only enable this setting on adapters that you trust. It is primarily of value with adapters used in NLB.

Practical advice for network performance design

Before exerting a lot of time and energy on tuning your network design, consider the demands of your workload. Most of these technologies are designed to reduce the load that networking places upon your systems' CPUs. It takes a fair number of gigabit adapters to carry enough traffic to strain most modern systems. Many networking loads are light enough so any performance gains will be as minimal as to be effectively non-existent. Keep this in mind especially on Internet-facing systems; you probably have a comparatively small Internet pipe that won't be able to stress your networking fabric. Connections to storage are also commonly over-optimized; there is little value in tuning a network connection that is already substantially faster than the underlying storage.

Set up jumbo frames on connections to storage (as long as the hardware manufacturer supports it), and for internal cluster networks. Create your virtual switches with your preferred QoS method. If there is anything else you are uncertain about, simply leave all other settings at defaults to start with. If you have reason to believe that networking performance is inadequate, follow the guidance in this chapter sequentially. Only then should you spend meaningful amounts of time tuning VMQ and other features.

Further possibilities

The Hyper-V Virtual Switch is extensible. This means that third-party developers can write software plug-ins that add capabilities to the switch that are not available directly from Microsoft. The three most common applications for extensions are packet capture, packet filtering (such as firewalls), and virtual gateway services. Some hardware vendors provide extensions that allow virtual switches and adapters special capabilities to communicate with their equipment. If the virtual switch doesn't suit your needs as shipped, search to see if there are any extensions that can provide a solution. Remember that SR-IOV adapters will be exempt from these extensions.

> Be aware that some extensions require Microsoft **System Center Virtual Machine Manager** (**SCVMM**) in order to operate correctly. SCVMM is a centralized management tool for Hyper-V that adds many capabilities. It is not required for any of the scenarios or configurations described in this book.

Another set of controls not covered in this book are the use of network **port access control lists** (**PACL**). These are of more use in a multi-tenant hosting environment, rather than in a typical Hyper-V Server cluster deployment. You can read about the basic features introduced in 2012, on the following TechNet URL: http://technet. microsoft.com/library/jj679878.aspx. R2 further enhances PACLs as described on the **What's New** page for R2: http://technet.microsoft.com/en-us/library/dn343757.aspx.

Summary

This chapter provided a close look at the traffic shaping and control techniques you can employ to manage networking for a Hyper-V or Windows Server system. You learned how to setup quality of service by using software and hardware methods. You learned how to increase networking performance by exploiting the hardware-assistance features of modern network adapters. Finally, the extensibility of the switch was touched upon.

This concludes the discussion of network configuration for Hyper-V Server. *Chapter 8, Performance Testing and Load Balancing*, will revisit some of these subjects to help you learn how to monitor and measure your network utilization. The next chapter will focus on memory configuration available to your Hyper-V systems.

7
Memory Planning and Management

As with all computer systems, memory is one of the most precious resources in your Hyper-V Server cluster. Despite recent advances in capacity, memory is the first resource that you're likely to run out of. Careful planning and allocation of memory is the best way to maximize virtual machine density. Otherwise, you may find that restrictions imposed by insufficient memory will cause your other resources to be underutilized.

This chapter will aid you in properly planning your system's memory selections. It will guide you through:

- Understanding physical memory characteristics
- Hyper-V Server memory utilization
- Understanding virtual machine memory utilization
- Non-uniform Memory Architecture (NUMA)
- Deploying Dynamic Memory
- Configuring Smart Paging

Understanding physical memory characteristics

Before diving into memory mechanics in Hyper-V Server, take the time to acclimate yourself to memory hardware. A system intended to host virtual machines is often the first time many administrators are introduced to high quantities of memory in a single system, and they are often surprised at how complicated the subject can actually be. Four sticks of 8 GB DIMMs may have the same capacity as two sticks of 16 GB DIMMs, but they won't always function in exactly the same way. Sometimes the distinction is meaningless; sometimes there are measurable performance differences.

> Be wary of going too far with memory optimization and tuning. Unless you are building a system that will perform very high quantities of transactional processing (as in hundreds per second), you may never even notice any delays in memory performance. Out of all the systems you will work with in your Hyper-V Server cluster, memory is one of the fastest by an order of magnitude.

As you read through this chapter, you will see lots of references to delays, impacted performance, and other words and phrases that may seem to be cause for concern. While it's always good to take performance issues seriously, keep in mind that memory speeds are all measured in double or low triple-digit nanoseconds. If a memory module needs fifteen nanoseconds to retrieve a chunk of data, that's less time than it took for the light to leave this page, reach your eyes, and for your brain to process it enough to realize that it's looking at letters. The delay would need to be over 3000 times longer for most humans to be able to realize that there had even been a delay. In aggregate, these delays can become meaningful; but few systems are so demanding. It is important to keep perspective.

> The specifics of physical memory involve many deep topics. Concepts will be presented with enough depth to help you make an informed decision, but you may wish to perform further research. Most memory manufacturers offer free materials on their websites.

Memory types

All modern main system memory is sold in a **Dual Inline Memory Module (DIMM)** package. The name was intended to contrast it with other packages, especially the now-obsolete SIMM package; "inline" means that the module's pins are all in a row and "dual" means there are two independent rows of pins. Current DIMMs come in four variants: U-DIMMs, R-DIMMs, FB-DIMMs, and LR-DIMMs in which the first letters of these are unregistered, registered, fully-buffered, and load-reduced, respectively.

U-DIMM

The simplest type of modern memory is a U-DIMM. It is essentially a dense bank of silicon that can hold information. The memory controller (usually on the CPU in current systems) does all the work of maintaining the status of the memory. U-DIMM's real draw is usually that it has a low price tag since it has no complex components. Unfortunately, reliance upon the electrically-distant memory controller also means that U-DIMMs have more severe restrictions on capacity and installation options. U-DIMMs are not commonly found in virtualization systems.

R-DIMM

R-DIMMs are the most common memory type found in modern high-capacity servers. These DIMMs include a dedicated piece of hardware that maintains a register (which is essentially a buffer) for the DIMM's memory modules. This hardware takes on the memory controller's burden of maintaining the status and timing of memory. Memory chips use a very high degree of miniaturization, so even a modest improvement in electrical characteristics can have a dramatic impact. R-DIMMs are more reliable, allow for higher densities, and when paired, are faster than U-DIMMs. Of course, this adds complexity, which translates to additional cost.

FB-DIMM

The FB-DIMM is a creation of Intel Corporation that is intended to solve the issues that R-DIMMs encounter at high capacities. R-DIMMs maintain the clock and integrity inside the DIMM, but inbound and outbound data is treated no differently than in a U-DIMM. An FB-DIMM contains a large central chip, called the **Advanced Memory Buffer (AMB)**. Instead of direct electrical conditioning, it accepts incoming requests in serial instead of the traditional parallel method. Internally, those requests are converted to parallel for operations on the actual memory chips. Outbound data is converted back to serial for transmission. This technique does add a bit of latency, but a more serious concern is that its power consumption is much higher. Also, because of the unique methodology, FB-DIMMs are not pin-compatible with the other three types. You cannot replace UDIMMs with FB-DIMMs or FB-DIMMs with LR-DIMMs.

LR-DIMM

LR-DIMMs are an advancement of R-DIMMs that uses registers to extend electrical stabilization to the data paths in addition to the control circuitry. The primary benefit is that upper limits on density are raised above those of R-DIMMs. As expected, they're also more expensive than R-DIMMs. Additionally, as with FB-DIMMs, they are a bit slower than R-DIMMs. Over time, LR-DIMM is likely to replace FB-DIMM.

Memory speed

For most server applications, memory speed isn't nearly as important as it is in some other applications, such as graphics processing loads on workstations. The information here is presented primarily to ensure you have a well-rounded understanding.

Memory speed is presented in a number of ways. The first is its clock speed, which is its maximum rated speed. Actual speed is determined by the system bus and is sometimes configurable. For memory, clock speed serves as the basis for how quickly memory operations, such as location and retrieval, occur. In most server applications, this is not actually a critical number. Other components are unlikely to be able to operate on the data as quickly as the memory can move it. There's usually little value in knowing the clock speed of the memory beyond ensuring that it is compatible with the clock speed of the system bus.

The second primary method of determining memory speed is its latency. If you're purchasing a prebuilt system, you may not even have access to these numbers. In most cases, you won't have access to all of them. The metric you're most likely to see is **column access strobe (CAS)** latency. You may sometimes see four numbers used to represent latency, which measure the four primary actions taken on memory modules that occur in sequence. The last of these activities, measured by the CAS, is the task that is most likely to need its entire rated time and as such, is a fair way to indicate the module's capability. This is the reason it is often published alone. However the numbers are displayed, they indicate the number of clock cycles at the module's maximum rated speed that are required for the module to carry out an operation.

Practical guidance on memory speeds

As previously mentioned, the effective differences between the higher end and lower end memory speeds for any given modern system are not dramatic in practice. High memory clock speeds and large CPU caches have reduced the differences to the point that they are difficult to detect even under high loads. It is almost guaranteed that performance bottlenecks in a Hyper-V Server system will not be traced to memory speeds. For a Hyper-V Server system, it is strongly recommended that you prioritize capacity above speed.

Memory ranks

Memory is sold in single-rank, dual-rank, and quad-rank configurations. The purpose of these rankings is to pack more memory cells onto the same module. This comes at the expense of some speed as only one rank can be accessed at a time. However, due to a variety of mitigating factors, this cost is negligible. A more important consideration is installing memory so that all modules in a channel use the same ranking. More information will be given in the upcoming sections. Refer to the figure in the *Physical memory installation* section for a visualization of how the channels might be laid out on a system board.

Mirroring, sparing, ECC, and other options

Protecting the contents of memory in server hardware is a priority, and a number of techniques have been introduced to facilitate it. Most of these options are provided by the system board, not the memory modules, so availability will be determined by your system manufacturer.

Memory mirroring is the easiest concept to understand. DIMMs must be installed in even pairs and each pair performs exactly the same operations as its twin. If a DIMM fails, the surviving twin will carry on alone.

Memory sparing keeps some DIMMs or ranks on DIMMs inactive. If a failure is detected on another DIMM or rank, the inactive ranks are brought online in its place. Unlike mirroring, sparing sets aside less than half of the total memory.

Due to the electrical characteristics of electronic components at high densities and speeds, memory contents are quite volatile. **Error Correcting Code (ECC)** is a generic term that describes a function of validating the integrity of memory data. Unlike the previous methods, ECC is provided by circuitry on the memory module, not the system board. Usually, the ECC designation will primarily be seen in relation to U-DIMMs, which can be sold in ECC or non-ECC variants. In many cases, the same system board will not accept both types, and almost none will allow them to be used simultaneously. All registered and buffered types provide ECC functionality by their nature.

Some system board manufacturers will use their own techniques that involve proprietary protection strategies and label it as an ECC variant. If you are purchasing a system or investigating BIOS settings and see any memory configurations not listed here, ensure that you consult your hardware manufacturer prior to enabling them. This is because some cause a reduction in available memory.

Practical memory protection

Many types of memory protection involve reducing the available RAM to make some available for fault tolerance or failover. While there is nothing inherently wrong with this, the costs of having less available RAM for your Hyper-V hosts must be weighed against the benefits of this protection. Memory chips do fail, but almost all that survive the initial burn-in period will operate for years. If you use U-DIMMs with ECC or any of the register/buffer types, they will typically log enough correction notices that you'll have plenty of warning of any pending chip failure. Also, don't forget that you're designing a failover cluster; the effects of memory failure can be mitigated by moving virtual machines to other hosts. Practically, the incentives to use capacity-reducing memory protection schemes in this scenario are very few.

Memory channels

Paying attention to memory channels is an important factor in memory performance, especially in multi-CPU systems. Incorrect configurations usually won't result in severe performance degradation, but they will be measurable.

In early systems, the memory controller had exactly one data path to and from memory, so it could perform only one memory operation at a time. As CPU clock multipliers outpaced memory clock speeds, it became increasingly possible for the CPU to become idle while waiting for a memory storage or retrieval process to complete. The introduction of an additional memory channel allowed another simultaneous memory operation. Since managing multiple independent communications channels generally causes more problems than it solves, the dual-channel implementation method treats the memory in each channel as a single large module with a double-wide data path.

For those early single-core, single-CPU systems; the performance increases of dual-channel memory where somewhat negligible. Some of it was simply that even though the CPU has a higher clock multiplier, it doesn't necessarily complete operations in a single cycle. In any case, it won't be attempting to communicate with system memory on every operation. Furthermore, even though dual-channel provides a 128-bit path to memory, 64 of those bits are on the memory module(s) in one channel while the remaining 64 bits are on the other. Since data is typically handled as bytes (8 bits), words (16 bits), or double-words (32 bits) and is rarely retrieved in the same fashion that it was stored, the odds are very high that any given memory operation cannot be evenly balanced across the channels. Most memory improvements on early systems resulted from large, efficient caches which sometimes completely obscured any benefits from dual-channel memory.

Two major advances improved the benefits of multi-channel memory. These are the integration of the memory controller directly onto the CPU and the advent of multi-core systems. Now that the CPU is able to directly control and optimize access to memory and has multiple concurrent threads that can keep the memory controller busy, the benefits of multi-channel memory are more obvious. A relatively recent advance in multiple-channel memory is the introduction of triple and quadruple-channel memory, which has helped memory to keep pace with the increasing core-per-CPU-package count.

Practical multi-channel memory implementation

Multi-channel memory has a definite, measurable benefit and should be implemented in your Hyper-V Server hosts whenever possible. In order for multi-channel memory to be possible, all channels must be populated with DIMMs of the exact same size and rank. If they aren't the same speed, most memory controllers will demote all banks to the speed of the slowest module, but such mixing is definitely not recommended. DIMM matching will be revisited in the discussion of NUMA.

> In almost all systems, multi-channel memory is automatically enabled when the system detects a properly balanced installation of modules.

NUMA

Inside a traditional multi-socket computer system, physical memory slots are divided evenly and matched to a specific CPU. A grouping of memory banks and their linked CPU is called a node. In a process called memory node interleaving, memory writes are alternated evenly across the nodes on a first-come, first-served basis in evenly-sized blocks, resulting in a uniform distribution of data across the memory banks. One problem with this approach is that when a CPU accesses memory on another node, it needs to coordinate the activity through a memory controller on that node. That adds a delay as high as two times long as it takes when accessing memory on its own node. Also, because all CPUs are evenly accessing all system memory, access must be coordinated through a single memory controller hub operating on a single bus.

> Although NUMA is the contrasting technology, this traditional memory distribution model is typically referred to only as **SMP (Symmetric Multiprocessing)**, which is the original name, instead of UMA. This is to avoid confusion with the term **Unified Memory Architecture**, which is an entirely different technology. However, the term Uniform Memory Architecture is acceptable.

The following figure shows a conceptual sample of how memory works in an SMP system. Threads on the CPUs make requests for memory. The memory controller hub satisfies those requests with fixed-size blocks of memory that it pulls from the two nodes in a simple round-robin fashion.

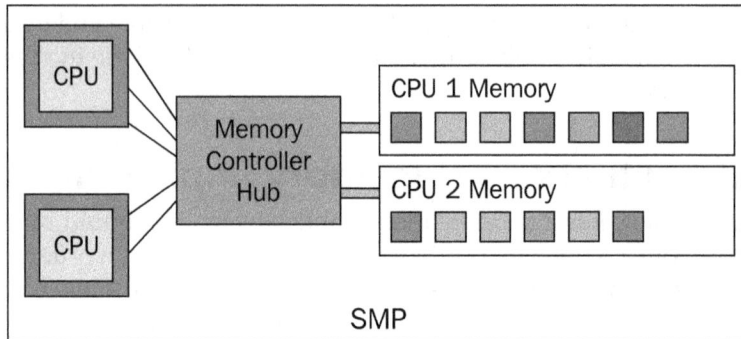

Non-uniform memory architecture addresses the bottleneck created by SMP's lone bus by allowing CPUs to communicate with their own memory without using a central hub. Processors and memory are carved into groups and assigned to a memory bus; each grouping of CPUs and memory locations is referred to simply as a NUMA node. SMP nodes are dictated by the physical layout of the system. NUMA may further subdivide those nodes, although it will not create nodes that span the physical boundaries. For example, a two-socket system with a pair of 12-core CPUs and 24 memory slots will have two SMP nodes, each with 12 slots of RAM. NUMA may split that into four nodes with six cores and the effective space of six memory modules. All cores and memory in a NUMA node will be on the same SMP node.

When a thread runs on a CPU, the system will attempt to keep all of its owned memory within the same node (local memory). If that's not possible, it can access memory on another node (remote memory) by making a request across interconnect to the memory controller of a CPU in another node. As with the SMP model, a delay is imposed for remote requests. The efficacy of NUMA is highly dependent upon how the operating system and applications make use of it. If processes and threads are scattered across nodes indiscriminately, their overall memory access will be slower than if the system had been left in SMP mode.

> The exact NUMA implementation for any given system is determined by the system board manufacturer. In some cases, an implementation will deviate from the previous description, although the basic concepts will still apply.

In the following figure, the same threads from the previous figure are shown in a NUMA environment:

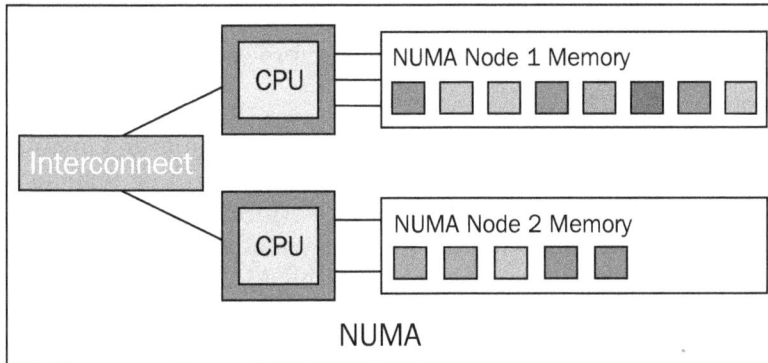

As you can see, Node 1's memory was completely filled, so the memory for one of its threads spilled over into another node. To access that memory, the CPU from node one must make requests to node two via interconnect. In terms of performance, this is known as a hop. A hop can incur a delay that causes remote memory access to require up to twice as long as local access. In a two-node NUMA system as shown here, there can never be more than one hop. Systems with more nodes add more possible hops. These are necessary trade-offs for having large quantities of RAM in a single system.

Practical NUMA configuration

In order to use NUMA, your system BIOS must support it and it must be enabled. To keep performance as stable and predictable as possible, ensure that you match the DIMM installation not only across the multiple channels, but across each of the CPU's slots as well. If you are ordering your system and memory simultaneously, consult with the manufacturer to determine the optimal configuration. If a discussion is not possible, ensure that the number of memory modules you order matches the number of slots in the system in an even distribution. For instance, if you order 64 GB for a 12-slot triple-channel system, you may receive eight 8 GB modules, which can be installed evenly but will be insufficient for triple-channel. A more optimal configuration would be four 8 GB modules and eight 4 GB modules, but you'll need to ensure they are installed so that all four of the 8 GB modules are in the same channel. A diagram in the succeeding section will illustrate this.

The exact requirements to enable NUMA will be determined by your system manufacturer, but hopefully it's obvious that an even distribution of memory modules will also benefit NUMA as well. If one node is significantly different from others, then performance characteristics will also vary. A node with more memory available will likely wind up burdened with more processes, resulting in imbalanced CPU loads.

The benefits of NUMA are more apparent as CPU/core counts and memory quantities rise. Unfortunately, there is no truly definitive turning point at which you can be certain that NUMA will provide superior performance. For most two-socket systems, NUMA's benefits begin to become apparent at around ten cores. For quad-socket systems, especially with multi-core CPUs, NUMA is usually beneficial right away since SMP interleaving causes three out of every four memory operations to be performed on remote nodes.

In simplistic terms, NUMA is of least value when there are only a few processes, and they are accessing or sharing large quantities of RAM. It is of most value in situations where there are a high number of threads that allocate RAM quantities that are less than a NUMA node and rarely, if ever, need to access the memory of another process. Virtual machines don't share memory, but a Hyper-V Server installation could fit either description. The determining factors will be how many virtual machines there are, how many vCPUs they use, and how they are assigned memory. If you're uncertain how to proceed, an understanding of how Hyper-V Server and its virtual machines use memory can help you make the decision.

> Although the performance impacts of interleaving and node hops are real, these delays are measured in nanoseconds. Very few loads are sensitive enough for memory access times to be a meaningful bottleneck, even if a more optimal configuration is available. If you simply are unable to make a decision between SMP and NUMA, use your system's default configuration.

Physical memory installation

The following figure shows a graphical representation of a system board layout:

This figure shows a two-socket system with a total of 12 memory slots in a triple-channel configuration. Banks and slots are identified by the CPU they are attached to. Slots in a bank are members of a memory channel. The slots are set off-center to more clearly delineate SMP/NUMA nodes. Remember that this is just a sample; manufacturers will use a combination of numbering, lettering, and color-coding.

In order to enable multi-channel memory in the previous example, all slots of any given bank must be filled with DIMMs of the same metric (size and rank). If some slots of a channel are empty, multi-channel is disabled for that group's slots. This will also happen if memory mirroring or a protection scheme that involves disabling slots is enabled. Sparing usually does not disable multi-channel; but if an entire slot is disabled, then the benefits of multi-channel are lost anyway.

How Hyper-V Server uses memory

In strict terms of its hypervisor functionality, Hyper-V Server uses very little memory. However, it is inextricably linked to the management operating system, which requires memory just like any other operating system.

Host memory

Memory for the hypervisor and the management operating system is not directly assigned by an administrator (although a reserve can be set). Virtual machines will be allocated memory according to their demands and the hypervisor, and management operating system will have access to whatever is left. It is not possible to entirely squeeze either of these functions out through virtual machine overload; Hyper-V will refuse to start any virtual machine that would cause complete memory starvation.

However, it may allow you to drain memory from the management operating system to the point that its performance is impacted. Take care in the way that you design and allocate memory.

The management operating system, whether you are using Windows Server or Hyper-V Server, requires a minimum of 512 MB. This does not take into account any applications or agents you may have installed, such as backup or intrusion prevention software. The hypervisor's memory usage is also added on top of this 512 MB minimum. To ensure there is enough breathing room for applications and the hypervisor, it is recommended that you plan for 2 GB of RAM to be left available for the host's usage. If you choose to use any server roles or applications that aren't specifically related to the host, hypervisor, or virtual machine management; they should be considered as needing memory beyond that 2 GB recommendation. In practice, systems without extraneous software often continue to operate well, although not optimally, with as little as 1 GB of RAM. In Hyper-V Server 2012, the system performs a better job of automatically enforcing the minimum that it needs than prior versions, so if you do not plan appropriately you may unexpectedly encounter a situation in which a virtual machine will not start or migrate. As you will see, RAM needs increase not only as RAM utilization increases, but also as VM density increases.

> It is possible, but not recommended, to enforce a minimum host reserve. In the following registry location: HKLM\SOFTWARE\Microsoft\Windows NT\CurrentVersion\Virtualization, create a key named MemoryReserve as a DWORD value. The decimal value you assign to it will be the memory reserve in megabytes.

Hypervisor memory usage

Hyper-V itself uses approximately 300 MB of system memory during normal operation. This should be treated as an unalterable minimum that is unrelated to the number, size, or state of its virtual machines and is added on top of the 512 MB needed for the management operating system. The rest of the memory that Hyper-V uses is overhead for the management of virtual machine memory. Hyper-V will consume 32 MB of memory for the first gigabyte of memory assigned to a virtual machine. This does not scale; it uses about 32 MB whether the virtual machine is assigned 256 MB or 1 GB. For each additional gigabyte in a virtual machine, Hyper-V will use another 8 MB. The amount of overhead memory the hypervisor needs just for virtual machines can be calculated with a very simple formula:

$$t = (x * 32) + ((y - x) * 8)$$

In the previous formula, *x* represents the total number of virtual machines, *y* represents the total number of gigabytes assigned to all virtual machines cumulatively; and the result *t* is the amount of memory, in megabytes, that Hyper-V will use as virtual machine overhead. If you have virtual machines with less than 1 GB of memory, treat them as having 1 GB and adjust *y* accordingly. So, if you are designing a host with an anticipated twenty virtual machines that will be assigned a cumulative 32 GB of memory, you'll need 736 MB of memory for the virtual machine RAM overhead. Add in the 2 GB for the management operating system (which includes the base 300 MB for Hyper-V itself), and this host will require about 23 GB of RAM to operate comfortably.

As you may have noticed, that first gigabyte in a virtual machine costs as much as the next four gigabytes of additional memory in the same machine. As a result, high density deployments require more overhead than a lower count of virtual machines assigned the same total amount of RAM. This is illustrated in the following two charts:

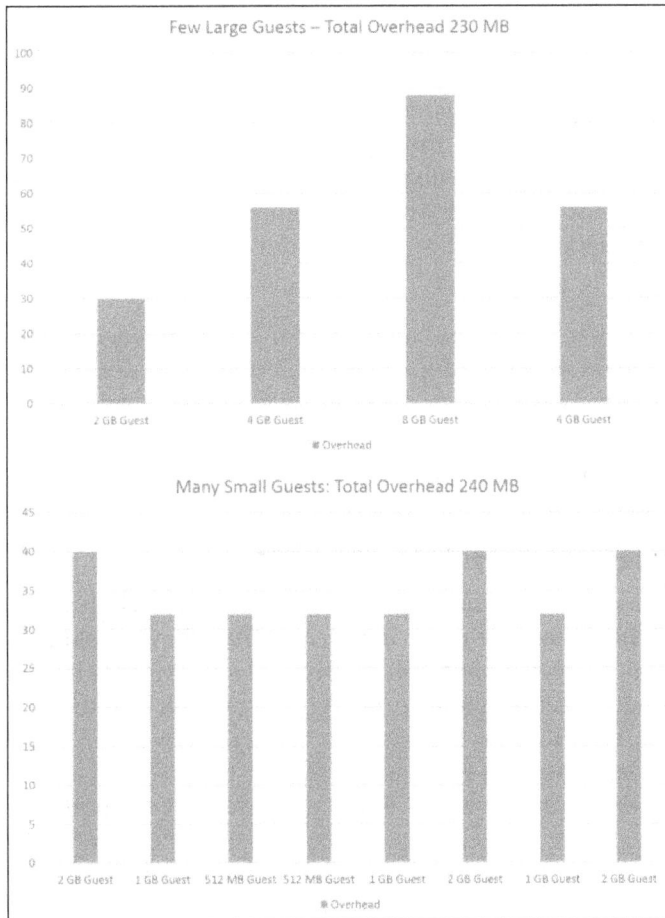

The larger guests use a total of 22 GB of RAM with 230 MB of overhead. The smaller guests only use a total of 10 GB of RAM, but need 240 MB for overhead.

At the other end of the planning spectrum, Hyper-V can manage hardware memory up to 4 TB in a host. A single virtual machine can be allocated up to 1 TB of RAM. At this time, most commercially available hosts have physical memory limitations that are much lower, usually below one terabyte. Very high RAM densities in physical hosts often causes the per-host expense to rise dramatically, therefore scaling your cluster out by adding hosts may be preferable to trying to pack in the maximum possible amount of system memory. When pondering a scale-out approach, don't forget to consider the additional networking and licensing costs.

> The 1 TB per-virtual-machine limitation applies to the management operating system as well; it will report no more than 1 TB of installed memory.

Hyper-V Server and NUMA

The Windows Server operating system and the Hyper-V Server hypervisor are both NUMA-aware. They will manage thread scheduling and process memory to respect NUMA boundaries wherever possible and to minimize the negative effects of node-spanning when it is inevitable. For virtual machines, this means that guests with vCPU and memory allocations that will fit within a NUMA node will be kept within that NUMA node.

New to Hyper-V Server 2012 is the capability for a virtual machine to be allocated more vCPUs and memory than a typical NUMA node contains. Hyper-V Server handles this by exposing NUMA characteristics to virtual machines. This capability is only one part of the larger subject of virtual machine memory usage, which is the focus of the next section.

Virtual machine memory

In contrast to storage and networking, most organizations will benefit from sizing virtual machine memory much differently than they would for physical deployments. It's not uncommon to order physical systems that have a calculated minimum rounded up to the next nice, even number such as four gigabytes. In other institutions, the price of RAM is low enough that it's not worth the administrative effort to calculate how much of RAM is optimal, so orders are made using a standard build template with a high amount of RAM such as 16 GB or more.

Practical virtual machine memory sizing

Obviously, allocating memory for virtual machines in the previous mentioned fashion would quickly deplete the resources of most hosts. In addition to the issue of overconsumption of available memory, this is also wasteful allocation. In a physical host, there's unlikely to be a large number of processes vying for access to that memory, so there's usually little or no harm done by building in a substantial amount of breathing room. It's also nice to have the ability to install another application or upgrade an existing one without needing to procure more physical memory and open the chassis. In Hyper-V, increasing memory allocation for a virtual machine is far simpler. Having spare memory assigned to a virtual machine, just in case, has little more effect than stealing that memory away from another virtual machine or the management operating system.

Overprovisioning virtual machine memory can also have unexpected performance consequences. For any system, adding more memory is usually a simple way to improve performance; it allows more processes to run simultaneously and/or with a larger working memory set without forcing the operating system to page as much to disk. Depending on the way the system is utilized, there is a point of diminishing returns where adding more memory has little or no practical value. A single 32-bit process cannot address more than 4 GB of memory and very few will allocate that much even if it is available. 64-bit applications have the ability to address far more than that, but the number of applications that will do so is still very low. Worse, there are situations where too much memory can cause performance to decrease. Most of these are application-sourced and result from software-based caching mechanisms. Common examples are legacy versions of Microsoft SQL Server and Microsoft Exchange Server. While Microsoft has a sufficient customer base for testing and the resources to enhance their newer products for these high memory conditions; not all software vendors do.

The balance of finite upper limits, wasteful allocation, and performance concerns versus the ease of allocating additional RAM to a virtual machine means that there is no benefit in assigning more memory to a virtual machine that it can actually make use of. Leverage the MAP tool and sizing guidance as explained in the *Determining requirements for existing systems* section of *Chapter 2, Cluster Design and Planning*, and size your virtual machines for the memory that they need; not for what you have available in your hosts.

Virtual machines and NUMA

When running on a NUMA-enabled host system, Hyper-V Server exposes the presence and configuration of NUMA to its guests. NUMA-aware guests can then use this data in their resource allocations.

As a rule, guests should only be sized to the point that NUMA becomes a concern when there is a definite, identifiable need for the guest to be assigned such large quantities of memory. Usually, this will be in situations where the guest is running an application that is NUMA-aware, such as recent versions of Microsoft SQL Server, and that instance's measured or projected load is certain to require a high volume of memory. If a virtual machine is allocated node-spanning quantities of memory and it is consumed by a guest application that is not NUMA-aware, the likely result is performance degradation in that guest. Depending on how it is using host resources overall, that degradation could impact other virtual machines as well. This is because they will lose the ability to schedule new threads and memory allocations in that node. If such a VM is the dominant machine on a host, SMP will likely result in a superior overall performance.

> All currently supported 64-bit editions of Windows operating systems are NUMA-aware as Hyper-V guests. Non-Windows guests that support the ACPI **Static Resource Affinity Table (SRAT)** standard will also receive NUMA configuration information from Hyper-V Server. Many Linux distributions qualify. However, not all operating systems use it with the same efficacy. Use large memory guests with caution.

NUMA in a cluster

By necessity, NUMA resource management is handled on the fly. For guests that fit within a NUMA node, there is little to be concerned about. If a virtual machine that's so large that it must span NUMA nodes moves from one cluster node to another, this can have a disruptive effect on the guests already running at the destination host. If problems are discovered, consider leveraging the **Preferred Owners and Possible Owners** settings to control where these machines can migrate.

The guidelines are different if you have a non-homogenous cluster that uses different CPUs, system boards, and/or memory quantities as the make-up of NUMA nodes may not be consistent. The issues facing the very large virtual machines doesn't change significantly, but smaller ones that fit in a NUMA node on one host may need to span if sent to another. Depending on your guest configurations and performance expectations, you may choose to ignore this and accept the possibility of impaired performance. Otherwise, you can use the **Possible and Preferred Owners** settings to restrict how guests move across your cluster.

> Through WMI, it is possible to specify the NUMA node that a virtual machine is allowed to run on. Because Hyper-V can now expose NUMA to the guest, the usefulness of this possibility is very limited. Also, preventing Hyper-V from automatically balancing a guest can cause problems on a standalone host. These problems can be magnified in a cluster environment. It is highly recommended that you allow the system to perform all NUMA balancing.

Practical virtual machine NUMA configuration

There's rarely value in manually configuring NUMA. It is recommended that you allow your systems to balance themselves. If you'd like to see how your Hyper-V Server is using NUMA, use the following PowerShell cmdlet:

```
Get-VMHostNumaNode
```

When entered without any parameters like this, it will return all NUMA nodes sequentially with information about each. You can use the `Id` parameter to specify which NUMA node you want to see information on. You can also use the `ComputerName` parameter to scan another system. There are only five returned items:

- **NodeId**:

  NUMA nodes begin numbering at 0 and count upward sequentially. This is the number of the node you are currently viewing the properties for.

- **ProcessorsAvailability**:

  This is a simple array. The number of items in the array indicates the number of physical processors in the node. The numbers themselves indicate the idle percentage of that processor core at the exact moment the cmdlet was run. Each time it is run, it will likely produce different numbers.

- **MemoryAvailable**:

    This is how much memory is unallocated at the exact time that the cmdlet will run. This number will also vary from run to run.

- **MemoryTotal**:

    This displays the total amount of physical memory that is within this NUMA node.

- **ComputerName**:

    This is the name of the management operating system on the host that contains the NUMA node.

If desired, you can configure a Hyper-V Server host so that it will not allow virtual machines to span NUMA nodes. This will completely eliminate any concerns about a virtual machine being impacted by the need to access remote memory, but it also reduces the maximum size of a virtual machine on that host to the size of an individual node, in terms of physical CPU access as well as memory. It also negatively impacts density. When no single NUMA node has sufficient space for a guest, it's possible that all NUMA nodes in the host cumulatively will. Migrations that might have been successful if NUMA was enabled may fail if it is disabled.

> Conceptually, preventing NUMA spanning breaks a host into multiple discrete computers, one per node. Hyper-V Server and the management operating system have visibility across all of them; but standard virtual machines can only exist on one. Networking and disk access are not affected.

The NUMA-node spanning restriction is a per-host setting. In Hyper-V Manager, right-click the host and choose **Hyper-V Settings**. Select the **NUMA Spanning** tab and check or uncheck **Allow virtual machines to span NUMA nodes**.

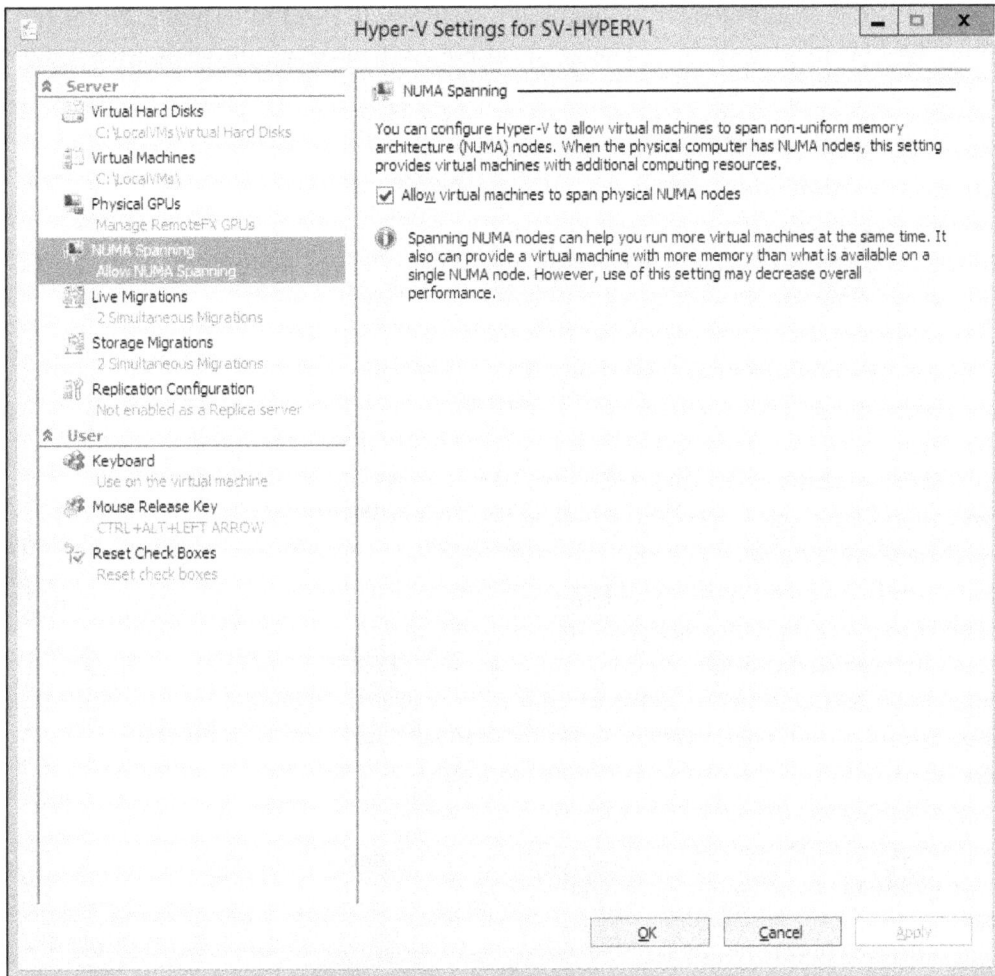

Set NUMA spanning from PowerShell with the `Set-VMHost` cmdlet:

```
Set-VMHost -NumaSpanningEnabled $false
```

The Hyper-V Virtual Machine Management service will need to be restarted for the change to take effect, which does not impact guests. It can be found in the traditional Services MMC snap-in on a GUI host or it can be restarted from PowerShell:

```
Restart-Service -Name "vmms"
```

> To increase the chances that virtual machines will migrate successfully, this setting should be uniform across all cluster nodes.

Once NUMA has been disabled on the host, you are given access to another cmdlet:

```
Get-VMHostNumaNodeStatus
```

As with the previous cmdlet, you can use the Id and ComputerName parameters to modify the output. This cmdlet displays the virtual machines assigned to a node and how they are utilizing resources within that node.

You can also set limits on how a virtual machine uses NUMA. These settings are of little use on hosts with only one NUMA node or that have NUMA spanning disabled. Even if you don't intend to change them, it is helpful to know where these settings are. Hyper-V Server will automatically configure these settings for optimal performance, but only when the guest is brought up from an off state. If a guest is migrated to another host with a different NUMA configuration, its setting are not changed.

To change a virtual machine's NUMA settings in Hyper-V Manager or Failover Cluster Manager:

1. Ensure the guest is off.
2. Access the virtual machine's settings dialog.
3. Click on **+** next to **Processor** in the left pane to expand it.

4. Click on **NUMA**. In the dialog that appears, adjust the limits as desired.

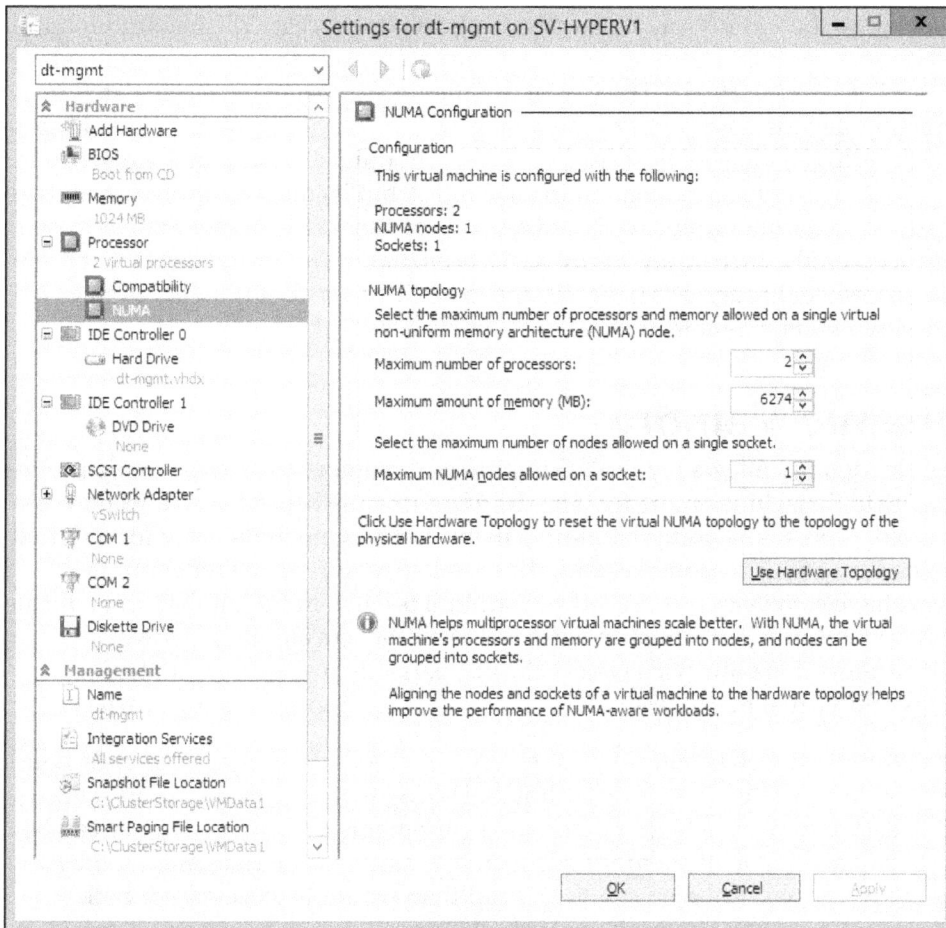

Click on the **Use Hardware Topology** button to allow Hyper-V Server to determine the appropriate values. These settings are pulled from the current host and may not be applicable on other hosts in your cluster if they have different configurations.

The `Set-VMProcessor` and `Set-VMMemory` cmdlets control NUMA settings from PowerShell:

```
Set-VMProcessor –VMName sv-mail – MaximumCountPerNumaNode 4

Set-VMMemory -VMName sv-mail -MaximumAmountPerNumaNodeBytes 2GB
-MaximumCountPerNumaSocket 2
```

There is no direct PowerShell equivalent to the **Use Hardware Topology** button as it is an ad hoc function of the GUI. The exact computations it uses are not published, so there is no way to exactly duplicate its process. The maximum number of processors per NUMA node can be determined by scanning through all nodes with Get-VMHostNumaNode. The maximum memory appears to be calculated by subtracting the host reserve from the total installed RAM. The method that Hyper-V Server uses to calculate its host reserve is also not published. Using the registry to force a setting is not recommended in 2012 or R2, but it could be approximated. The final item, maximum number of NUMA nodes per socket, does not appear to be determined easily; there are Windows API calls that could be leveraged, but nothing easily accessible through WMI. While approximating the functionality of this GUI function would be possible, it would be a non-trivial task.

Dynamic Memory

Dynamic Memory allows Hyper-V Server to add memory to or remove memory from a virtual machine on the fly. The driving principle behind such a technology is twofold. First, many administrators will allocate too much memory for a virtual machine for various reasons; second, the memory requirements for computer systems have some variance. As administrators become more familiar and educated on hypervisors, the first situation has become a little less common. However, administrators don't always have the time to perfectly research good memory settings and virtual machines will always have at least some memory variance.

As an example, a web server may have very high memory usage in business hours but dwindle almost to idleness after hours. During that time frame, a virtualized backup server may have higher memory requirements. Dynamic Memory can be used to balance available memory between these systems on demand, thereby allowing lower physical memory to be used than would be necessary if both were statically assigned enough to satisfy their peak demand. The end result is a potentially higher virtual machine density than would otherwise be possible. This scenario is illustrated in the following figure:

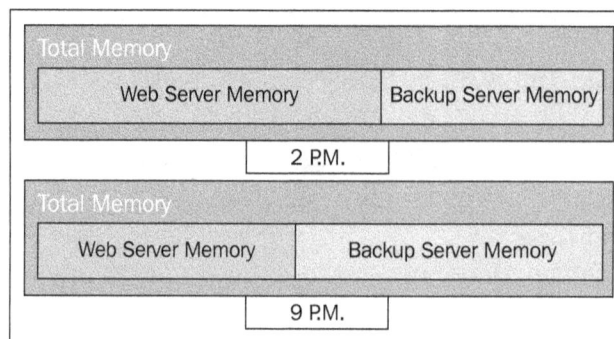

Although Hyper-V Server has the final word on how memory is allocated to virtual machines, its operation requires collusion between the hypervisor and the guest. Initially, a guest operating system is aware of exactly how much memory Hyper-V has assigned to it. If it detects that its applications require more memory than it has available, it will ask the hypervisor for more memory. If Hyper-V has memory to spare, it will be assigned to the virtual machine. The guest learns of this additional memory through a process that is the same process as physical machines with hot-add memory support.

> In Windows Server operating systems prior to 2012, only Enterprise and Datacenter editions support hot-add memory; but the Standard edition will work with Dynamic Memory.

When the guest detects that its applications are reducing their memory demand, a component called a "balloon driver" allocates the unused memory within the guest so that no other process has access to it. Hyper-V Server then deallocates the underlying physical RAM and puts it back into the available pool. If memory demands with in that guest later rise again and Hyper-V Server has memory available, it assigns memory to the VM and a matching amount is removed from the balloon driver's control for other guest processes to access. Hyper-V Server can also instruct the balloon driver to allocate more memory, forcing the guest to page other processes so that the memory can be returned to Hyper-V Server. The following figure illustrates Dynamic Memory on a virtual machine that starts with 2 GB, expands to 3 GB, returns to 2 GB, and then increases to 2.5 GB.

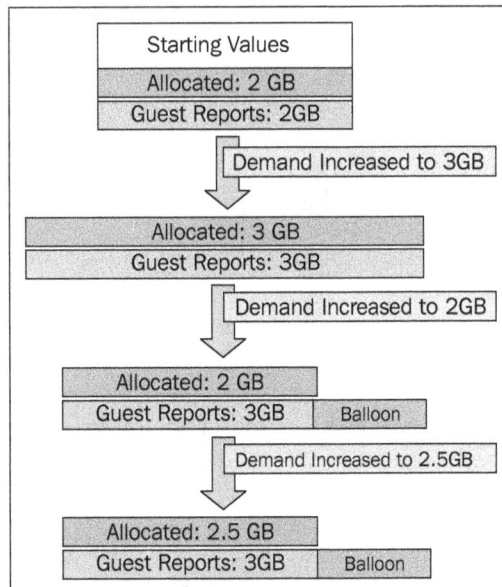

As you can see, the guest can only see that memory is being added. There is no Hot Remove action. The guest will never report that it has less memory than the highest amount it has been allocated since it was last powered on from an off state. The physical memory claimed by the balloon driver has been released back to Hyper-V Server, but the guest believes that it is being used by one of its own processes.

In order to smooth the expansion process of Dynamic Memory, Hyper-V Server attempts to create a buffer for all virtual machines using Dynamic Memory. By default, that buffer is 20 percent of the size of the virtual machine's currently allocated memory. So, in the previous figure, the buffer would have been 400 MB while the guest had 2 GB allocated to it. The buffer would have grown to 600 MB while the guest was at 3 GB, and would have shrunk again when that extra gigabyte was released. As memory demand in the guest increases, the buffer can be instantly assigned to it without needing to wait for Hyper-V Server to determine if memory is available. Therefore, the buffer reduces the likelihood that a guest will need to perform a disk page operation. If memory contention on the host becomes an issue and allocations to guests with Dynamic Memory cannot be reduced, these buffers are sacrificed.

Dynamic Memory requirements and restrictions

Because Dynamic Memory involves interaction between the hypervisor and the guest, Hyper-V Integration Services must be installed inside the guest. Desktop systems must be Windows Vista Enterprise with Service Pack 1 or newer (Windows 8 removed the requirement for a particular edition). Server systems must be Windows Server 2003 with Service Pack 2 or newer (any edition). Linux support for Dynamic Memory was introduced concurrently with R2 and support was retroactively extended to 2012, although it has a limitation of only being able to adjust Linux guest memory in 128 MB chunks. TechNet has a combined article on Dynamic Memory in both versions that includes a list of supported operating systems, which is available at http://technet.microsoft.com/en-us/library/hh831766.aspx. The Linux matrix is not all-inclusive, but these are the only distributions for which Microsoft will guarantee proper operation.

Hyper-V will allow you to enable Dynamic Memory and set minimums and maximums for any virtual machine. However, if a guest is not aware of Dynamic Memory, then it will not be able to use any number other than its startup amount. Because this awareness is granted by the Integration Services, a virtual machine cannot use Dynamic Memory until those services start. In earlier versions of Hyper-V Server, this was a problem that could prevent a virtual machine from starting. Hyper-V Server 2012 has expanded the capabilities of RAM to deal with virtual machine starts.

Startup RAM, Minimum RAM, and Smart Paging

Introduced in Hyper-V Server 2012 is the ability to set not only a Startup RAM value, but also a Minimum RAM setting. The purpose of having two settings derives from the fact that many systems require more memory to start than they do to operate but no guest can make use of Dynamic Memory until the start of Integration Services. So, if a guest needs 1 GB to boot successfully but you set a startup value of 512 MB, Dynamic Memory will be unable to assign it that extra 512 MB. However, using a startup value high enough to allow the guest to start might be far more than it needs to actually function, which results in wasted memory.

In 2012 and R2, you now have easy access to a Minimum RAM value for a guest that is using Dynamic Memory. When the guest is turned on, it uses the startup value, which does not involve Dynamic Memory. Once the Integration Services start, their normal ballooning operations take over and work in between the minimum and maximum settings, ignoring the startup value.

While this can help to dramatically reduce the amount of wasted memory and therefore allow greater density, there are other factors to consider. What happens when several virtual machines start at once? What happens when a virtual machine starts that could fit once its memory usage settles, but there's not enough for it to start? Since the fundamental problem assumes that the cumulative amount of minimum memory consumes too much host memory, then it's highly probable that the cumulative amount of startup memory will do the same. The Startup/Minimum RAM set would be of little value if it still prevented guests from starting.

The starting of virtual machines with Dynamic Memory assignments is the one and only time that Hyper-V will perform paging of guest memory (second-level paging), and it is triggered only in very specific conditions. This technology is named **Smart Paging** in Hyper-V.

Smart Paging will only activate when a virtual machine is being brought online due to a guest reboot or a host action (such as re-activating guests after a host restart). It will not be triggered by a manual or scripted start of a VM from an off state. Hyper-V will exhaust all other options before triggering Smart Paging, starting with main system memory and then by trying to pressure other Dynamic Memory virtual machines to release memory. Smart Paging dramatically slows the boot process of the virtual machine, but that is usually preferable to not allowing it to start at all.

> Resuming from a saved state will never trigger Smart Paging as that is not a boot operation and should not have any inordinate memory demands. Using Save State as the automatic cluster and host action can reduce the need for Smart Paging.

If Smart Paging is active for a virtual machine, the Integration Services will begin pressuring its RAM usage downward as soon as they start. Once the guest no longer needs second-level paging, that page file is deleted and Smart Paging will not be available to that virtual machine again until it is rebooted. If Smart Paging cannot be deactivated because the guest cannot release memory or because the guest will not release memory (Integration Services are not installed, too old, or are not, and the host continues to be unable to find sufficient memory to make up the difference, Hyper-V will begin logging errors. Worse, performance for that guest will be severely impacted.

Practical virtual machine memory implementation

The primary goal when assigning memory to a virtual machine is to not assign it so little that it is paging often, while also not assigning it so much that memory goes wasted. Excessive paging will negatively impact any computer's performance and this is likely to be a noticeable impact. A virtual machine with excessive amounts of memory may prevent others from getting what they need.

Where possible, use static memory assignments and do not rely on Dynamic Memory. It's easy to become overly reliant upon Dynamic Memory, which can lead to performance degradation and memory starvation as guests are added to an existing cluster. If virtual machines are properly sized, Dynamic Memory may not provide much of a benefit in low and medium-density deployments of guests running server operating systems since their requirements usually won't have a great deal of variance. Of course, it's very easy to talk about proper guest sizing, but in practice, the effort involved may be daunting. Strive for reasonable effort, not perfection.

The basic premise that makes Dynamic Memory worthwhile is that most applications allocate memory as they need it and deallocate it when they are finished. Usually, the largest variances are seen when an application starts and when it exits. On servers, applications typically run as services, which mean they start with the system and don't stop until it shuts down. Their memory requirements may remain fairly static.

As density increases, even the smaller variances can start to make a difference and the value of Dynamic Memory increases accordingly. In VDI deployments, Dynamic Memory is often of great value as a user interacting with a system is far more likely to perform the application starts and exits that trigger requests and releases of memory.

Some applications will preclude the use of Dynamic Memory. Chief among these are database applications such as Microsoft SQL Server, unless they are specifically hot-add aware. These applications present a problem for Dynamic Memory because they do not request memory on an as-needed basis; they check to see how much is available and request a high portion of it. Since a virtual machine using Dynamic Memory isn't aware of how much memory it can be assigned, these applications will only see how much is allocated to the virtual machine at the moment of the capacity check. They will not adjust their allocations up or down based on later changes, nor will they generate the pressure that triggers a request for more memory. As an example, if you install a non-Hot-Add aware copy of Microsoft SQL in a guest and assign it a minimum of 2 GB memory and a maximum of 4 GB, you'll likely find that, without intervention, it almost never grows beyond 2 GB and that SQL never allocates more than about 1.7 GB.

There is no requirement that Dynamic Memory be an all-or-none decision. Activate it on the guests that will benefit from it and leave it disabled on those that won't.

For guests using 4 GB or below of memory, the default buffer setting of twenty percent is probably sufficient. For larger guests, consider lowering it. A machine currently using 64 GB of memory will have a buffer of nearly 13 GB, which is probably excessive. The primary sign that a guest's buffer is too small is excessive paging operations. The buffer can be changed while the machine is on.

To set Dynamic Memory on a virtual machine, access its settings sheet in Failover Cluster Manager (Hyper-V Manager for non-highly-available machines) and switch to the **Memory** tab. The dialog is shown in the following screenshot:

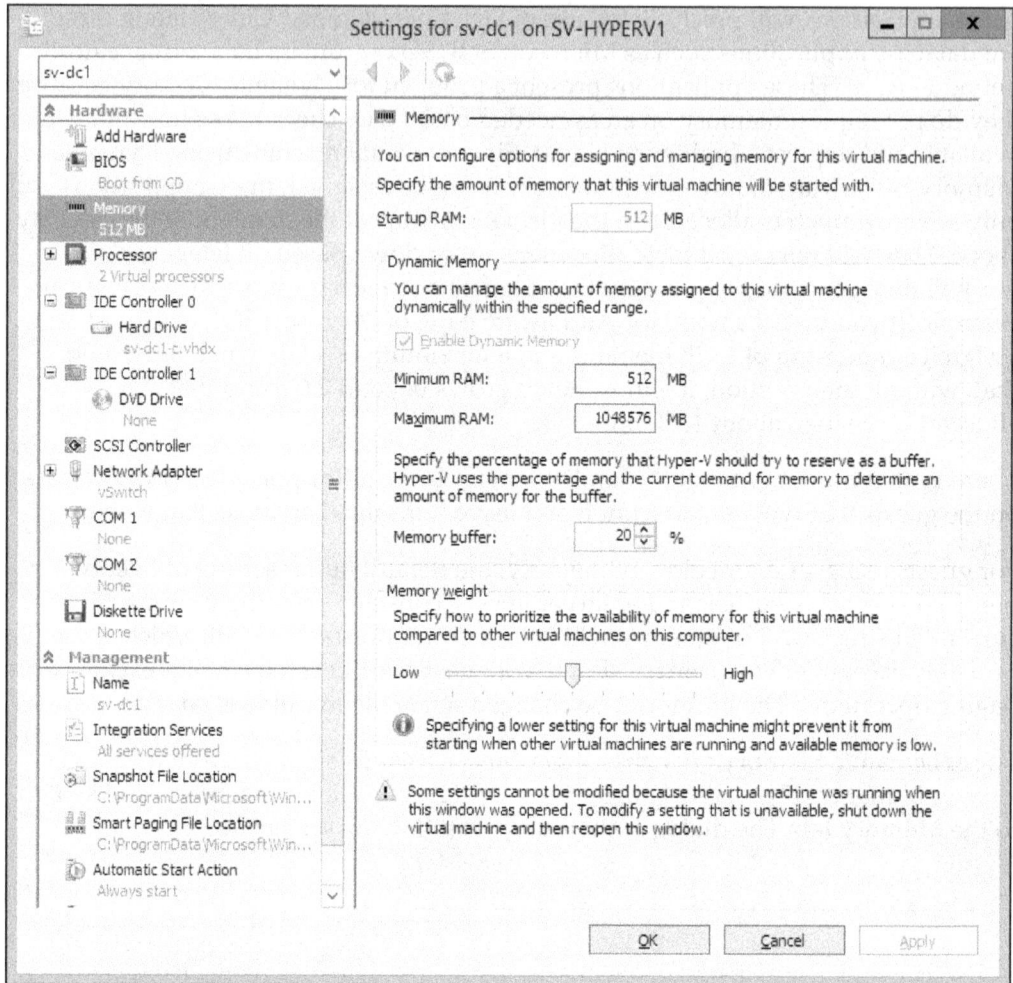

The **Startup RAM** value and **Dynamic Memory** status can only be changed while the virtual machine is turned off. For virtual machines that do not have Dynamic Memory enabled, the Startup RAM value represents the statically assigned value.

All other settings can be modified while the virtual machine is running, although the maximum cannot be reduced until the guest is shut down. The minimum and maximum values are only absolute limits placed on Hyper-V; there is no guarantee that it will reduce to the minimum or increase to the maximum.

> The default maximum is Hyper-V's limit of one terabyte, even if your system doesn't have that much RAM.

The **Memory weight** setting applies a priority to the virtual machine's memory assignment. When multiple virtual machines are starting and there isn't memory for all of them, those with higher weights are chosen first. For running virtual machines using Dynamic Memory, the weight assignment controls which machines can expand if there isn't enough memory for all requests.

The PowerShell equivalents for the previous are all part of the Set-VMMemory cmdlet.

To enable or disable Dynamic Memory (remember, the VM must be offline):

```
Set-VMMemory –VMName sv-apps –DynamicMemoryEnabled $true
```

Use the following command to adjust the startup, minimum and maximum values as well as the buffer size (the VM only needs to be offline if you are reducing the maximum):

```
Set-VMMemory –VMName sv-apps -StartupBytes 2GB -MinimumBytes 512MB
-MaximumBytes 4294967296 –Buffer 10 –Priority 60
```

With the exception of the buffer and the priority, these can also be set using Set-VM. Use either the DynamicMemory or StaticMemory toggle options to set either of those options. The following cmdlet shows how to set Dynamic Memory:

```
Set-VM –VMName sv-apps -MemoryStartupBytes 2GB -MemoryMinimumBytes 512MB
-MemoryMaximumBytes 4294967296
```

The various byte parameters will accept values in kilobytes, gigabytes, and terabytes provided that you use the respective abbreviation. Otherwise, numbers are assumed to be bytes. The **Buffer** parameter is a percentage as explained earlier and can be set as low as 5 and as high as 2000. The **Priority** parameter accepts values from 0 to 100; higher numbers have higher priority.

> Enabling Dynamic Memory disables virtual machine NUMA.

As you may have noticed, it is possible to set the maximum well above what you actually have available in the host. This allows the virtual machine to migrate to larger hosts and scale up to the maximum without human intervention. However, it also provides the potential for a virtual machine to cause unnecessary memory contention on a host. Most systems will not be so poorly behaved, but it is conceivable for a 64-bit application with a memory leak to completely consume all available RAM up to the one terabyte limit. Set reasonable maximums on your guests. Since you don't have to power them off to raise the number, feel free to experiment with lower values and increase them as necessary.

Do not be afraid to use Smart Paging in high density environments, but do not rely on it. Balance your nodes so that there is sufficient room to accommodate everything. Calculate for the minimum RAM settings of all virtual machines that could possibly arrive on any given host, the minimum memory for the management operating system, the minimum and overhead memory for Hyper-V, and leave a little breathing room. If the combined startup RAM values push this calculation above the host's installed memory, keep a careful watch on operations and growth.

Smart Paging is always available for any virtual machine that is using Dynamic Memory so there is really nothing to configure. The location of the Smart Paging file(s) for a virtual machine can be changed, though. By default, they are in the same location as the virtual machine. They exist only as long as they are needed but while active, will consume space equivalent to the size of the virtual machine's startup RAM.

To change the location of the Smart Paging file for a virtual machine, access its settings page in Failover Cluster Manager (or Hyper-V Manager for non-highly-available virtual machines). The setting is on the **Smart Paging File Location** tab near the bottom and is a simple text entry field with a **Browse** button.

To change the location in PowerShell, use Set-VM:

```
Set-VM -VMName "sv-apps" -SmartPagingFilePath "C:\ClusterStorage\vmdata1"
```

> The Smart Paging file location can also be changed using the Move Virtual Machine Storage wizard and the Move-VM PowerShell command. It is shown as second-level paging in the wizard. The benefit of using these instead of the earlier methods is that they can relocate the paging file while it is in use.

Cluster memory shortages

With the lone exception of Smart Paging operations, Hyper-V Server does not oversubscribe memory. Contrast this behavior to its provisioning of CPU and hard drives: the total number of vCPUs assigned across all guests probably exceeds the number of physical CPU cores in the host and dynamic VHD[X] files can have combined maximum sizes that exceed the size of the physical storage they exist on. With memory, Hyper-V will not allow more memory to be allocated by virtual machines than the guest has. The reason that Hyper-V does not oversubscribe memory is that it would require permanent implementation of second-level paging. Such paging is indiscriminate; it will send active memory pages to the disk along with idle pages. Of all the performance considerations discussed in this book, nothing impacts performance like requiring the CPU to access its working set on a slow disk instead of fast RAM.

Because second-level paging is not an option in Microsoft's hypervisor, Hyper-V must take other actions when memory runs low. The consequences of an out-of-memory condition vary based on the situation.

When the guests on a host demand more memory than is available, Hyper-V Server assigns memory according to the memory priority weight assigned on the virtual machines. If the weights are all even, memory is assigned as evenly as possible.

> System Center Virtual Machine Manager has the ability to detect this condition and can attempt to automatically relocate virtual machines to other hosts to balance memory utilization.

If a saved or stopped guest attempts to start, but there's insufficient memory available, the start attempt will fail. For guests using Dynamic Memory, this is determined by the minimum RAM setting. If the guest is clustered and a start attempt fails, the cluster service will attempt to locate another host with capacity and start the virtual machine there. If multiple guests are attempting to start simultaneously (such as after a host start or failure of another node in the cluster), they will be started in the order of their memory priority setting. If all priority settings are equal, the decision is left to Hyper-V to maximize utilization. If no host can be found to start guests, they are left powered off.

Quick migrations are treated as resume events at the destination host. If the cluster service moves a machine in response to a failover or a host shutdown, it will be treated as either a resume or a start event depending upon the state of the virtual machine when it arrives. If insufficient memory is available to start a migrated guest, it will be treated as a failover event and the cluster will attempt to failback and/or locate another host.

If an attempt is made to live migrate a virtual machine to a host that does not have sufficient memory, the migration fails. After any configured failover/failback attempts are made, the machine continues running on the source host without interruption.

Summary

This chapter covered all aspects of memory within a Hyper-V Server host and how it relates within a cluster. You learned about physical memory first, then how it was used and controlled by the hypervisor. You were then shown how to configure virtual machine memory usage. Throughout, considerations and challenges for memory in a host and in a cluster were explored.

It is worth repeating that memory is too valuable of a resource to be wasted, so allocation should be done with care. It should also not be forgotten that it is difficult to make tweaks to memory performance that produce tangible benefits. The most important aspect to virtual machine memory allocation is to ensure it has enough that it does not need to page often, yet not so much that other guests are required to do without.

With the close of this chapter, we end our examination of the virtual machines and their drain on individual resources, and we shift gears to an examination of the hosts that comprise your cluster. In the next chapter, you'll see how to determine what the capabilities of your hosts are, how to ensure that they are ready for your virtual machines, and ways to balance your virtual machines to use hosts effectively.

8
Performance Testing and Load Balancing

Now that we've covered how to design and plan your virtual machines, we're going to turn to the host's view of things. There are add-on and third-party tools that can perform automatic load balancing, but a failover cluster of Hyper-V Servers will only perform balancing in response to a failover event. Whether you'll use automated tools or not, you'll need to have an understanding of your host's abilities.

Balancing is not the entire story. Even if you have additional tools that can perform load balancing for you, you'll still need to keep abreast of the performance metrics of your cluster. As new virtual machines are added, your total capacity will be lessened and you'll want to know well in advance if you need to add hardware. Remember that your cluster is probably intended to survive the loss of at least one host without negatively impacting virtual machines, so just having a fully functional cluster with sufficient capacity may not be adequate.

There are two basic components to proper balancing. The first is being aware of what your hosts are capable of. The second is being aware of what they're doing. This chapter will work through a number of ways to satisfy these needs. You'll be introduced to the following concepts and activities:

- General system testing
- Disk I/O testing
- Memory testing
- Network testing
- Preferred and possible owners
- Anti-affinity

Initial and on-going performance measurement

Performance measurements begin prior to system deployment. In terms of a failover cluster of Hyper-V systems, it begins prior to creating any virtual machines. Your first goal is to obtain baselines. The term baseline has different meanings in different contexts; in this case it means gathering data on a system during a known healthy period. Its purpose is to serve as a point of comparison for later data gathering operations.

The first set of performance measurements you take will be with no virtual machines. Once you have reached your target deployment level, you will obtain another. These will be your baselines. All future performance measurements will be compared to these in order to determine how your systems are working.

> Microsoft provides a thorough document for performance tuning of Windows Server 2012. These concepts carry forward to R2 and many apply to Hyper-V Server as well. Download it from the following site: `http://download.microsoft.com/download/0/0/B/00BE76AF-D340-4759-8ECD-C80BC53B6231/performance-tuning-guidelines-windows-server-2012.docx`

General performance measurement

Baselines and ongoing performance evaluations tend to be fairly generic in nature. They can be carried out in a number of ways. You were already introduced to the **Microsoft Assessment and Planning Toolkit** (**MAP**) in *Chapter 2, Cluster Design and Planning*. This section will examine two others. The first is the free **Server Performance Advisor** (**SPA**) provided by Microsoft. The second is the Performance Monitor tool in-built in Windows operating systems.

Server Performance Advisor

This tool can be run quickly to determine the performance characteristics of a new system and on a schedule to track the performance trends of an active system.

> Do not install or run Server Performance Advisor directly on a
> Hyper-V host or any guests that are to be measured. Doing so adds
> a load that will make the results inaccurate.

The following instructions can be used to quickly set up SPA to run in a basic environment. They assume that you'll be running the application with a domain account that has administrative privileges on the systems to be measured. To scan a system that has an active firewall, run the following cmdlet:

```
Enable-NetFirewallRule -DisplayName "Performance Logs and Alerts
(TCP-In)"
```

Service Performance Advisor is published on the developer center, which is accessible at http://msdn.microsoft.com/en-us/library/windows/hardware/hh367834.aspx. For best results, this tool should be run from a remote computer that's not on the host being measured. It can be run from any modern Windows system. It requires a connection to an installation of Microsoft SQL Server 2008 R2 or newer. The Express edition is perfectly acceptable. The latest version can be obtained at no charge from the Microsoft download center at http://search.microsoft.com/en-us/downloadresults.aspx?q=sql%20express.

There is another requirement that's listed on the download page but not in the included documentation. The CAB file that SPA is delivered in must be extracted with its directory structure intact. If you use Windows Explorer to open the CAB, it will not extract the files properly. Use the built-in extrac32 tool according to the directions (they're on the download page) or use another extraction application that can reproduce the proper folder structure.

The final prerequisite you must satisfy is the creation of a folder to hold the results. This folder can be in any location on the system you'll be running SPA from, and it can have any name. This folder must be shared. Determine the domain account that you'll be running SPA with and give that account full permissions to the folder and its share.

All that's left is to run SPA. In the folder where you extracted the CAB's contents, run `SPAConsole.exe`. When it opens, choose **File** and then **New Project** to get started. The first screen is just a basic introductory screen. Click on **Next** and you'll see the following screen, which has been filled in with examples:

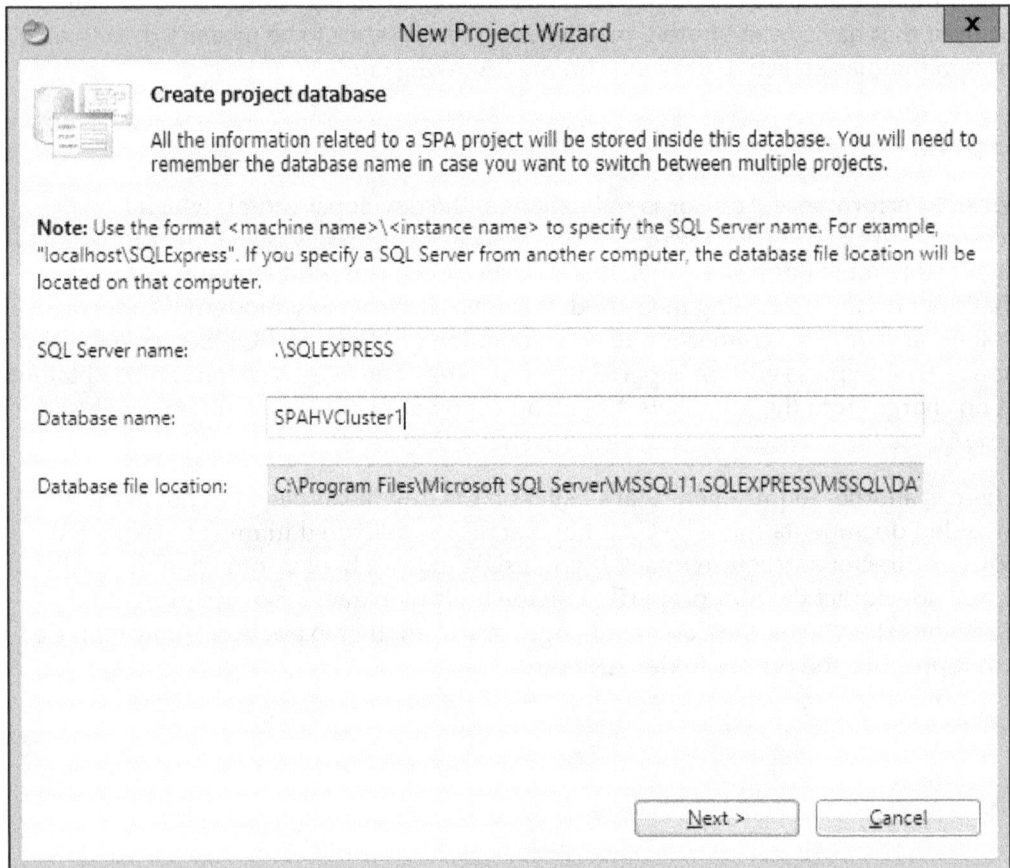

New Project Wizard	**X**

Create project database

All the information related to a SPA project will be stored inside this database. You will need to remember the database name in case you want to switch between multiple projects.

Note: Use the format <machine name>\<instance name> to specify the SQL Server name. For example, "localhost\SQLExpress". If you specify a SQL Server from another computer, the database file location will be located on that computer.

SQL Server name:	.\SQLEXPRESS
Database name:	SPAHVCluster1
Database file location:	C:\Program Files\Microsoft SQL Server\MSSQL11.SQLEXPRESS\MSSQL\DA'

Next >	Cancel

The previous entries direct the application to create a database on the local computer, in this case an instance of SQL Server Express. For a large environment with many systems to scan, it is recommended to use SQL Server Standard instead. The database name can be anything you like; this one has been named to reflect that it will contain data on the first Hyper-V cluster in the sample organization. Be aware that this will create a new database on the selected server. Once you have selected the database server, instance, and name, and then click on **Next** to move to the following screen:

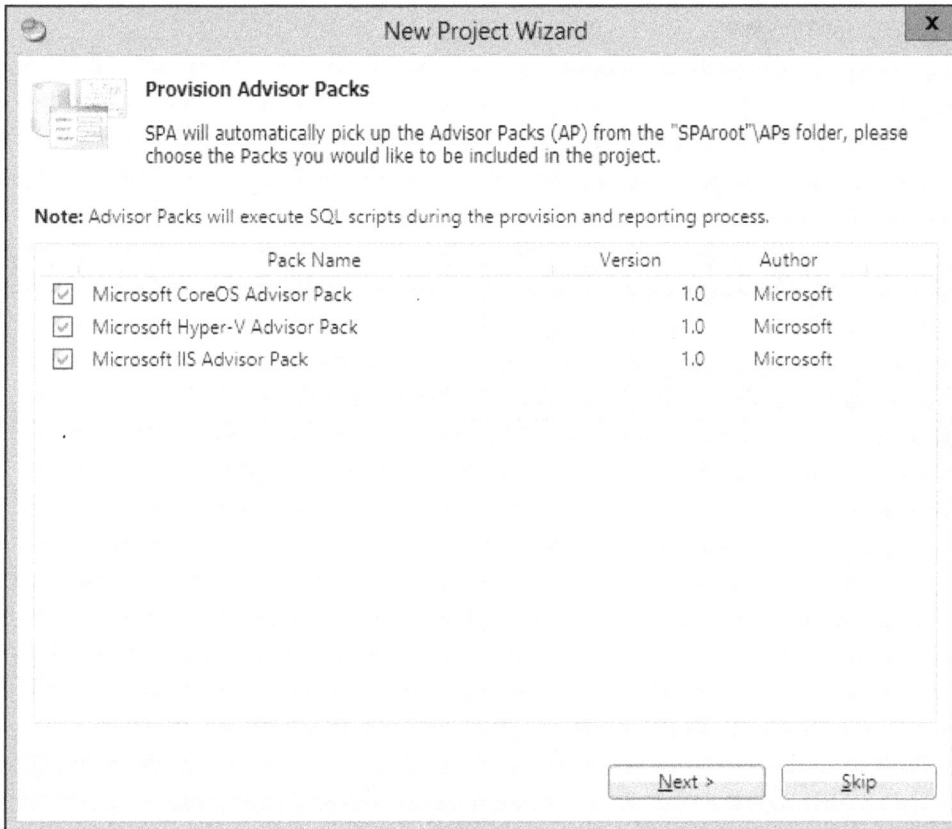

This screen allows you to select the advisor packs that you'd like to make available in this project. Even though you only need the Hyper-V advisor and perhaps the CoreOS advisor, it's best to select all three. The interface sometimes hangs if only a subset is selected. You won't be required to use all three during a scan. Click **Next**. This will bring you to the final screen:

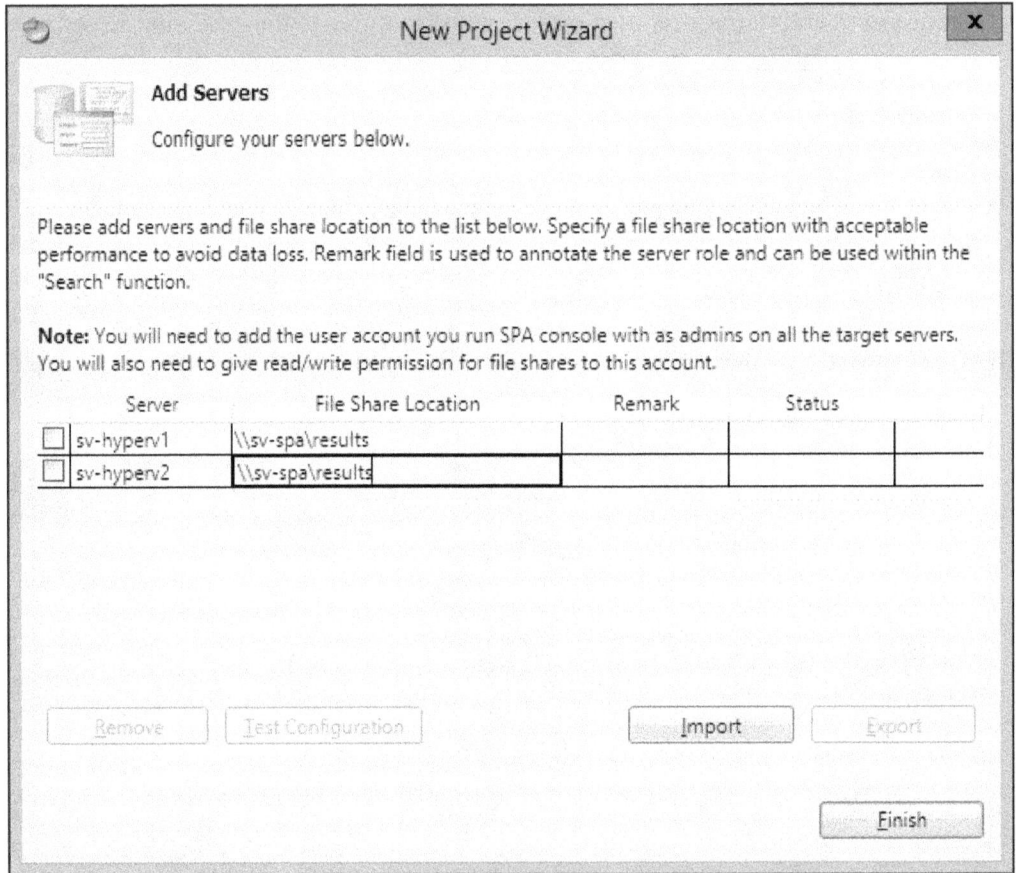

New Project Wizard				**X**

Add Servers

Configure your servers below.

Please add servers and file share location to the list below. Specify a file share location with acceptable performance to avoid data loss. Remark field is used to annotate the server role and can be used within the "Search" function.

Note: You will need to add the user account you run SPA console with as admins on all the target servers. You will also need to give read/write permission for file shares to this account.

	Server	File Share Location	Remark	Status
☐	sv-hyperv1	\\sv-spa\results		
☐	sv-hyperv2	\\sv-spa\results		

Remove   Test Configuration   Import   Export

Finish

On this screen, enter the servers that you want to scan. The **File Share Location** is a file share that will hold the results of the scan. As with the SQL database, it's not required to be on the same system as the scanner. Servers can be added to the list later. You can use **Test Configuration** to ensure that the indicated servers are reachable. Once you're happy with the entries, click on **Finish**.

You'll be returned to the main screen of SPA. Now, you should see the host(s) that you selected for this project. Select their checkboxes, and then press the **Run Analysis** button in the lower-right corner. Here, you'll be able to select the actual advisor packs that you want to use. At the bottom of the screen, you'll be able to enter how long you want the scan to run, and if you wish to collect numerous data points over a period of time — how often you want it to run. Click on **OK** when you're satisfied with your selections and the data collection process will begin.

Once it is complete, you can click on the small down arrow in the **Analysis Result** column of one of the hosts. This will show three buttons, indicated in the following screenshot:

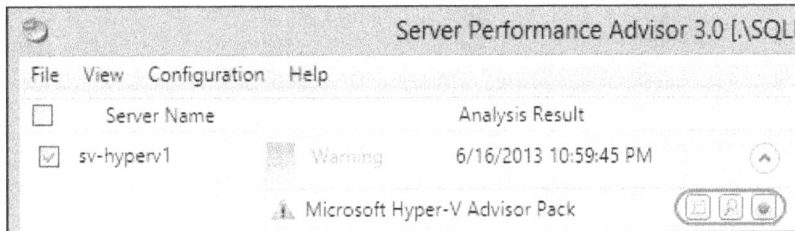

These buttons are, from left to right:

- **View Latest Report**: See the report from the latest analysis. This is the screen you're most likely to be interested in after a one-time scan of a new system. It will show warnings for any items and settings it finds that might impede optimal performance of Hyper-V. It can also compare one report against another and export result sets to XML.

- **Find Reports**: Search through all result sets for this host according to the criteria that you choose.

- **View Charts**: These are detailed charts that examine and graph very specific performance metrics of the host.

> The wording of the **Logical Processor count limit when Hyper-V is enabled** warning is misleading. The management operating system is restricted to using 64 logical processors, but Hyper-V itself can still schedule guest processes up to the maximum of 320 logical processors.

The first two buttons are very simple to understand and you should have no trouble navigating them on your own. Do remember to check the various tabs inside the report. The third button, **View Charts**, brings you to a tool that isn't as easy to decipher. You'll begin by picking a range of dates, and assuming that you've got more than one report to chart, you'll get a screen that looks something like the following screenshot:

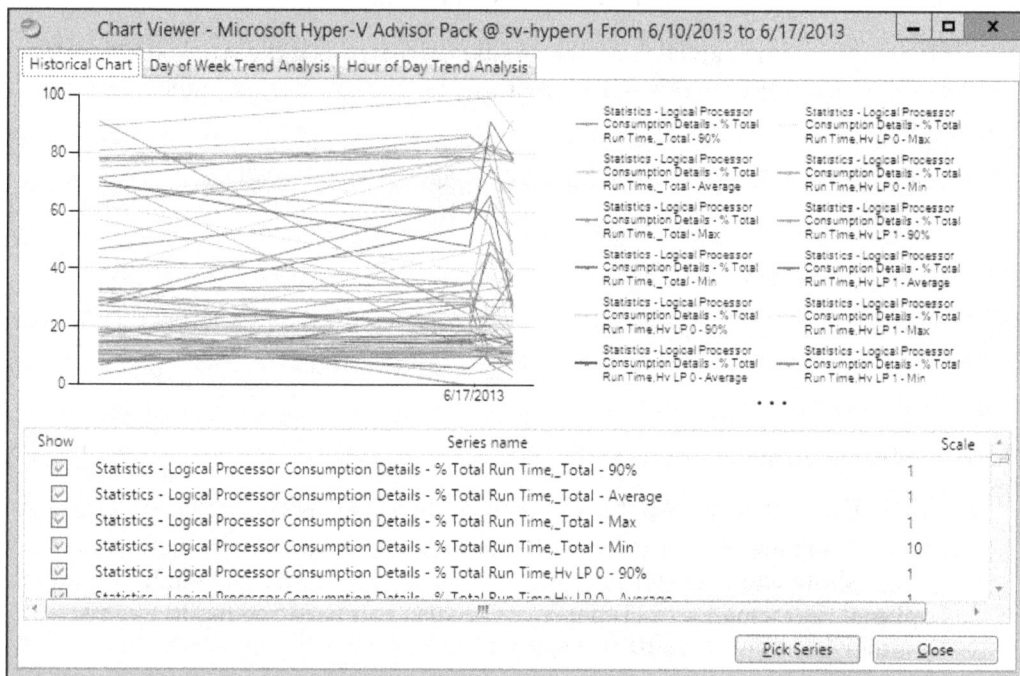

The sheer amount of data shown can make this difficult to interpret. In the lower section, you'll notice that there is a large number of performance counters. Select only those that you're actually interested in viewing and you'll find that the chart becomes much easier to understand. To deselect all items, select the first item and press *Ctrl* + *A*, and then press the Space bar.

> The items marked as **90%** remove all utilization above the 90 percent mark. These are assumed to be momentary spikes that can skew the outcome in a way that makes the data meaningless. Compare these to the same metrics marked as **Max**.

Use the **Pick Series** button at the bottom of the window if you wish to reduce the number of selectable items. This button is more useful on the other two tabs; in fact, they'll have no data to display if you do not select an item. As indicated, these two tabs show the way that the selected metrics have been trending over a specified period of time. These can show you how your systems behave differently during the day or across a week. Comparing these reports against those generated by other servers can help you to determine how your guests should be load balanced.

Performance Monitor

The built-in Performance Monitor tool is much more powerful than most others; but it's up to you to choose what to measure. One of its major strengths is that there's nothing to install. All you need is a Windows system with a GUI.

> As with Server Performance Advisor, it is not recommended that you run this on a Hyper-V host or guest that you are going to measure.

There are two ways to run Performance Monitor. One is as a real-time tool that graphs the monitored performance counters as they occur. The second is as a collector that gathers metrics and stores them for trend analysis. The differentiating features of Performance Monitor from Server Performance Advisor are:

- Real-time graphing
- Precise selection of metrics
- No software downloads required
- No database system required
- Performance logs can be opened on any Windows system

Performance Monitor is found in Administrative Tools. Depending on how your system is configured, **Administrative Tools** may be found on the Start screen or menu. It's available in the **Control Panel** in all versions of Windows. It's also available under the **Performance** node of **Computer Management**. If you will be running it for real-time graphing, ensure that you start it with an account that has administrative privileges on the target system. For collectors, you'll be able to specify the account to run it under. You may also need to modify the firewall as indicated under the *Server Performance Advisor* section mentioned earlier.

Real-time monitoring with Performance Monitor

To start a real-time monitoring session, expand the **Monitoring Tools** node and click on **Performance Monitor**. In the center pane, click on the button with the green plus, which will open the **Add Counters** window. In this window, you'll want to change the counters' source to the target computer. Your screen should look like the following screenshot:

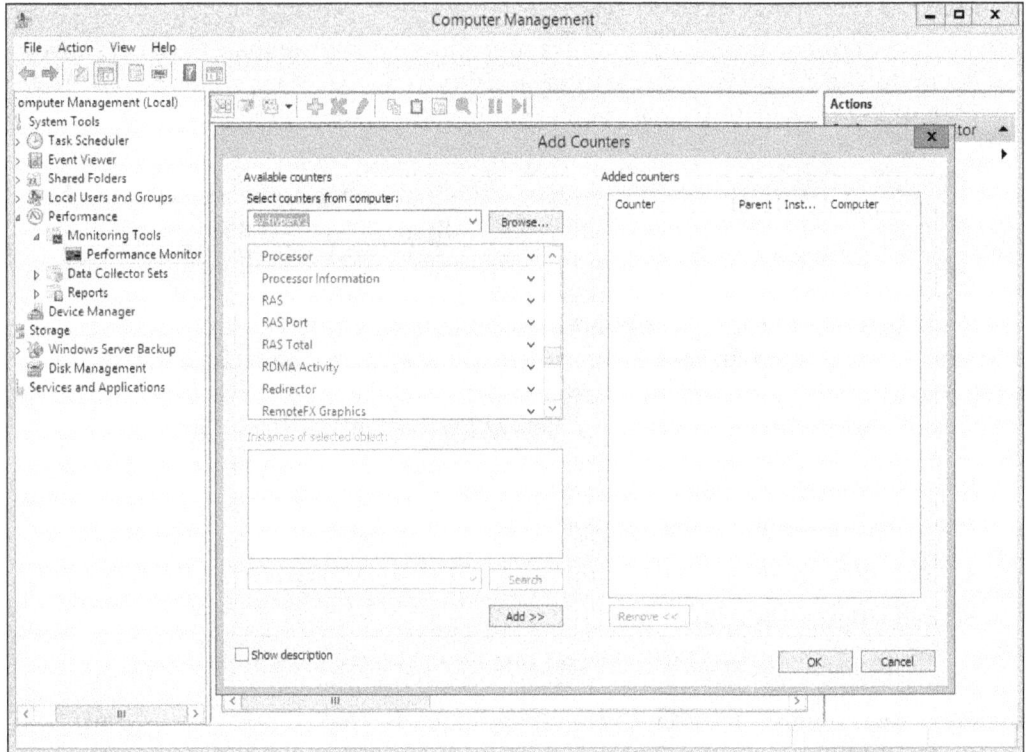

Navigate through the various counters in the upper list box. When you click on one, it will show the instances of that counter that are available to be monitored. Double-click on an instance or highlight it and click on the **Add >>** button to move it to the list box on the right. These are the objects that will be tracked. When you are satisfied with your selection, click on **OK**. See Step 4 in the next section for a screenshot of this window and more information about its contents.

You will be returned to the main screen. The display will be updated every second. Each counter you picked will be displayed as a line of a various color. The legend will be shown at the bottom. You can uncheck an item to hide it from the running display; however, its counter will still be monitored.

Using the buttons across the top of the graph pane, you can modify the output. Most of the options are self-explanatory; change them until the display suits your desires. You have the ability to modify the graph from its default line output to a histogram or to a running digital display. Click on the **Highlight** button and then select a counter to make it stand out against the others. Several of the buttons open various tabs on the **Performance Monitor Properties** window where you can change many settings, such as the delay between samples. Of interest here is the **Source** tab, which will be used in the next section.

Trend tracking with Performance Monitor

The second use for Performance Monitor is to pull performance statistics across a span of time. This concept was first introduced in *Chapter 2, Cluster Design and Planning*, to aid in capacity planning for physical to virtual conversions. In active deployments, it can be used to track the performance of Hyper-V hosts. You'll create scheduled gathering of data collector sets for this. What makes Performance Monitor especially useful for this is that a single collector set can gather from all the hosts in your cluster simultaneously.

Before you start, ensure that the Performance Monitor console is not connected to the target computer system as it would be for a real-time monitor. For instance, if you are using Computer Management as shown in the first screenshot in this chapter, the tree root should say **Computer Management (Local)** and not contain the name of another system. The first reason is that running and managing the collector sets creates a small drain on the system's resources. Second, you're going to be running collectors against multiple systems and it's better to use a single remote computer for those purposes. Third, it's easiest to look at the results of performance logs on the system that took them. Otherwise, you have to move them around.

Look under the **Data Collector Sets** tree item. There are a number of predefined collector sets and you can add more. Just right-click on the **User Defined** node and choose **New** and **Data Collector Set**. The following steps will take you through the creation of a collector set:

1. On the first screen, come up with a name for the set, then choose to manually create the set, then click on **Next**:

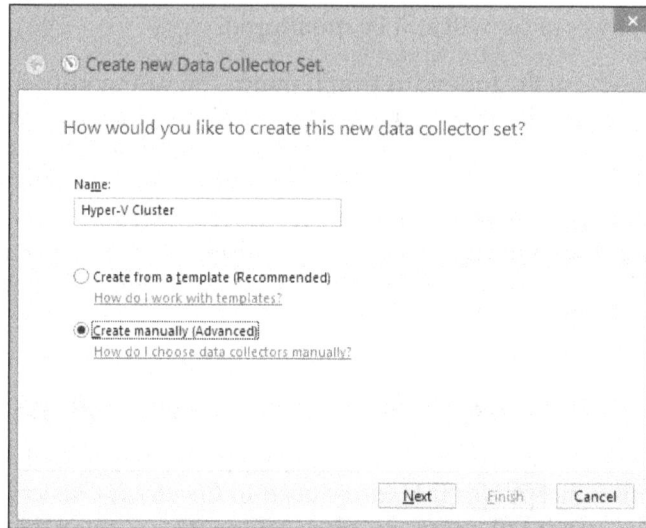

This wizard will create a data collector named `DataCollector01` which cannot be renamed. If you wish, you can skip through the wizard to the end, delete the generic collector, and then create new ones with friendlier names.

2. On the second screen, you want to create performance counter data logs:

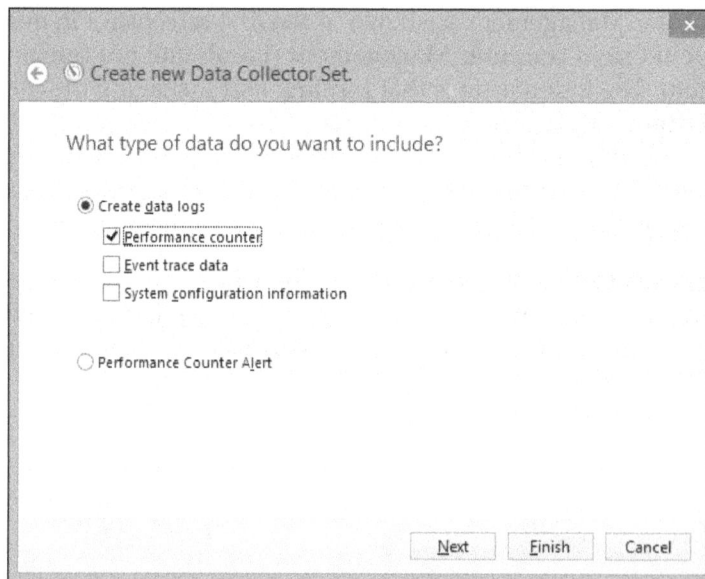

3. On the third screen, you can change how often the collector polls for data. As you can see in the following screenshot, the default is every 15 seconds:

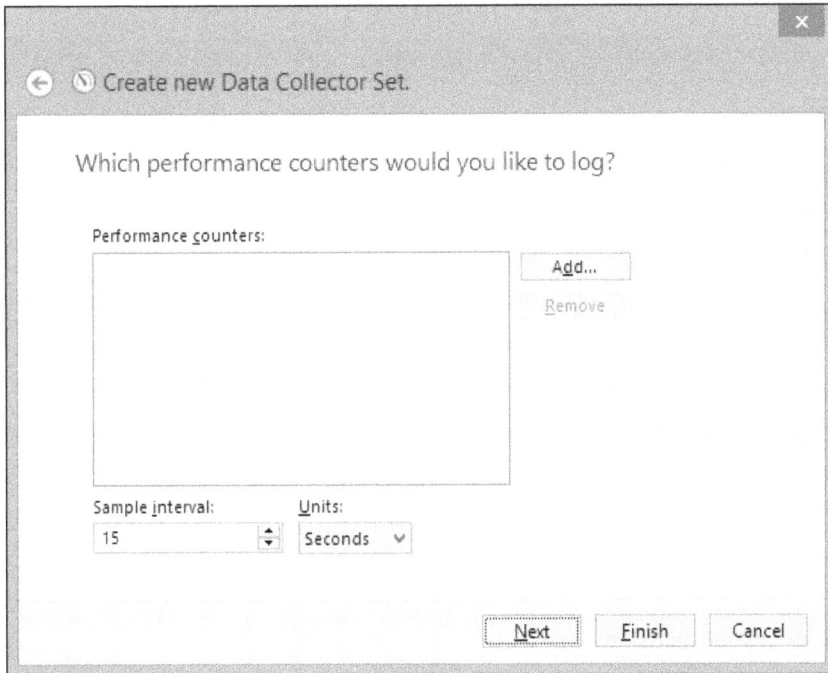

4. Click on the **Add...** button in the previous screen to pick the counters that you want to poll. This is the same screen that you see when selecting counters in the real-time screen. Enter the name of the computer you want to poll data from in the **Select counters from computer** text box. Upon pressing *Tab* or *Enter* or clicking on another control, it will load the counters from that system. Select the counters and instances that you desire and click on **Add >>**. You can monitor counters from multiple computer systems in the same collector set if you like, but you may also choose to use one collector per computer per set. Remember that you'll want to select Hyper-V related counters for CPU, memory, and networking or you'll be retrieving collectors from the parent partition only. Physical disk counters are read from the management operating system.

> You cannot retrieve statistics for pass-through disks by setting performance counters on the management operating system.

5. If you click on the **Add >>** button and nothing happens, it is because instances are required but didn't load. Click on another counter and then back on the desired counter until the instances are displayed.

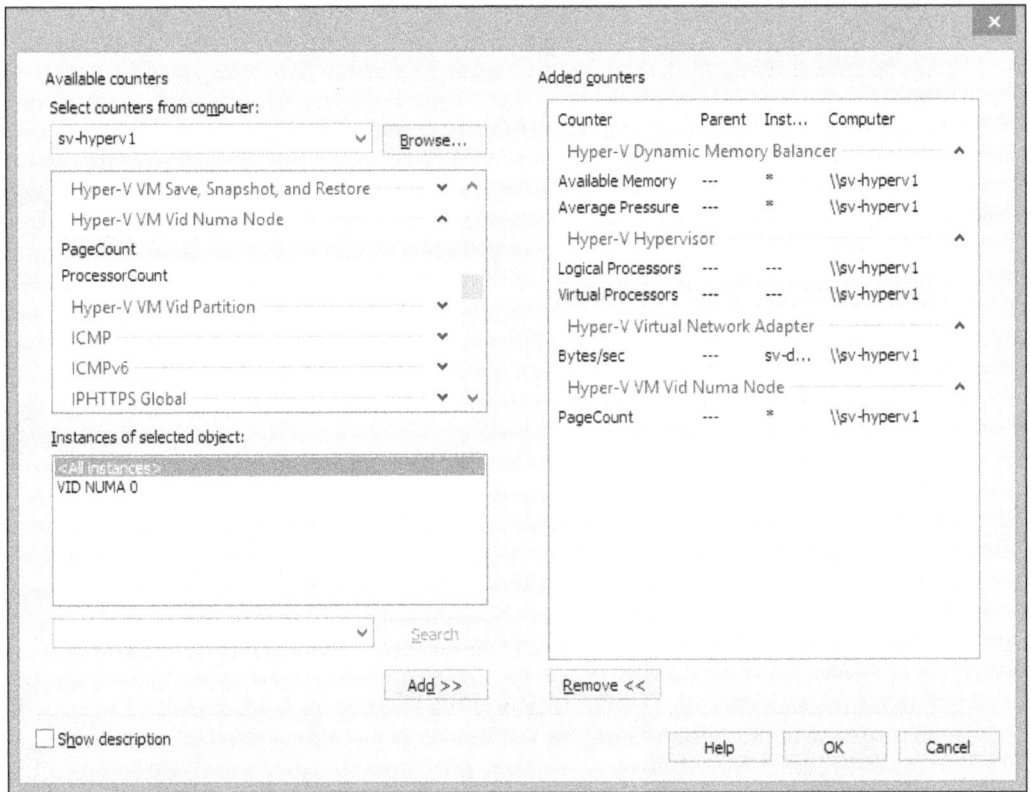

6. On clicking **OK**, you'll be returned to the previous screen that will now be populated with the counters that you chose. Ensure everything looks as you wish and click on **Next**.

7. You'll now be asked for a location to save the logs to. Although it will allow you to enter a UNC, logfile creation is usually unsuccessful anywhere but on the local system. You may place them in a local folder that is shared for easy accessibility from other systems, if you wish.

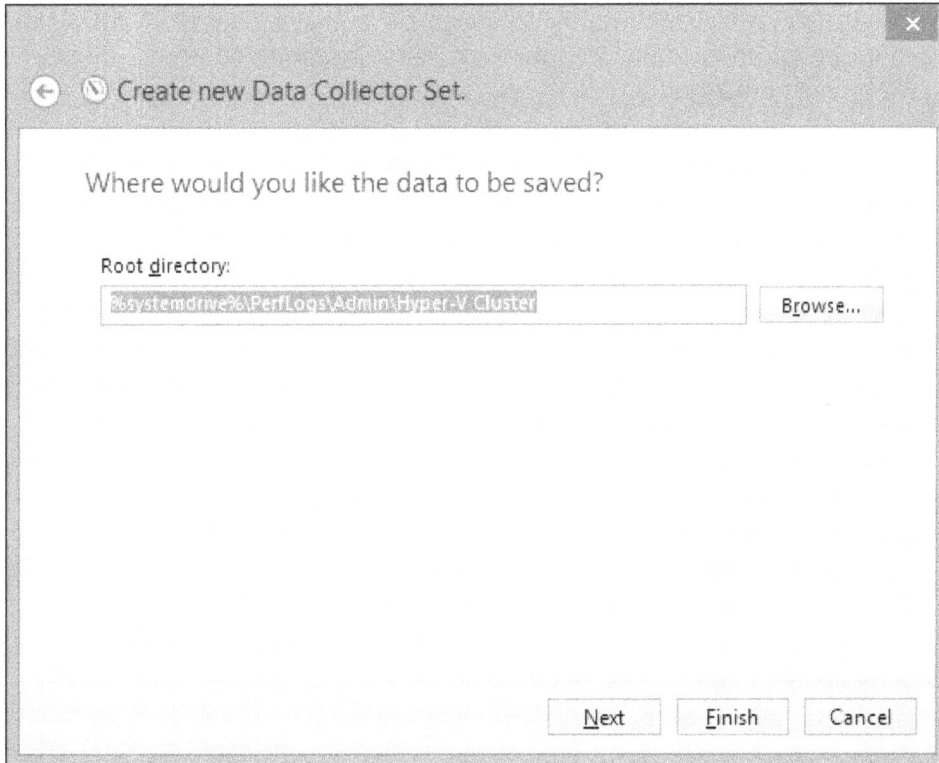

8. The final screen will have you provide the credentials that the set will use. If you leave it on its default setting, it will use the Local System account that will not have the necessary rights to run the collection on the target computer. You have two choices: you can add the computer account of the collector machine to the Performance Log Users group on all target machines or you can use an account that is a member of that group on all machines. For the purposes of this step-through, we're just going to use the domain administrator account:

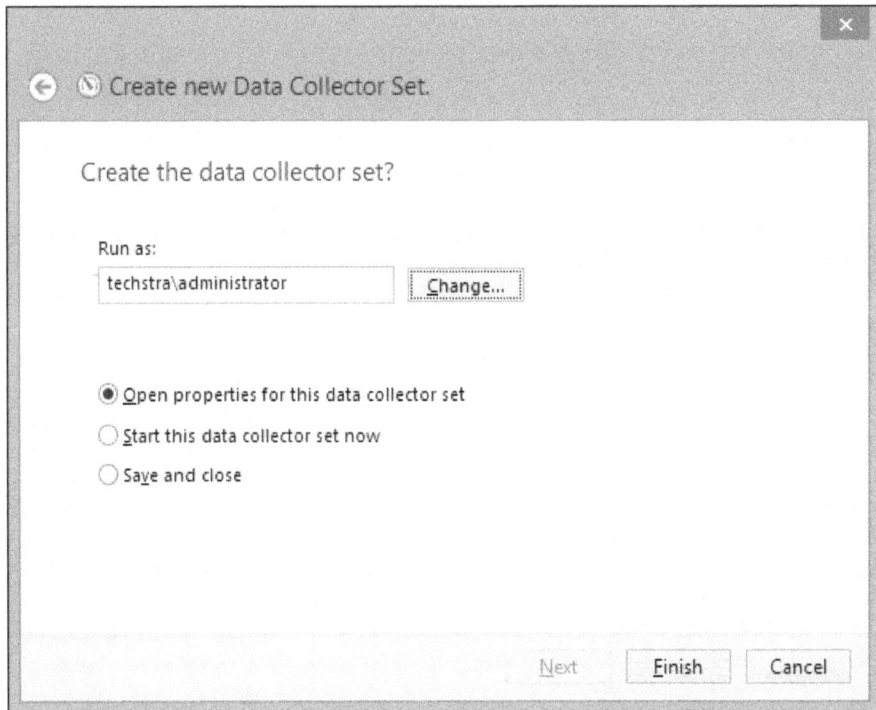

9. Before clicking on **Finish**, you are encouraged to set the radio button to **Open properties for this data collector set**. This will allow you to jump straight to the properties window where you can schedule the scan. Alternately, you can open the properties window by right-clicking on the completed collector set and clicking on **Properties**.

10. In the properties window, change the options as you like. The **Schedule** tab is where you establish the Start and End times. You can create multiple schedules for a collector set:

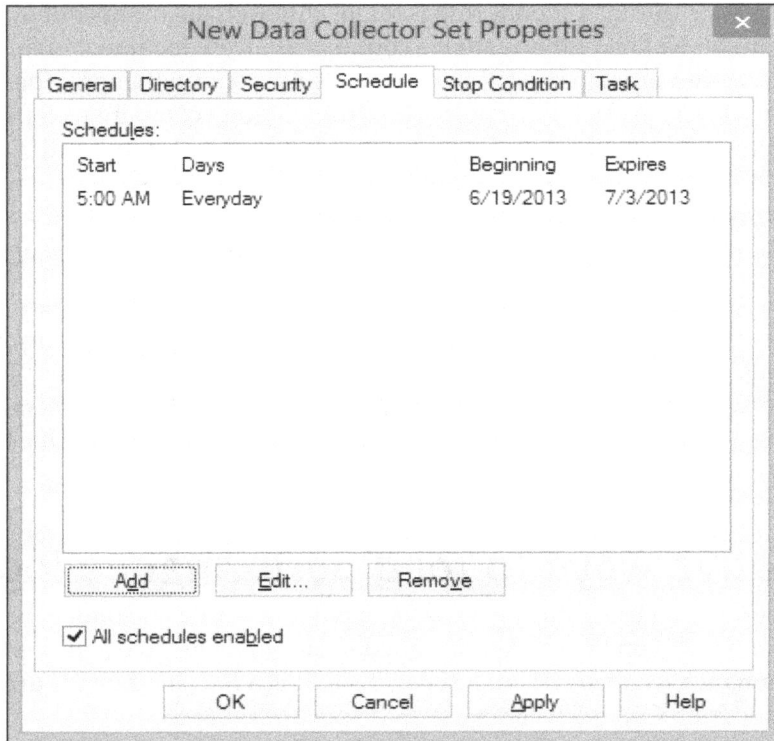

11. If you want to use a separate collector in this set for another host, right-click on the new **Collector Set** in the left pane and click on **New** and **Data Collector**. The wizard is very nearly identical to the one you just completed.

You aren't required to follow a schedule. You can manually start and stop collector sets by right-clicking on the menu in the left pane.

Once the collector has begun its work, you can go back to the real-time monitor screen and open the **Performance Monitor Properties** window to the **Source** tab. Select the logfile that you instructed the collector set to use. The display will switch to the static output of the logfile. However, it will be blank because by default, no counters are selected. Add counters with the green plus button just as you did with the real-time display. This time, you'll only be able to choose from counters that are contained in the logfiles. You can now manipulate the log contents as you did with the live display. Note that you can view a log of an actively running collector, but the screen will not update in real time.

Selecting counters practically

If you use the exact counters as shown in the example, you'll notice that some of them aren't very useful. For instance, the number of processors in a host is highly unlikely to change during a monitoring session, although the number of virtual processors might. Not all of the available counters are well documented, but there is a **Show description** check box on the counter selection screen that provides a bit of information. Also, some of the counters you can pull don't compare well from one host to another. In the sample, we instructed SV-HYPERV1 to monitor the amount of data traveling across the virtual adapter in SV-DC1. This is useful data in its own right, but probably in isolation, not as a comparator. Of course, if the virtual machine migrates to another host, it will no longer be readable. You may find the aggregate counters to be more useful than specific virtual machine counters.

The counters that are truly useful are simply too numerous to make a meaningful list out of, and not all counters are universally useful in all organizations. The four generic categories you're likely to be interested in are CPU, disk, memory, and networking. Be judicious about selecting counters that look at specific highly available virtual machines.

Alternative ways to read performance logs

Performance logs can be confusing, especially when you first encounter them. There are a number of tools on the market designed to aid you. One free and popular tool is the **Performance Analysis of Logs** (**PAL**) Tool. It is a free and open source tool downloadable from Codeplex at http://pal.codeplex.com.

Subsystem testing

Along with generic system testing, you can examine specific subsystems. This may be more useful in situations in which you suspect an issue, rather than for general knowledge or trend analysis. It's also useful if you just want to know the capabilities of your systems, since the tools you'll be shown focus more on what the system can do than on how it has been performing. The biggest barrier to testing subsystems is that many of the tools won't work from the hypervisor level. The subsystems we'll examine are disk, memory, and network.

Disk I/O testing

A tool commonly used for examining disk performance is IOMeter, which was created by Intel and is now an open source project. The official site and download are accessible at `http://www.iometer.org`. More recent but somewhat less stable versions are available at `http://sourceforge.net/projects/iometer/`. It runs on all current Windows operating systems including Hyper-V Server, and all non-Windows operating systems that can run as guests under Hyper-V. Unfortunately, it does not work directly with Cluster Shared Volumes or mapped network drives. You'll need to assign drive letters to them for testing. It can, of course, test iSCSI and Fibre Channel LUNs that have been assigned a drive letter in the local system. So, as a test of a LUN, you can test by using a drive letter prior to moving it to Cluster Shared Volumes. You can also use Storage Live Migration to evacuate a CSV, remove it from Cluster Shared Volumes, and test it.

> IOMeter is a stress-test tool. It will impact performance during use. If measuring a production system, consider doing so during a maintenance window.

To assign a drive letter to a CSV, you can use either DISKPART or SUBST. The DISKPART method will survive a reboot while the SUBST method will not. SUBST is a basic built-in command; use SUBST /? if you are unfamiliar with its usage. For DISKPART, perform the following steps:

1. Execute DISKPART.EXE at an elevated command prompt.
2. Type LIST VOLUME.
3. Items with CSVFS in the Fs column are your CSVs. Note the volume number of the CSV that you want to test.
4. Type SELECT VOLUME 3, substituting the number for the CSV you wish to test.
5. Type ASSIGN LETTER J, substituting the desired drive letter. To reverse this later, use REMOVE LETTER J in the same fashion.
6. Type EXIT to end your DISKPART session.

To measure the performance of an SMB share, use standard drive mappings:

```
NET USE J: \\SV-STORAGE\VMs
```

> The previous steps are non-standard and unsupported for both CSVs and shared locations. Remove assigned drive letters and mappings once testing is complete.

IOMeter can also be used inside guests to test pass-through disks. You may also choose to use this tool inside a virtual machine to test shared storage. The results of this test will be subject to contention for the shared location, but it will give a fairly accurate idea of how well the particular machine can utilize that storage.

The following screenshot shows the screen you'll see when starting IOMeter:

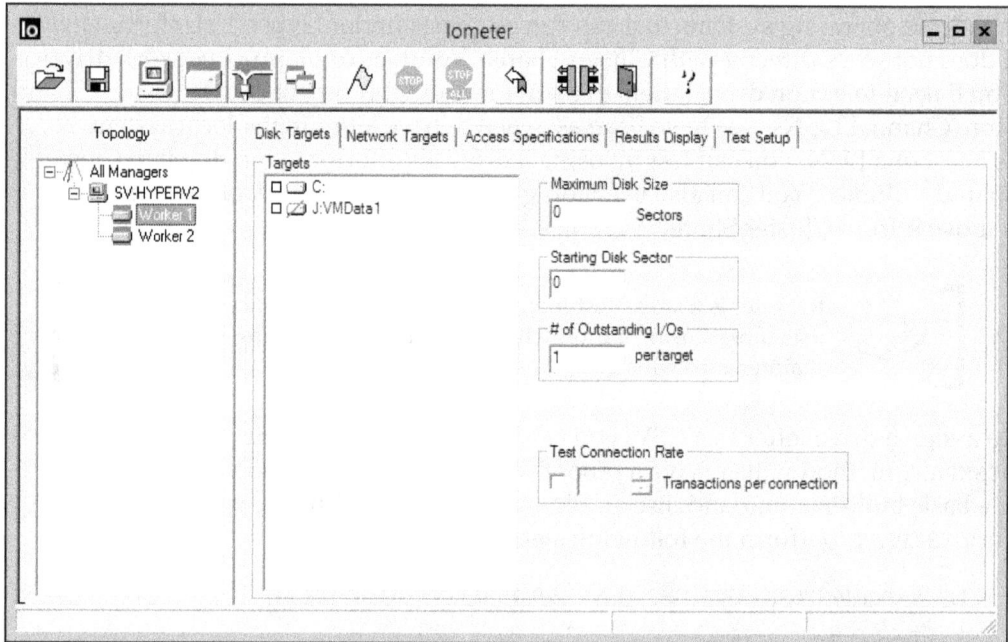

The red line through the J: indicates that it needs to be prepared, which simply means that it is not a raw drive (because it has one or more partitions) and does not contain an iobw.tst file at its root. This file will be automatically created once the job starts. If undirected, this file will consume all available space on the drive. To keep it to a reasonable size, you can use the **Maximum Disk Size** field as a limiter. Unfortunately, that field is by sector, so you'll have to do some math to arrive at a reasonable size. For a 10 GB file on a standard 512 bytes-per-sector drive system, you would enter 20971520.

A clumsier, but effective method is to simply allow the file creation to proceed automatically. After a few minutes of **Preparing Drives** status, stop the job and exit the program. The file will be truncated at whatever size IOMeter reached when you cancelled its creation. When you start the program again, it will use that file at its current size. Of course, you may also use file generation software to create a file of any size you like; it should contain mixed bits (preferably random), must be named iobw.tst, and must be created in the root of the drive to be tested.

By default, two workers are generated. You only need to use one but you can add as many as you like. Each worker maintains its own disk targets and test criteria. You can have multiple workers targeting the same disk.

To set how your worker will test the file, switch to the **Access Specifications** tab. Predefined test types are in the right column. You can edit these entries to create whatever test you like, and a single worker can run multiple tests. The following screenshot shows an **Edit Access Specification** screen:

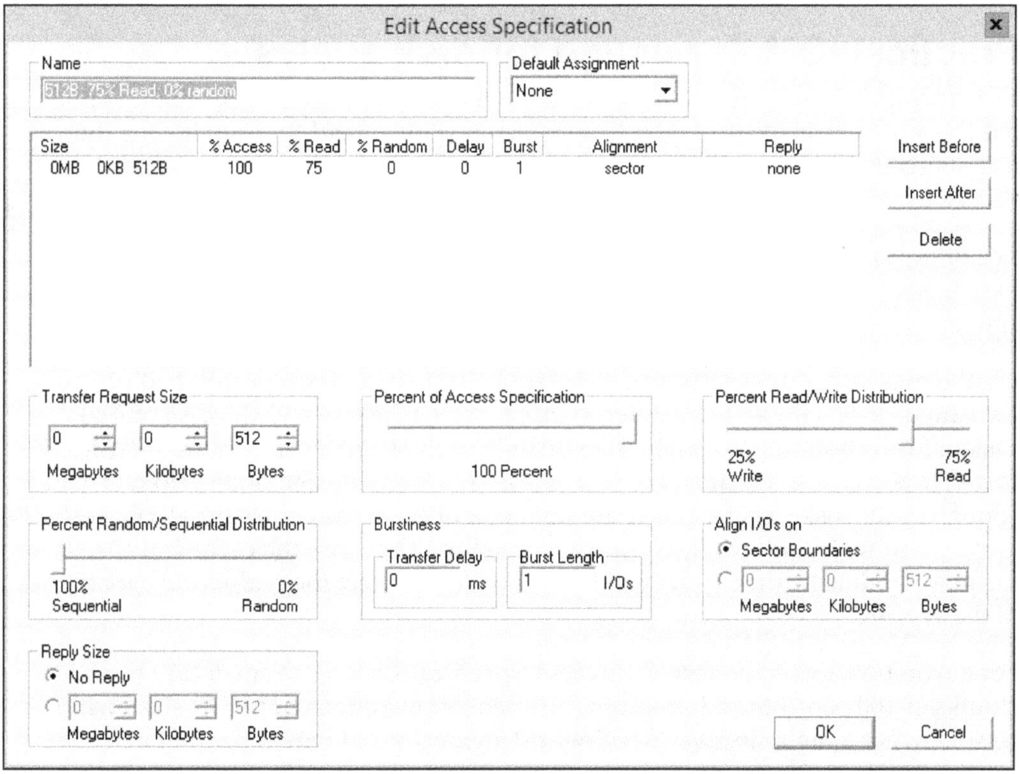

The final step to perform prior to starting your test is to configure the duration and test conditions. These are all found on the **Test Setup** tab and are self-explanatory.

> IOMeter has the ability to save test configuration files using the relevant toolbar items and buttons. It is highly recommended that you save the configurations that you use so that you can make meaningful comparisons in the future.

Once you've set up the test as desired, click on the button with the green flag icon to start the test. You'll be asked for a location to save the `results.csv` file which can be imported into Excel or any other application that can process comma-separated values. Switch to the results display screen if you'd like to watch the gatherer work. You'll need to set **Update Frequency** to something other than infinite in order to see the numbers change. You can also click on the **>** button at the end of each row to see a gage display of that statistic. Click on the text button at the start of each row to change the statistic that it displays.

Practical IOMeter usage for disk analysis

The official site provides documentation for the tool that is very thorough. For all but the most simplistic testing, it is worth your time to read through it. One thing it contains that is not in this book is instructions on importing your results into Excel and using them to create a graph.

The prerelease software on SourceForge does not contain an installer. Remember to unblock the files in Windows Explorer or with the `Unblock-File` PowerShell cmdlet or they will not function. IOMeter requires elevated privileges to run.

For the most accurate results, use a raw disk that has not been partitioned or formatted. This will cause IOMeter to utilize the entire space of the disk or disk system for its testing, which can then include such factors as maximum read-head travel. If you cannot test the raw disk, use a very large file. Small files do not span enough of the disk to get an accurate understanding of the effects of read-head motion and will result in a high rate of cache hits. The more the cache is utilized, the more optimistic the results will be and will not reflect the real-world capabilities of the system.

For a worst-case scenario test, set **Access Specifications** to use small (512 or 4KB) chunks of 100 percent random access. Sequential operations of higher sizes will be somewhat more reflective of real-world scenarios, but remember that in a virtualization environment, disk access is scheduled across all virtual machines and will therefore be unpredictable. Most real-world workloads are heavier on reads than writes. 75 percent read is a good expectation for standard systems. IOMeter's documentation indicates using a 66 percent read pattern to simulate a database load. In reality, a database system's disk access will be as dependent on its usage scenario as any other system. Your application vendors may be able to help you design reasonable metrics. Use a varied combination of **Access Specifications** to simulate real-world loads.

Testing shared storage is dependent not only on the capabilities of the disk system but also on the connections to that disk system. In most cases, they won't present a meaningful bottleneck but keep their limitations in mind as you test.

If you are using automatic-tiered storage that will move heavily-accessed data to a faster disk, ensure that you consult with your manufacturer prior to running any disk metric tests. Otherwise, it may inappropriately place low-utilization data on high-speed storage in response to a stress test.

Make sure to save your test configuration. You will be unable to perform a proper comparative analysis without using the same criteria in other tests.

Network testing

Network testing is most useful at deployment time and when you suspect that there may be an issue in the hardware that is undetectable by other means. Network adapters and switching hardware has very fixed limits on performance that do not have the variances of spinning disks due to their solid-state nature. We will look at two tools for networking testing.

IOMeter for network testing

Since you've already got IOMeter for testing your disks, there's not much more to using it for testing a network connection. You'll need to install or place IOMeter's executables on another system. By setting that remote system as a target, you can test the network between them.

Before setting up IOMeter for network testing, make a firewall change on the system by running the IOMeter GUI. You can use the /p switch in the following commands to indicate exactly which port you wish to use; otherwise, it will randomly select a port above 53,000.

To use IOMeter to test the network connection between two systems:

1. On the remote system, open an elevated command prompt. Navigate to the folder that contains the IOMeter executables. Run dynamo.exe with both the /i and /m switches targeting the system that is running the IOMeter application. In this test environment, **SV-HYPERV2** is running IOMeter and **SV-HYPERV1** is the remote system. The command for that is as follows:

   ```
   Dynamo.exe /i SV-HYPERV2 /m SV-HYPERV2
   ```

2. It will indicate that it is attempting to log in to the target system and will show the port it is attempting to use.

3. On the IOMeter system, either add a new manager or change the existing one. The managers are displayed in the **Topology** pane at the left. To add a manager, use the button with a computer as its icon. To change a manager, you have to click on its name and then after a brief pause, click on it again. If done properly, the manager name will become an editable text box. Change it to the name of the remote system. For our example, this would be SV-HYPERV1.

4. With that manager selected, add a new **Network Worker** using the relevant toolbar button.

5. Switch to the **Network Targets** tab. At this point, your screen should look similar to the following screenshot:

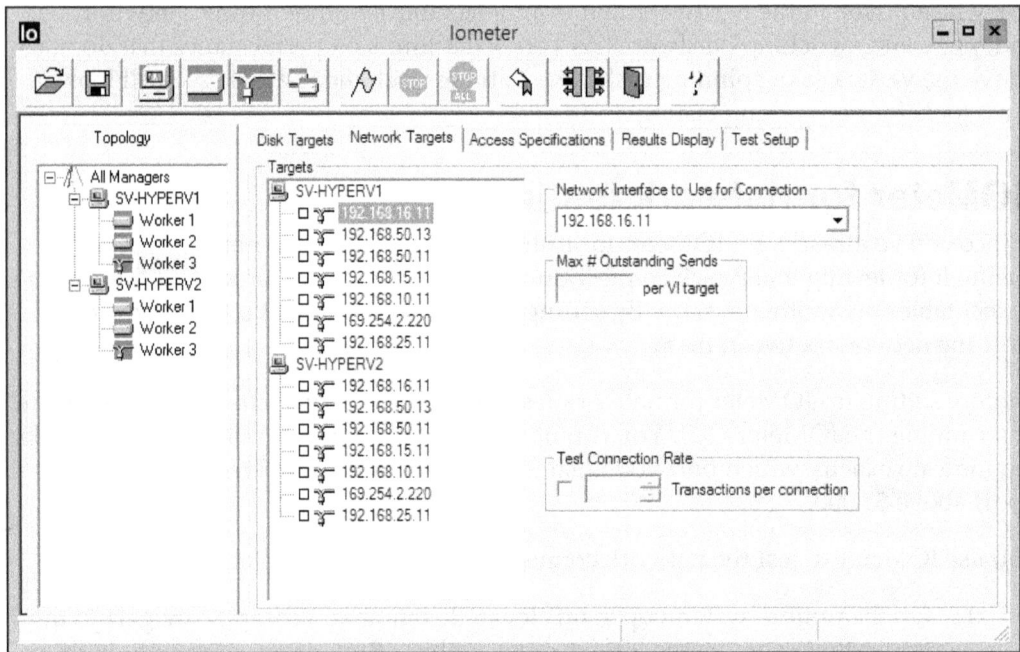

6. Under the remote machine's entry in the **Targets** pane, check the adapters you wish to test.

7. Configure, save, and execute the tests as you would for a disk target.

Practical IOMeter usage for network analysis

Unlike the disk scan, you won't get as much useful data out of changing the **Access Specification** metrics. What you want to watch for are MBs and latency. These will indicate if your network speeds are as expected and if there is high delay between the measured nodes. Another interesting metric to watch is CPU utilization. The efficiency of IOMeter itself is unknown, but this is a test of an application fully utilizing a network channel. By changing enabled network options and re-running the test, you can see the effect that various offload technologies have (or do not have).

NTttcp for network testing

NTttcp is a Microsoft tool used for measuring network performance. It has been made available to the public through the Microsoft TechNet gallery. The version that was most recent as of this writing is available at `http://gallery.technet.microsoft.com/NTttcp-Version-528-Now-f8b12769`.

To compare and contrast this tool with IOMeter, it is command line only and can only export to XML files. The benefit is that it is easier to run multiple simultaneous instances, which means that you can test using multiple ports. With multiple tests running on multiple ports, you can more properly test a hashed load-balancing algorithm for a single virtual adapter on a network team.

NTttcp usage is straightforward. Instructions are provided directly on the download page.

Memory testing

Testing memory for its performance capabilities is generally not a useful undertaking. Because memory is solid state and its performance characteristics are not dependent on external factors, memory will behave exactly the same way throughout its life. Only a faulty memory module will have variances. Simply knowing the published data for your memory as explained in *Chapter 7, Memory Planning and Management*, is likely to be sufficient. For actual performance testing, a number of benchmarking applications are commercially available.

Testing memory for faults is usually much more valuable than testing it for performance. Often, administrators will perform a burn-in procedure on new hardware. Such a procedure runs all portions of all memory modules through a repeated series of stress tests over a period of time. If any of the modules produce inconsistent results, it is a sign that the module is faulty and needs to be replaced. In general, memory modules will fail shortly after being placed into service or they will last a number of years. The burn-in process helps to single out those that will fail early, before they enter production.

A commonly used tool for testing memory is the Prime95 software. This tool's primary purpose is actually to use a distributed computing model to find Mersenne prime numbers. You can read about that endeavor and download the software at `http://www.mersenne.org/freesoft/`. You do not need to sign up for an account or participate in the search to use this software. If you will be running it from within a Windows Server or Hyper-V Server installation, use the 64-bit download. If you will be placing the file on a bootable CD or USB flash drive, use the 32-bit download.

To use it, you can simply extract, unblock, and run the `Prime95.exe` program from within Windows or a command prompt. When run with the 64-bit GUI, you can use the **Custom** setting to specify how you want the utility to run; although the default stress test settings are adequate. There isn't a lot to see as the tests run. One child window will be created for each master thread and a line item will be entered for each test as it runs. The following is a screenshot of the application running on Hyper-V Server 2012:

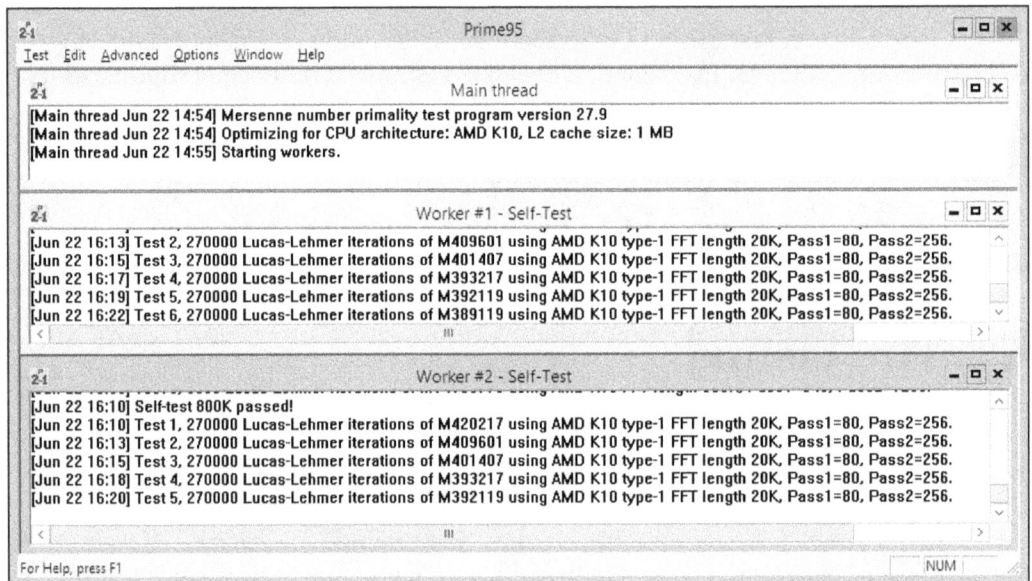

Creating a bootable CD or USB flash drive is beyond the scope of this book. Rather than going through the effort of making a special-use bootable disk, it is possible to boot to other bootable media then replace it with media that contains the 32-bit `Prime95.exe` program. Many prebuilt bootable images are readily available. They are not specifically referenced in this text as very few are both free and have direct support from any manufacturer.

Baseline and comparative performance measures

Using the previous tools, conduct the tests of your systems that can be duplicated later. You'll want to know how they perform right out of the box and how they perform under normal load. Store these results as baseline measures. Then, if you or your users suspect that there are performance problems, you can run the exact same tests and compare them against the baselines. You will then have an easier time determining if there is a problem and where that problem may be.

As your deployment grows, these comparative measurements will help you determine how quickly your systems are expanding, which can help you plan well in advance for any scale-out operations.

Cluster load balancing

The next phase beyond node resource usage is resource usage across your cluster. As previously noted, an extra application layer, such as System Center Virtual Machine Manager, can perform this load balancing automatically. Without this software, you will need to perform load balancing manually. Also, in some cases, you may wish to exert manual control over specific virtual machines. For instance, if you are using the built-in high availability features of some applications, such as Microsoft SQL Server or Exchange Server, you may want to ensure that particular virtual machines never share the same host. You may also be using clustering with Hyper-V Server with the intent of keeping particular application servers logically arranged more than providing failover. For instance, the following is a planning diagram for a Microsoft Lync system running on a Hyper-V Server cluster:

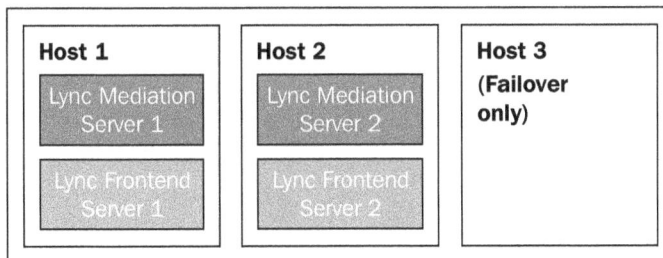

A Lync frontend server involves very heavy usage of CPU and having two on the same physical host would probably overload it. The mediation servers are less demanding; so in this theoretical design, one mediation server and one frontend server have been paired on two hosts. The challenge is to provide automatic failover capabilities while ensuring that the two frontend servers are never on the same hardware. Preventing the mediation servers from sharing hardware isn't quite as important; but because the purpose of having two is to introduce high availability at the application level, keeping them apart is desirable. There are two things built-in to Hyper-V Server to address these issues.

> Lync does not support Live Migration. This scenario represents a failover build in which the cluster service could revive a crashed guest on another host.

Preferred owners

By marking particular hosts as the preferred owners for a given virtual machine, they are given top priority when a cluster-initiated move event occurs. Usually, this is in response to a host shutdown (including crashes) or a Drain Roles operation. It is not considered when an administrator manually initiates Live Migration or Quick Migration. Preferred owners can be designated in the GUI or in PowerShell.

Setting preferred owners using Failover Cluster Manager

Select the **Roles** node in Failover Cluster Manager. In the center pane, right-click on the virtual machine whose settings you wish to change and click on **Properties**. In the properties dialog, check the boxes next to the host(s) you wish to designate as preferred for this particular virtual machine.

There is also a **Preferred Owners** link in the grey divider area between the top and bottom panes of Failover Cluster Manager as seen in the following screenshot:

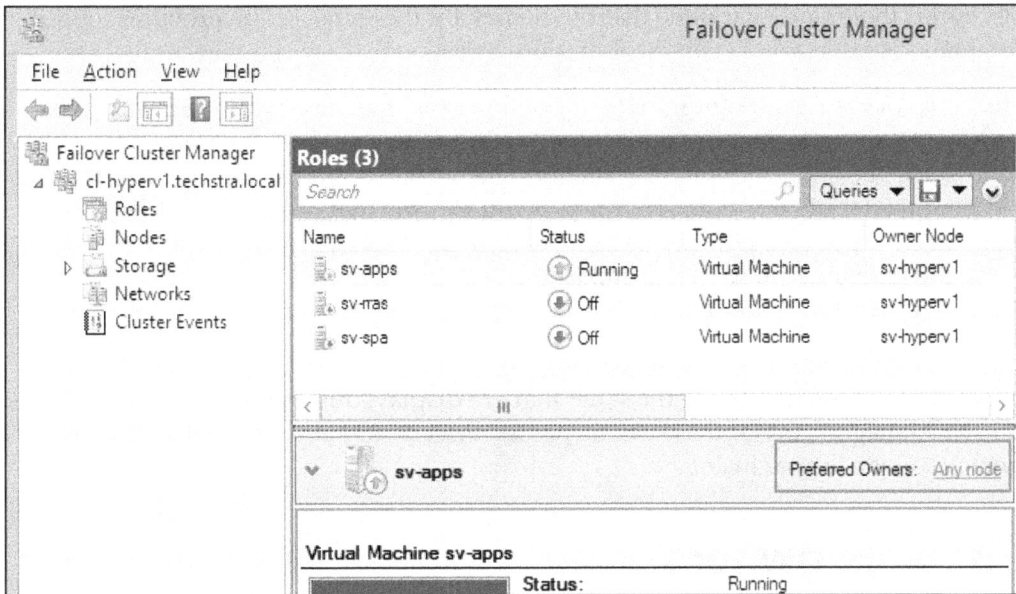

Setting preferred owners using PowerShell

This can be a somewhat involved process, but it looks more difficult than it actually is. For example, one-line method to set the possible owner of the virtual machine named `sv-spa` to `sv-hyperv1` and `sv-hyperv3` is as follows:

```
Get-ClusterGroup -VMId ((Get-VM -Name "sv-spa").VMId) |
Set-ClusterOwnerNode -Owners "sv-hyperv1", "sv-hyperv3"
```

The reason for the depth is because you actually set the owner property on a group of resources that the virtual machine is part of. The other component is the configuration data for that guest. Together, these are members of a resource group that the cluster controls. Usually, this group has the exact same name as the virtual machine, so you're probably safe to just use:

```
Set-ClusterOwnerNode -Group "sv-spa" -Owners "sv-hyperv1", "sv-hyperv3"
```

Of course, there's no guarantee that the names are the same, so the previous longer command is safer. We'll examine that piece by piece:

First, it retrieves the identifier for the specific virtual machine with (Get-VM -Name "sv-spa").VMId. If the virtual machine was running on a different node, you'd also have to use the ComputerName parameter. The retrieved VMId is then used in the VMId parameter of Get-ClusterGroup. If you execute that portion by itself, it will show you the group that contains the virtual machine in question. What we've done is use the pipeline to ship that group to the Set-ClusterOwnerNode cmdlet. There, the preferred owners are set.

If you'd just like to see all the available groups, use Get-ClusterGroup with no parameters. These names are the same that are displayed in the **Roles** tree of Failover Cluster Manager. Any of these can be passed directly to Set-ClusterOwnerNode from any node in the cluster.

Possible owners

Possible owners goes one step beyond preferred owners by setting which nodes are allowed to host a virtual machine. Any node not included cannot be a destination for that guest by any means, automatic or manual.

Setting possible owners using Failover Cluster Manager

To use Failover Cluster Manager to set Possible Owners:

1. Click on the **Roles** node. In the lower section of the center pane, switch to the **Resources** tab.

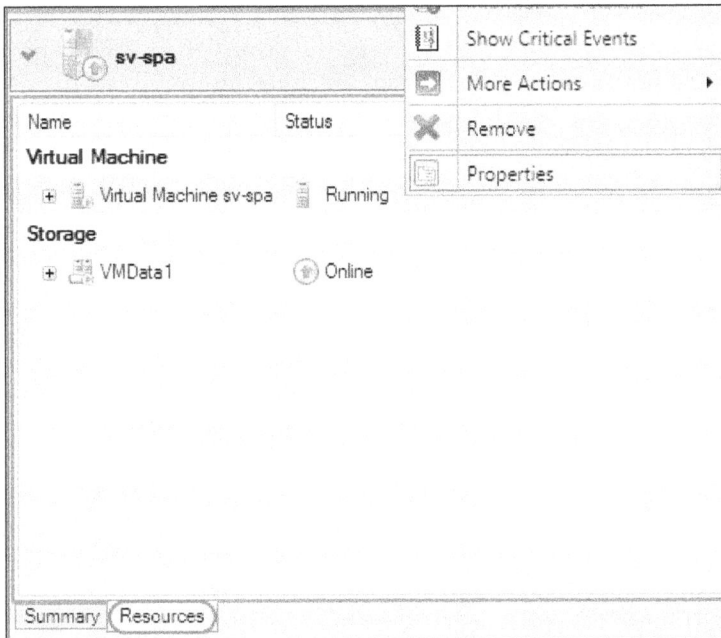

2. In the upper portion of this screen, under the **Virtual Machine** heading, right-click on the virtual machine object and click on **Properties**.

3. In the **Properties** window, uncheck any server that you do not wish to host this virtual machine.

Setting possible owners using PowerShell

As with the Preferred Owners PowerShell setting, we need to go a little deeper into the system. These cmdlets look very similar to the preferred owners cmdlets:

```
Get-ClusterResource -VMId ((Get-VM -Name "sv-spa").VMId) |
Set-ClusterOwnerNode -Owners "sv-hyperv1", "sv-hyperv3"
```

This time, instead of setting the owners on the overall group, we are setting it on the virtual machine resource itself. Unlike the group, the resource probably does not have the same name as the virtual machine, although it will probably be similar. A virtual machine resource created using the GUI tools will usually have a name such as `Virtual Machine sv-spa`. You can see these by executing `Get-ClusterResource` by itself or by looking in the GUI in the location mentioned for setting possible owners.

Anti-affinity

Where Preferred Owners and Possible Owners set restrictions on specific virtual machines in relation to specific nodes, the anti-affinity setting is applied to a group of virtual machines. When the cluster service takes automatic actions that move virtual machines, it will attempt to prevent any members of the same anti-affinity group from being started on the same host. As with Preferred Owners, this setting is not guaranteed to be honored and you can override it with manual migrations.

The property itself is a string array that is attached to the cluster resource group. String arrays are more commonly seen in programming than in systems administration. An array is a group and a string is a set of characters. A common example would be an array that contains colors. Such an array might just be named `Colors` and it would contain values such as blue, green, and red. Those values have meaning to you as a human but the computer just sees them as assorted characters. As you'll recall from Preferred Owners, the cluster resource group contains the virtual machine and its configuration information. So in order to set anti-affinity, you first need to come up with a name for an anti-affinity class. Then you need to insert that name into this array on the cluster resource group for the virtual machines you want to be members of that class. The reason that this field is an array and not simply a string value is so that you can assign the same virtual machine to multiple anti-affinity classes.

Despite the lengthy explanation, setting anti-affinity is very simple:

```
(Get-ClusterGroup "sv-lyncms1").AntiAffinityClassNames = "Lync Mediation
Servers"
(Get-ClusterGroup "sv-lyncms2").AntiAffinityClassNames = "Lync Mediation
Servers"
```

The previous cmdlet will set the two indicated cluster groups to the same anti-affinity class so that automated failovers will attempt to keep them separated. The cmdlets assume that the cluster groups have the same name as the virtual machines. Refer to the *Setting Preferred Owners Using PowerShell* section earlier to learn how to find the cluster group name for a virtual machine.

Of course, you can perform similar operates on one line:

```
((Get-ClusterGroup).Name -like "*lyncms*").AntiAffinityClassNames = "Lync
Mediation Servers"
```

You can then add a system into another anti-affinity class with the += operator:

```
(Get-ClusterGroup "sv-lyncfe1").AntiAffinityClassNames += "High CPU"
```

To view the classes that a virtual machine belongs to:

```
(Get-ClusterGroup "sv-lyncms1").AntiAffinityClassNames
```

Remove the guest from classes by setting an empty array:

```
(Get-ClusterGroup "sv-lyncms1").AntiAffinityClassNames = ""
```

Unfortunately, removing a single class is difficult. You can replace the entire array, specifying only the classes that you wish to remain:

```
(Get-ClusterGroup "sv-lyncfe1").AntiAffinityClassNames = @("Lync Front-
End Servers", "High CPU")
```

> Cluster.exe also contains switches for setting anti-affinity. This module is deprecated and should no longer be used. System Center Virtual Machine Manager can be used to modify this setting by changing **Availability Sets**.

Summary

In this chapter, we looked at performance monitoring and load balancing.

First, we learned how to use Server Performance Advisor and Performance Monitor to learn how hosts are functioning. We then learned about various tools to monitor the capabilities and stability of the core components of your systems.

When discussing performance, it is always important to remember that the goal is to achieve a level that provides a satisfactory experience for users of the system; not to achieve an arbitrary score on a benchmark. Provision and balance our resources wisely.

After performance monitoring, we showed how to automatically set restrictions on your virtual machines to control which hosts they can operate on. This is an important tactic to keep our host systems properly load-balanced.

In the next chapter, we will look at special uses of Hyper-V Server clusters beyond the norm of consolidation.

9
Special Cases

So far, we've only considered the most common uses for Hyper-V clusters. Sometimes, consolidation and resource maximization are not the primary drivers for a high availability virtualization solution. Some environments may have their own particular requirements that aren't covered in the documentation. The purpose of this chapter is to examine some of these special cases and explain how and why they can be implemented in a Hyper-V Server cluster. We will look at:

- Non-highly-available virtual machines in a cluster
- A cluster with only one virtual machine
- A cluster with a single host
- Domain controllers in a Hyper-V Server cluster
- Storing a single virtual machine's files across multiple locations
- Geographically distributed clusters
- Using non-virtualized hardware with virtual machines
- Pass-through disks in a cluster

The ideas presented in this chapter are by no means an all-inclusive coverage of the ways that a Hyper-V Server cluster can be leveraged in atypical scenarios. They are intended to address some of the more common questions and to provide you with a springboard to craft your own solutions. Keep in mind that there are some configurations that Hyper-V Server and Microsoft Failover Clustering are capable of that Microsoft and third-party vendors may not support.

Non-highly-available virtual machines in a cluster

You are not required to make all virtual machines highly available just because they run on cluster nodes. There are two acceptable methods to creating non-highly-available guests in your cluster: local virtual machines and restricted virtual machines.

Local virtual machines

Locally running virtual machines is the simplest method to implement and understand. These are configured exactly as though the host were not a member of a cluster. To create such a virtual machine, you can use either Hyper-V Manager or the New-VM PowerShell cmdlet. Do not use Failover Cluster Manager. In order to ensure that the virtual machine is truly local, you must make certain that all of the virtual machine's configuration and data files are placed on storage that is local, preferably internal, to the host. Hyper-V Server will allow you to place the files in any location that the management operating system's computer object has access to, but not all locations make sense. If you want to use a shared location for a non-highly-available virtual machine, the method explained in the next section may be preferable to using a local virtual machine.

By using internal storage for a guest, you guarantee that if its host computer can start and the virtual machine is not damaged, it will be able to start as well. There will be no external constraints on whether or not that guest virtual machine will operate. Such a local virtual machine is useful for mission-critical infrastructure servers that use some form of resiliency that is independent of the high availability features of Hyper-V Server.

You can use a remote SMB 3.0 shared folder to hold local virtual machine configuration files and data. The rules are the same for a standalone host in this configuration as they are for a cluster: the share and the NTFS folder it sits upon must provide sufficient permissions to the Active Directory computer object for the connecting Hyper-V Server host. If a domain controller is not accessible at the time that the host attempts to connect, then the connection will fail. It is functionally possible to locate a non-highly-available virtual machine on a Cluster Shared Volume, but Microsoft does not support this configuration. A non-highly-available virtual machine configured to use remote storage doesn't have the resiliency it would have on an internal storage due to reliance on external factors, but that does not eliminate its usefulness. Such a virtual machine is not bound to the clustering service, so it will continue to operate even if the cluster loses quorum (quorum will be detailed in *Chapter 11, High Availability*).

The drawbacks of a local virtual machine are fairly obvious. They exist in an environment where they have access to Hyper-V Server's high availability features but are not using any of them. This means that if the containing host is down, the guest is down with it. One very important thing to remember is that Failover Cluster Manager does not display these virtual machines at all, so you'll need to manage them through PowerShell, Hyper-V Manager, or another tool. When using Drain Roles, these guests are completely untouched.

Switching to or from high availability mode

The decision you make here is not permanent. Converting to and from high availability mode does not incur downtime for the guest. This conversion requires two steps. The first is to ensure that the virtual machine is contained entirely on or off of shared storage (this is not a strict requirement if the storage is on a remote SMB 3.0 share). The second is to create or destroy its cluster resources.

Converting a local virtual machine to high availability

As mentioned earlier, the first step is to move the storage. This can be done through Hyper-V Manager or PowerShell. For Hyper-V Manager, perform the following steps:

1. Right-click on the virtual machine and click on **Move...** as shown in the following screenshot:

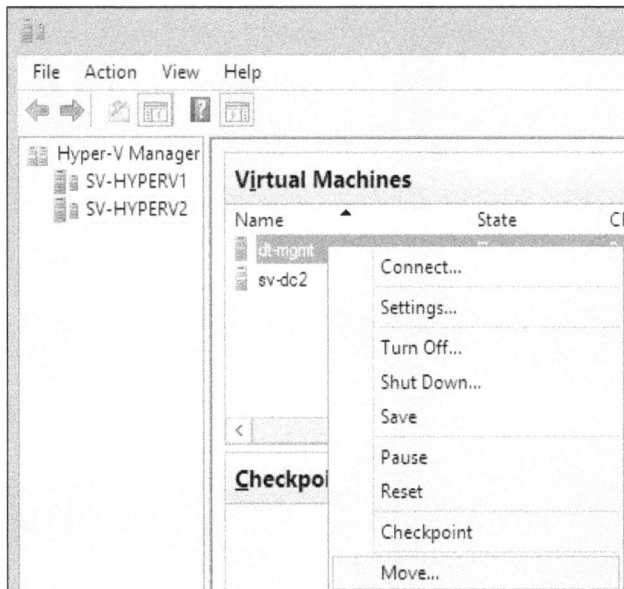

2. The first screen is simply informational, so click on **Next**. On the second screen, choose whether you want to move the entire virtual machine (which includes relocating it to another host using Shared Nothing Live Migration) or just the storage. These steps only cover the selection of **Move the virtual machine's storage** as shown in the following screenshot, but moving the entire virtual machine doesn't substantially alter what you'll see. Make your selection and click on **Next**:

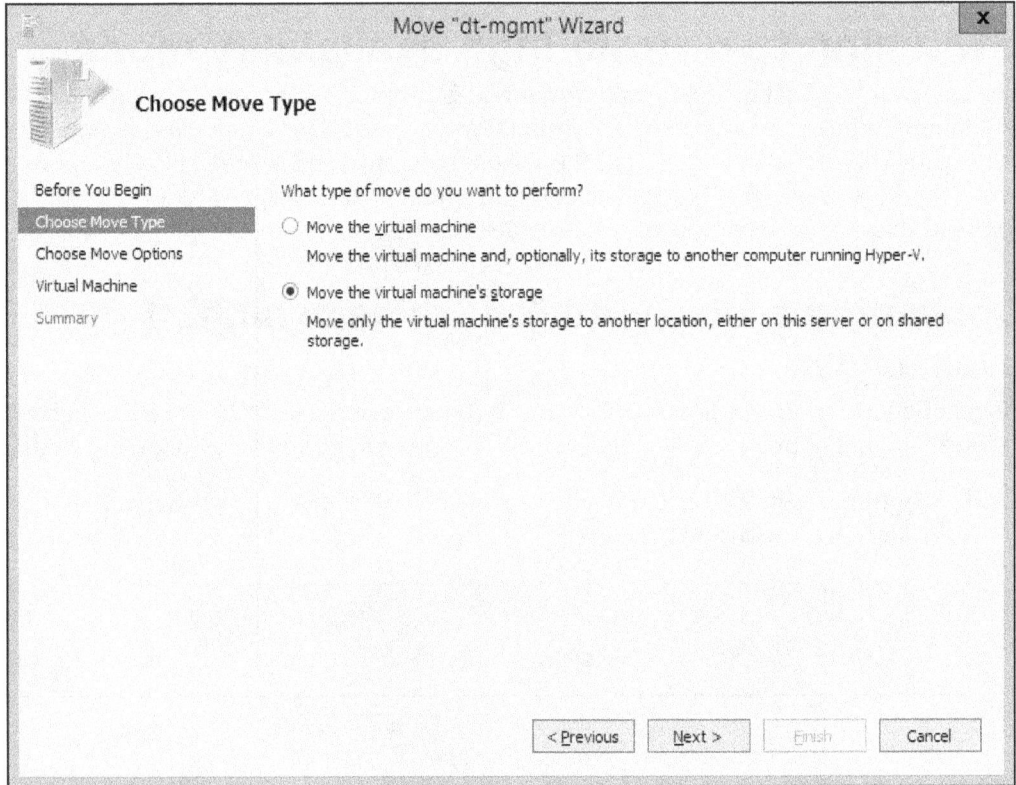

3. It is possible for the cluster to work with virtual machines that have their component files spread across multiple locations. This will be discussed in a later section. The option to only move the virtual hard disks is inappropriate in this situation as it would leave the configuration files on non-highly-available storage, which would prevent the guest from becoming highly available. These steps only cover **Move all of the virtual machine's data to a single location**. Choose that option, shown in the following screenshot, and then click on **Next**:

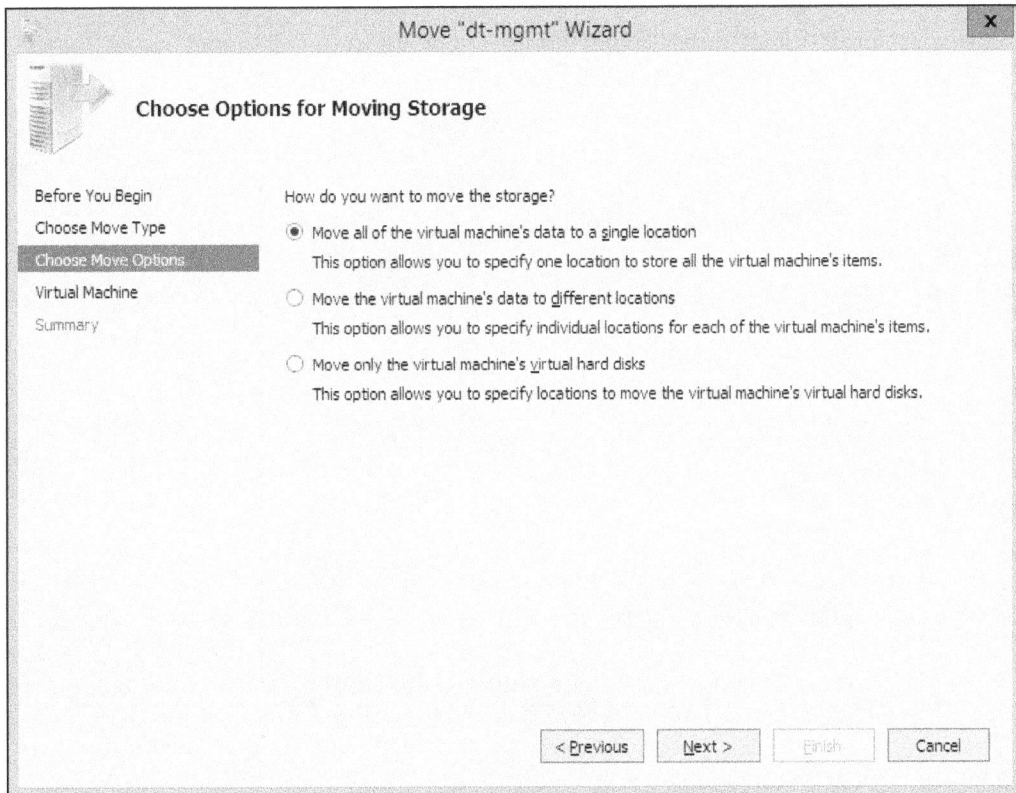

4. On the next screen, shown in the following screenshot, you'll be asked for the location to place the files in. The wizard will automatically create any necessary subfolders; you only need to type in or browse to the root location. Because you are moving the guest to convert it to high availability mode, enter or browse to a location on shared storage. Click on **Next**.

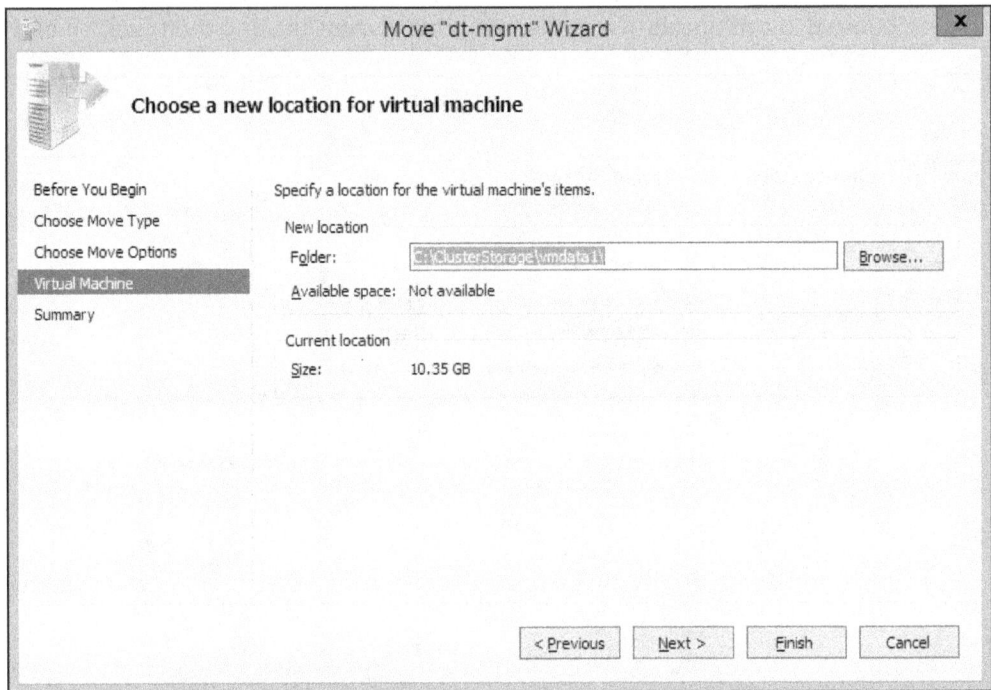

5. On the final screen, review your settings and click on **Finish** and the data move will begin. Remember that this occurs without taking the guest offline.

To perform the previous steps using PowerShell, type the following cmdlet:

```
Move-VMStorage -VMName "dt-mgmt" -DestinationStoragePath "C:\
ClusterStorage\VMData1"
```

If you will be moving the files to an SMB 3.0 share, you'll need to configure constrained delegation for the previous cmdlet to work:

1. In Active Directory Users and Computers, locate the source system's computer object. Right-click on it and click on **Properties**. Switch to the **Delegation** tab.

2. Change the selection to **Trust this computer for delegation to specified services only**.

3. Click on **Add**. In the dialog that appears, click on **Users or Computers**. Locate the destination computer account and click on **OK** (you can enter multiple computers if you have need).

4. If you are moving only the files, locate and highlight **CIFS**. If you are also migrating an actively running virtual machine, locate and highlight **Microsoft Virtual System Migration Service** as well (use *Ctrl* while clicking so you don't lose the highlight on **CIFS**). Repeat for any other computer accounts you added. When completed, your screen should look similar to the following screenshot:

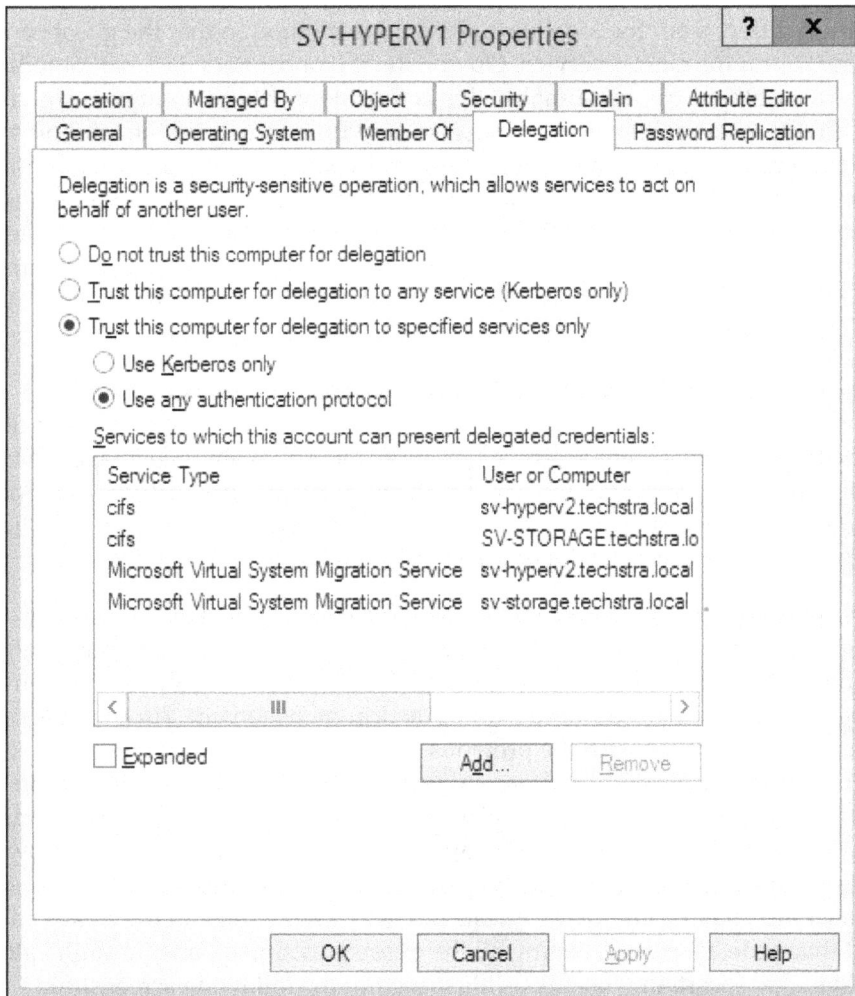

```
┌─────────────────────────────────────────────────────────────┐
│          SV-HYPERV1 Properties              │ ? │   X   │     │
├─────────────────────────────────────────────────────────────┤
│ Location │ Managed By │ Object │ Security │ Dial-in │ Attribute Editor │
│ General │ Operating System │ Member Of │ Delegation │ Password Replication │
│                                                               │
│ Delegation is a security-sensitive operation, which allows services to act on │
│ behalf of another user.                                       │
│                                                               │
│ ○ Do not trust this computer for delegation                   │
│ ○ Trust this computer for delegation to any service (Kerberos only) │
│ ● Trust this computer for delegation to specified services only │
│     ○ Use Kerberos only                                       │
│     ● Use any authentication protocol                         │
│   Services to which this account can present delegated credentials: │
│   ┌─────────────────────────────────────────────────────┐   │
│   │ Service Type                    User or Computer      │   │
│   │ cifs                            sv-hyperv2.techstra.local │
│   │ cifs                            SV-STORAGE.techstra.lo │   │
│   │ Microsoft Virtual System Migration Service  sv-hyperv2.techstra.local │
│   │ Microsoft Virtual System Migration Service  sv-storage.techstra.local │
│   │                                                       │   │
│   │ <  [    III          ]                           >    │   │
│   └─────────────────────────────────────────────────────┘   │
│   □ Expanded              [ Add... ]      [ Remove ]          │
│                                                               │
│        [ OK ]    [ Cancel ]    [ Apply ]    [ Help ]          │
└─────────────────────────────────────────────────────────────┘
```

5. Click on **OK** twice.

Restricted highly available virtual machines

As you saw in *Chapter 8, Performance Testing and Load Balancing*, it is possible to use the Possible Owners setting to restrict which hosts a virtual machine can migrate to. You can take this to its farthest extreme by allowing only one host to be an owner. The end result is a virtual machine that appears in Failover Cluster Manager and can be manipulated like a highly available virtual machine but cannot be moved off of its designated host without first modifying the Possible Owners list. This accomplishes nearly the same effect as creating a local virtual machine, but its files can remain in a shared location without placing your cluster in an unsupported configuration.

This method differs from the local virtual machine method in that the guest continues to be reliant upon the cluster service. Obviously, if its host node is down, it will not be moved to another host; presumably this is the intent behind configuring a virtual machine in this fashion. However, it will also stop functioning (in the method set on the **Automatic Stop Action** tab of its settings in Failover Cluster Manager) if its host is online but loses quorum. Also, be aware that the Drain Roles command has absolutely no effect on virtual machines configured to run on only one host; they do not generate any messages or errors of any kind. If you are manually attempting to migrate, then such a guest will generate error **0x8007138d** (a cluster node is not available for this operation).

A highly available virtual machine restricted to a single host is useful in a few situations. One is when you wish to leverage Cluster Shared Volumes to consolidate multiple computers into a single storage location and you want to leverage the benefits of virtualization but you do not wish to use the high availability features of Hyper-V Server. One example of such a configuration would be mirrored or clustered Microsoft SQL Servers running inside Hyper-V virtual machines.

Another usage of such guests is when the cluster's primary purpose is logically grouping a particular set of virtual machines. In these cases, there may not be any need or desire for Hyper-V Server's high availability, but having all the guests in a single logical location aids conceptual and practical management. An example of such a configuration that mixes with the previous example would be a farm of web servers and their backend databases. The frontend web servers could be paired up with backend SQL servers; each pair is installed in separate virtual machines that share the same physical computer. Both the web application and SQL servers use their own high availability features, and not only do they not need Hyper-V Server's ability to move virtual machines, having any of the guests move to another host in the cluster might overload that node. However, having all the guests in a single pane through Failover Cluster Manager is certainly useful, as illustrated in the following screenshot:

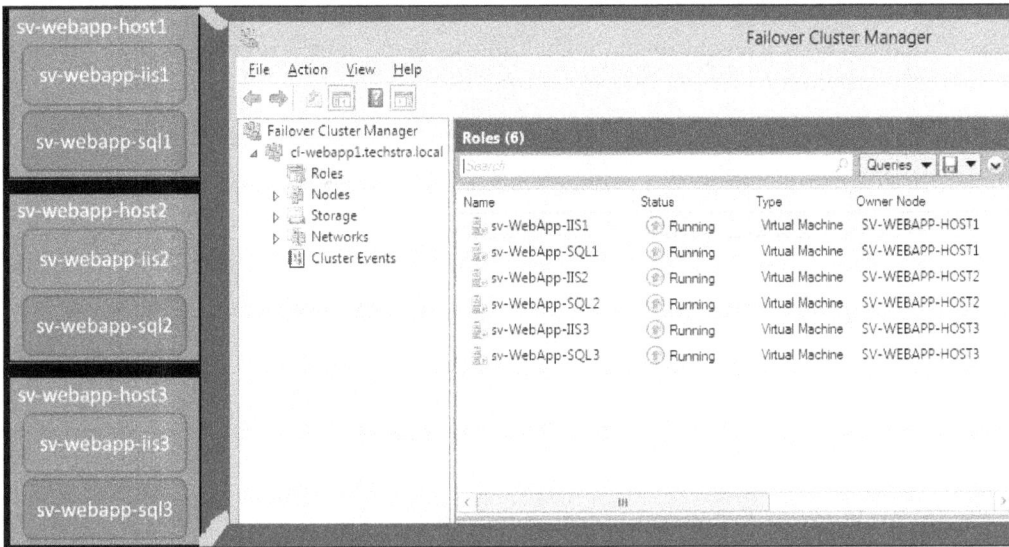

If you choose to restrict a virtual machine in this fashion, ensure that it is well-documented and the knowledge is shared among all individuals who need to manage the system.

A cluster with only one virtual machine

An uncommon but viable use of Hyper-V Server and Microsoft Failover Clustering is a cluster that has only one virtual machine. Clearly, the goal of such a design is not maximization of resource utilization, but maximizing protection for a single guest. The most likely usage for this scenario is a mission-critical server application that requires a substantial amount of computing resources but does not have any high availability capabilities of its own. Be especially conscious of licensing requirements in this situation. Remember that even if only one host will ever have a guest at any given time, guest licensing is tied to the physical processor. Review the licensing overview from *Chapter 2*, *Cluster Design and Planning*, if this is unclear.

Because such a deployment is highly focused on one virtual machine, there are some additional considerations that may justify more thought and preparation than a standard consolidation deployment. Uptime of hosts and virtual machines is always important, but a design such as this implies that avoidance of unplanned downtime for the singular guest is of special importance. In that case, it is recommended that you use automated tools that can respond to system events by moving virtual machines.

The Microsoft System Center suite can give you this ability. You can also leverage hardware and software vendor tools, the built-in Windows Server tools, and scripting to automatically respond to failures. Some examples are as follows:

- A Performance Alert that is triggered when iSCSI connections drop
- A Recovery Action on a vendor's service set to run a program
- A Basic Task in Task Scheduler that responds to event ID 50 from source Mup (Delayed Write Failed) by running a script
- A third-party monitoring tool that initiates a script or command

The first three possibilities will be revisited in the monitoring section of *Chapter 10, Maintaining and Monitoring a Hyper-V Server Cluster*. For vendor tools, consult the manufacturer's documentation and information sources. A sample response script is shown in the following code snippet:

```
# Ping the destination host to ensure it's online
if(Test-Connection -ComputerName sv-hyperv2 -Count 2)
{
  # If the host is online, check to see if it has set a flag to not
allow incoming transfers
  if(Test-Path \\sv-hyperv2\dontmove.flag)
  {
    # If the flag is there, log that we can't move the VM
    Add-Content -Path C:\VMLogs\ScriptedTransfer.Log -Value ((Get-
Date).ToString() + ": SV-HYPERV2 has the don't move flag set")
  }
  else
  {
    # Looks like things are OK. Live Migrate the virtual machine
    Move-VM -Name sv-supercritical -DestinationHost sv-hyperv2
    # Since the VM was moved because a problem was detected on this
host, set the "don't move" flag here
    Set-Content -Path C:\VMLogs\dontmove.flag -Value 1
  }
}
else
{
  # sv-hyperv2 is not reachable, so Live Migration can't occur
  Add-Content -Path C:\VMLogs\ScriptedTransfer.log -Value ((Get-Date).
ToString() + ": Tried to move sv-supercritical to sv-hyperv2, but sv-
hyperv2 was not reachable")
}
```

For the previous script to function, a folder must exist on C: named VMLogs, and it must be writable by the process running the script. A folder must exist on the target Hyper-V Server system that is shared as VMLogs, and that must also be readable by the process running the script. Also, the firewall on the destination host must accept a ping request from the host running the script.

Some tools, such as the Recovery Action in the Control Panel's Services applet, do not allow directly running PowerShell scripts. In these cases, trigger your script from a batch file:

```
POWERSHELL.EXE C:\Scripts\AutoMove.ps1
```

Remember that you must qualify the directory (enter the entire path) that PowerShell scripts are in or they will not run. If the PowerShell script is in the same location as its calling batch file, you can use .\AutoMove.ps1. However, it's better to fully qualify it.

Notice that the script checks for and sets a dontmove.flag file. One of the drawbacks to scripted responses to failures that involve moving virtual machines between hosts is that it's easy to get stuck in a failover/failback loop. Ensure that your scripts are carefully designed, that they leave some notice somewhere of their activity, and that you check their status on a regular basis. Note that the script contains no method for cleaning up a flag file that's no longer necessary, so manual intervention will be required at some point.

> Even the most carefully designed scripts are not up to the task of guaranteeing that a virtual machine will have no downtime, and all incur at least some risks. You may find it difficult or impossible to receive support for a cluster with such scripts activated. They should be used very sparingly, if at all.

Single-VM cluster in a small environment

Another potential purpose of a cluster with only one virtual machine is a very small environment. You'll recall that although it is a best practice, there is no requirement that the nodes of a cluster be homogenous. Usually, this is thought of in terms of the hardware. It also extends to the installed software. Many Windows Server roles are not supported when the Hyper-V role is installed (notably and most importantly, the domain controller role), but some, such as the various file services roles, can be installed.

You may recall from the discussion on licensing in *Chapter2, Cluster Design and Planning*, that if you purchase a single license for Windows Server 2012 Standard Edition, you can run a single virtual machine on a two-socket physical host if the management operating system is providing services other than those strictly necessary for its guests. So, if you have two physical systems in your organization that are running the Standard Edition of Windows Server 2012, they are under-utilized, and they only provide basic services, you have the option of consolidating them into a failover cluster running Hyper-V.

The drawback with this is that it may place you in an unsupported configuration. There is no official Microsoft document that indicates the extent of what roles are and are not supported with Hyper-V Server. The Best Practices Analyzer is the closest official documentation, and it merely recommends that non-Hyper-V-related roles be removed. Alessandro Cardoso, a Microsoft MVP for Virtual Machine, has written a blog post that details known supported roles that can co-exist with Hyper-V: http://cloudtidings.com/2013/04/20/sharing-roles-with-hyper-v-on-the-same-physical-host/.

If you choose to share roles, there are two considerations to be made. First, if you have any problems with the Hyper-V role or if problems arise with other roles after the Hyper-V role is enabled, Microsoft Product Support will likely ask you to remove either Hyper-V or the potentially conflicting roles. Second, enabling the Hyper-V role is a major change to the management operating system. Enabling it on an actively functioning operating system that is running other roles and applications may have very undesirable outcomes. If possible, test in a lab environment before attempting in production.

Where this configuration could be useful and remain in a supported configuration would be if you have two low-utilization file servers (in terms of active access, not consumed space) and an aging but critical physical system running legacy software that you'd like to virtualize. Remember that whereas guests contend equally with each other for all resources and issues inside a guest isolated to that virtual machine, problems in the management operating system can affect all guests. This can be especially catastrophic in the event of a blue screen.

A preferred solution would be to virtualize the existing physical installations and let them run side-by-side in a two-guest configuration. Such an installation would allow all of the machines to have access to Hyper-V Server and Failover Clustering's benefits without changes the licensing needs of the operating systems. However, it is understood that, especially in smaller environments, the ideal solution is not always possible.

A cluster with a single host

Since it has no actual failover capabilities, a single-host failover cluster is normally of very little use in a production environment. However, it does have a few potential applications.

The most common use for a single-node Hyper-V Server cluster is for testing. You can use such a cluster to prescreen operating system and application upgrades and patches before placing them onto your production systems. Another related use is vetting new hardware. Since Microsoft Failover Clustering and Hyper-V Server do not require that all nodes be identical, you can temporarily join new server hardware into a cluster with your test host, ensure it behaves as expected, and then move it into a production cluster.

The second potential usage of a single-node Hyper-V Server cluster may occur while a two-node cluster is in a failure situation. If one of the nodes is lost and will not be repaired, it needs to be evicted. It can run as a single-node cluster until such time as the replacement hardware is brought online.

The single-node configuration also presents a method to migrate a cluster from one version of Hyper-V Server to another. In short, you remove one node from an existing cluster, upgrade or rebuild it to the current iteration of Windows Server or Hyper-V Server, use the wizard in Failover Cluster Manager for migrating the virtual machines to it, upgrade or rebuild the remaining nodes one at a time, and join them into the new cluster.

The migration wizard is not covered in this book, but it has an easy-to-use wizard. You can start it by right-clicking on the root node in Failover Cluster Manager, selecting **More Actions**, and then clicking on **Migrate Roles...**.

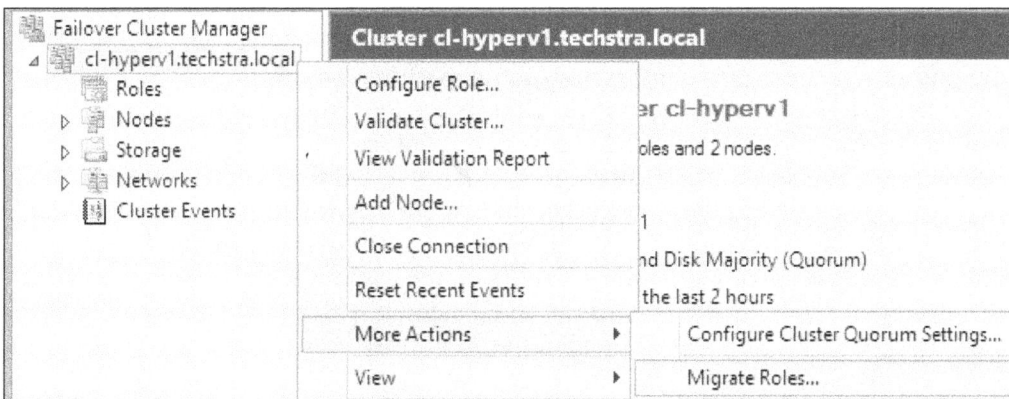

A complete migration walkthrough is provided by Microsoft's blogging team at
`http://blogs.msdn.com/b/clustering/archive/2012/06/25/10323434.aspx`.

Virtualized domain controllers in a Hyper-V Cluster

The subject of domain controllers in a virtual environment does not enjoy universal agreement. You have three generic possibilities: all physical, all virtual, and a mixture. When a virtualized environment is present, the most common deployment scenario is the mixed method. Domain controllers are typically not resource-intensive, even in a high density environment, so performance is not a driving concern. There are a number of reasons that many organizations will choose to maintain physical domain controllers.

Discomfort with virtualization of a vital infrastructure role

The fear of placing something like Active Directory in a virtualized environment is quite real. If there is a general resistance to it in your organization, there may not be much value in pushing back against it. If you have hardware and Windows Server licenses available, it may be more prudent to go with the physical or mixed approach and avoid the fight altogether. As organizational confidence in Hyper-V Server grows, resistance will naturally decline and the subject can be revisited in the future.

If you choose to make a case for virtualization of domain controllers, your task is really to allay fears. One of the more powerful points to present is that Microsoft directly supports virtualization of domain controllers. In the event that there is a problem, you can get help. The second major point is that there are organizations with purely virtualized Active Directory infrastructures, so this is not new territory. Remember that many individuals who are resistant to virtualization of domain controllers are already convinced that disaster looms, so your task may be less about proving that it can work and more about proving that failures will not result in doom: with only one standard backup of the System State of any domain controller, using standardized processes, you can revive a completely failed Active Directory infrastructure in relatively little time. This, of course, assumes a worst-case scenario. We will step through the other concerns and conclude with an explanation of how your Hyper-V Server cluster can prevent the worst-case scenario.

Concern that Hyper-V Server will not start

The fear that a Hyper-V Server host will not boot if a domain controller is unavailable or that it will prevent guest domain controllers from starting is unfounded. The hypervisor does not run in the context of a domain account; it runs using the Local System account. As long as the host can boot, Hyper-V can start. If the guest is not damaged in some fashion, the domain controller can start. If the host is unable to reach any other domain controller while the guest is starting, you may be unable to log in to the management operating system using a domain account (cached credentials usually allows login without a domain controller). You will, however, be able to log in using the local administrator account. From there, you can perform any actions or repairs that are necessary.

In previous versions, the lack of a domain controller could prevent the cluster from starting. That was alleviated with the release of 2012.

Concern that domain controllers will be unavailable

The worry that domain controllers will be unavailable in the event of a hypervisor outage is valid. Using multiple physical domain controllers has always been recommended in order to avoid dependency on a single piece of hardware. The same is true with virtualized domain controllers. Fortunately, a cluster offers this protection.

Concern over clock drift in a virtual environment

Clock drift is definitely something to be concerned about. In a typical Active Directory domain, the domain controllers are responsible for time synchronization for all domain members. The way that any Windows machine tracks its time is by first synchronizing to some source and then using its own internal mechanics to mark time from that point. Substantial clock drift can occur because being controlled by a hypervisor means that the normal operation of those processes may not function predictably. Such drift can be especially problematic for many applications, notably Exchange Server, which are heavily dependent upon synchronized time. Hyper-V Server does have a built-in mechanism for controlling time, but if the host is dependent upon one of its guests for accurate time, this creates a loop that can cause the entire domain to drift unacceptably. Fortunately, this issue is not without a solution, as you will see in the upcoming Windows Domain Time Synchronization subsection.

Concern over effects of snapshots on domain controllers

Snapshots can present a very real threat to a virtualized domain controller. A new feature in Hyper-V and Windows Server mitigates this risk, but you must be aware of the basic issue so that you understand how to address the problem.

Active Directory is exactly that: a directory. It is essentially a large list of all the objects that comprise a domain organized in a fashion that facilitates the lookup of any given object or group of objects. It is called Active because this list and its members can be easily modified at any given time. One feature of Active Directory is that it is multi-master. This means that there can be more than one system (domain controller) that can make authoritative changes to the directory. These masters periodically synchronize with each other through replication. In order to ensure that any conflicting changes end up with the item in its most current state, Active Directory uses **Update Sequence Numbers** (**USN**). These are just numbers that a domain controller will increment each time it makes changes to its copy of a directory object. The version of the local database itself is tracked by an Invocation ID. When domain controllers contact each other for replication, they use these numbers to determine which objects have changed remotely and therefore need to be updated locally.

A problem arises when a domain controller is reverted to an earlier snapshot. When that snapshot is activated, the domain controller is completely unaware that anything has occurred. At most, it notices a shift in the time. Its database is in the exact condition that it was when the snapshot was taken, and as far as it knows, that database is current. It will begin servicing additions, changes, and deletions from clients as normal, but it will increment old USNs and use old Invocation IDs. When another domain controller connects, it will see those old numbers, believe it has already replicated them, and ignore them. Once that occurs, the Active Directory data is inconsistent; this is known as a USN rollback condition. If you believe this has happened to you, you can follow Microsoft's Knowledge Base Article 875495 for information and rectification steps, which is available at `http://support.microsoft.com/kb/875495`.

In the current versions, this problem has been addressed. A new Active Directory attribute, `msDS-GenerationID`, has been introduced. Hyper-V Server 2012 and later provides a VM-Generation ID for its guests, which is tracked both by the hypervisor and by the Integration Services within domain controller guests. If these IDs become mismatched, the hypervisor and/or guest domain controller will take action to prevent a USN rollback. While these present a fairly bullet-proof solution for the issue, they require that the domain controllers be running at least Windows Server 2012 and that the hypervisor supports the VM-Generation ID. The earliest version of Hyper-V that provided such support was Hyper-V Server 2012.

Even if you have both Windows Server 2012 domain controllers and a hypervisor that supports VM-Generation, USN rollback is generally important to understand because snapshots are not the only way they can be caused. Directory restorations by backup software that is not Active Directory-aware are another leading cause of USN rollbacks. No environment, whether physical or virtual, is immune to the risks. The combination of Windows Server 2012 or later and Hyper-V Server 2012 or later actually makes the virtualized domain controller safer than the physical because of the VM-Generation ID.

Concerns over Saved States of domain controllers

Saved States with domain controllers is another valid source of worries. Fortunately, it is (usually) far less nefarious than the other issues. If a domain controller is saved (or paused) for a length of time longer than the domain's tombstone (60 days by default) and an object is deleted while it is in that state, then the domain controller will revive that object when it is started again. This is because even though its database, USNs, and Invocation ID are perfectly consistent, the other domain controllers are no longer aware that the deleted object ever existed. They will conclude that it is a new object and replicate it. This is illustrated in the following figure:

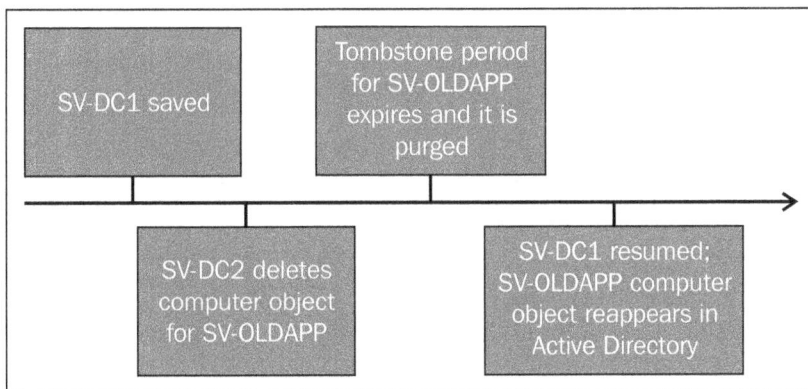

Security concerns for virtualized domain controllers

The final sticking point that may be insurmountable is the possible security risks of having domain controllers live as guests on Hyper-V Server. Worries related to compromising a fellow guest are not valid as Hyper-V Server isolates these guests quite well. A virtualized domain controller that shares a host with a compromised virtual machine is at no greater risk than a physical domain controller that shares a network with a compromised physical computer. The exception is the management operating system. If it is broken into, the attacker has as much control over the domain controller as he or she would have over any other virtual machine.

The risk is real, but it can be overstated. The hypervisor and its management operating system are already sensitive installations and should be well-secured following such practices as restricted access and strong password policies. The attacker will not have direct access into the interface of the domain controller. The immediate capabilities will be only what are granted at the management operating system's console: starting, stopping, and deleting virtual machines and the like. However, the VHD files for the domain controller are accessible through the management operating system, so a highly skilled attacker poses a serious threat. It should be understood that an attacker with that much ability is a threat regardless of whether or not your domain controllers are virtualized. With the understanding that there is no such thing as a system that cannot be compromised, all security decisions should grant greater weight to what is probable to occur than simply what might occur. The aforementioned scenario is exceedingly unlikely.

Implementing virtualized domain controllers in a cluster

While this book focuses on Microsoft's Hyper-V Server, most of the following rules apply regardless of hypervisor. Using these guidelines and processes, you should have little difficulty implementing a purely or mostly virtual Active Directory infrastructure:

- Using the previous guidelines, create domain controller guests as non-highly available. Because Active Directory is multi-master, it has its own high availability feature and does not need Failover Clustering in any way. Use multiple domain controllers and distribute them across your cluster nodes. You may also consider using non-clustered hypervisors for hosting virtual domain controllers.

- Set domain controller guests to start automatically. This setting is on the **Automatic Start Action** tab of the **Settings** dialog in both Hyper-V Manager and Failover Cluster Manager, as seen in the following screenshot:

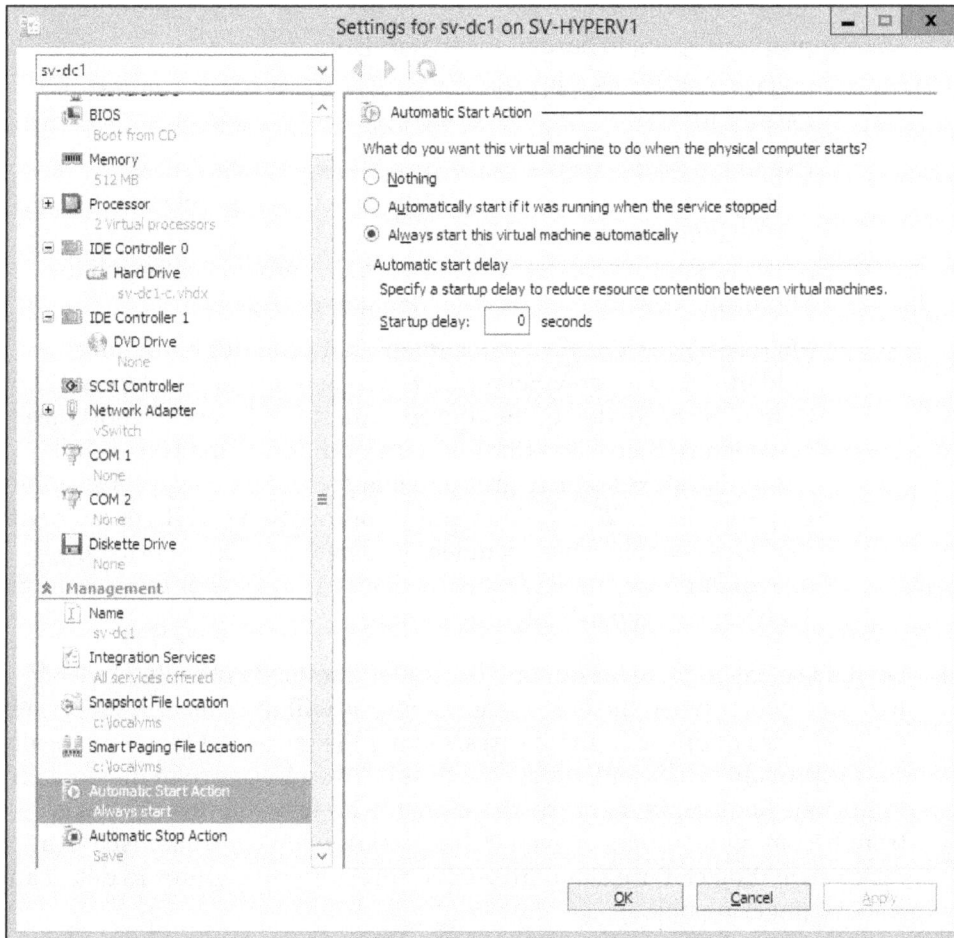

- It can also be set using PowerShell:

```
Set-VM –Name "sv-dc1" –AutomaticStartAction Start
```

- If your domain controllers are all virtualized, have them start instantly when the hypervisor starts, but have all other guests begin starting a few seconds later. Doing so allows the domain controller to start its directory services before the other computers request them. This setting is also on the **Automatic Start Action** tab. To use PowerShell type the following cmdlet:

```
Set-VM –Name sv-sharepoint1 –AutomaticStartDelay 30
```

> [💡 The more domain controllers you have and the more dispersed they are, the less you need to be concerned about automatic delays.]

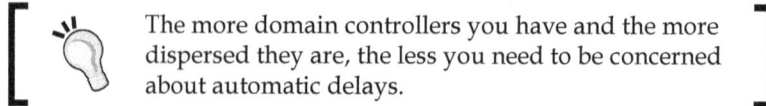

- Take appropriate steps to harden the hypervisor:
    - ° Use the built-in Best Practices Analyzer. This will be covered in *Chapter 10, Maintaining and Monitoring a Hyper-V Server Cluster.*
    - ° Use Microsoft Security Compliance Manager, which has specific settings for Hyper-V Server 2012. This Solution Accelerator is available from `http://technet.microsoft.com/en-us/solutionaccelerators/cc835245.aspx`, or you can search for Microsoft Security Compliance Manager on TechNet.
    - ° Microsoft has published a document that provides hardening guidance for Hyper-V Server 2008. While many of the steps and technologies are dated, the concepts are still relevant. The primary new feature it does not discuss is the addition of the **Hyper-V Administrators** security group that is present on all systems running Hyper-V Server 2012 or later and Windows Server 2012 or later with the Hyper-V role. This document is available at `http://technet.microsoft.com/en-us/library/dd569113.aspx` or by searching TechNet for Hyper-V Security Guide.

- Do not use Saved State for domain controller guests. By default, Hyper-V will save guests when the host is shut down, as will the clustering service if the host loses quorum. In those cases, having the guests set to automatically start is probably sufficient, unless the host is down longer than the domain's tombstone lifetime. In that case, there's really no way to prevent objects from becoming reanimated, even if the guest domain controller isn't in a saved state. You can use standard Active Directory procedures to detect and remove lingering objects.

- Do not use snapshots for domain controllers. Even with the new safeguards, domain controllers should not be running any processes that will benefit from a snapshot.

- Do not disable the time synchronization Integration Service for domain controllers. This is old advice that has been superseded by better preparatory steps as will be outlined in the next section.

- Do not place domain controllers on systems with high resource contention, especially for CPU. Such systems are at higher risk of clock drift.

- If you make a domain controller highly available, be judicious about placing it on an SMB 3.0 share. The storage location will require Active Directory authentication before it will allow the Hyper-V host to connect to it. Using multiple domain controllers with some on internal storage along with carefully planned startup delays can render this moot.

- As with any Active Directory installation, ensure that you are backing up the directory regularly from multiple domain controllers and that your backup software understands Active Directory. Ensure that you know of any special requirements it has for performing Active Directory restores. The built-in Windows Backup tool can be used if you don't have third-party software.

Windows domain time synchronization

Most of what follows are generic steps that can be used in any Windows domain, regardless of whether or not any domain controllers are virtualized. The purpose is to prevent clock drift as much as possible. It is very important to remember that Windows is not, and never has been, capable of real-time clocking. Some clock drift will always occur and it may be more apparent in a virtualized environment. These steps represent only one way this may be achieved and have been adapted from Microsoft's official recommendation, viewable at `http://support.microsoft.com/kb/816042`. Whatever configuration you choose, domain controllers should remain the ultimate authority for time synchronization in your domain and, when virtualized, domain controllers should only receive enough information from the hypervisor to know when an event has occurred that should force them to update their time.

Many of the following steps reference registry locations. Remember that the registry is a potentially dangerous place and care should be taken when editing its contents. All keys in this section branch off of a common root: `HKEY_LOCAL_MACHINE\SYSTEM\CurrentControlSet\Services\W32Time\`. Individual steps will only refer to sub keys under that branch. Perform the following steps to configure your domain for reliable clock synchronization:

1. Choose a reliable time source. Some manufacturers sell hardware that can be deployed on-premises, including some that can be installed inside a computer. These devices are preferred when an organization does not want to rely on external sources for security or comfort reasons. This book will use the servers provided by the Network Time Protocol project, viewable at `http://www.ntp.org/`.

2. Choose a Windows Server system that will serve as the single authoritative system for your network. This system may be a domain controller, a domain member, or even a workgroup member. The key is that it must be reliably available and free from contention that contributes to clock drift. This could be a system that hosts a specially-designed internal real-time hardware clock. Do not use more than one authoritative system; if your authoritative server must be offline for an extended period of time, configure a replacement. If you choose to use a domain controller, the one that hosts the PDC emulator FSMO role is already considered the highest authority in the domain, so it is the logical choice.

3. Set the server to use **Network Time Protocol** (**NTP**) as its preferred time-keeping method. In the registry, access the **Parameters** key. Modify the **Type** value to be NTP.

4. Switch to the **Config** key. Set the value for **AnnounceFlags** to 5. If the connection between the authoritative server and the external source proves to be unstable and clock drift issues arise, change this to A.

5. Enable NTP Server on the authoritative system by switching to **TimeProviders\NTPServer** and changing the **Enabled** value to 1.

6. Indicate what source your authoritative server should set its time from. If you are using dedicated hardware, the manufacturer can aid you in making this setting. If you are using a network target, switch to the **Parameters** key. You will be modifying the value of **NtpServer**. This key is a single-line string, so it requires you to enter all the source servers on a single line. Each entry must be separated by a space. In order for the system to check for time updates at a frequency that you select, each entry must be immediately followed by , 0x1. For multiple entries, this must come before the space separator. So, to use the servers provided by the Network Time Protocol project, enter (in one line):

```
0.pool.ntp.org,0x1 1.pool.ntp.org,0x1 2.pool.ntp.org,0x1 3.pool.
ntp.org,0x1
```

> If you are concerned about DNS spoofing, you may also use IP addresses instead of DNS names. Be advised that the Network Time Protocol project periodically cycles the servers that the earlier names refer to, so you will need to monitor the event viewer on the authoritative time server for repeated **Windows Time** entries that indicate a host cannot be reached.

7. Ensure that it only uses the previous sources by opening an elevated command prompt and entering the following cmdlet:

```
w32tm /config /syncfromflags:MANUAL
```

8. Specify how often you want the authoritative time server to verify its time against the source in **TimeProviders\NtpClient**. Change **SpecialPollInterval** to reflect the number of seconds between checks. Remember that the view on this field is presented in hexadecimal, so you may wish to switch it to a decimal view. Microsoft recommends 900, which is a 15-minute interval.

9. If desired, adjust the maximum amount that the authoritative server can change its own clock to correct a difference with the source clock. There are two settings; both keys are located under **Config**. The two key names are **MaxPosPhaseCorrection** and **MaxNegPhaseCorrection**. Their values set how far forward and how far backward, respectively, that the authoritative server can change its clock to match the source. If a required change is outside this range, the authoritative system will not change its clock. The values are measured in seconds. The referenced article suggests 30 minutes (1800 seconds) or an hour (3600 seconds), but there is no universal consensus. The concern with a small limit is that the authoritative system's clock may drift or suffer an issue that causes it to skew outside the valid range, in which case it would be refusing updates and sending invalid time to your other clients. The concern with a large allowable offset is that the connection to the time server or the source itself could be damaged or compromised in some fashion, such as a defective hardware clock or a malicious man-in-the-middle attack, which could cause a very dramatic time skew throughout your entire organization. The decision is yours; a setting recommended by Microsoft field engineers for domain controllers is 48 hours (hexadecimal 2a300). You might wish to make this a little bit tighter when referencing an external source.

10. Restart the Windows Time service on the authoritative server. This can be done in the `services.msc` console or by typing `net stop "Windows Time" && net start "Windows Time"` on one line in an elevated command prompt, or, if the operating system is recent enough, running `Restart-Service -Name "Windows Time"` in PowerShell.

11. If you did not choose to use a domain controller for your network authoritative time server, choose the domain controller you want to be authoritative for the domain. This isn't strictly necessary, but all domain members inherently trust the domain controllers. As explained in Step 2, the PDC emulator is the preferred option. If the domain authoritative time server is different from the network authoritative time server, follow Steps 3 through 10 again on the domain authoritative system, pointing it to the network authoritative system. Further steps will differentiate between the network authoritative time server and the domain authoritative time server; ignore the difference if you are using only one to perform both services.

12. If you've used the PDC emulator as an authoritative time server, then your non-virtualized domain members, including your Hyper-V Server hosts, will follow it automatically. You can determine what source a Windows machine is using by running the following cmdlet at a command prompt:

```
w32tm /query /source
```

13. To enforce the selection across the domain, use group policy. The exact method you use will be determined by your organization's policy on creating and applying group policies. In the Group Policy Management Console, the relevant settings are in the `Configure Windows NTP Client` object found under `Computer Configuration\Policies\Administrative Templates\ System\Windows Time Service\Time Providers`. They will look much like the previous registry settings. Remember to point the policy to your domain authoritative server.

> Remember that if you apply this policy to your entire domain, it will be set on your domain controllers and possibly the network authoritative server as well, which will override the manual settings that you entered. In order to prevent this, open the policy in the Group Policy Editor, right-click on the root node, and then click on **Properties**. On the security tab, add the **Domain Controllers** security group and, if necessary, the computer account for the network authoritative time server. On both, check the **Deny box for Apply group policy**.

14. Your domain members are now covered, but they're not the only systems in your network. You may also set your DHCP servers to deliver the IP address of either local authoritative time server in their NTP settings. This is option 42 in all standard DHCP servers. Some systems and devices may require manual entry.

15. Ensure that all Hyper-V guests, including domain controllers, are set to synchronize time through the Integration Services. This option is on the **Integration Services** tab in the **Settings** dialog in both **Hyper-V Manager** and **Failover Cluster Manager**. Check the box for **Time Synchronization**. Other hypervisors will have similar settings; only do this if those hosts have been configured to use an authoritative time source. Otherwise, disable their time synchronization and set your guests accordingly.

16. If either authoritative time server is virtualized in Hyper-V, access the root registry location for the `w32time` service indicated before the start of these directions and then access the **TimeProviders\VMICTimeProvider** sub key. Modify the **Enabled** key to a value of **0**. What this does is ensure that the guest's time service is notified by the host when it is rebooted or, more importantly, restored from saved state. It will become dependent on the accuracy of the host clock for up to the maximum duration of the poll interval, but this is usually preferable to leaving the clock at whatever state it was in when the guest was deactivated.

The previous steps are lengthy, but the end result is a network with a stable and uniform time service. If your clocks are not behaving after making these changes, first verify they are using the proper source using the directions indicated in Step 12. Make sure that your authoritative systems are not contending for resources. Reduce the polling interval to make them check more often; this is better performed on the domain authoritative time server rather than the network authoritative system unless it is using a hardware clock of some sort. Also, you may need to open firewall port TCP 139 inbound to your authoritative time servers and outbound from your authoritative network time server to the external source.

Storing a single virtual machine's files in different locations

As you may have noticed by looking at the options in the Storage Live Migration GUI wizard or at the `Move-VM` cmdlet's parameters, you are not required to keep all of a virtual machine's files together in the same location. What may not be obvious is that this possibility goes beyond simple folder segregation. You may also distribute them across different storage targets. This is not an approach to be taken lightly, however. Whereas all the folders on a single storage target are likely to share the same fate in the event of an outage, multiple storage locations result in multiple points of failure. Separate locations may not even behave predictably in the event of a routine startup procedure. Separating a virtual machine's files across different storage locations simply for logical grouping is heavily discouraged. For instance, don't create a LUN just for configuration files and another just for VHDX files on the same storage device. Use different folders instead.

Where file separation makes sense is in configurations that use manually-assigned tiered storage. This is a situation in which you have multiple storage devices of differing speed characteristics that require manual balancing by the administrator. As an example, you might have some high-speed SSDs in one cabinet and 10,000 RPM SAS drives in another. With that hardware at hand, you might wish to place the system VHDX for a virtual machine running Microsoft SQL Server on the SAS drives and have the data VHDX file reside on the SSD system. This is a perfectly valid and logical desire, and configuring your virtual machine in this fashion is supported.

What you must keep in mind is that all storage locations for any given highly-available virtual machine must be universally accessible to all cluster nodes that could host that virtual machine. To be in a supported configuration, all storage for a local virtual machine should be on storage local to its host.

Geographically distributed clusters

As truly high-speed **wide-area network (WAN)** connections become more reliable and more readily available, an emerging trend is the creation of clusters that span sites. As a rule, this is something that should only be implemented after a substantial amount of consideration and planning. In most cases, creating one cluster in each site is far preferable to trying to coerce a multisite cluster to work. Remember that with Hyper-V Server 2012, you can live migrate across clusters using Shared Nothing Live Migration, so you can achieve downtime-free inter-site portability. If downtime-free is not strictly necessary, consider using Hyper-V Replica instead. This is a subject covered in *Chapter 12, Backup and Disaster Recovery*.

Things to consider for a geographically distributed cluster are as follows:

- Inter-site network latency and reliability are absolutely critical. Average latency should be at or below 100 milliseconds; 60 or below is preferable.
- Inter-site connection speeds must be multi-gigabit or higher.
- Ensure that the **Service Level Agreement (SLA)** you have with the carrier that connects your sites clearly documents the expected levels of service and your options for compensation are in the event the SLA is not met. Depending on the purpose of your multisite cluster, outages may cost you more than the inter-site link is worth.

- It is highly recommended that you use a point-to-point form of inter-site link, not a technology that routes your data across the public Internet. Not only is such a configuration slower and more prone to outages beyond the control of your carrier, but it also places your data at risk of compromise. Consult with your carrier so you're aware of the degree of isolation your network has so you can determine if you need to enable inter-node encryption.

- The Microsoft Failover Clustering service does not concern itself with site configurations. You will need to use anti-affinity and/or preferred/possible owners (as shown in *Chapter 8, Performance Testing and Load Balancing*) to keep guests placed near the clients that are most likely to use them.

- There is no built-in functionality in Microsoft Failover Clustering that mirrors or automatically moves storage between sites. If a guest is running in one site and its storage is in another, latency may result in unacceptable performance.

- If an Internet connection is lost for a site, quorum will determine how the cluster responds. However, it is generally guaranteed that the cluster service will shut down at least one site. Quorum will be covered in *Chapter 11, High Availability*. In a nutshell, this is the mechanic that avoids a split-brain scenario in which the same virtual machine is running on one or more hosts. You will need to choose which site will remain running if it is completely isolated; all others will shut down if they suffer the same fate.

If you intend to implement a multisite cluster, it is highly recommended that you work with a manufacturer that provides top-tier storage devices. These vendors have trained and experienced staff that can provide you with storage solutions that will handle the needs of a multisite cluster, aid you in its proper configuration, and guide you past the pitfalls. This book will not directly discuss the storage possibilities of such a cluster.

Networking is another major concern for a multisite cluster. You have two basic choices: the first is to use stretched VLANs, in which your networks co-exist in both sites. The benefit of such a design is that it's very easy for you as the Hyper-V and clustering administrator to configure a network for your hosts. They are set up no differently than if the cluster wasn't distributed. It's not quite so easy for the network administrator, though. The other drawback is that the clusters won't distinguish one site from another. Even with a good inter-site connection, latency will be higher for some connections than others. Without a way to differentiate them, balancing for failover conditions may prove to be tricky.

The second option is to create your cluster so that it spans subnets. This is less work for the network administrator, but more for you. You must understand and configure the cluster as follows:

- In a multi-subnet cluster, the CNO that represents it in Active Directory might be owned by any given node. That means its IP address might change, causing issues for applications that connect to the CNO.

- Virtual machines that move across sites will change IP addresses as well. They have the same concerns as the CNO.

- Since you will have access to multiple subnets, you can change settings on the cluster so longer network delays are allowed before the cluster considers a virtual machine to be down and starts moving it.

Cluster networking with multiple subnets

There are three general networking considerations with a subnet-spanning cluster. The first is how the **Cluster Name Object (CNO)** behaves. This isn't quite as critical in a Hyper-V Server cluster as it would be for other application cluster types such as Exchange Server or Microsoft SQL Server, but you are advised to read through the relevant section and determine how it applies to your situation. The second is the way that the inter-node subnets handle their traffic. The final consideration is how virtual machines are configured and how they react to cross-subnet failover.

Cluster name object in a multiple subnet cluster

If you have all of your nodes in place with their final IP addresses prior to validating and creating your cluster or before adding a node, the cluster creation wizard will automatically set up your CNO to use the proper IP configuration. If you modified your cluster after creation, you'll need to ensure that the IP address dependencies for the CNO are correct. In the left pane of Failover Cluster Manager, click on the cluster name. In the lower section of the middle pane, locate the **Cluster Core Resources** section. Right-click on the **Name** object and click on **Properties**:

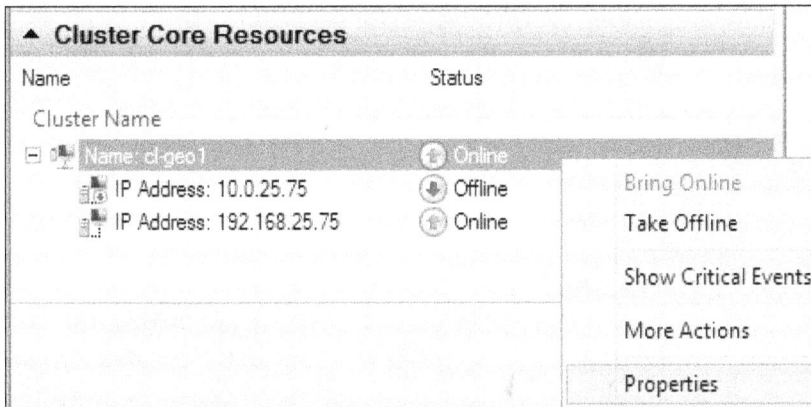

In the dialog box that opens, switch to the **Dependencies** tab. Ensure that all management IP addresses for each node are listed here with **OR** conditions, as seen in the following screenshot:

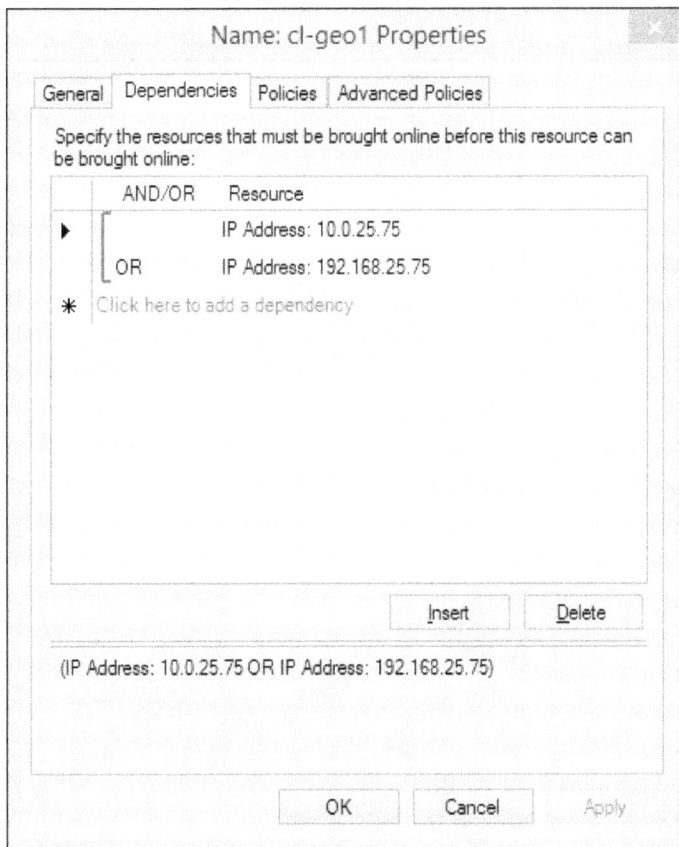

You will also want to modify the DNS record for the CNO so that it has a short TTL. This is to ensure that if it does fail to another node, your management applications will be able to find it quickly. To see what it is currently set to, run the following cmdlet:

```
Get-ClusterResource "Cluster Name" | Get-ClusterParameter -Name
"HostRecordTTL"
```

> Do not substitute the name of your cluster for `"Cluster Name"` in the preceding command. Type it as shown.

The number displayed is the number of seconds that the DNS record for your cluster name is considered valid in DNS. So, if a client computer retrieves the IP for the cluster at 2:00 PM, it will not ask for it again until it needs the IP again after 2:20 PM. So, in the event of a failover, client computers may not be aware of the change for up to 20 minutes. Remember that this only pertains to the cluster name itself; in a Hyper-V Server cluster, this will only be of concern to management and monitoring systems.

To change the cluster name's TTL:

```
Get-ClusterResource "Cluster Name" | Get-ClusterParameter -Name
"HostRecordTTL" -Value 600
Get-ClusterResource "Cluster Name" | Stop-ClusterResource |
Start-ClusterResource
```

A related setting is `RegisterAllProvidersIP`. In its default setting of 0, only the IP address that is currently online will be registered in DNS. If you set it to 1, which you can do using the same method used to change the `HostRecordTTL` value, all possible IP addresses for the CNO will be registered at once. For systems that have been designed to check other IPs if the primary fails, this can reduce or even eliminate the time they require to determine that a failover has occurred.

Configuring subnet traffic handling

Configure the individual cluster networks as you would if all nodes were in the same location. Networks set for Live Migration can locate others used for Live Migration, and so on.

You can use static routes to connect disparate networks. For instance, if the Live Migration network in your primary site is 192.168.15.0/24 and the Live Migration network in your secondary site is 10.0.15.0/24, you do not need to configure default gateways on the hosts for those networks. Having multiple default gateways on a single host sometimes leads to confusing networking issues.

Instead, have your network administrator establish a gateway in each of those subnets that can route to the destination network. In this case, we'll use an example of 192.168.15.1 and 10.0.15.1. On all hosts in the cluster that contain the 192.168.15.0/24 network, enter the following cmdlet:

```
New-NetRoute -DestinationPrefix 10.0.15.0/24 -InterfaceAlias "vEthernet
(Live Migration)" -NextHop 192.168.15.1
```

Modify the numbers accordingly for other nodes and other networks.

If latency will be of concern at all, you'll want to adjust the way that inter-subnet heartbeats work. There are four settings, accessible only through PowerShell: SameSubnetDelay, SameSubnetThreshold, CrossSubnetDelay, and CrossSubnetThreshold. The two delay settings determine the number of milliseconds to wait between heartbeats; they both default to 1000 (one second). The two threshold settings determine how many heartbeats are missed before a failover event is generated; they both default to five heartbeats. To see how your cluster is configured, enter the following cmdlet:

```
Get-Cluster -Name "cl-hyperv1" | Format-List "*Subnet*"
```

To change any of the four, use the following format:

```
(Get-Cluster -Name "cl-hyperv1").CrossSubnetDelay = 2000
```

The previous cmdlet adjusts the delay between heartbeats that cross subnets to two seconds. Just replace the parameter and number with any of the other three that you wish to change.

If your data will cross public networks, encryption of cluster traffic is desirable. Check your cluster's current encryption status with the following cmdlet:

```
Get-Cluster -Name "cl-hyperv1" | Format-List "SecurityLevel"
```

A **0** means clear-text, a **1** means signed (tamper-resistant), and a 2 means it is encrypted. Change this setting just like you would for the previous subnet items.

Virtual machine networking in a multiple subnet cluster

The concern for virtual machines is similar to those for the CNO, except that it's much more likely that your virtual machines are being actively used by client applications. Unfortunately, you can't just attach an IP resource to a virtual machine and have the cluster care for it as it crosses subnets like you can for other clustered resources. Hyper-V Replica does allow for a situation like this, so if some downtime is acceptable in the event of a failure, consider that as an alternative.

The two easiest ways to deal with this issue are to stretch the VLAN(s) that the virtual machines belong to across the sites or to set up the virtual machines to use DHCP. You can use DHCP reservations and **IP Address Management (IPAM)** (a feature of Windows Server 2012 and later) to control what IPs the virtual machines receive. If they are DHCP clients, they will detect subnet changes and request new IPs rapidly. Unless your DNS and DHCP settings have been configured otherwise, this will automatically trigger a DNS update.

If your virtual machines are using static IP addresses, they will not detect the subnet change. Your only options are scripted IP changes or manual updates.

Using non-virtualized hardware in a cluster

The drawback to abstracting hardware is that not all hardware can be successfully or practically abstracted to the same degree. For instance, there is currently no practical way to expose a PCI-Express fax card to a Hyper-V guest. As SR-IOV technology advances and becomes more ubiquitous, this may eventually change. For now, the only guaranteed components you have access to are CPU, memory, network, and disk (and video if RemoteFX is configured). That's not quite where the story ends, though.

The most common device type requested for connection is USB, such as for a faxing device or a manufacturer's hardware-enforced license key. Such a device is problematic enough in a single-host environment, but it is compounded in a cluster. By its nature, USB is inherently a single-host architecture. Even if the USB connection were able to be passed through to the guest, the connection would be lost if the guest migrated. So, hardware directly attached to the host is simply not feasible. However, you do have options. Fibre Channel and Ethernet network connections can be abstracted and exposed to virtual machines, which provides an open door for solutions.

> Hyper-V Server 2012 R2 does allow for USB devices attached to a computer running a remote session (accessible by right-clicking on a virtual machine in Hyper-V Manager and clicking on **Connect**) to be used. This is part of the new Enhanced Session feature, which can be enabled per-host by accessing its Settings dialog in Hyper-V Manager. This USB connection is broken as soon as the client disconnects. It is not the same thing as providing virtual machine access to a USB device connected to the host.

A few manufacturers provide USB-over-IP devices. These devices contain one or more USB ports with an Ethernet adapter. It is connected to your network, and using the manufacturer's configuration tool, assigned an IP address. With the aid of a manufacturer's driver, you can then have a virtual machine connect to that IP address, at which time the USB ports will appear to be local to that guest. Again, because of USB's single-host nature, none of the ports will be available to any other guest or host, but the guest that is using the ports can be Live Migrated without concern.

A less common but still valid use is devices that connect by Fibre Channel. Your hosts' FC adapters must support **N_Port ID Virtualization** (**NPIV**). Using the Virtual SAN Manager (there is a link to this on the right-hand side of Hyper-V Manager) or the `VMSan` PowerShell cmdlets, you can create and manage virtual Fibre Channel **host bus adapters** (**HBA**) and connect them to individual virtual machines. Their World Wide Name and zoning settings are the same as any other Fibre Channel device. If you are not familiar with these terms and configurations, consult with your device manufacturer or documentation. While the virtual FC HBA was intended for SAN storage, it is simply an interface; it can be used to connect to other FC devices as well. However, Microsoft does not provide direct support for such configurations, and your hardware manufacturer may not provide support for connections for guest machines.

The PowerShell cmdlets related to virtual SAN are part of the larger Hyper-V cmdlet groups. For 2012, documentation is at `http://technet.microsoft.com/en-us/library/hh848559.aspx`. For R2, it is at `http://technet.microsoft.com/en-us/library/hh848559%28v=wps.630%29.aspx`.

Pass-through disks in a cluster

A pass-through disk is a hardware storage location that is directly connected to a guest. This is in contrast to using a VHD file controlled by Hyper-V. While popular in earlier editions, the pass-through disk has become effectively obsolete with the continued maturity of virtual hard disks. However, if you choose to use them, they continue to be supported. If used in a cluster environment, there are extra concerns.

Pass-through disks cannot be internal storage since that is not accessible to all cluster nodes. Your choices will be to use an iSCSI or Fibre Channel LUN. Follow the connection directions from *Chapter 3, Constructing a Hyper-V Server Cluster*, as if you were adding the LUN to cluster disks, but stop before bringing it online on any node. Do not add it to Cluster Disks in Failover Cluster Manager or you will be unable to use it as a pass-through disk.

Once all nodes have been connected, add the disk directly to the virtual machine using its Settings dialog in Failover Cluster Manager. A VM configured for pass-through is shown in the following screenshot:

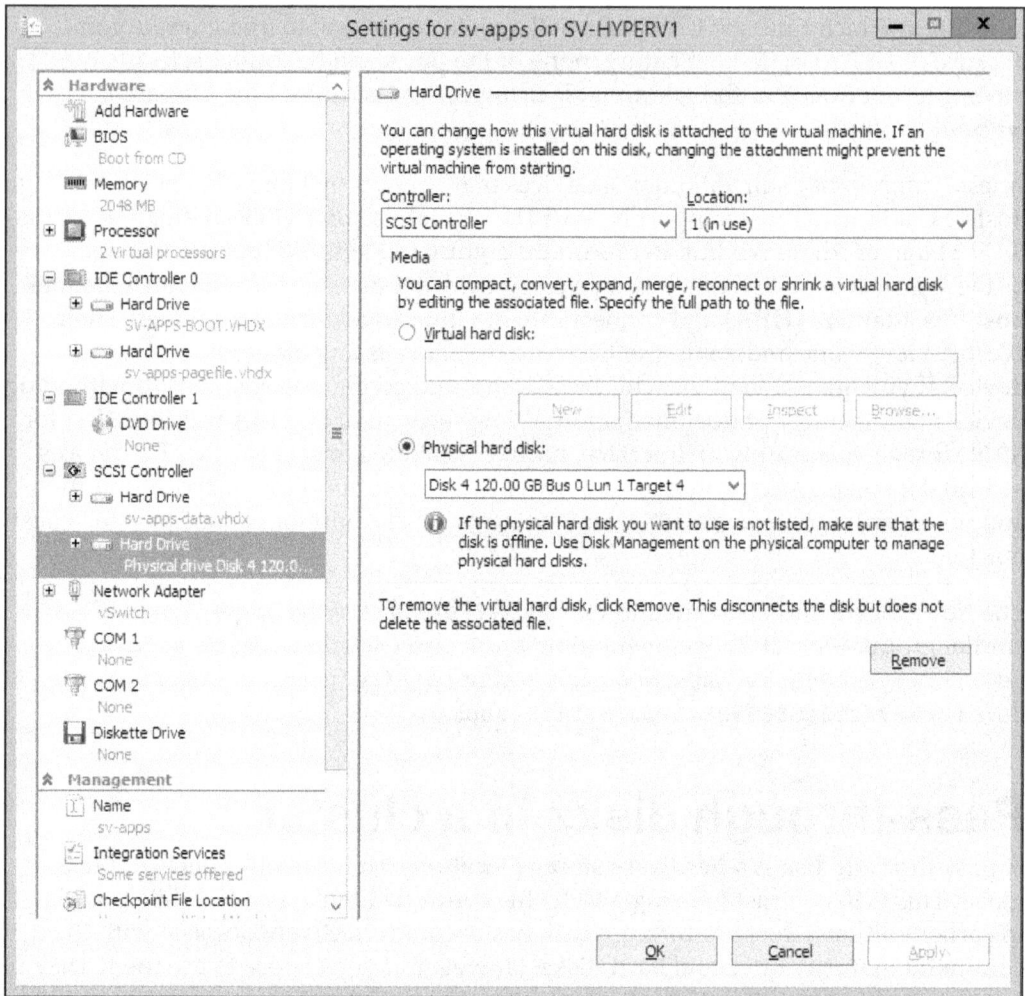

Once attached, you will be able to bring it online in the guest as a normal disk. If it shows up as **Read Only**, you can attempt to resolve it by restarting the Virtual Disk service. A restart of the guest may be necessary.

When a virtual machine with a pass-through disk is Live Migrated to another node, there is an interrupt as the pass-through disk is disconnected from the source host, its ownership is transferred, and the new node brings it online. This disconnect could be long enough that the guest decides the disk is lost, which could lead to data loss, blue screens, or other issues in the guest.

Summary

This chapter took a look at some of the less common challenges that face Hyper-V Server cluster administrators and presented possible solutions for them. It covered a wide range of topics, including non-highly-available virtual machines in a cluster, single-guest clusters, geographically distributed clusters, and non-virtualizable hardware.

The next chapter will show you how to maintain and monitor a cluster, no matter how we've got it configured.

10
Maintaining and Monitoring a Hyper-V Server Cluster

As with all systems, deployment isn't the end of a cluster's administrative needs. Once in production, your cluster will need to be kept up-to-date. Even though you've designed a system that will automatically failover virtual machines in the event of a serious outage, you'll still want to take advantage of any opportunities to proactively respond to situations before they become serious. This chapter will introduce you to methods to care for your cluster and its nodes. It will cover the following concepts:

- Cluster validation
- Best Practices Analyzer for Hyper-V
- Windows Server Update Services
- Cluster-Aware Updating
- Monitoring and metering Hyper-V hosts and guests

Cluster validation

Microsoft provides the Cluster Validation Wizard feature, which is important for two major reasons. The first is that it can help you identify issues that might cause problems for your cluster before you even create it. The second is that Microsoft is only committed to providing support for a cluster that has passed validation tests. If you need to contact Microsoft support, they may decline to aid you with a cluster that has not passed.

When to perform validation

Validation should be performed prior to the initial creation of the cluster, but it should also be performed after most cluster configuration changes. Major events that warrant a new validation report are the addition of a new cluster node and connection to a new storage device. However, minor modifications such as driver upgrades and even Windows updates will also invalidate the existing report. How closely you keep your validation report current is a risk balance that is up to you or your corporate policies. If you run into an issue that requires you to contact Microsoft support, you may be asked to update your validation report or restore your cluster to its last validated status.

One option that makes it easy to keep your report up-to-date is skipping storage validation tests. All tests that cause interruption to active virtual machines are in this category. Gather full validation reports only at initial creation and when changes are made to storage. When any other change is made, retrieve a partial report that includes all other options. It is recommended that you store copies of the latest full report and any partials that came afterward in an alternate location. These are generally sufficient for any support requests that you might encounter. In the event that you do need to perform full validation, the interruption is only a few minutes in duration for most clusters and can be run during a scheduled maintenance window or, depending on your organization's IT processes, after advance user notification.

Microsoft will generally expect a full report after any change is made that affects the cluster's storage layout or environment, which includes storage drivers and operating system patches. If the modification can be verified by testing only one target, such as a firmware update, then you can choose one disk to test and leave the others online. If you add a single new storage location, you can test just that location, which will not impact the other locations. For any changes that have no relation to storage, you can skip the storage tests entirely.

> You can create a small cluster disk and leave it unused for any purpose except specifically for running storage validation tests.

Chapter 3, Constructing a Hyper-V Server Cluster, briefly introduced you to the Cluster Validation Wizard feature. Now, we'll take a deeper dive into the wizard and its reports. To recap, you can run a cluster validation from within the Failover Cluster Manager interface or from PowerShell. The GUI is more detailed and allows for easier modification of defaults. PowerShell is quicker if you know what you want to do.

Running the validation wizard in Failover Cluster Manager

These steps assume that you have already created your cluster. If not, refer to *Chapter 3, Constructing a Hyper-V Server Cluster*. Follow these steps in Failover Cluster Manager to generate a validation report:

1. If this instance of Failover Cluster Manager is not yet connected to the cluster, right-click on **Failover Cluster Manager** in the top of the left pane and click on **Connect to Cluster**. In the dialog that appears, shown in the following screenshot, enter the DNS name of the cluster's name object or the computer name of any one of that cluster's nodes. Click on **OK**. It may take a few moments for the interface to open the connection:

2. Highlight the root node of the cluster in the left pane (the node that is the DNS name of the cluster name object). In the center pane, click on **Validate Cluster....** This is also an option when you right-click on the cluster, as shown in the following screenshot:

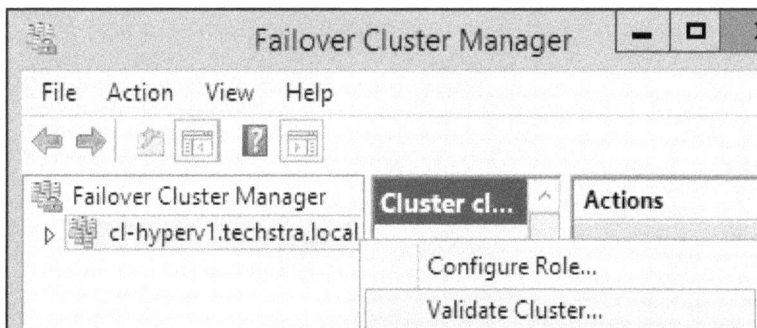

3. The first screen is informational. Read it and click on **Next**.

4. The **Testing Options** screen, as seen in the following screenshot, asks you to choose between running all tests or a subset. These steps will look at the various tests, so choose **Run only tests I select** and click on **Next**:

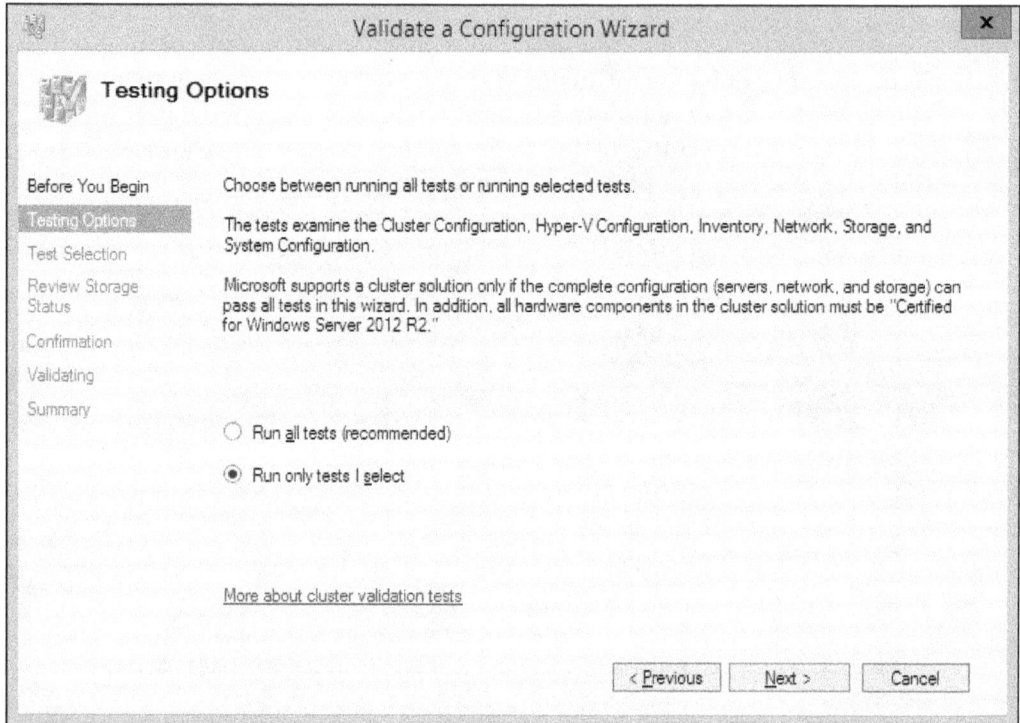

Validate a Configuration Wizard   ☒

Testing Options

Before You Begin

Testing Options

Test Selection

Review Storage
Status

Confirmation

Validating

Summary

Choose between running all tests or running selected tests.

The tests examine the Cluster Configuration, Hyper-V Configuration, Inventory, Network, Storage, and System Configuration.

Microsoft supports a cluster solution only if the complete configuration (servers, network, and storage) can pass all tests in this wizard. In addition, all hardware components in the cluster solution must be "Certified for Windows Server 2012 R2."

○ Run all tests (recommended)

◉ Run only tests I select

More about cluster validation tests

< Previous   Next >   Cancel

5. The **Test Selection** screen begins with a collapsed tree view of the test categories. Here, you can choose which categories you'd like to run. You can also expand the various categories and choose specific tests to run. This screen and some options are shown in the following screenshot. You'll notice that each option is either a **List** or a **Validate** action. **List** items are informational only and do nothing except record information on the final report. **Validate** items actually perform the indicated test. As you select an item, a description of its function is displayed to the right of the dialog box. If you'd like to run the most comprehensive test possible without interrupting any cluster resources, perform all tests in all categories except **Storage**; in that category, select only the **List** items. Make your selections and click on **Next**:

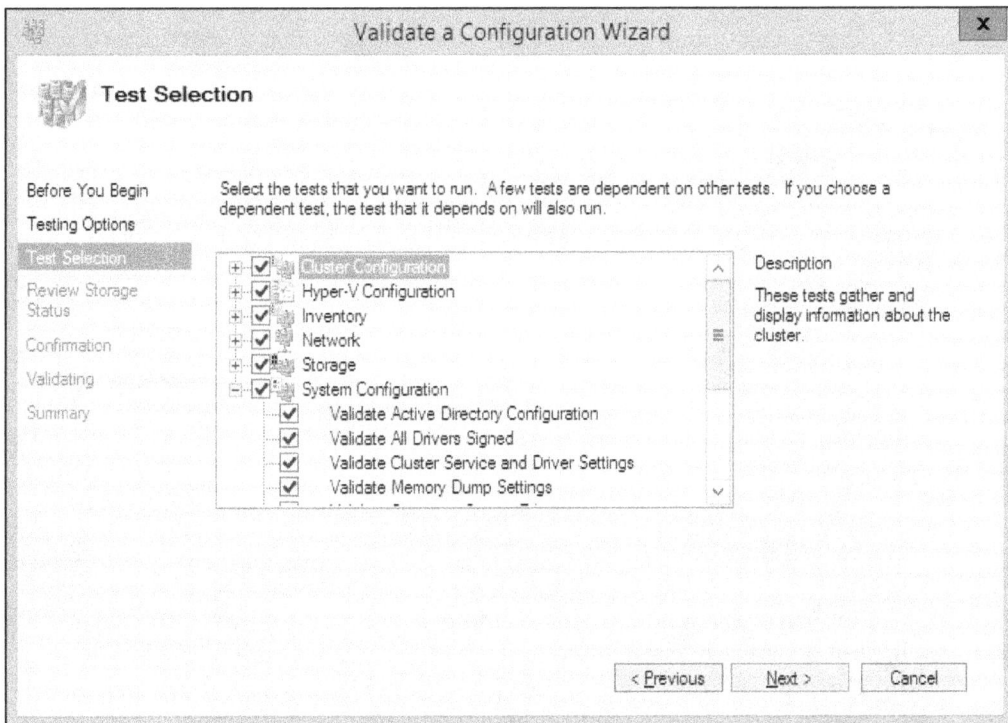

6. On the **Review Storage Status** screen, you're given the opportunity to select (or deselect) individual shared storage locations. SMB 3.0 share locations are exempted as the cluster does not validate those. As you can see in the following screenshot, quorum disks, standard cluster disks, and Cluster Shared Volumes are listed here. Virtual machines running on checked locations will be taken offline for the test. Check (or uncheck) storage locations as desired and click on **Next**:

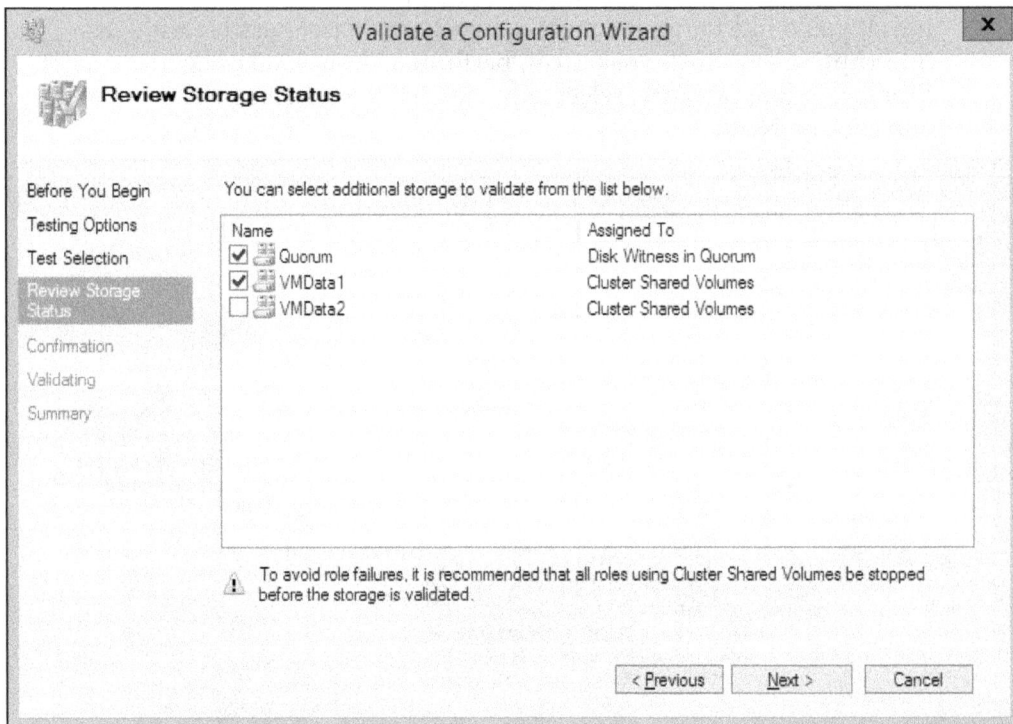

7. The **Confirmation** screen allows you to review your choices. If the wizard will shut down any virtual machines, they'll be listed here in the **Roles to Stop During Testing** section. When the related tests begin, those virtual machines will be saved or shut down depending on the option chosen for them on the **Automatic Stop Action** tab on their **Settings** dialog box. The lower section will show all selected tests. Click on **Back** to modify any screens; click on **Next** to proceed with the tests.

8. As the tests run, they'll show their basic status. Possible conditions are **Pending, Passed, Failed, Warning**, or a description of what the wizard is currently doing. This will take time, possibly a substantial amount. Be aware that storage to be taken offline is kept offline throughout the entire testing process. Hyper-V Manager will show the guests on CSVs and cluster disks as being in a state of **Off-Critical** in 2012. In R2, they disappear from Hyper-V Manager. When the tests complete, the status will return to normal.

9. Once the tests complete, you'll be taken to the final screen. You can scroll through the basic results, which display only **Success, Failed**, or **Warning** for each individual test. You can click on **View Report** to see detailed results. These are saved, so you can click on **Finish** if you'd like to view them later. The section after the PowerShell validation instructions will examine the results.

Validating a cluster in PowerShell

The PowerShell validation is a single command and requires less time to enter than stepping through the wizard. Its primary drawback is that selecting individual tests to run or exclude is tedious. The cmdlet used for validation is `Test-Cluster`. It has a number of parameters that modify its operation:

- `Cluster`: This is the name of the cluster to test. If you use the pipeline from `Get-Cluster`, this can be omitted.
- `Disk`: This is the identifier(s) for one or more cluster disks to be examined by any storage tests that are selected. This field will accept the signature of an MBR disk or the GUID of a GPT disk. It will also accept an array of these values if you wish to test multiple cluster disks simultaneously. To determine this number for a disk, first start by identifying your disk using the `Get-Disk` cmdlet. By itself, this will show a list of all disks the current computer system recognizes. Identify your disk by its parameters and note its **Number**. Use this number in a more thorough request from `Get-Disk`:

  ```
  Get-Disk 3 | Format-List Guid, Signature
  ```

  One of the two fields will contain information. This is the information that will be passed to the `Disks` parameter.

- `Force`: This skips confirmation messages. If any disks were selected for testing and are online, this will take them offline for the duration of the tests.
- `Ignore`: This is a list of tests that will not be run. You can use the `List` parameter by itself to see the possibilities. Enclose each entry in double quotes and separate them with commas. This parameter is mutually exclusive with the `Include` parameter.

- `Include`: The exact opposite to the `Ignore` parameter; this is a list of the only tests that will be run. Its usage and restrictions are identical to those of the `Ignore` parameter.

- `List`: This displays a list of all possible tests to be run. It is used by itself or in conjunction with the `Cluster` parameter to retrieve the possible tests from a remote cluster.

- `Node`: This is a comma-separated list of the nodes to be tested. This is more common for validating candidates for a cluster that has not yet been created. If you enter only one node of an existing cluster, its entire cluster will be validated.

- `Pool`: This is the identifier(s) of one or more cluster storage pools to be validated by any storage tests. You can specify its name as shown by using the `Get-StoragePool` cmdlet or its resource name as shown by using the `Get-ClusterResource` cmdlet. Tested storage pools have the same behavior as tested disks.

- `ReportName`: The reports are usually named `"Validation Report"` with a date and time stamp. You can use this parameter to override that name. However, the location cannot be modified.

So, if you just want to run the entire battery on a cluster, all you need is `Test-Cluster`.

Unlike most of the other PowerShell cmdlets in this book, `Test-Cluster` has a substantial amount of output. The results of a validation of this book's sample cluster are shown in the following screenshot:

If you want to run the tests remotely, you simply add in the `Cluster` or `Node` parameter. Of course, the cluster PowerShell modules must be installed on the remote system. Instructions were given at the beginning of *Chapter 3, Constructing a Hyper-V Server Cluster*. As shown, no disks or pools will be taken offline, but any that are currently offline will be tested. In order to test actively used storage, you'll need to enter the GUIDs or signatures of those disks.

If you'd like to scan all online storage, you can use a simple script that retrieves all necessary values. What makes it simple is that all storage actively used by the cluster, whether it be quorum, CSV, or a basic cluster disk, contains the phrase `MSFT Virtual HD` in the `FriendlyName` property. This fact can be easily scripted against, as follows:

```
$ClusterDisks = @()
foreach ($Disk in Get-Disk)
{
  if($Disk.FriendlyName -match "MSFT Virtual HD")
  {
    if($Disk.Guid.Length -gt 0)
    { $ClusterDisks += $Disk.Guid }
    elseif ($Disk.Signature.Length -gt 0)
    { $ClusterDisks += $Disk.Signature }
  }
}
Test-Cluster -Disk $ClusterDisks -Force
```

Be aware that the previous script does not target a cluster or node, so it must be amended or run directly on a cluster node. Also, it will take all non-SMB storage offline for testing, so perform this during a scheduled maintenance period if you are validating an active cluster.

If you'd like to specify a subset of tests, `Ignore` and `Include` are the parameters that will aid you. Before you can use either effectively, you'll need to know how to specify those tests. Retrieve a list of all available tests by running the following cmdlet:

`Test-Cluster -List`

There are a total of three columns in the output: **Category**, **DisplayName**, and **Description**. By default, the `description` field is truncated. If you like, you can modify the output to list format:

`Test-Cluster -List | Format-List`

The **Category** and the **DisplayName** fields can be used with the `Ignore` and `Include` parameters. Specifying a category will ignore or include all of the tests in that category while specifying a display name will ignore or include that specific test. Categories and display names can be combined into a single command, but you cannot mix the `Ignore` and `Include` parameters in the same validation run. Remember that you must use double-quotes around the item names that contain spaces:

```
Test-Cluster -Include "System Configuration", "Validate Windows Firewall
Configuration"
```

Reading the validation report

Before you can read the report, you'll need to locate it. It is available through the **View Report** button on the last page of the wizard; if that's the method you used to create it. In Failover Cluster Manager, the last report can be opened by right-clicking on the cluster name's root node and clicking on **View Validation Report**. In all cases, the report itself is saved as an MHT file in the `\Windows\Cluster\ Reports` folder on the system drive (usually `C:`) of every node in the cluster. MHT files are archives that contain an HTML file and any supporting media that it requires. They can be viewed in Microsoft Internet Explorer and most other popular web browsers. You can also copy them to another computer for viewing. Unless you used the `ReportName` parameter (PowerShell only) to override the default behavior, the file will start with the words `"Validation Report"` and end with a date and time stamp of when the report was generated.

The following screenshot is a sample report which has been shrunken down so that you can clearly see the different sections of the report. This was taken from a partial test that only looked at a few components:

The header section contains the start and end times of the validation process as well as the names of each node and whether or not they were validated. Also included is a link to a Microsoft TechNet document that discusses validation, including a detailed table that outlines when validation should be performed and which tests should be selected.

Next is a short summary of the results of each overall category. These use icons so you can determine the status at a glance. Each icon contains an image of a sheet of paper with a green check mark, but the lower-right has a status icon: a green circle with a white check mark indicates the category completely passed, a yellow triangle indicates that one or more tests ended with a warning, a red circle with a white **X** signifies that one or more tests failed, and a white circle with a red perimeter and a red diagonal line indicates that one or more tests were canceled. Clicking on the text for a category will take you directly to the details for that category, which are in the immediately following section.

A sample screen with all these icons and links is shown as follows:

The category details section shows each category that was selected for testing and the individual tests that were run within that category. The outcomes are indicated by the same icons used in the category summary section. Clicking on the text of a test will take you to the details of that test. These are below the overall test result section.

After the category details, there is a section titled **Overall Result**. This is the final word on whether or not the current cluster configuration is supported. If the result indicates that your cluster is not suitable for clustering, a Microsoft support engineer may make a best effort attempt to assist you with any issues, but he or she is not required to do so. As a general rule, any failed test results in an unsupported cluster.

Multisite clusters have some exemptions from passing storage tests since they commonly use storage that is only available in one site.

After the overall results, each individual test and its outcome are displayed. These are not marked by icons. Conditions that render the cluster in an unsupported configuration are color-coded as white text on a reddish-orange background. Warnings are in black text on a yellow background. All other entries are black text on alternating gray backgrounds.

In most cases, any warnings or errors include sufficient information for you to take corrective action. For instance, if any virtual machine has Integration Components installed but they are not at the same level as the host, an error will be displayed that indicates which guests are out of date. In other cases, warnings will be displayed when a condition cannot be tested.

Warnings will not prevent you from successfully running a cluster, nor will they leave you in an unsupported configuration. It is not necessary to try to eliminate every single warning. As an example, if you use multiple adapters for iSCSI and choose not to place them into separate subnets, the validation report will return warnings that can be ignored. Do investigate every warning message to see if there is a situation that can be rectified.

Do not assume that because a cluster is functional that it is valid or that an unsupported configuration cannot be functional. The demo cluster used in the writing of this book used one node running Windows Server Datacenter Edition and one node running Hyper-V Server. The validation tool marked this cluster as unsupported because it mixes different operating systems. Builds such as these are acceptable for test and training scenarios, but never deploy a cluster that has failed validation into production.

Other cluster reports

The validation report isn't the only file stored in `\Windows\Cluster\Reports`, although it is the only report run on-demand. The other files are:

- `AddNodes.mht`: If a node is added to the cluster after it has been created, this file will be generated. It is overwritten at each new add.

- `Cluster.log`: Cluster events for the past three months are saved in this file.

- `CreateCluster.mht`: This file contains the results of all steps from initial cluster creation.

- `HAVirtualMachine.mht`: If you use Failover Cluster Manager to convert an existing virtual machine to a highly available role, the results of each step will be logged in this file. Each new conversion overwrites this file.

- `QuorumConfiguration.mht`: If you reconfigure the quorum mode, this file shows what was changed and the outcome.

- `ValidateStorage.log`: The storage validation process is quite involved. All tests and their results from each storage validation are saved in this file. It contains much more detail than the standard validation report. The contents of this file are appended to on each run, not overwritten.

Best Practices Analyzer for Hyper-V

The 2012 series of server products provide a **Best Practices Analyzer (BPA)** right out of the box. One of these analyzers is designed specifically for Hyper-V. It can be invoked through the GUI using Server Manager or from PowerShell.

Hyper-V Best Practices Analyzer in Server Manager

The built-in Server Manager console that ships with Windows Server 2012 includes a number of Best Practices Analyzers for many Windows Server roles. Among those is the Hyper-V role. The server does not need any special features or roles installed in order to analyze the Hyper-V role on another system. Remote systems will need to be added to the local list of servers, however. In order to do this:

1. Start on Server Manager's **Dashboard** page. In the center pane, click on **(3) Add other servers to manage**.

2. In the **Add Servers** dialog, enter the server name or a beginning portion of it, in the **Name (CN)** field and click on **Find Now**. If your hosts have similar names, you can enter the common portion of them and they'll all appear in the lower-left box as seen in the following screenshot:

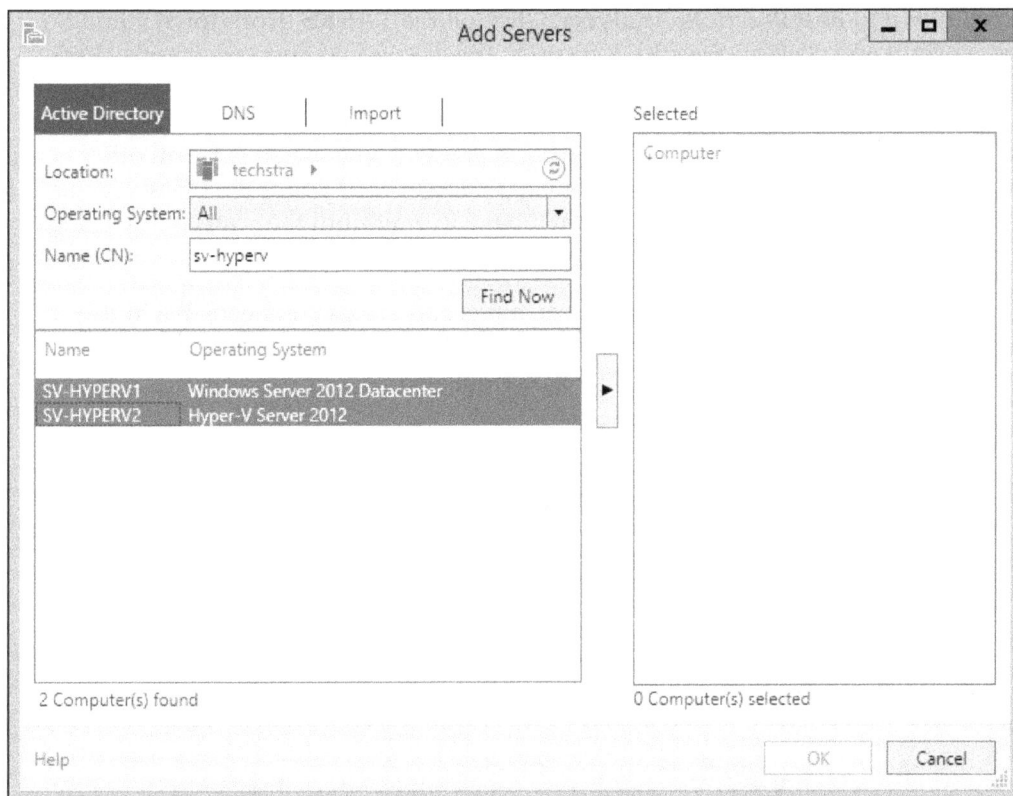

> Server Manager will connect to servers running previous versions of Windows, but not all options will be available.

3. Use the rectangular box with the arrow in the center of the dialog box to move servers from the left to the **Selected** box on the right. Once you are satisfied with your selections, click on **OK**.

Once all the machines are added and their roles have been scanned, a new **Hyper-V** selection will appear on the left of the main **Server Manager** screen along with all the other options and roles if it wasn't there already. Click on it to switch to that tab.

Because your Hyper-V Server computers are in a cluster, you'll see the cluster name object computer account in addition to the host computer accounts. The computer account that is selected is the object that all the following sub windows are reading from, so if the cluster name object is highlighted, the active item will be the node that currently hosts the CNO. The analyzer allows you to select all the servers you wish to scan, so it is not necessary to pick any particular object.

Scroll down to **Best Practices Analyzer**. Click on the **TASKS** drop-down menu on the far right and click on **Start BPA Scan**. In the dialog that appears, place a check next to the server(s) you wish to scan and click on **Start Scan**. A small blue and white progress bar directly above the BPA output window in Server Manager will start to scroll. The analysis will run as a background process, so you can perform other tasks while it runs and even close Server Manager. However, if you leave this screen and return, the progress window stops. You'll have to wait until the scan completes and the interface updates before the results will be visible.

Once the scan is finished, all detected warnings and errors will be visible in this pane. Selecting an item will split the pane and show you details for that particular message, as you can see in the following screenshot:

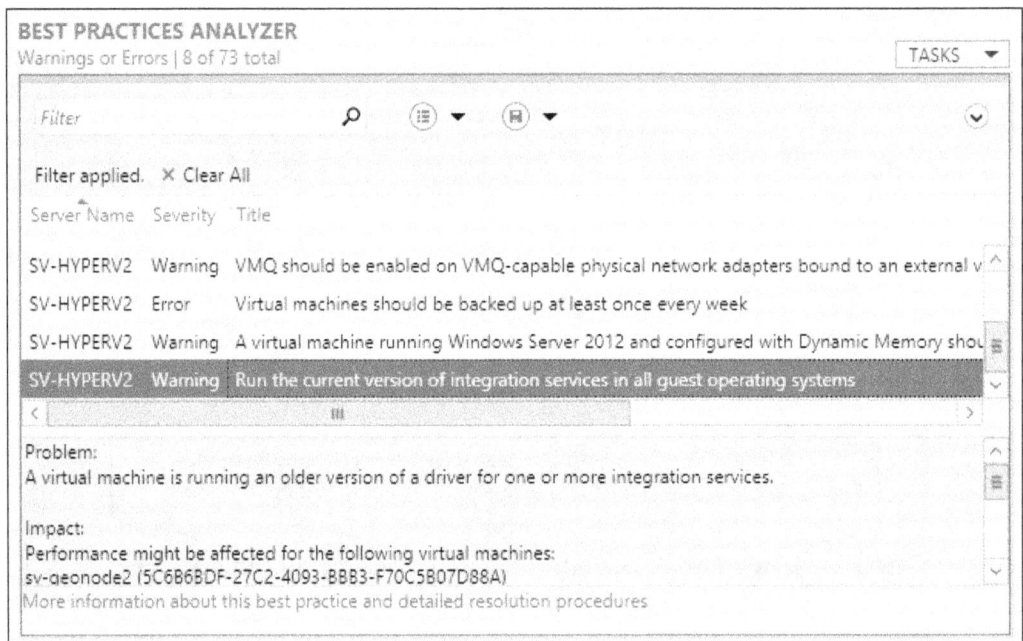

As seen at the bottom of the screenshot, each item presents a clickable link that allows you to find more information about the item. These can help you find ways to reconcile any issues that the analyzer finds.

> Remember that Best Practices are not hard rules. They are guidelines that result in successful operation in the majority of cases in which Microsoft's engineers and community experts have shared experiences. You are not required to satisfy every item. However, errors generally indicate a serious problem that should be addressed.

The BPA view defaults to warnings and errors only. If you'd like to see everything that the analyzer checked and found, click on the small down arrow in the circle right below the **TASKS** menu on the right-hand side of the screen. This will expose the filter where you can change the criteria that determine what is displayed. By default, an included filter is **and Severity does not equal Information**, which is why only warnings and errors appear. You can click the **x** to the right of any filter to remove it. You can also click on **Add criteria** to add more filters. The default filters are shown in the following screenshot:

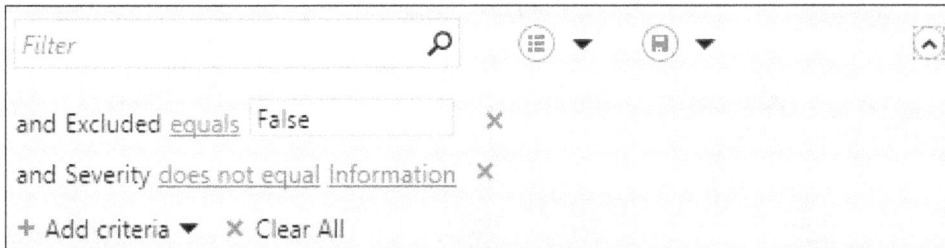

The icon with three dots and three lines immediately to the right of the **Filter** text box in the previous screenshot allows you to choose between predefined and saved filters. If you create a filter that you'd like to use again, you can use the button with the disk icon to name and save the current filter selections.

As you address concerns that the BPA highlights, run the analyzer again to update the results. There is, unfortunately, no way to save the entire output of a BPA scan using Server Manager. You can, however, right-click on any item in the list and choose **Copy** to place the contents of the line item on the clipboard, or you can click **Copy Results Properties** to place the contents of the item's extended output to the clipboard. The XML files that contain the results are stored in the `\Windows\Logs\` BPA folder on the system drive. The PowerShell options grant the ability to output the results.

Hyper-V Best Practices Analyzer in PowerShell

This book only covers the Hyper-V BPA, but there are a number of other analyzers available. A single set of unified PowerShell commands controls them all. Unfortunately, the online documentation set is not complete. You can use `Get-Help` with the four BPA cmdlets: `Get-BpaModel`, `Get-BpaResult`, `Invoke-BpaModel`, and `Set-BpaResult` for the most up-to-date information.

To start a Hyper-V BPA scan on a remote system, run the following cmdlet:

```
Invoke-BpaModel -ComputerName sv-hyperv2 -ModelId Microsoft/Windows/
Hyper-V -RepositoryPath \\sv-storage\bparesults\hyperv2
```

You can skip the `ComputerName` parameter if you are running on the local system. `RepositoryPath` allows you to change the output folder and is optional, although you may have trouble viewing the results remotely if they are not in an easily accessible location. The location specified by `RepositoryPath` must exist.

In order to review the result generated by the previous cmdlet, run the following cmdlet:

```
Get-BpaResult -ModelId Microsoft/Windows/Hyper-V -RepositoryPath \\
sv-storage\bparesults\hyperv2
```

As with BPA in Server Manager, only the latest BPA results are displayed. You can use the `All` parameter to retrieve every report of the specified `ModelId`.

Using the PowerShell approach grants you the ability to format the output. You can see the results in a grid pattern (GUI installations only):

```
Get-BpaResult -ModelId Microsoft/Windows/Hyper-V | Out-GridView
```

The results can be saved to a CSV file:

```
Get-BpaResult -ModelId Microsoft/Windows/Hyper-V | ConvertTo-Csv |
Out-File "C:\BPAResults\Hyperv1BPA.csv"
```

An HTML file is also possible:

```
Get-BpaResult -ModelId Microsoft/Windows/Hyper-V | ConvertTo-Html |
Out-File "C:\BPAResults\Hyperv1BPA.html"
```

Updating Hyper-V Server hosts

Keeping systems up-to-date on patches for security and stability is a critical requirement for the data center, but it can also be a burden on administrators. With a cluster of Hyper-V Server 2012 systems, you can combine new capabilities with mature solutions to reduce the workload and eliminate the downtime involved with patching. This new capability is provided by CAU in conjunction with Windows Update. You can extend your control over patch acquisition and deployment using **Windows Server Update Services (WSUS)** to act as an intermediary between your systems and Windows Update.

System Center Virtual Machine Manager can also handle cluster patching.

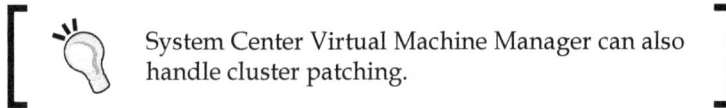

Typically, Windows Update and WSUS make sense to introduce first, since CAU relies on them as a source. However, these are both well-known technologies that most administrators already have at least some familiarity with. CAU will require a different configuration than most administrators are used to, so it will be discussed first.

When Hyper-V Server is updated, the Integration Services may also be updated. Use the Hyper-V Best Practices Analyzer to quickly determine if your guests are using current Integration Components.

Cluster-Aware Updating

The new **Cluster-Aware Updating** (**CAU**) feature of Windows Server 2012 has been designed specifically to automate the patching of clustered systems without causing downtime for clustered services. In the past, cluster patching was performed manually, by script, or automatically with some downtime as rebooting nodes stopped their guests. CAU automatically chooses the node with the fewest running roles: it drains its roles, patches and reboots it, fails its roles back, and then moves on to the next node. This cycle repeats until all nodes are updated. If it encounters any issues along the way, the entire process is halted.

Configuring Cluster-Aware Updating

The CAU role can be enabled through a GUI or PowerShell. You will need to have installed the Failover Clustering management tools in order to access CAU. *Chapter 3, Constructing a Hyper-V Server Cluster*, included a section on installing the clustering and other related tools.

CAU performs its functions by using its own Active Directory computer account for the cluster. If desired, you can prestage this account. To do so, using Active Directory Users and Computers or the New-ADComputer cmdlet, create a computer account. You can use any name you like, although it is recommended that it be identifiable as related to CAU and the cluster it applies to (for example, CAU-Hyperv1). You can place it anywhere you like. The organizational unit that contains the existing cluster name object is where the wizard would create the account, so this is a known safe location. Once the account is created, disable it. Unless your organization's security requirements necessitate it, prestaging is not recommended because it gains you very little while adding to the steps you must take.

Whether you prestage or not, you need to modify the **organizational unit (OU)** where the current cluster name object resides so that the cluster's computer object has the **Create Computer Objects** and **Read All Properties** permissions. If you don't want to dive all the way into the advanced security settings, the **Read All Properties** permission is part of the default permissions granted when the computer account is added to the ACL. Granting **Create all child objects** will grant permissions including **Create Computer Objects**. The following screenshot shows the security tab of an OU configured in this fashion:

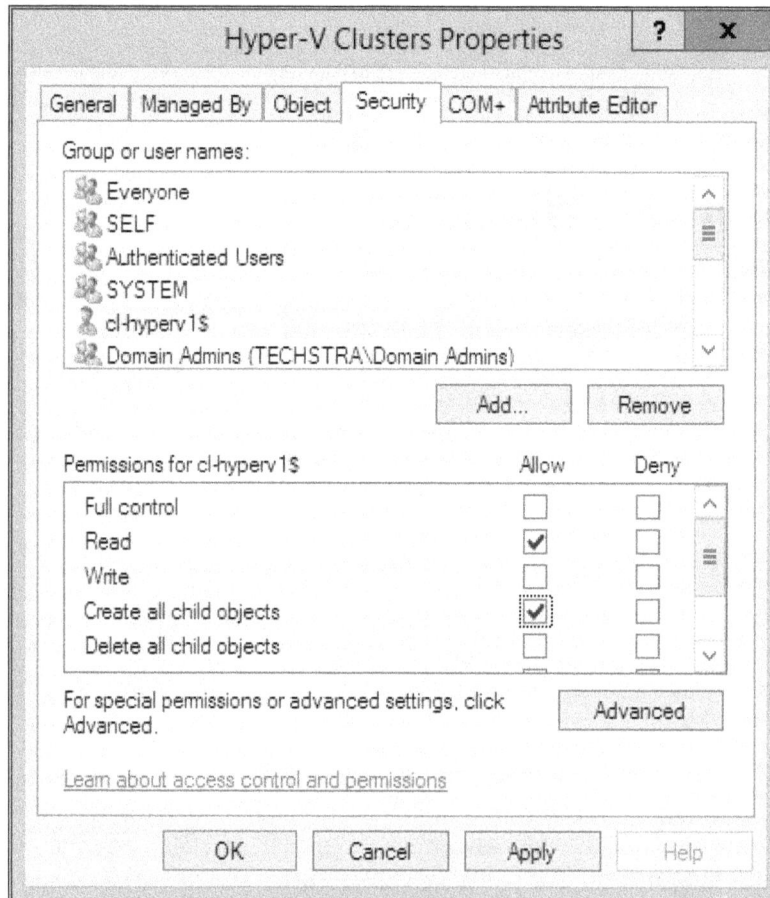

> Prestaging requires extra permissions. Microsoft's instructions indicate that you only need to assign the same permissions to the prestaged computer account as used for the cluster's account, but testing has shown this to be insufficient. Granting **Full Control** does work. All permissions can be rescinded once the CAU role has been enabled.

Enabling CAU using the GUI

To begin, open the Cluster-Aware Updating application. It can be found in **Administrative Tools** from the Start screen or the **Control Panel**. It can also be found in Server Manager in the Tools window. R2 adds a link to the main screen in Failover Cluster Manager when you click on the cluster name. In the **Connect to a failover cluster** combo box, click on the drop-down menu and select your cluster or type its name. Click on the **Connect** button. Your screen should now look similar to the following screenshot:

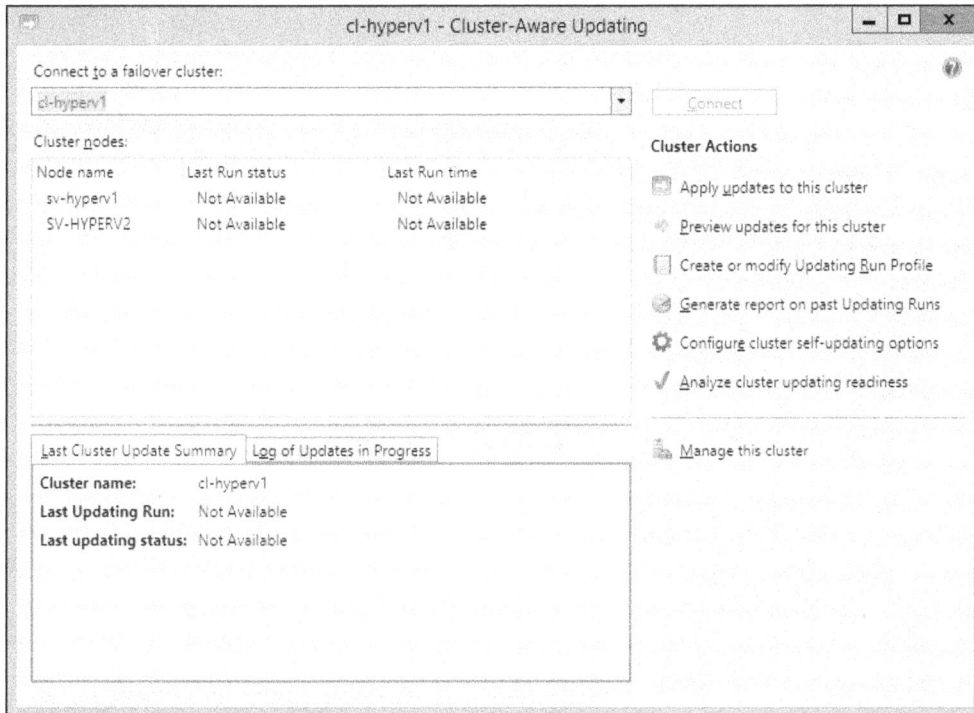

At the bottom of the list of actions on the right, click on **Analyze cluster updating readiness**. In the results box, look for warnings and errors. Because you have not yet installed the CAU role, ignore any error that indicates CAU is not installed. If you receive an error that **The machine proxy on each failover cluster node should be set to a local proxy server** and your Hyper-V Server hosts do not need a proxy to reach your WSUS host, you may ignore the error. If the test indicates that you must enable a firewall rule for remote shutdown, first verify that this does not conflict with your organization's security policies. In the Windows Firewall with Advanced Security applet (found in the same location as Cluster-Aware Updating), find and enable the rule group named **Remote Shutdown**.

Once you've corrected any prohibitive issues, click on **Configure cluster self-updating options** at the bottom of the list of actions to the right of the main CAU screen. Follow the wizard:

1. The first screen is informative. Read its contents and click on **Next**.

2. Check the first box to add the role. If you've prestaged the computer account, check that box and enter the name of the account you created. Click on **Next**. This screen appears as follows:

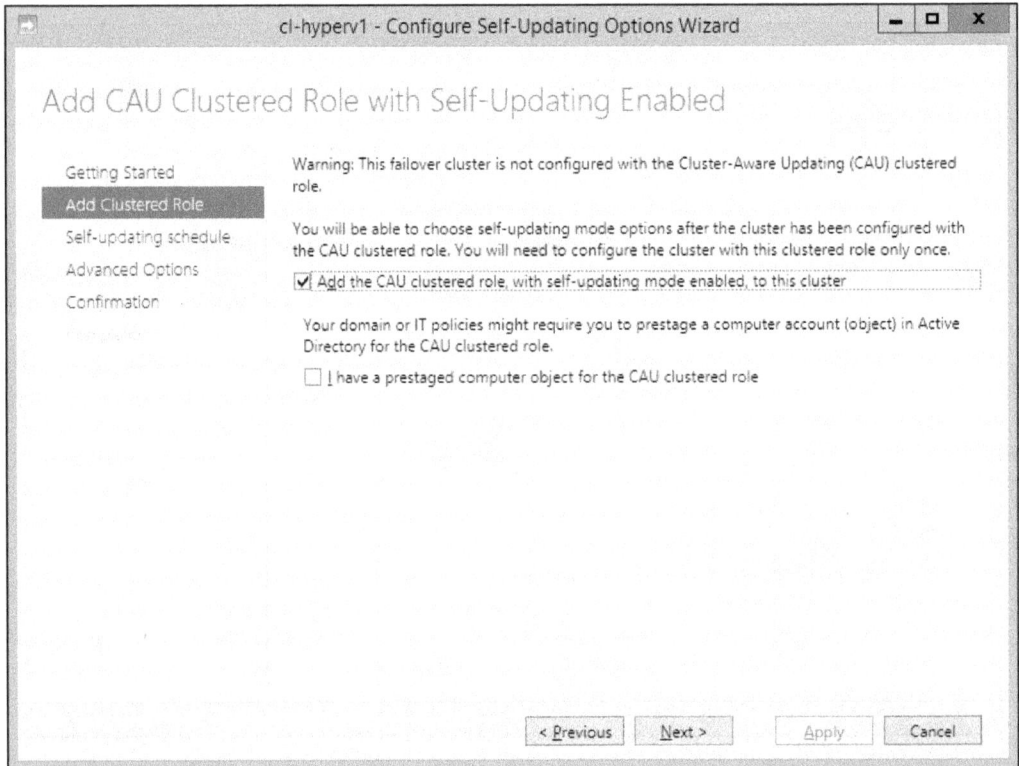

3. Choose your scheduling option according to your corporate policy. Remember that standard Windows updates are released on the second Tuesday of every month (called Patch Tuesday). Click on **Next**. This screen is shown as follows:

4. The **Advanced Options** screen, shown in the following screenshot, offers many ways to control CAU's operation. You are not required to change any of them. The default configuration applies every patch that is applicable to the cluster nodes. Click on the **Learn more about profile options** link near the top of the window to be taken to the help file. If the help file provides insufficient information, it also contains links to online sites that go into further detail. Make any desired changes and click on **Next**:

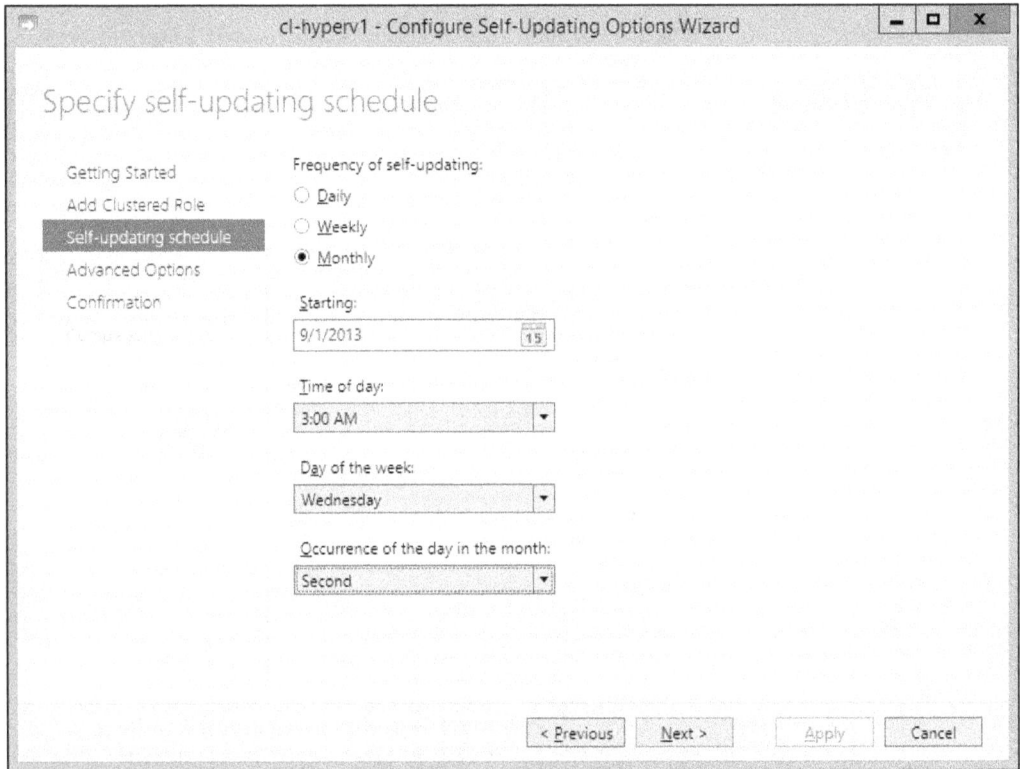

5. The **Confirmation** screen includes two portions. The first is a summary of all the items you selected. At the bottom, in the **Command to run** field, the PowerShell cmdlet that the wizard will call is displayed with all options. The following screenshot has been scrolled to this section. You can select and copy the contents of this field in the event that you wish to study it, modify it, and use it or anything similar again. Review your settings and click on **Previous** to change them or **Apply** to enable the role with these options:

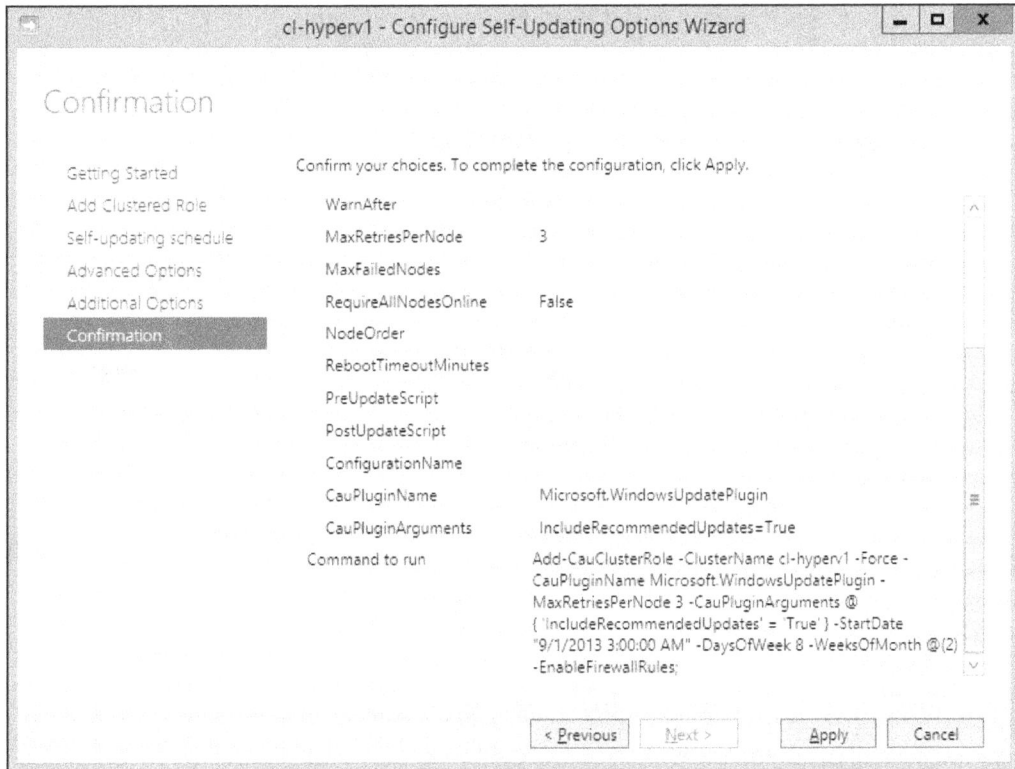

Once CAU has been enabled, you can use the other links in the main screen to work with the role. You can use the **Apply updates to this cluster** link to perform a manual update. Be aware that you cannot close the interface at any time during a manual update or the update will be canceled. This does not apply to scheduled runs.

Enabling CAU using PowerShell

Start by running `Test-CauSetup` on any node in the cluster to check for any condition that might prevent you from successfully enabling CAU. Look specifically for warnings and errors. Because you have not yet installed the CAU role, ignore any error that indicates CAU is not installed. If you receive an error that **The machine proxy on each failover cluster node should be set to a local proxy server** and your Hyper-V Server hosts do not require a proxy to reach your WSUS host, you may ignore the error. If the test indicates that you must enable a firewall rule for remote shutdown, first verify that this does not conflict with your organization's security policies. The steps to enable CAU will include turning this firewall rule on.

`Add-CauClusterRole` is the cmdlet used to enable CAU, and it has a great many options. They are well-described on the documentation page viewable at http://technet.microsoft.com/en-us/library/hh847235.aspx. If you like, you can use the wizard as described in the previous section to structure the cmdlet specifically to suit your needs, then copy and paste it to run it manually. The following is a sample:

```
Add-CauClusterRole -ClusterName cl-hyperv1 -Force -CauPluginName
Microsoft.WindowsUpdatePlugin -MaxRetriesPerNode 3 -CauPluginArguments @{
'IncludeRecommendedUpdates' = 'True' } -StartDate "7/9/2013 11:00:00 PM"
-DaysOfWeek 4 -WeeksOfMonth @(2) -EnableFirewallRules;
```

One reason that you may wish to run this manually is because the wizard allows only a drop-down box for the `CauPluginName` parameter. You can have a single CAU role use the Windows Update and Hotfix plugins simultaneously, along with any custom plugins you may have access to. Modify the `CauPluginName` parameter to read `Microsoft.WindowsUpdatePlugin, Microsoft.HotfixPlugin`.

There are a number of other cmdlets related to managing CAU. All related cmdlets for 2012 are viewable on the TechNet site at http://technet.microsoft.com/en-us/library/hh847221.aspx. The R2 documentation is at http://technet.microsoft.com/en-us/library/hh847221%28v=wps.630%29.aspx. Among the cmdlets is the `Set-CauClusterRole` cmdlet, which allows you to modify any of the options you set with `Add-CauClusterRole`.

Windows Update and Windows Server Update Services

It is possible to keep your systems up-to-date by simply pointing them to Windows Update and leaving the default configurations. A superior solution is Windows Server Update Services. This feature began life as a downloadable add-in for Windows Server 2003, but it became a fully-integrated feature in Windows Server 2012. As this is a general Windows Server technology that falls more under the purview of ordinary Windows administration, this book will not fully investigate the WSUS feature. If you are completely new to WSUS, you can start with the related TechNet articles, which are viewable at http://technet.microsoft.com/en-us/library/hh852345.aspx. A few information points on WSUS with Hyper-V are as follows:

- If you have an existing WSUS infrastructure running on an earlier version of Windows Server, you are not required to upgrade it.

- WSUS relies on a database, which makes it a very poor choice for a role that runs within the management operating system of Hyper-V. However, it is a very low-usage database in most cases, so it is acceptable to place WSUS inside a virtual machine.

- In addition to single patch download and storage, WSUS grants you control over what updates can be installed in your environment and on which computers. It also allows systems to receive updates without connecting to the Internet at all.

- If storage space is more of a concern than Internet bandwidth, you can instruct WSUS clients to download directly from Windows Update while still controlling which patches they can install.

- There is no specific Hyper-V Server category in WSUS. Hyper-V Server patches are distributed through the Windows Server category.

- WSUS only indirectly controls when patches are installed. None can be installed until they are approved (auto-approval is an option). WSUS should be thought of as the "which" component of patch management, not "when".

- If at all possible, have a test system that receives patches first so that you can have a reasonable chance of seeing how they will affect your systems prior to assigning them to production systems.

There are a number of ways to direct your Hyper-V hosts to use your WSUS installation. The preferred method is to use Group Policy. This allows you to create a single group of settings and have them apply automatically to all hosts. To do so, perform the following steps:

1. Create a dedicated OU in Active Directory to hold your Hyper-V Server hosts and their related cluster accounts (this can be done in Active Directory Users and Computers or in PowerShell).

2. Create a computer group in the WSUS console to contain Hyper-V Server hosts. In the examples in this chapter, this group will simply be named `Hyper-V`.

In the Group Policy Management Console (installed by default on domain controllers), create a new GPO and link it to the OU that holds the Hyper-V computer accounts. In this policy, navigate to `Computer Configuration\Policies\Administrative Templates\Windows Components\Windows Update`. Enable **Specify intranet Microsoft update service location** and point it to your WSUS server. Enter the name of the computer group you created in Step 2 into **Enable client-side targeting**.

The following screenshot shows a section of the Group Policy Management Console with these settings enabled:

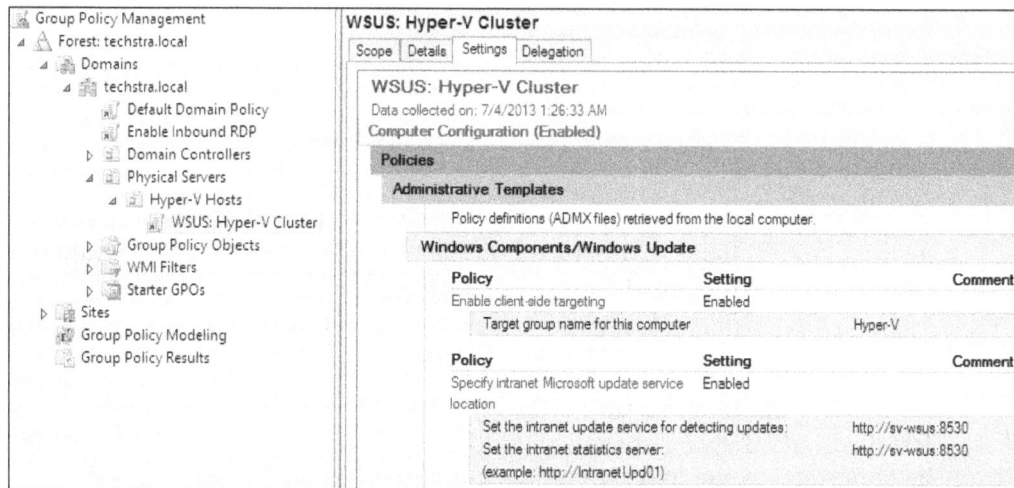

You can wait for the policy to update on the system or you can log on to the hosts and run `gpupdate /force` at an elevated command prompt. Notice that only the location of the WSUS server and the computer group has been assigned through Group Policy; CAU handles the rest of the settings. As an alternative to the Group Policy setting, you can also use the WSUS console to assign the hosts to the appropriate computer group.

Hotfixes

Not all available patches are available through Windows Update. Many start out as hotfixes. These are generally fixes to problems that are urgent enough that they cannot wait for a standard Windows Update cycle but have not yet been through a thorough testing cycle. Without that testing, there are greater chances that a hotfix will cause problems besides, and possibly even worse than, the problem it solves. For this reason, be cautious about applying hotfixes, especially for problems you are not experiencing.

Hotfixes are not automatically distributed. If you search the Microsoft Knowledgebase for a specific error message, you may encounter a download for a hotfix for that issue. The Microsoft TechNet wiki also contains lists of hotfixes, including one for Hyper-V Server and one for Failover Clustering. The wiki is located at `http://social.technet.microsoft.com/wiki`.

A list of Hyper-V patches is available at `http://social.technet.microsoft.com/wiki/contents/articles/15576.hyper-v-update-list-for-windows-server-2012.aspx` (or search the wiki for Hyper-V update list 2012). The Failover Clustering patch list is available at `http://social.technet.microsoft.com/wiki/contents/articles/15577.list-of-failover-cluster-hotfixes-for-windows-server-2012.aspx` (or search the wiki for failover cluster hotfixes 2012).

These hotfixes can be integrated in CAU. The basic procedure is not difficult but is fairly involved, and there are several options to precisely control its behavior. Microsoft provides a complete walkthrough to configure the hotfix plugin for CAU on the TechNet site at `http://technet.microsoft.com/en-us/library/jj134213.aspx`.

Monitoring Hyper-V Server

The built-in tools for monitoring Windows Server and Hyper-V Server are not well-suited to providing automated and proactive monitoring capabilities. Microsoft provides a comprehensive package of management and notification tools in the System Center 2012 with Service Pack 1 product suite. Many third-party solutions also exist, and a few of them are free or ad-supported. Many hardware providers also include software that can alert you to any issues with their equipment.

There is no single list to help you determine exactly what you'll need in a monitoring system, but there are some guidelines:

- Integrated solutions are preferred, but you may need to mix and match components from different providers to get the monitoring solution you need.

- Ensure that the system has a reliable way to notify you of problems. E-mail and SMS are common, but they are of minimal use if they require that a monitored system be accessible. For example, a local monitoring system that sends you an e-mail when your e-mail server is down isn't very useful if it doesn't have its own SMTP service.

- Microsoft products support SNMP, which is a common monitoring protocol. Microsoft also implements the **Common Information Model (CIM)** standard as **Windows Management Instrumentation (WMI)**. Tools that leverage these technologies may be able to give you in-depth reports and controls.

- Many tools will run scripts in response to detected problems in addition to sending notifications.

- A comprehensive tool will allow monitoring of services and event logs.

If you don't have access to these tools, you're not out of luck. There are a number of ways you can leverage the built-in capabilities of Windows Server 2012 to keep an eye on your systems. Based on what you learned in *Chapter 8*, *Performance Testing and Load Balancing*, you can use the Performance Monitor to receive notifications whenever a counter goes above or below a certain threshold that you specify. This is useful to watch for high CPU and low disk space. You can use standard performance traces to watch for patterns such as consistently high Dynamic Memory allocations.

Hyper-V Server does not contain any single location for at-a-glance information. The management tools have separate displays for various items. Failover Cluster Manager in R2 has a minimalist dashboard that lists the status of all clusters. It appears in the bottom right of the following screenshot:

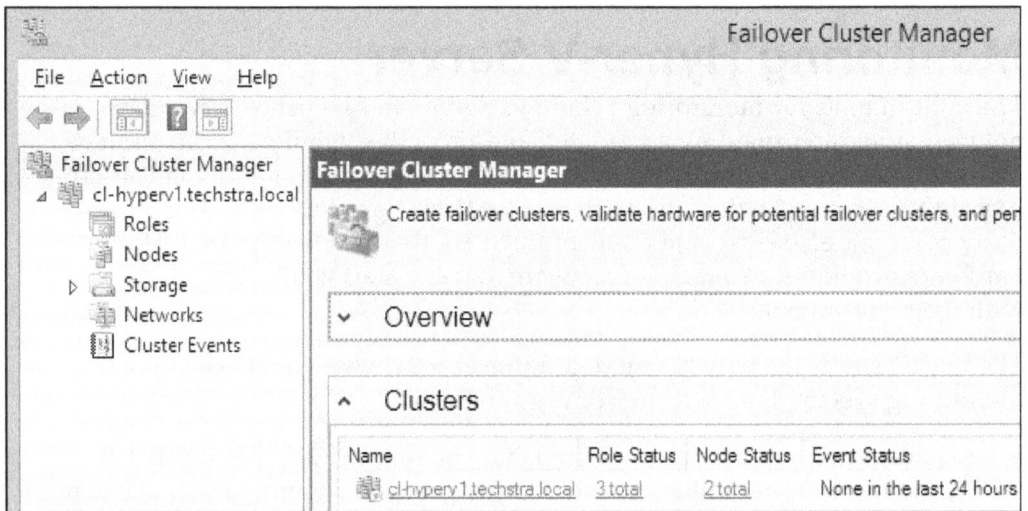

In Hyper-V Manager, all virtual machines for the selected host are displayed in the top center pane. They both show the current CPU usage percentage, the amount of currently allocated memory, uptime, and the status of any current process (such as a Live Migration or export) for each guest. You can use the **View** menu to add a column for **Replication Health**. Highlighting any guest displays the snapshots that it contains in the middle-center pane and updates the tabs in the lower-center pane. The first of those tabs is a very basic summary screen that shows the guest's name, creation date, high availability status, and administrator-entered notes. The other tabs provide details on the guest's memory status, networking components (including IP addresses), and replication status.

To see the details of a guest's virtual disks, access its **Settings** dialog and highlight any of its virtual disks. Click on the **Inspect** button in the right-hand pane. This will show you the type of disk, where it is physically located, and its current size.

Failover Cluster Manager has many similarities with Hyper-V Manager. The **Roles** node lists all the virtual machines, but the grid display doesn't have as many details. Highlighting a virtual machine will update the lower pane with some of the same information as Hyper-V Manager's detail tabs, although it is not as inclusive. It does contain a summary field for **Monitored Services**, which will be discussed shortly.

Failover Cluster Manager provides information about cluster storage. Expand the **Storage** node and click on **Disks** or **Pools**. Here, you will see a grid display of all storage locations and a synopsis of their statuses. Highlighting any of these will show a progress-bar-style display of remaining space in the lower pane. Right-clicking on any and choosing **Properties** will present a dialog with a few more details.

The Cluster Events node in Failover Cluster Manager shows a recent display of warnings and errors that occurred in the cluster service on any node. You can click on the **Query** link in the right-hand pane to view and modify the criteria that it is using for the current display. Any changes you make are not permanent. You can use the **Save Query As** link for later usage. The events you see here are a customized view into the event logs.

Event logs

Hyper-V also has its own event trees, accessible in Event Viewer. You can find both groups in Event Viewer when connecting to a Hyper-V node, as seen in the following screenshot:

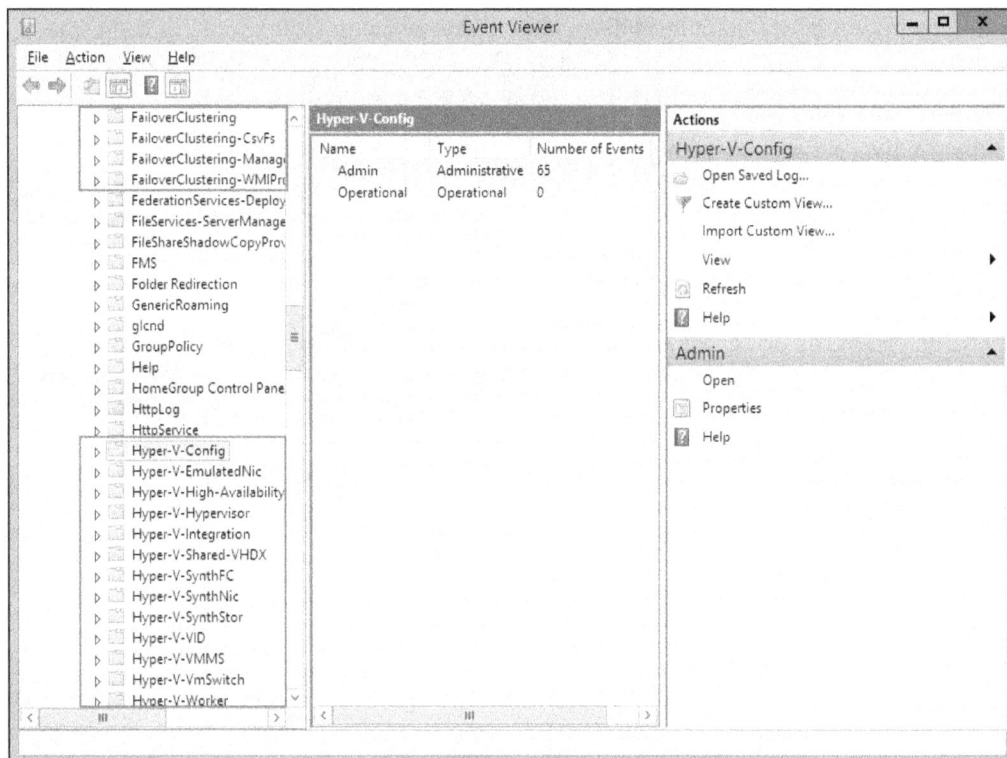

The subjects of events you'll find in the individual Hyper-V logs are as follows:

- **Hyper-V-Config**: This is virtual machine configuration files

- **Hyper-V-EmulatedNic**: This is emulated (legacy) network adapters

- **Hyper-V-High-Availability**: This is Hyper-V resources managed by Failover Clustering

- **Hyper-V-Hypervisor**: This is events specific to the hypervisor itself

- **Hyper-V-Integration**: This is Integration Components installed in individual virtual machines

- **Hyper-V-Shared-VHDX** (R2 only): This pertains to VHDX files that are accessed by multiple virtual machines

- **Hyper-V-SynthFC**: This is virtual Fibre Channel adapters connected directly to guests

- **Hyper-V-SynthNic**: This is synthetic virtual network adapters

- **Hyper-V-SynthStor**: This is machine storage, including both virtual disk and pass-through connections

- **Hyper-V-VID**: This is events from the virtualization infrastructure driver, which controls guest memory and CPU

- **Hyper-V-VMMS**: This is events from the virtual machine management service

- **Hyper-V-VmSwitch** (R2 only): This is a virtual switch

- **Hyper-V-Worker**: This is status changes of virtual machine objects

Services

A new feature in the 2012 product series allows the cluster service to monitor services inside a highly available virtual machine. This capability is limited to guests running Windows Server 2012 or higher; the guest and host must be in the same domain or be able to authenticate against each other and the cluster's responses will be used to restart the guest operating system.

Before you can monitor a guest service, there are a few prerequisite steps:

1. Monitoring is performed over a standard network connection between host and guest, not through Integration Components. The firewall must be accordingly opened on the guest. The Windows Firewall with Advanced Services applet has five predefined rules, all in the **Virtual Machine Monitoring** group. Alternately, you can use PowerShell:

   ```
   Enable-NetFirewallRule -DisplayGroup "Virtual Machine Monitoring"
   ```

2. The **Recovery Action** for the service(s) to be monitored must be configured within the guest. This is normally done through the Services applet. The **Properties** dialog for each service has a **Recovery** tab. At least one failure action must be set to **Take No Action**; the first with this setting is the point at which the Hyper-V Server cluster will act.

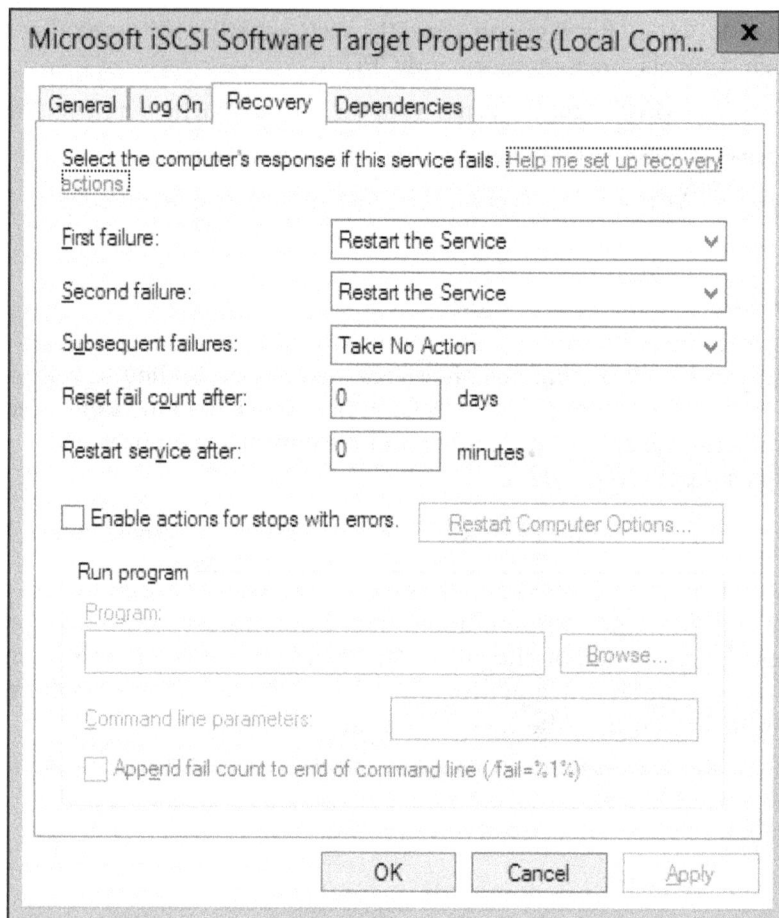

3. While in the service's property dialog, stop on the **General** tab and note its **Service name**.

Once the guest is prepared, the next portion is done at the cluster level. You can use either Failover Cluster Manager or PowerShell. Failover Cluster Manager is easier, but it only has the ability to work with services that run in the context of their own executable. A great many built-in services run under the context of Svchost.exe and are ineligible.

Any service can be set for monitoring with PowerShell. For either method you choose, you must start the tool under an account that has administrative access on the monitored system. That system must be running when you issue the command.

To start monitoring using Failover Cluster Manager, right-click on the virtual machine to be monitored under the **Roles** node (it must be powered on) and navigate to **More Actions** and click on **Configure Monitoring**. Check off the service(s) to be monitored and click on **OK**. To start monitoring services using PowerShell, use the short name(s) you gathered previously during Step 3 and execute the following cmdlet:

```
Add-ClusterVMMonitoredItem -VirtualMachine "sv-apps" -Service CryptSvc,
EventSystem
```

When the cluster responds to a service failure, it will first restart the virtual machine. If it responds again within the timeout configured on the **Failover** tab of the virtual machine's property sheet, it will relocate the virtual machine to another node and restart it there. When failures occur, the virtual machine will have a status of **Application Critical**. This can be cleared from within the virtual machine by simply running `Reset-ClusterVMMonitoredState`. Monitoring can be stopped by unchecking the item(s) in Failover Cluster Manager or by using `Remove-ClusterMonitoredItem` with the same usage as `Add-ClusterVMMonitoredItem`.

Metering

Monitoring and metering are not synonyms, but they function in similar fashions. Whereas monitoring is intended to watch a system for performance measuring or for issues, metering watches a system in order to quantify its behavior. Typically, this is used in chargeback systems in which a system owner or tenant is billed for the amount of resources that a virtual machine uses. New in Hyper-V Server 2012 is a built-in capability to monitor systems. As shipped, it can only be used with PowerShell with `Enable-VMResourceMetering`, `Measure-VM`, `Measure-VMResourcePool`, and `Disable-VMResourceMetering`. These are very straightforward cmdlets to use and you'll find everything you need with `Get-Help`, but they are somewhat inconvenient. Fortunately, Microsoft MVP Yusuf Ozturk has provided a graphical web-driven interface that is very simple to install and use. Find the free download and more information at `http://www.poshstats.net`.

Summary

The maintenance and monitoring cycle of your Hyper-V Server cluster deployment is just as important as planning and deployment. In this chapter, we learned how to use freely available Microsoft tools to keep your hosts systems up-to-date. You were also introduced to the concepts involved in selecting monitoring applications and basic ways to leverage built-in components for simplistic monitoring.

In the next chapter, we will use the combined knowledge we've gained so far to examine the high availability capabilities granted by your new Hyper-V Server 2012 cluster environment.

11
High Availability

One of the primary reasons that many organizations will deploy a cluster of Hyper-V Servers is for the high availability features that such a configuration provides. Building on the previous chapters, this chapter will explore the details of high availability.

This chapter will cover the following topics:

- High availability terms and definitions
- Creating a highly available virtual machine
- High availability beyond Hyper-V
- Migrations (live and quick)
- Cluster responses to failures, including R2 network protection
- Understanding and configuring cluster quorum
- Using snapshots and checkpoints

What does high availability mean?

High availability is a systems design approach that attempts to maximize the likelihood that a service or system will be available for end user usage. The Sisyphean goal of any such system would be to make the services and systems always available. Some very well-crafted designs promise what is commonly known as five 9s, which is guaranteed 99.999 percent availability. The percentage is tied to a specific length of time, typically one year. In order for a system to meet a five 9s standard, it must be unavailable for no more than about five minutes in an entire year's time.

> Just because a system is up does not automatically mean that it is available.

Service level agreements

The exact definition of high availability can be set by your organization. Ordinarily, this is done through **Service Level Agreements (SLA)**. An SLA is a formal or semi-formal document in which the provider of a service sets forth the metrics it promises that any given system will be available. SLAs are very common between separate businesses; for instance, your organization's Internet provider most likely has an SLA that describes their commitment to ensuring your ability to reach Internet sites. However, a similar document, called an **Operational Level Agreement (OLA)**, is effectively an SLA between business units within the same organization. For a failover cluster of Hyper-V Server systems, you may design an SLA/OLA document for the departments in your company that will have their systems hosted on your equipment. If you provide cloud services, especially self-service, you will almost undoubtedly need to provide an SLA. The general components of an SLA and how they pertain to high availability are:

- A general availability metric that expresses expected availability of a system over a specific course of time. An example is 99.5 percent availability per year.

- Specific mention of the distinction or lack of distinction between planned and unplanned downtime. Some SLAs do not consider planned downtime to count against the availability metric. In such cases, an SLA should set forth how service consumers are notified of pending downtime windows. If possible, the SLA should also indicate how common such downtime is, for instance, one hour of downtime every second Tuesday night for patching. Other SLAs consider any unavailability to count against the metric and should make that clear.

- Available compensation (if any) if an SLA is not met. Compensation is generally more important for inter-business SLAs than for those within the same organization. Some organizations use a charge-back system for their own divisions, so compensation might reduce chargebacks in accordance with the amount of unexpected unavailability. Be aware that many SLAs do not provide compensation in direct ratio with the amount of time that a system is unavailable.

Even in a small organization, a basic SLA/OLA is useful. It provides a very quick comparison point for the health of a system that can be shared with anyone. These can be used for things such as end-of-year inter-departmental summary reports.

Fault tolerance

Fault tolerance is a term that is often confused with high availability. The two terms are not interchangeable. Fault tolerant describes a component or system that can continue operating without interruption through a sub component failure. High availability can be defined as an availability expectation; fault tolerance can be defined as a capability expectation. A RAID-5 array can be considered fault tolerant, but only as far as its disks are concerned. A disk system with a RAID-5 array and multiple controllers can be considered fault tolerant, but only for disks and controllers. Such a subsystem might have redundant power supplies, which further extends the fault tolerance to include those. High availability systems are usually composed of multiple fault tolerant components. A failover cluster of Hyper-V Servers is not considered fault tolerant because if a host were to crash unexpectedly, the virtual machines it is hosting will also crash.

Creating a highly available virtual machine

There are actually two steps to building a highly available virtual machine from scratch. The first is to create the virtual machine. The second is creating a cluster resource that enables the cluster service to control the virtual machine. Both the GUI and PowerShell can be used for this purpose.

Using Failover Cluster Manager to create a highly available virtual machine

Right-click on the **Roles** node, navigate to **Virtual Machines**, and click on **New Virtual Machine**. This will present a dialog asking you which node you'd like to deploy the new guest on. Highlight one and click on **OK**. This will start the virtual machine creation wizard.

1. The first screen is informational; read its contents and click on **Next**.

2. The **Specify Name and Location** screen, shown in the following screenshot, asks for the name and file location of the virtual machine. Choose the name of the virtual machine. The default location is determined by the node that you chose to deploy on (this setting can be changed by opening the Hyper-V **Settings** dialog and right-clicking on that node in Hyper-V Manager). Choose a location that is reachable by all nodes, such as an SMB 3.0 network share or a CSV under `C:\ClusterStorage`. Click on **Next**:

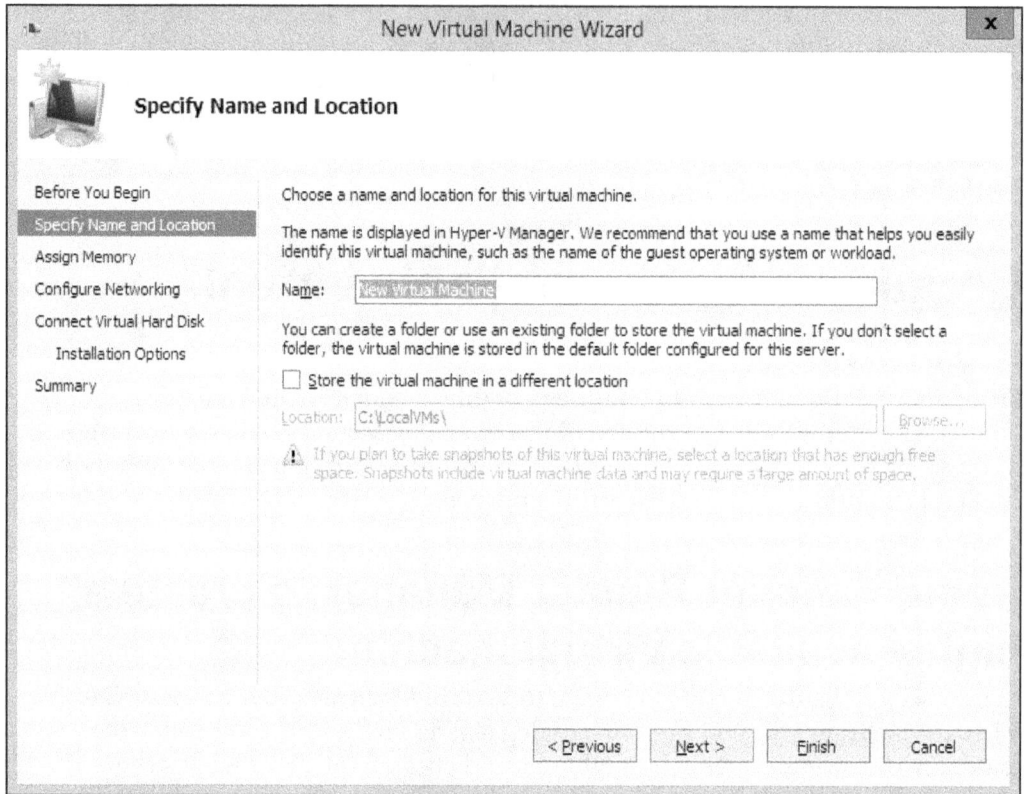

3. On the **Specify Generation** screen (R2 only), shown in the following screenshot, choose whether you want to use the original Hyper-V virtual machine type or the new Generation 2 VM type. Generation 2 VM's can only run Windows Server 2012 or later, or Windows 8.1 or later, and cannot use any emulated hardware (legacy network adapters and IDE drive controllers). Generation 2 VM's support secure boot. Details on this new type are available on TechNet at `http://technet.microsoft.com/en-us/library/dn282285.aspx`:

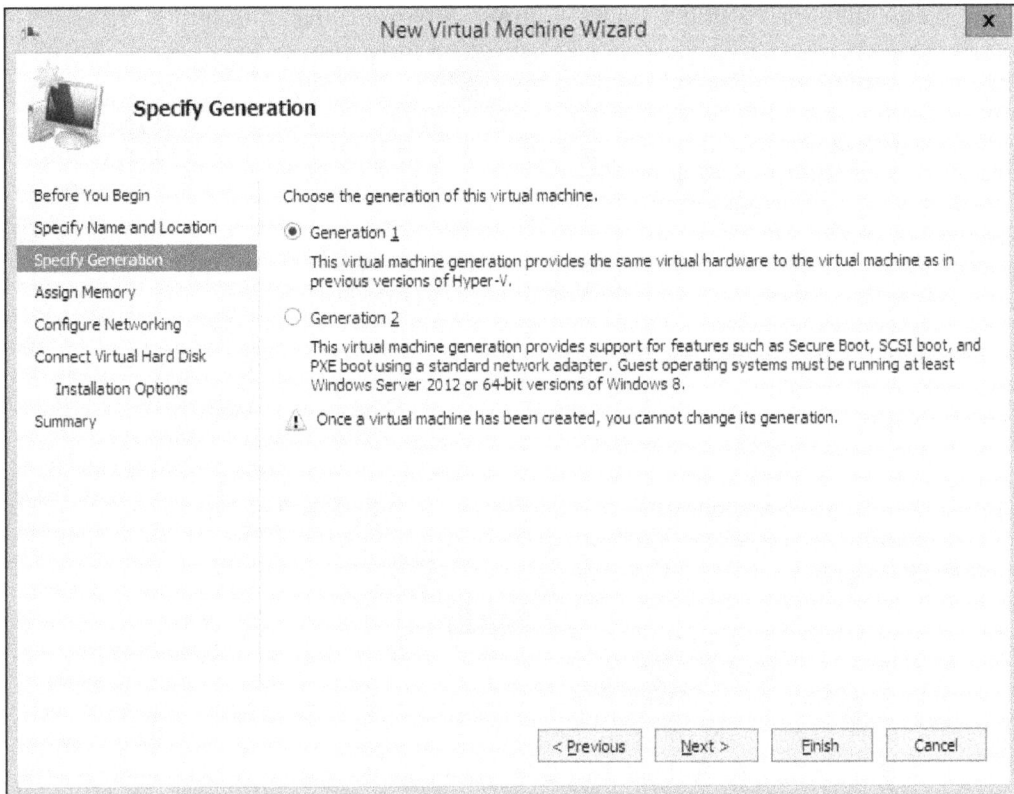

New Virtual Machine Wizard   X

Specify Generation

Before You Begin   Choose the generation of this virtual machine.

Specify Name and Location   ⦿ Generation 1

Specify Generation   This virtual machine generation provides the same virtual hardware to the virtual machine as in
                                    previous versions of Hyper-V.
Assign Memory

Configure Networking   ◯ Generation 2

Connect Virtual Hard Disk   This virtual machine generation provides support for features such as Secure Boot, SCSI boot, and
                                    PXE boot using a standard network adapter. Guest operating systems must be running at least
   Installation Options   Windows Server 2012 or 64-bit versions of Windows 8.

Summary   ⚠ Once a virtual machine has been created, you cannot change its generation.

                                       < Previous   Next >   Finish   Cancel

Generation selection is permanent.

4. The **Assign Memory** page allows you to select the startup memory and whether or not the virtual machine will begin with Dynamic Memory available. You cannot set the bounds for Dynamic Memory in this wizard; you'll need to modify the virtual machine's properties later. Make your selections and click on **Next**.

5. On the **Configure Networking** page, you can choose to connect to a virtual switch or leave the adapter unconnected. This is a synthetic network adapter, and the wizard will only create one. Choose an option and click on **Next**.

6. You have three options on the **Connect Virtual Hard Disk** screen. The first is to create a new VHD or VHDX file. You must specify the name of the file including its extension, the location, and the maximum size. It will be created as dynamically expanding. The second option is to use an existing disk. You'll need to enter the location and name or browse to it. The third option will create the virtual machine without attaching a disk at all. Decide, enter any necessary information, and click on **Next**.

7. If you are creating a new disk, the next screen will be **Installation Options**. You can choose to install from a CD or DVD that is contained in an ISO file or the host's physical drive, from a virtual floppy image, or from a network location (if you attached the adapter to the network). If you choose to install from the network, the network adapter that is created for the virtual machine will be of the legacy type instead of synthetic. Make your selections and click on **Next**.

8. Review your options and, if satisfied, click on **Finish**. The wizard will check your options and create the virtual machine. If there are any issues, such as placing the virtual machine in a non-shared location or connecting to an ISO that is on the local computer, these will be displayed as warnings. The virtual machine will be created as highly available, but migrations will fail until the problems are fixed.

The installation option you chose in Step 5 is not guided. The wizard will simply set the boot order for the first start to the necessary option.

Using Failover Cluster Manager to make an existing virtual machine highly available

Any virtual machine on any node can be made highly available. Right-click on the **Roles** node and then click on **Configure Role**. Click on **Next** in the **Role Selection** screen. Choose **Virtual Machine** and click on **Next**. All non-highly-available machines on all nodes in the cluster will be displayed. Check any virtual machine(s) you'd like to convert and click on **Next**, then click on **Next** again on the confirmation screen. Once the process is complete, the report will be displayed. You can use Storage Live Migration to move any files on local storage to shared storage.

> When using Failover Cluster Manager to create or convert a highly available virtual machine, the report is saved to `C:\Windows\Cluster\Reports\HAVirtualMachine.mht`.

Using PowerShell to create and convert a highly available virtual machine

PowerShell does not have a single step operation to both create a virtual machine and make it highly available, although it can all be done in a single line:

```
New-VM -Name "sv-sql2" -BootDevice IDE -MemoryStartupBytes 512MB
-SwitchName "vSwitch" -NewVHDPath 'C:\ClusterStorage\VMData1\Virtual Hard
Disks\sv-sql2-boot.vhdx' -NewVHDSizeBytes 25GB -Path 'C:\ClusterStorage\
VMData1\' | Add-ClusterVirtualMachineRole
```

> In 2012 R2, specify the virtual machine generation with the `Generation` parameter: `New-VM -Name "sv-sql2" -Generation 2...`

If you have an existing virtual machine, you can use it with `Get-VM` and the pipeline as shown previously for the `New-VM` cmdlet, or you can just use the `Add-ClusterVirtualMachineRole` cmdlet:

```
Add-ClusterVirtualMachineRole -VMName "sv-sql3"
```

> No report file is created when saving or converting a virtual machine using PowerShell.

Removing high availability from a virtual machine

You can make a virtual machine non-highly-available very easily. Right-click on it in the **Roles** section of the Failover Cluster Manager and click on **Remove**. The virtual machine itself is completely unaltered, but it is no longer a cluster resource and has no high availability protection. You can perform the same action in PowerShell:

```
Remove-ClusterGroup -VMId (Get-VM -Name "sv-sql2").VMId -RemoveResources
```

High availability beyond Hyper-V

Making a virtual machine highly available is not the only way to enable high availability for a service or application. Many server-grade applications include their own high availability features; in fact, Hyper-V is one of them. Others are Microsoft SQL Server and Exchange Server. SQL provides mirrored, AlwaysOn, and clustered database capabilities. Exchange Server offers **database availability groups** (**DAG**) and lagged database copies. These capabilities can provide fault tolerance; a guest can be lost without interrupting application availability. Research the applications you plan to place on your servers to see if the vendor has their own protection methodology.

Some application-based high availability schemes are not supported in conjunction with highly available virtual machines. With those, you will need to make a choice. You can follow the directions from *Chapter 9, Special Cases*, on placing non-highly-available virtual machines in your cluster. You may also choose to not use the application's high availability features. One good reason to do so is complexity. High availability application configurations typically require many steps and processes to build and maintain, and it may be more than an organization wants to invest in or needs to have. Another good reason to only use Hyper-V high availability is licensing costs. Each installation of the application server is likely to require its own license. By using only a single highly available virtual machine and not employing any other protection mechanisms, you may only need a single license for that application. As an example, many Microsoft server applications waive the 90-day hardware license transfer requirement, if the application only moves across nodes in the same cluster. Consult with the vendor of your application for specifics.

Cluster within a cluster

One of the most common ways to employ application-level high availability in a Hyper-V Server cluster is to create a cluster of guests. These clusters will have their own design needs and should be built mostly as if they were standalone physical computers. Work with the application vendor to determine if the guests can be highly available, or if they need to be prevented from participating in Live Migration. Use the knowledge that you gained in the *Anti-affinity* section of *Chapter 8, Performance Testing and Load Balancing*, to configure guests to not share a host.

Hyper-V Server 2012 does not allow guests to share storage presented through Hyper-V (R2 does, as explained in the next subsection). What that means is that you cannot assign the same VHD file or a pass-through disk to two guests. In order for clustered guests in that version to have access to shared storage, you must allow them to connect directly to iSCSI targets using their virtual network adapters, or grant them access to virtualized Fibre Channel adapters.

If you will be connecting your guests to iSCSI targets, configure them just as you would a physical host. Use at least one virtual network adapter dedicated to iSCSI. If your virtual switch is built on top of a team of physical adapters, you can use more than one virtual adapter for iSCSI and configure multipath I/O. This makes it possible for the guest to have access to aggregated bandwidth for its iSCSI traffic. However, the virtual switch and the network team retain control of traffic distribution, so it is not guaranteed.

For both iSCSI and Fibre Channel targets, you must install any vendor-supplied software and/or **Device Specific Modules** (**DSM**), installed inside, guests that will connect directly.

The storage concepts discussed in this section were illustrated in *Chapter 4, Storage Design*.

Shared VHDX in R2

Hyper-V Server 2012 R2 adds the shared VHDX feature. This eliminates the need to connect guests directly to iSCSI or Fibre Channel targets, although that is still an option. In the virtual machine's Settings dialog in either Hyper-V Manager or Failover Cluster Manager, hard drives now have an **Advanced Features** tab. On this tab, you'll find a check box for **Enable virtual hard disk sharing**.

The dialog and this setting are shown in the following screenshot:

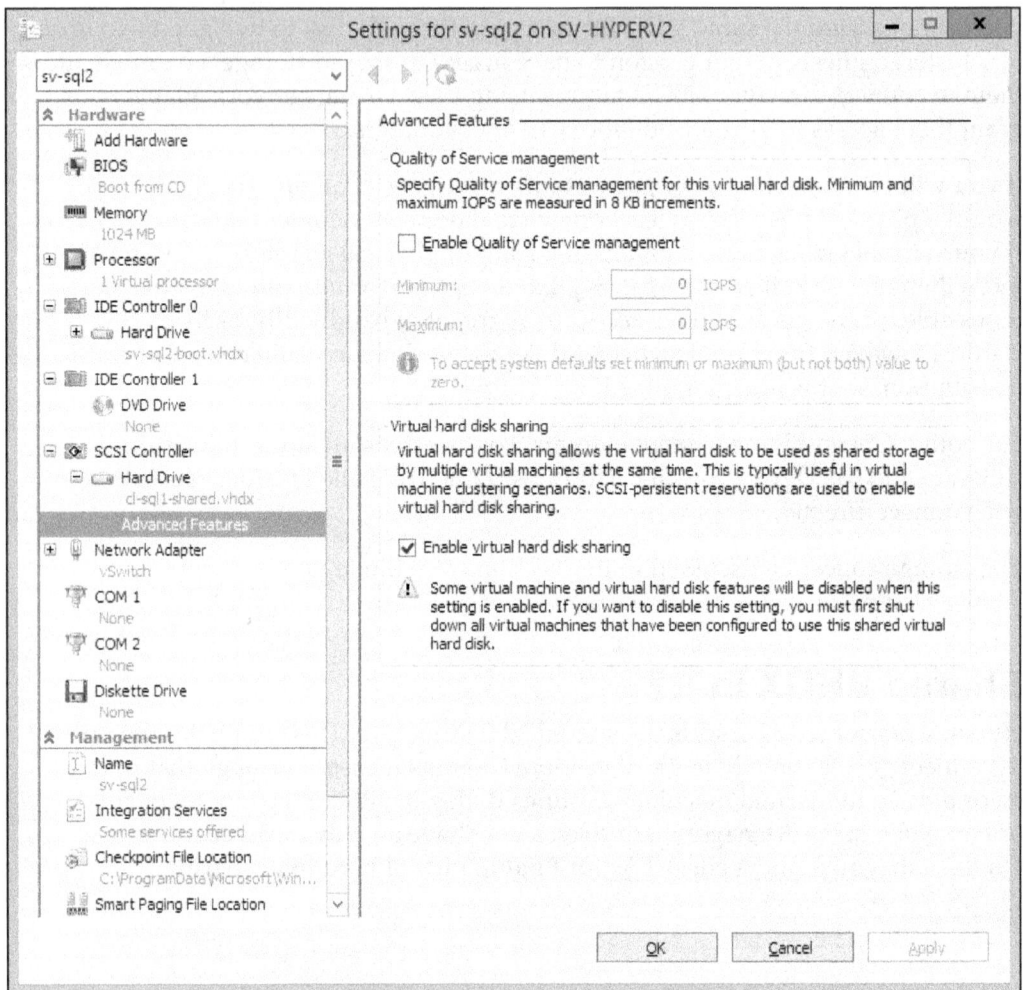

While this can be a useful feature, there are a number of concerns:

- The disk file type must be VHDX, not VHD. It can be dynamic or fixed.
- The file must reside on a CSV or on an SMB 3.0 share hosted on a Scale-Out File Server. If Hyper-V detects that you are attempting to set this option on a disk in any other location type, you'll receive an error that the disk settings cannot be modified. Microsoft will not support shared VHDX in any other location even if you manage to fool the system.
- Setting or clearing this option requires that all connected guests be shut down.
- Hyper-V Replica and host-based backups cannot work with a shared VHDX.
- Shared VHDX cannot move by Storage Live Migration.

Jose Barreto, a Microsoft Principal Program Manager, has written a blog post that illustrates creating a shared VHDX environment, which is available at `http://blogs.technet.com/b/josebda/archive/2013/07/31/windows-server-2012-r2-storage-step-by-step-with-storage-spaces-smb-scale-out-and-shared-vhdx-virtual.aspx`.

Network adapter configurations for guest clusters

If you will be using Microsoft **Network Load Balancing** (**NLB**) in conjunction with a guest cluster, you must enable **media access control** (**MAC**) spoofing. This allows a network adapter to use a hardware address different than the one it was initially assigned, which is vital for NLB to work properly. MAC spoofing is set directly on the virtual adapter. Access the virtual machine's **Settings** dialog in either Failover Cluster Manager or Hyper-V Manager. Click on **+** next to the virtual adapter whose properties you wish to change and then click on **Advanced Features**.

In the right pane, check the box for **Enable MAC address spoofing**, as shown in the following screenshot, and click on **OK**:

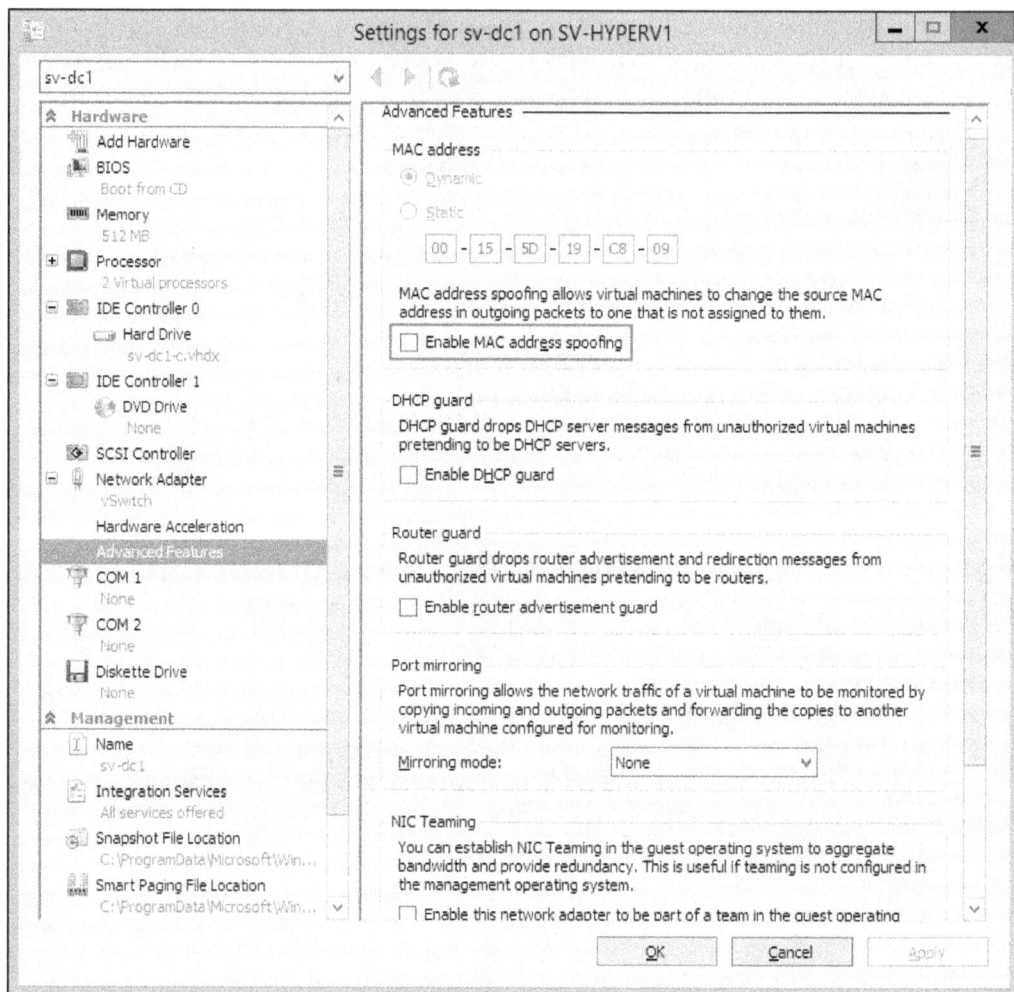

To perform the same task in PowerShell:

```
Set-VMNetworkAdapter -VMName "sv-dc1" -MacAddressSpoofing On
```

Migrations

One way that Hyper-V Server offers high availability is through its Live Migration feature. This technology allows a running virtual machine to transfer from one physical host to another without incurring downtime. There is a brief interruption as the logical network components make the transition and MAC addresses are relocated on switching hardware, but the transfer occurs within the standard TCP timeout window. Any lost TCP packets will be retransmitted, while any lost UDP packets will be simply lost as UDP is not a guaranteed lossless protocol. Other protocols will behave according to their design; ICMP packets (such as ping), will also be lost as ICMP's purpose is to check for network issues. For some applications, such as real-time voice communications (for example, Microsoft Lync Server), this can cause an interruption of service. For most, it does not affect availability in a way that would count as downtime in an SLA. Therefore, Live Migration contributes to high availability by allowing you to completely vacate a host to perform operations such as BIOS upgrades and management operating system patching without impacting end users at all.

Another migration technology available in Hyper-V Server is Quick Migration. Whereas Live Migration transfers the active state of memory and CPU threads across a cluster network to another host, Quick Migration does not rely on any cluster network at all. Instead, it places the virtual machine in a saved state on one host and resumes it on another. The save operation is somewhat similar to hibernation on a standard computer system, with the major difference being that the entire process is completely owned and controlled by the hypervisor. The virtual machine itself is never made aware that a save and resume operation occurred. It must be pointed out that this is not a downtime-free operation. The downtime would need to count against any SLA metrics, but this alone does not disqualify it as a high availability technology since it allows for a move from one physical machine to another in seconds.

Practical high availability migration guidance

Within a cluster, both migration types are considered proactive technologies in the sphere of high availability. They are intended to eliminate or reduce the impact of an outage on guest virtual machines and their contained services. The System Center 2012 suite can be configured to automatically move virtual machines in response to detected problems. Scripting can also be used to achieve a similar result.

In most situations, Live Migration is the preferred method. However, unless you have a really fast network for Live Migration (10 GbE or better), and the guests cumulatively only have a few gigabytes of memory to move, Live Migration may require time that you don't have. For very large or numerous virtual machines, consider using Quick Migration instead. Of course, if time is of the essence, then manually migrating guests by any fashion is out of the question. Fortunately, there is an automated way to move all virtual machines off a node.

To evacuate a node in Failover Cluster Manager, expand the **Nodes** tree (it is not a tree in R2 and does not expand; left-click instead) so that all nodes are visible. Right-click on the desired node and choose **Pause**, then click on **Drain Roles**, as shown in the following screenshot. The clustering service will choose the optimal location for each virtual machine and relocate them accordingly:

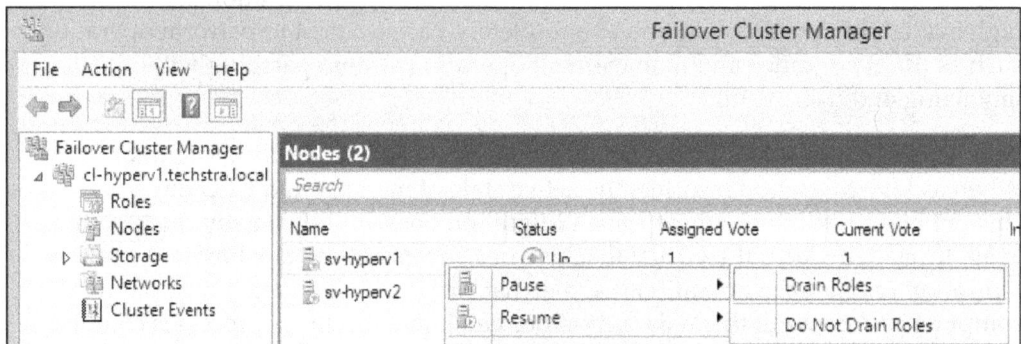

The cluster service on the paused node will remain in the paused condition until it is explicitly resumed. This is true even if the host is rebooted. To start it again, you'll find the **Resume** menu in the same location you found the **Pause** menu (visible in the previous screenshot). You can choose to have it reclaim all the roles it moved by clicking on **Fail Roles Back**, or you can click on **Do Not Fail Roles Back** to have them remain where they are.

The PowerShell operation is equally simple:

```
Suspend-ClusterNode -Name "sv-hyperv2" -Drain
```

The Drain parameter is simply a toggle. Omitting it will cause the cluster service to leave the virtual machines exactly as they are. The PowerShell cmdlet does have some options that are unavailable in Failover Cluster Manager. The first is ForceEvacuation. This is a toggle that ignores any errors that occur in migration and continues moving roles. The second is TargetNode, which allows you to direct which node the guests are moved to.

> When an R2 node is shut down gracefully, its roles will be drained in the same fashion. The guests of a 2012 node will perform their Automatic Stop Action.

To resume using PowerShell:

```
Resume-ClusterNode -Name "sv-hyperv2" -Failback Immediate
```

The `Failback` parameter exposes another set of features not available in the GUI. The displayed value is `Immediate`, which will cause the resume operation to work exactly as the GUI method does. The other two options are: `NoFailback` and `Policy`. The former is self-explanatory. According to the cmdlet's documentation, the latter follows the virtual machine's failback policy. In practice, the policy value acts no differently than `Immediate`. Failback policies will be discussed in the upcoming section on cluster responses to failure.

The discussion of Live Migration as opposed to Quick Migration is entirely moot if there's not a way to control which the cluster service uses. Fortunately, such control is entirely possible. You can set the priority of a virtual machine's resource to one of four priorities: **High**, **Medium**, **Low**, and **No Auto Restart**.

> The cluster resource priority setting is not the same as the priority setting for memory, although there is some overlap. The cluster resource setting will only apply in response to a cluster-initiated action; while the memory priority setting will apply in any conditions (such as cold boot of a node, or a migration that was initiated by an administrator, or an application). There is no defined precedence between the cluster priority setting and the memory priority setting, so outcomes will be circumstantial if they are in contention (for example, a virtual machine with a high priority cluster resource and low memory priority). For the best, most predictable results, keep these settings in sync or leave one at default.

When a role drain is initiated, first the high and then the medium priority virtual machines are moved by Live Migration. Once the Live Migrations have started, guests set to No Auto Restart and Low priority will move by Quick Migration. In most cases, the quick migrated machines will arrive at the destination first, but do remember that there is a brief outage and their uptime counters will be reset.

> In some rare cases, medium priority virtual machines may be migrated ahead of high priority guests. This behavior is most commonly seen when the drain is performed immediately after a change is made to these priorities.

If Quick Migration for low priority machines is not desirable, the behavior can be overridden by modifying a cluster parameter. Internally, each priority setting has a numeric value: 0 for No Auto Restart, 1000 for low priority, 2000 for medium priority, and 3000 for high priority. By default, Microsoft Failover Clustering will initiate Live Migration only for resources that have a priority of 2000 or greater. On any cluster node, open Registry Editor and access `HKEY_LOCAL_MACHINE\Cluster\ResourceTypes\Virtual Machine\Parameters`. Change the **MoveTypeThreshold** value to a number at or below 1000 (decimal) to cause virtual machines with low priority to be live migrated during a role drain. If you set it to 0, virtual machines with No Auto Restart priority will also be live migrated. This key is also accessible using PowerShell:

```
Get-ClusterResourceType -Name "Virtual Machine" | Set-ClusterParameter
-Name "MoveTypeThreshold" -Value 1000
```

Cluster responses to failures

As the name indicates, the purpose of Microsoft Failover Clustering is to provide failover capabilities. Whenever the cluster service on a node is not reachable within a five second window, a failover event is triggered. There are two ways for a node to become unavailable. The first is a simple crash. This could be a blue-screen error or a power outage. The second is network isolation. In this state, the host is still up, but it is not available.

Another failover trigger is the failure of a monitored service, as described in *Chapter 10, Maintaining and Monitoring a Hyper-V Server Cluster*. In this case, the cluster's first response is to try to restart the guest on the same node. Its second response is to move it to another node, much as it would if that guest's host became isolated.

The way that the cluster responds to a failover will vary based on the condition and configuration of protected resources. The cluster nodes are constantly exchanging configuration and status data. Within a second, they have synchronized any changes and are aware of the condition of all virtual machines on all nodes. If a quorum disk is used, it also contains up to date state information.

When surviving nodes notice that a node has become unavailable, they will begin assessing the status of the resources that the failed node contained. The primary consideration is whether or not the resources are available to start. If that node can no longer communicate with the network but it can still reach its storage, its guests may still be online. It will shut them down in accordance with their configured automatic stop actions, and the other nodes will wait. Once the resources are available, the other nodes will process through possible owners, preferred owners, and priorities. They will then bring the guests online accordingly. In the event that not all guests can be brought online for various reasons, the cluster will continue to attempt to bring guests online. A virtual machine may be shifted to another node, or Dynamic Memory pressure on a host may drop as guests normalize from startup, allowing further guests to start.

Possible owners and preferred owners were covered in-depth in *Chapter 8*, *Performance Testing and Load Balancing*, and priorities were examined earlier in this chapter. The Automatic Start and Stop Actions require deeper inspection.

Automatic Stop Action

Automatic stop actions are triggered whenever a host is shut down or when the clustering service determines that a node needs to stop participating in the cluster. That determination is made using quorum, which will be discussed in the next section.

To configure the Automatic Stop Action for a virtual machine, it must be turned off. To change its settings in a GUI, access its Settings dialog in either Hyper-V Manager or Failover Cluster Manager, and switch to the **Automatic Stop Action** tab at the bottom of the left pane.

The three available options, as seen in the following screenshot, are **Save the virtual machine state**, **Turn off the virtual machine**, or **Shut down the guest operating system**:

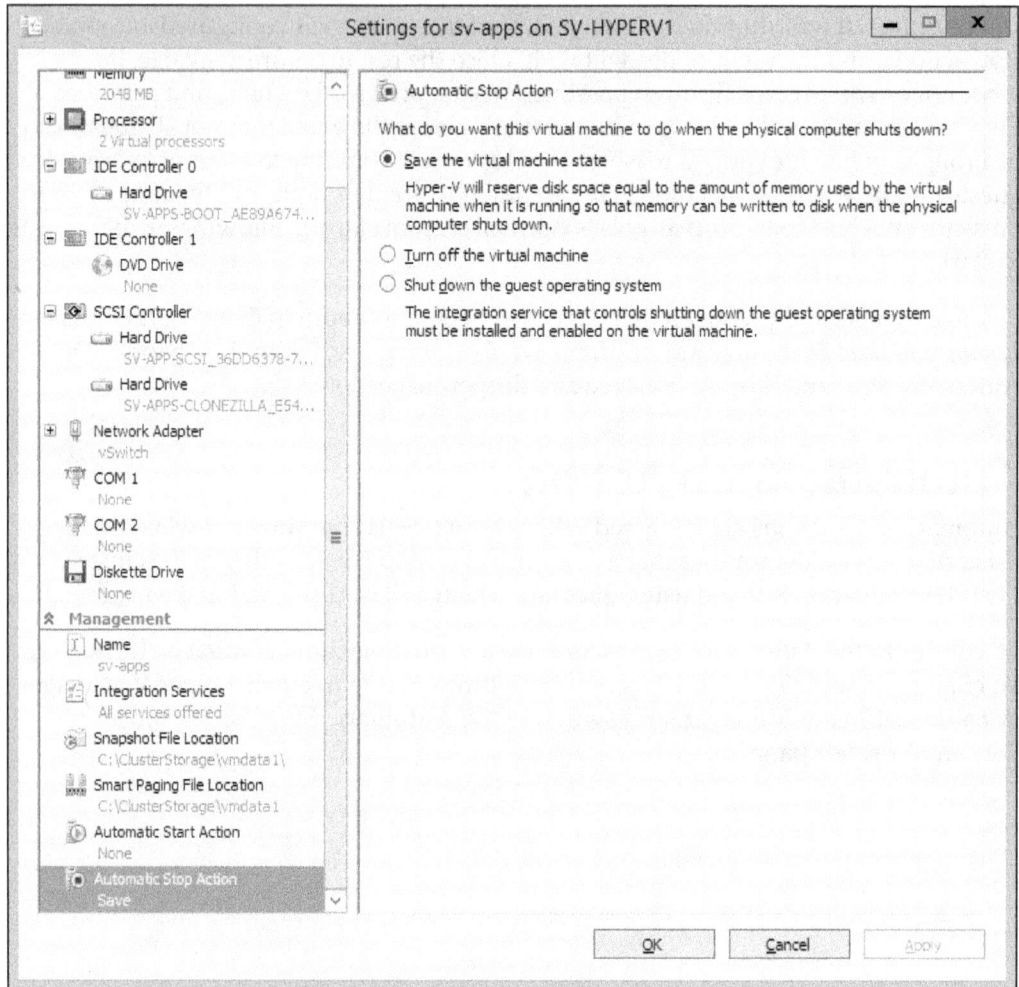

The **Save State** action has been discussed throughout this book. To recap, all CPU, memory, and disk I/O options for the virtual machine are paused and its entire active state is saved to a file. This process is very rapid as it requires no actions by the virtual machine, but it can be undesirable and even dangerous for some server applications, as the guest is not given any opportunity to gracefully cease client interactions.

The **Turn Off** action is the virtual equivalent to removing power from an actively running server. This process is nearly instantaneous, but the guest has no opportunity to save anything and its active state is completely lost. It's the only option for virtual machines that don't support Integration Services. It may desirable for systems that have no data to be saved, such as firewall virtual appliances, but it should be used with caution, as data loss is all but guaranteed.

The **Shut Down** action attempts a graceful shut down of the guest. Of all the options, this takes the longest time and can potentially cause the host shut down process to hang. It works through Integration Services. The `shutdown` command is sent to the guest; if it responds to this command and continues to respond to requests through the Integration Services, Hyper-V will block a host shutdown. For an isolated but functional host, this will prevent other nodes from being able to access the guest to bring it online. If the guest does not respond to the request, Hyper-V performs the **Turn Off** action instead.

These actions can also be configured using PowerShell:

```
Set-VM -Name "sv-apps" -AutomaticStopAction ShutDown
```

The other options for `AutomaticStopAction` are `Save` and `TurnOff`. As seen in other chapters, the `Set-VM` cmdlet allows you to use a comma-separated list of guests for the `Name` parameter, and it also accepts virtual machines through the pipeline. You can design a script that uses `Get-VM` to gather multiple guests and set their Automatic Stop actions simultaneously.

> In 2012, virtual machines will execute their Automatic Stop Action if their node is shut down. In R2, a drain action will occur.

Automatic Start Action

An Automatic Start Action is triggered when a host is brought online from a stopped state and still owns virtual machines. This will be the case for non-highly-available virtual machines, virtual machines restricted to a specific host, or when most or all nodes of a cluster have been offline. It is not triggered when a failover event occurs. If the cluster detects that the virtual machine was on when its host failed, it will be turned on after a failover; otherwise, it will be left in the off state.

> If a highly-available virtual machine is off when its owning node fails, it is transferred to another host but left in the off state.

The **Automatic Start Action** tab is also found on the Settings dialog of a virtual machine in Hyper-V Manager and Failover Cluster Manager, directly above the **Automatic Stop Action** tab. It also has three possibilities. These are: **Nothing, Automatically start if it was running when the service stopped**, and **Always start this virtual machine automatically**. The **Nothing** setting leaves the virtual machine off or in a Saved State setting, whichever the guest was left in when the host shut down. The other two are self-explanatory. If you choose to automatically start the virtual machine you are also given the option to set the **Startup delay**. This is the number of seconds that Hyper-V will wait to start the guest. This is useful to stagger guest startup to reduce I/O loads and to increase the probability that Dynamic Memory can successfully pressure guests downward in order to bring others online.

As with the Automatic Stop Action, the Automatic Start Action can be configured with the Set-VM cmdlet:

```
Set-VM –Name "sv-apps" –AutomaticStartAction Start -AutomaticStartDelay 15
```

The other options for AutomaticStartAction, are Nothing and StartIfRunning. AutomaticStartDelay will be ignored if either is used. As mentioned for Automatic Stop Action, you can use a comma-separated list of virtual machines, or use the pipeline from Get-VM to apply one setting to multiple guests.

> You can set the Automatic Stop Action and the Automatic Start Action in the same call to Set-VM.

Failback

By default, virtual machines that were moved by the cluster service in response to a failure will remain where they are. However, if you have manually balanced the virtual machine load across your cluster, you may prefer that the guests find their way home automatically. In scenarios such as guest clusters in a small Hyper-V Server cluster, you may also wish for certain guests to be able to share a node when absolutely required, but to then automatically separate when possible. This is possible by configuring failback. Despite its name, this process does not necessarily send the virtual machine back to the host it started on. Instead, it will attempt to place it on one of its Preferred Owners. If no Preferred Owner is configured, failback is ignored.

In Failover Cluster Manager, right-click on a virtual machine, and click on **Properties**. If you have not set Preferred Owners, they are accessible on the first tab of this dialog. Switch to the **Failover** tab, and you'll see a screen, as shown in the following screenshot:

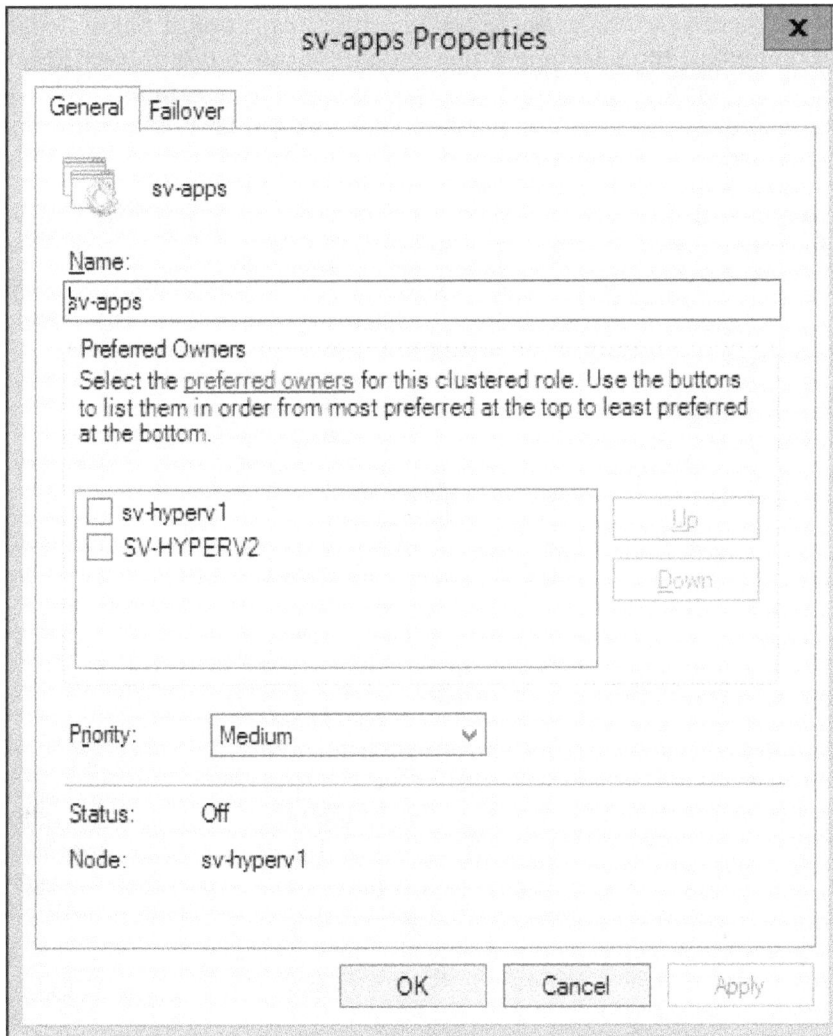

You can configure failback to occur immediately, or you can establish time windows. If failback is allowed immediately, the guest will attempt to relocate as soon as its preferred owner rejoins the cluster. If you use the **Failback between** settings, you are indicating a time window based on a 24-hour clock. So, if you set the first number to 22 and the second to 5, failback will only occur between 10:00 PM and 5:00 AM. If a failover event occurs and the preferred owner comes back online before 10:00 PM, the guest will remain on its failover target and not be moved until 10:00 PM. If the failure and recovery occur between 10:00 PM and 5:00 AM, the failback will occur as soon as the preferred owner is available. If they are both set to the same time, failback will only occur at that time.

These settings can also be adjusted using PowerShell to manipulate the properties of the virtual machine's cluster group. The following cmdlet demonstration assumes that your virtual machine and its cluster group have the same name. If it does not, use `Get-ClusterGroup -VMId ((Get-VM -Name "sv-apps").VMId)`, instead of `Get-ClusterGroup -Name "sv-apps"`.

```
(Get-ClusterGroup -Name "sv-apps").AutoFailbackType = 1
(Get-ClusterGroup -Name "sv-apps").FailbackWindowStart = 22
(Get-ClusterGroup -Name "sv-apps").FailbackWindowEnd = 5
```

Set the `AutoFailbackType` property to 0 to prevent failback. Set the type to 1 and use a value of 4294967295 for both the `FailbackWindowStart` and `FailbackWindowEnd`, to set immediate failback.

Failover limits

A common problem in automatic failover events is flapping. A service is considered to be flapping if it is continually cycling between up and down conditions. For example, a server that encounters a blue screen stop error, automatically reboots, makes its services available for a few moments, and then encounters another stop error, is flapping. In a cluster environment, this can cause a multitude of issues. If a host is flapping and its guests are configured for failback without limitations, the cluster will continually attempt to relocate those guests. If a guest's monitored service is flapping and no limits are set, the cluster will continually attempt to restart and relocate it across other nodes, causing an unusual resource drain. Fluctuating shared storage connectivity is another source of flapping. Problems can compound if multiple hosts are flapping and there are insufficient resources across the cluster to handle all of the guests that are attempting to failover. To keep these issues from entering an infinite loop, or worse, causing a cascade failure that affects otherwise functional services, use failover limits.

To set the failover limits in the GUI, look at the **Failover** tab of the virtual machine's properties, as shown in the preceding section on Failback. The **Maximum failures in the specified period** setting sets an upper limit on the number of times the cluster service will attempt to recover a virtual machine within the number of hours indicated in the **Period (hours)** setting. To set these options using PowerShell, modify the virtual machine's group properties:

```
(Get-ClusterGroup -Name "sv-apps").FailoverThreshold = 5
(Get-ClusterGroup -Name "sv-apps").FailoverPeriod = 6
```

If your virtual machine's cluster group uses a different name than the virtual machine, refer to the Failback section's instructions on using the VMId parameter instead.

> There is some inconsistency with using a **Maximum failures in the specified period** value of 1 in the GUI. The FailoverThreshold property will be set to 4294967295 instead, which is effectively infinite. For predictable behavior, it is recommended that you determine and set a reasonable value above 1.

Network protection in R2

New in R2, is the ability for the host to detect if a virtual machine has lost its network connection and automatically live migrate it to another node, where the network is available. This is configured on the individual virtual network adapter. You can access it from the Settings page of the virtual machine in Failover Cluster Manager. Expand the virtual adapter and click on **Advanced Features**.

Check the **Protected Network** checkbox, as seen in the following screenshot:

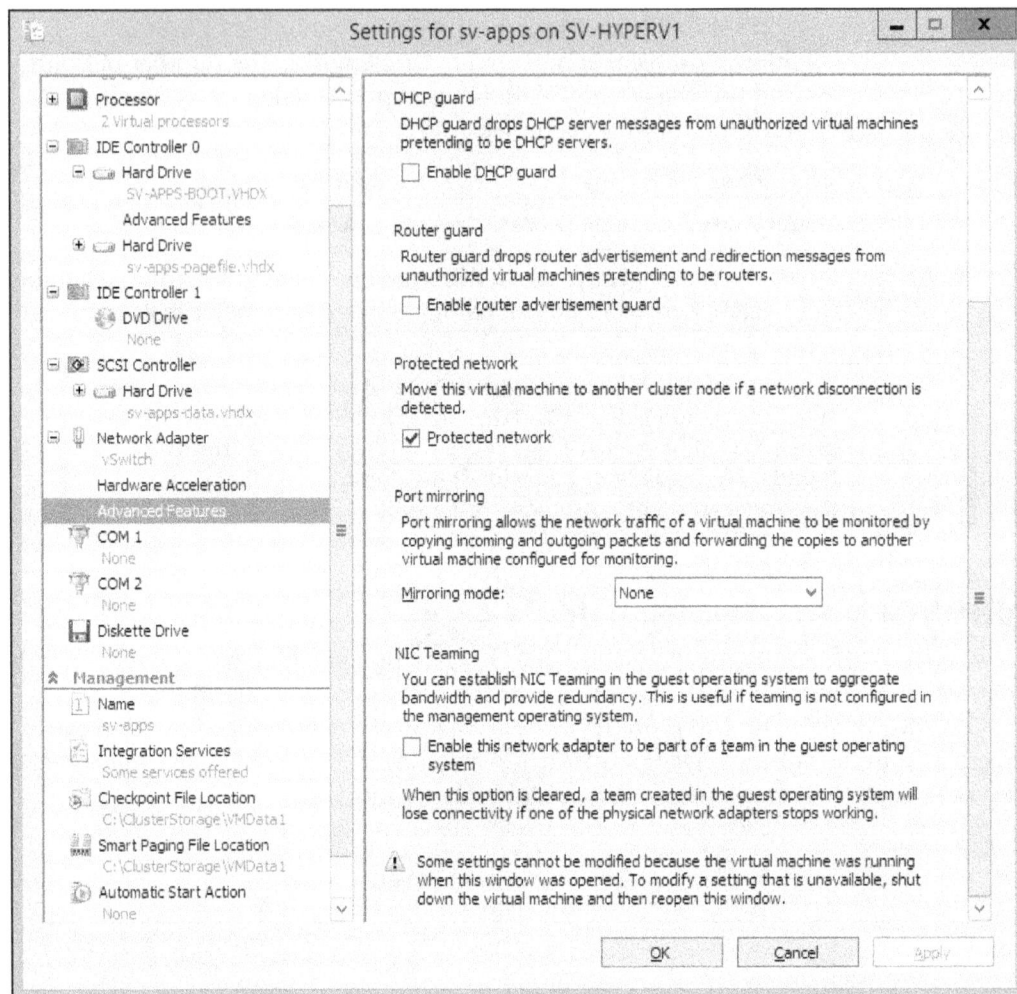

The PowerShell cmdlet is a little awkward to use, as it is phrased as a negative. To enable network protections for all virtual adapters connected to the guest named sv-apps, consider the following cmdlet:

```
Set-VMNetworkAdapter -VMName "sv-apps" -NotMonitoredInCluster $false
```

You can, of course, use the Name parameter or pipeline from Get-VMNetworkAdapter to select one or more specific virtual adapters.

Quorum

A major concern in an automated failover system is the split-brain scenario. This occurs when two or more resource controllers believe they are in control of the only running instance of that resource. This is also known as a partitioned cluster. In the case of clustered Hyper-V Servers, such a situation would look like the following figure:

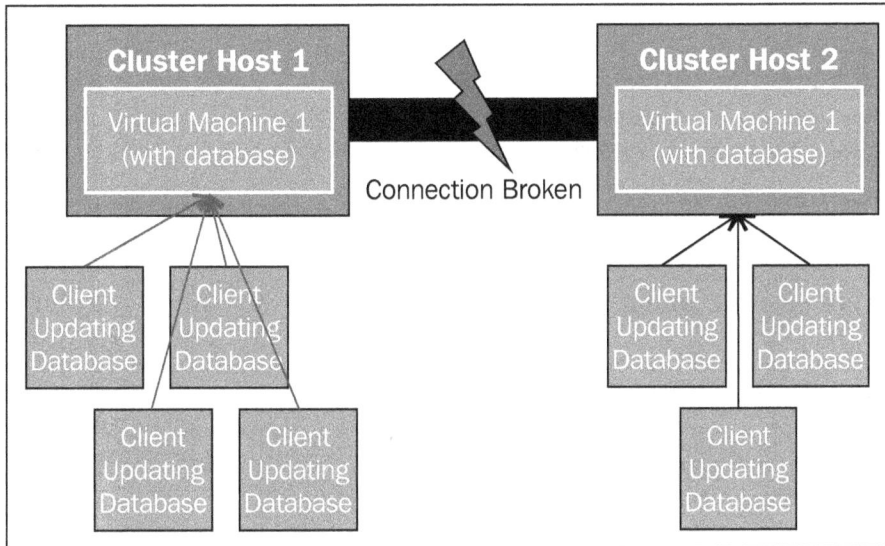

In the figure, the hosts cannot see each other, so each assumes that the other is down and starts the highly available virtual machine. Clients connect and begin making updates to two separate database copies, resulting in modifications that may be irreconcilable. Fortunately, this situation is practically impossible for most virtual machines. Even if multiple nodes try to bring the same virtual machines online, only one will be able to use its files, most importantly its VHDs, which exist on shared storage. For the virtual machines that use pass-through disks, the outcome isn't as clear. Some multisite clusters use replication technologies that make a single LUN available simultaneously across sites, so the same disk would seem to be available, even if the intersite link drops. Even for a virtual machine that uses shared disk technologies, the inability to determine which of the previous two hosts should be in control can still lead to failover and failback issues.

To address the split-brain problem, Microsoft Failover Clustering uses a quorum methodology. The term is borrowed from human organization practices in which a specific number or percentage of the whole must be present in order for the group to perform its function. In the case of Hyper-V Server and Microsoft Failover Clustering, the group is the cluster nodes and the function is to keep highly available virtual machines online without a split-brain.

There are a number of different methods to configure the quorum in Microsoft Failover Clustering. In all cases, each node determines for itself whether or not the requirements for quorum have been met. If it does not believe quorum is satisfied, it will shut down its guests according to their Automatic Stop Action and stop its cluster local service. If other nodes believe they have quorum, they can take ownership of those offline virtual machines and start them.

The oldest method in Microsoft clustering is the single disk witness. As long as a node can reach this witness, it will remain online. This witness is a single point of failure; if it goes offline, all nodes lose quorum and the entire cluster is shut down. The single witness method is still available, but not recommended.

The preferred methods involve a majority of nodes. Clusters with an odd number of nodes can use the simple `Node Majority` method. As long as a node sees enough other nodes that, along with itself, constitute a majority of the total number of nodes in the cluster, it will remain online. Clusters with an even number of nodes can use a disk or file share witness as a tiebreaker.

While the `Node Majority` option should be sufficient in most cases, it is possible to configure individual nodes so that they don't have a vote. When a node's vote is removed, it is no longer considered when determining if quorum is met. This configuration should only be used after careful consideration, as each non-voting node reduces the number of failures that the cluster can withstand. As an example, a five-node cluster with only three voting nodes must have a minimum of two of the three online, in order for any node to function.

A new addition in Windows Server 2012 is Dynamic Quorum. If a single node exits the cluster, the cluster service will remove its vote after a time. This effectively reduces the number of nodes necessary for the cluster to achieve quorum. In a situation such as a controlled, orderly shutdown of nodes, it is possible for a cluster to operate all the way down to a single node. However, if multiple nodes are lost simultaneously, as in a partitioned scenario, and the loss causes the cluster to dip below majority before the votes can be removed, the remaining nodes will lose quorum and the cluster will shut down.

R2 adds the ability to remove the disk witness' vote as well.

> Quorum is configured when the cluster is created, and reconfigured when nodes are added and removed. There is no need to manually override its settings without a specific reason.

Configuring quorum using Failover Cluster Manager

In the left pane, right-click on the cluster's name, navigate to **More Actions** and click on **Configure Cluster Quorum** Settings. This will launch a wizard. The first screen is simply informational. Click **Next**.

On the second screen, you'll have three options to choose from. In 2012, the first is **Use typical settings (recommended)**; in R2, it is **Use default quorum configuration**. This allows Failover Clustering to determine what it believes is the best mode for your system. The **Add or change the quorum witness** (2012) / **Select the quorum witness** (R2) option are a subset of the screens presented for the third option, **Advanced quorum configuration and witness** selection, so both will be discussed together. The first two screens are only shown for the advanced configuration option. On the **Select Voting Configuration** screen, select the nodes you wish to have a vote: all, none, or a subset. On the **Quorum Management** screen, check whether or not you wish to enable Dynamic Quorum. As it indicates, any nodes that have had their votes manually removed are not managed or counted by Dynamic Quorum. The third screen from the Advanced selection, **Select Quorum Witness**, is the first screen you'll see if you opted for the **Advanced quorum configuration and witness** selection. On this page, you indicate whether or not you wish to use a witness.

In 2012, the wizard will indicate whether a particular option is recommended or not, depending on your current configuration, as shown in the following screenshot:

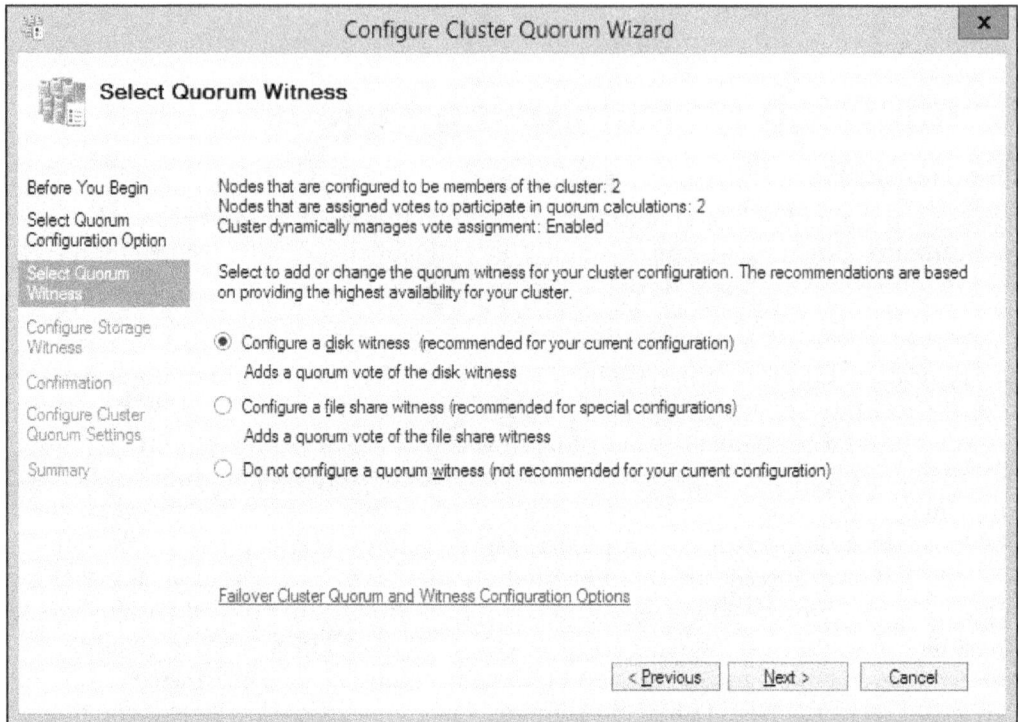

R2 does not make any recommendations, but otherwise the screen has the same options.

The **disk witness** refers to a cluster disk. As you saw in *Chapter 4, Storage Design*, a cluster disk is an iSCSI or Fibre Channel LUN that is visible from all cluster nodes. It cannot be configured as a CSV. It's not required, but is highly recommended that a quorum disk be used for nothing else. The disk must be formatted as NTFS and should be 512 MB in size. Cluster data itself will generally consume less than 100 MB, so anything larger than 512 MB is wasted.

The second option is the **file share**. This can be any SMB share location formatted with NTFS. The computer accounts for each node must have full control over this share point (unless the cluster service has been configured to run as a user, then that account must have full control). The share location needs about 5 MB of free space.

The final option is to not use a witness at all. Use this with an odd number of nodes.

The remainder of the wizard is simply verification and confirmation.

Configuring quorum using PowerShell

Use the `Set-ClusterQuorum` cmdlet to configure the quorum method that you want. It has four mutually exclusive parameters: `NodeMajority`, `NodeAndDiskMajority`, `NodeAndFileShareMajority`, and `DiskOnly`. `NodeMajority` is used alone but the others require that you specify the witness.

To set a disk witness, use the name of the cluster disk. You can use the following cmdlet to see a list of all disks:

```
Get-ClusterResource | Where-Object -FilterScript { $_.ResourceType -eq
"Physical Disk" }
```

If you need to add a disk, refer to *Chapter 4*, *Storage Design*. Once you've determined the disk to use, use the following cmdlet to set it as the disk witness:

```
Set-ClusterQuorum -NodeAndDiskMajority "Cluster Disk 3"
```

For a file share, use:

```
Set-ClusterQuorum -NodeAndFileShareMajority \\sv-file1\cluster1fsw
```

To use only a disk witness without node votes:

```
Set-ClusterQuorum -DiskOnly "Cluster Disk 3"
```

To enable or disable Dynamic Quorum, set the `DynamicQuorum` property of the cluster to a `1` or `0`, respectively:

```
(Get-Cluster -Name "cl-hyperv1").DynamicQuorum = 1
```

To add or remove a node's vote, set its `NodeWeight` property to `1` or `0`, respectively:

```
(Get-ClusterNode -Name "sv-hyperv2").NodeWeight = 1
```

R2-only quorum PowerShell operations

If Dynamic Quorum is active and you are using a disk witness, the cluster will automatically add or remove the disk witness' vote. You can view its current status as follows:

```
(Get-Cluster).WitnessDynamicWeight
```

If the response is `1`, the witness has its vote. A `0` indicates that it does not.

To prevent an even number of nodes, Dynamic Quorum will automatically remove votes from nodes to ensure an odd number of votes. To designate a system as the first to lose its vote, retrieve its ID and pass it to the new `LowerQuorumPriorityId` parameter. Use the following cmdlet as an example:

```
(Get-Cluster).LowerQuorumPriorityNodeID = (Get-ClusterNode -Name "sv-hyperv2").Id
```

Replace everything after the equals sign with a `0` to return the configuration to its default.

Practical quorum guidance

It is recommended to allow the wizard to decide how to set your quorum.

For an even-node cluster, your first choice for a witness should be a cluster disk. They are commonly placed on the same physical storage as the guest machines, so it's a reasonable way to protect the cluster if it's not reachable. The virtual machine storage is likely to be unavailable as well, so it's of little consequence whether or not the cluster continues to operate.

For a file share witness to be truly useful, it should not be in a location that any cluster resource depends on. This means that it should not be on the shared storage for the cluster or any virtual machine. The file share witness is most useful in multicluster and multisite configurations. If you have a number of clusters, all of their witnesses can reside on a single file server that isn't part of any of them. For a multisite cluster, the benefit of a file share witness is that it does not require a single iSCSI or Fibre Channel LUN to be reachable by all nodes. All sites will be able to reach the witness with only the standard intersite networking configuration. For resiliency, the file share witness can be placed on a clustered file server.

Quorum disks should not participate in antivirus scans or backup. Use caution in setting access permissions. A witness disk will contain the active configuration database for the cluster, just as a computer node does. A file share witness will contain only a log file.

As with the file share witness, the greatest use for removing a node's vote is also in a multisite cluster. Due to the possibility of isolation, it is necessary to determine in advance which site you wish to survive in all cases. For 2012, placing the cluster's witness in this site is the first step to ensuring it is the primary. However, because of Dynamic Quorum, that alone is not a guarantee. For instance, if a node in the primary site goes offline for maintenance, Dynamic Quorum will automatically remove its vote. If the primary site then becomes isolated, no site will have quorum and the entire cluster will shut down.

Let's understand the concept in more detail with the help of the following figure:

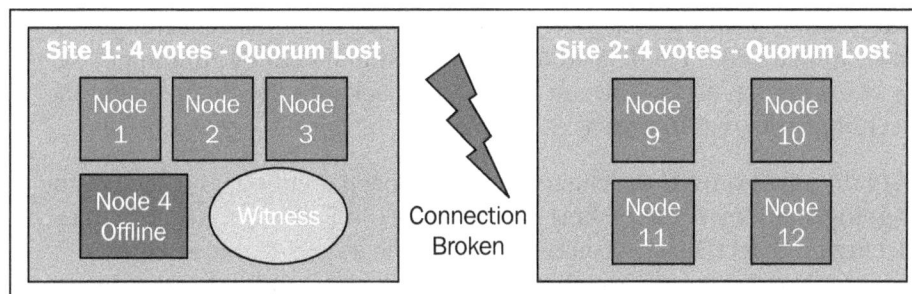

As node 4 is offline due to maintenance, each site has four votes if Dynamic Quorum is disabled. The cluster requires five votes for majority. When the connection drops, both sites will instantly be below the minimum required for the cluster and all nodes will shut down. If Dynamic Quorum is enabled, one of the other nodes will have its vote removed so that majority is satisfied by only three nodes. However, Dynamic Quorum will decide from which node to pull the second vote and it could be in either site. This very condition is the purpose of the new automatic witness vote handling and the `LowerQuorumPriorityId` parameter in R2.

To prevent the situation in 2012, the best choice is to remove votes from sites other than the primary. The easiest way is to simply remove votes from all nodes in those secondary sites. You may come up with a strategy to leave voting nodes in the other sites to cover less emergent situations where nodes in the primary site go offline.

Recovering from quorum loss

When a node loses quorum, it will shut down its cluster service. If all nodes lose quorum, your cluster will be in a failed state. In all cases, determine the reason that quorum was lost prior to performing any recovery steps. If the reason isn't obvious, you can examine the `cluster.log` file, which is in the `\Windows\Cluster\Reports` folder on the system drive of each node, to see if it contains any clues.

How you recover will depend on how the failure occurred. If nodes will not be returnable to the cluster, perhaps due to hardware failure, then evict them. This option can be found under the **More Actions** menu on the node in Failover Cluster Manager. You can also use PowerShell:

```
Remove-ClusterNode -Name sv-hyperv1
```

Eviction should be a last resort option reserved for a node that cannot be fixed. If a node has been evicted while offline but can be returned to service, it will still retain the configuration from the last point at which it was a member. It cannot rejoin the cluster in that state. You'll need to remove residual data by running `Clear-ClusterNode` on that node. You can then add it back into the cluster using the same techniques shown in *Chapter 3, Constructing a Hyper-V Server Cluster*.

If the situation that caused the cluster to fail has been rectified, you can get the cluster going again by right-clicking on the cluster in Failover Cluster Manager and clicking on **Start Cluster**. You can also run the `Start-Cluster` cmdlet on any node. The cluster service on each node will start, and their contained resources will perform their designated Automatic Start Action. You can use the `IgnorePersistentState` toggle parameter with `Start-Cluster` to prevent them from starting, if desired.

Another possibility is that the nodes aren't unrecoverable but you can't bring them all online and you need to get the cluster started again. This could occur in the situation outlined previously, if the secondary site is unreachable and its nodes were allowed to vote. In this case, you'll need to force the cluster to start. There is a **Force Cluster Start** menu option right below the **Start Cluster** menu item in Failover Cluster Manager. This will start as many members as possible.

To force the cluster to start using PowerShell, connect to the node you wish to begin the startup with and run the following cmdlet:

```
Start-ClusterNode -FixQuorum
```

If you've started the cluster using a node that has previously had its vote removed, set its `NodeWeight` property back to **1**, as shown in the previous command-line example. This will only start the single node. To start others, you need to ensure that they do not attempt to establish quorum by themselves. Do so with the `PreventQuorum` parameter:

```
Start-ClusterNode -Name sv-hyperv1 -PreventQuorum
```

Once enough nodes have rejoined the cluster to be considered a quorum, you can start nodes normally. As soon as the cluster has true quorum, it will be in normal operation mode. Any further failures that occur will be measured against the standard quorum.

Snapshots or checkpoints

Snapshots, called checkpoints in R2, are not commonly considered part of the high availability features of Hyper-V Server. However, they can be used to ensure and provide regular client access to services, so they fall within the scope. For the remainder of this section, only VHD files will be mentioned, although everything about snapshots also applies to VHDX files as well. Snapshot will be the term used, but remember that R2 uses the term checkpoint.

A snapshot captures the state of a virtual machine at an exact point in time. This includes its running processes, memory state, and even how its virtual hardware, such as virtual network adapters, is configured. Any VHD files that the virtual machines write to are frozen and new writes intended for those disk files will instead be placed in an AVHD file. The virtual machine continues to run uninterrupted. If necessary, you can revert to a snapshot. This stops the virtual machine, discards its current running state and everything that has occurred since the snapshot was taken, and starts the virtual machine from the exact point at which the snapshot was taken.

> Pass-through disks are completely unaltered by the snapshot process. They are not captured when a snapshot is taken, nor are they reverted when a snapshot is applied. If a pass-through disk is connected or disconnected after a snapshot is taken, the connection status will be reversed when the snapshot is applied.

In order to take a snapshot, just right-click on virtual machine in Hyper-V Manager, and then click on **Snapshot**. To get a snapshot in PowerShell (the cmdlet name and parameters are the same in both versions), use the following cmdlet:

```
Checkpoint-VM -Name "sv-apps" -SnapshotName "OS Upgrade"
```

The SnapshotName parameter is optional. Without it, the snapshot will have the name of the virtual machine and the time stamp of the snapshot. Snapshots can be renamed in Hyper-V Manager by right-clicking on the snapshot and choosing **Rename**, or by highlighting it and pressing *F2*.

If you take snapshots of a machine that is already snapshotted, it will be a child of the earlier snapshot. If you revert to an older snapshot and then snapshot the virtual machine again, you will have formed a branch snapshot. Complicated trees such as these are more easily managed in Hyper-V Manager's GUI. They are displayed in the **Snapshots** section in the center pane when a virtual machine is selected.

An example of screenshot is as follows:

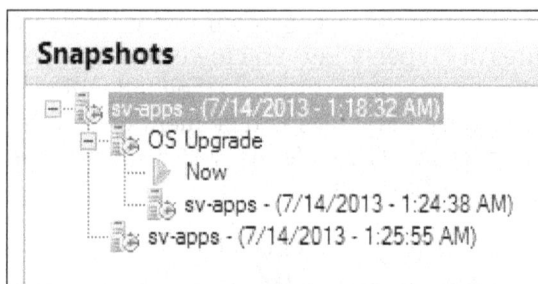

Snapshots

```
⊟─ sv-apps - (7/14/2013 - 1:18:32 AM)
   ⊟─ OS Upgrade
      ▷ Now
      ─ sv-apps - (7/14/2013 - 1:24:38 AM)
   ─ sv-apps - (7/14/2013 - 1:25:55 AM)
```

In order to revert to a snapshot, right-click on it, and then choose **Apply**. You will receive a warning dialog that will allow you to take another snapshot prior to applying the selected snapshot. You can also apply a snapshot by using PowerShell (also the same cmdlet in both versions):

```
Restore-VMSnapshot -VMName "sv-apps" -Name "OS Upgrade"
```

You will be asked to confirm the reversion, but you will not be asked to create a snapshot as in the GUI. If you need to see a list of a virtual machine's snapshots, run the following cmdlet:

```
Get-VM -Name "sv-apps" | Get-VMSnapshot
```

Delete a snapshot by right-clicking on it and choosing **Delete Snapshot** or, to remove a snapshot and all of its children, choose **Delete Snapshot Subtree**. With PowerShell, execute the follwowing command:

```
Remove-VMSnapshot -VMName "sv-apps" -Name "OS Upgrade"
-IncludeAllChildSnapshots
```

> Never manipulate AVHD files manually. This can cause permanent data loss.

If the snapshot to be deleted is a child of the current running state, or is in a different snapshot tree, it will be deleted immediately. If it is a parent, then the current status will be merged with the parent status. This can take some time, but it is performed online. There must be enough space in the virtual machine's storage location to build the combined VHD file(s). Usually, this is a little larger than the size of the base VHD file.

By default, the files for a snapshot are stored in the same location as the rest of the files for the virtual machine. This location can be changed by using Storage Live Migration to specifically move the snapshot files, which will move any existing snapshots to the new location. You can also change the virtual machine's settings, which will change where new snapshots are placed but will not affect any existing snapshots. On the virtual machine's **Settings** dialog in Failover Cluster Manager and Hyper-V Manager, there is a **Snapshot File Location** tab where you can change this setting. To modify it using PowerShell, execute the following command:

```
Set-VM -Name "sv-apps" -SnapshotFileLocation "\\sv-storage\VMSnapshots"
```

Snapshots can be exported. This is useful in shared test and development scenarios. A specific snapshot can be exported and then imported as a complete virtual machine. The virtual machine must be off. In Hyper-V Manager, there is an **Export** option available on a snapshot's right-click menu. You'll be asked where the export files are to be saved; if the destination is not on the local machine, the host's computer account must have write access in the target location. In PowerShell, type the following command:

```
Export-VMSnapshot -VMName "sv-apps" -Name "OS Upgrade" -Path C:\Exports
```

Practical snapshot guidance

Snapshots are a very powerful tool. They allow you to make changes to a production machine and quickly revert to a known working state if the changes turn out to be undesirable. In a non-virtual environment, this would require restoring from backup and could take hours. With snapshots, it takes only moments, dramatically reducing service interruption to clients.

While powerful, snapshots are also potentially very dangerous. As illustrated in *Chapter 9*, *Special Cases*, they can be catastrophic when used with domain controllers. Other applications may also respond poorly. Definitely avoid using snapshots with virtual machines that are members of a cluster of guest virtual machines.

Even with virtual machines that can be used sensibly with snapshots, there is a problem. The AVHD file that a snapshot uses has no upper limit on growth and it tracks all changes that the disk file has encountered since being snapshotted, so it can potentially grow very rapidly. If a storage location for a virtual machine runs out of space completely, then that virtual machine will be paused. Since virtual machines typically share a location, this can cause service interruption for several guests.

There are a number of ways to ensure safe usage of snapshots:

- Set a very short limit on snapshot age. As a reverted snapshot loses all data and changes that occurred after it was taken, snapshots quickly lose value as they age. If a snapshot is more than a few days old, relying on a true backup is a superior option. Unfortunately, Hyper-V cannot manage age restrictions for you.

- Snapshots are not backups. Always use dedicated backup software.

- Educate all staff on the proper use and dangers of snapshots.

- Periodically check for the existence of snapshots. This can be done in PowerShell very easily (per host):

```
Get-VM | Get-VMSnapshot
```

- Target snapshots to a location other than where virtual machines store their active VHD files. This will restrict the effect of an out-of-control snapshot to the guest(s) using snapshots on that location.

- Be very judicious about snapshotting high I/O virtual machines, such as SQL Servers. They will likely have much quicker AVHD file growth.

> Other methods are available to restrict the usage of snapshots, such as targeting the snapshot location to an invalid directory, or using pass-through disks. Using an invalid location for the snapshot directory is a hack that specifically breaks the way that Hyper-V functions, and is neither supported nor recommended. The pass-through disk approach reduces portability and resilience of virtual machines. Pass-through disks are generally not useful in Hyper-V Server 2012 and later, but using them specifically to prevent snapshots is poor usage of the technology. Educate and train staff instead.

Typical high availability uses for snapshots are software roll-outs and upgrades in which the outcome is uncertain, and the effects of any problems must be mitigated in the shortest amount of time possible. If used cautiously and judiciously, they are a valuable asset in the Hyper-V administrator's toolkit. Used improperly, they can cause problems that are difficult to rectify. Use them sparingly and monitor them closely.

Summary

In this chapter, we discussed the high availability features of Hyper-V Server in a Microsoft Failover Cluster. We learned the related definitions and how they are employed in a Service Level Agreement. We instructed the creation and deployment of a highly available virtual machine. We learned about other ways we can leverage a Hyper-V Server cluster to provide high availability. We saw how a cluster operates when a failure occurs and how to configure virtual machines to react as you wish. We learned about quorum, how to configure it, and how it works in a failure condition. Finally, we learned about snapshots and how they can provide high availability for your virtual machines.

At this stage, we have enough information to design, deploy, and operate a fully functional Hyper-V Server cluster. In the next chapter, we will learn how to protect it and its virtual machines in situations that high availability cannot address.

12
Backup and Disaster Recovery

An unfortunate fact of the computing world is that failures occur. High availability features go a long way toward mitigating the negative impacts of small and simple failures, but they do not offer. This chapter will look at the ways you can guarantee the safety of your virtual machines and their data beyond clustering.

The primary topics covered in this chapter are:

- Knowing your risks
- Planning for disaster recovery
- Planning and deploying backup
- Planning and deploying Hyper-V Replica
- Verifying your disaster recovery plan

The most critical message of this chapter is that without a thorough plan to protect your systems, all high availability measures are potentially useless.

Knowing your risks

The basic concept behind disaster recovery planning is to try to mitigate the effects of events that are outside your control; for example, you cannot control whether or not the public power grid will continue to supply electricity to your installation. So you can employ uninterruptible power supplies, secondary public sources, and diesel generators to compensate. As a general rule, powers outages are temporary and won't qualify as true disasters. While you'll certainly need to plan for them, you'll need to focus your planning on larger issues. There are three general risk categories:

- Physical loss
- Data loss
- Data corruption

Physical loss

The most common disaster preparedness scenarios focus on physical loss. Common risks for all installations will be fire and theft. Depending on your location, you may have other concerns such as tornados, hurricanes, floods, earthquakes, and other natural disasters. Many of these risks can be mitigated with technological, construction, and placement strategies. Such approaches will need to be coordinated with those responsible for your building and facilities layout, purchasing, and maintenance teams.

Remember that not all loss is malicious or an act of nature. Basic mechanical and electronic failure is more likely, although usually less catastrophic. Your failover cluster design has hopefully planned for most of the likely failures and will be able to handle them without extended downtime. Other failures may be out of your control, for example, a broken cooling unit that services the server room and forces a shutdown, or a broken water line whose problems spread into your electrical or server system.

Data loss

Data loss varies from routine to catastrophic. The most common data loss scenario is simply a user inadvertently deleting or overwriting a file. Similar issues involve improper usage of an application that causes data to become invalidated.

Data loss can also result from environmental causes. When a system unexpectedly goes offline, perhaps as a result of a blue screen or power failure, data being actively processed is usually lost. In some instances, related data, especially in a database system, might be lost as well.

A third, and fortunately much less common, cause of data loss is malicious assault. Internal users pose as much risk as external attackers, and sometimes more. Such risks also include untargeted attacks such as viruses and other malware.

Data corruption

Data corruption is a persistent threat in the data center. Data corruption can occur as a result of the same causes as data loss. It can also be a result of an application misbehaving or improper usage. Parity-based RAID arrays (such as, RAID-5 and RAID-6, with very large drives and a very large number of disks) may not be able to complete scrub operations in a timely fashion, which can allow data to become slowly corrupted over time.

> During a scrub, the RAID controller performs read operations on all blocks on all disks to ensure that they are physically operating as expected. This is a background operation and on arrays with very large disks, it may take so long to complete that corruption risks may go undetected for many days.

Risk analysis

Often, the previous issues come in groups. A RAID controller failure might cause data on the contained drives to be lost or destroyed. Theft is a definite risk for component and data loss. When planning, expect and plan for the worst.

Some industries may need to place more emphasis on planning for specific contingencies than others. For instance, a bank branch should expect regular external attacks. A factory plant that mass-produces commodity parts is likely to be at much less risk of direct assault. However, such a facility may not place as much emphasis on computer safety in its information worker training programs, which may place it at greater risk for untargeted malware and social engineering attacks.

> A social engineering attack occurs when a malicious individual convinces a user to perform a task that grants the attacker access without involving technological means. This can involve posing as a trustworthy individual: "Hi, this is your IT department. Can I have your username and password so I can test something?"

Regardless of your organization's expected risks, even those with low probability should be planned for. Many issues may necessitate the same response, but the act of investigating your potential risks may reveal previously unknown vulnerabilities.

Risk mitigation

Proactively preparing for potential problems can dramatically reduce, and in some cases eliminate, their impact. For instance, in the previous example regarding power outages, installing uninterruptible power supplies is a logical first step. However, during risk assessment, you may also come across information that indicates that power outages in your area are commonly between three and four hours in duration. This information can be used to help you design a power plan that allows your organization to work through a typical outage without interruption.

Some mitigation strategies will only reduce the impact of an outage, not prevent it. For instance, if your data center is in a flood zone, it may be impossible to truly guarantee that power will be available. However, you may be able to position critical systems above the expected water line, which will at least allow you to save the equipment.

Security measures can be taken to reduce your risk of theft and malicious attacks. Security is a very large and complex topic that cannot be covered in a few short paragraphs; so consider the following to be quick introductory material. Physical security should not be overlooked, as the average computer system is much easier to compromise when an attacker has physical access to it. Keeping your infrastructure systems behind locked doors is a vital first step; access controls such as proximity or magnetic stripe badges may also be justified depending on your risks.

Establishing digital security is far more difficult than physical security, and it is vital to understand that no digital system with any form of external connectivity can be fully secured. Your first step should be to leverage your Active Directory infrastructure. In the case of your Hyper-V Server hosts, only members of the local Administrators and Hyper-V Administrators groups can manipulate Hyper-V. Keep a close control over members of these groups and enforce sensible password strength policies. Your organization should also have written policies that prohibit password-sharing. Optionally, you may use the **Authorization Manager (AzMan)** to further restrict access to your Hyper-V deployment. Microsoft provides instructions for doing so on the TechNet site, which is found at `http://technet.microsoft.com/en-us/library/dd283030%28v=ws.10%29.aspx`.

The next step to digital security involves basic preventative infrastructure design and planning. Your Hyper-V Server hosts (along with other critical systems) should be protected by an adequate firewall system. Internet browsing from any server system should be discouraged and perhaps prevented. You may opt to install antivirus software. However, the scanning exclusions required for successful deployment of antivirus applications on a Hyper-V Server host are broad enough that the effectiveness of such an application is reduced.

Microsoft hosts a wiki page that lists these exclusions: `http://social.technet.microsoft.com/wiki/contents/articles/2179.hyper-v-anti-virus-exclusions-for-hyper-v-hosts.aspx`. It is usually much more effective to protect the endpoints around your Hyper-V host, such as all user and administrator workstations, than try to scan the hosts. Unlike the hosts, guest operating systems have no particular restrictions against having antivirus packages installed.

For organizations with greater security needs, other options are available. These options include things such as **Intrusion Prevention Systems** (**IPS**) and **Intrusion Detection Systems** (**IDS**). These systems can be software applications, virtual appliances, hardware systems, or hybrid offerings. You may also consider hiring a computer security consulting firm to help you analyze your risks and prepare your systems. Many computer training companies offer courses on computer security that can provide knowledge and expert advice on the proper tools and resources that have a proven track record.

Planning for disaster recovery

With an idea of risks in hand and mitigation components in place, you are ready to plan your disaster recovery strategy. Despite its name, disaster recovery is not truly limited to the recovery phase but also includes the response phase in which you are actively reacting to a disaster in progress. Strategies should include multiple tiers as not all disasters will be handled the same way. For instance, you may suffer catastrophic data loss that doesn't require you to perform any physical hardware replacement; so your response will necessarily be different in that case.

Disaster recovery planning is another large, complex topic that encompasses much more than Hyper-V Server clusters. Every department in your organization should be involved in disaster recovery planning as it includes things such as personnel evacuation, customer notification, and filing the appropriate insurance claims for your damaged or lost buildings and equipment. As with security, consulting firms offer disaster recovery planning services and can assist you with this process. For the purpose of this book, we will look at the tools you have available to recover your Hyper-V Server clusters.

Backup

If the data on your systems has any value at all, then it is imperative that you employ at least one backup tool. You must not attempt any shortcut methods. The snapshots introduced in *Chapter 11*, *High Availability*, do not qualify. Hyper-V Replica, which will be discussed later in this chapter, is insufficient. Investigate and select solutions that involve dedicated backup software packages.

Choosing a backup solution

In order for a backup application to be considered acceptable, it must satisfy all of the following conditions:

- Allows for complete recovery without any source data or equipment:

  Complete loss of the source environment is a possibility that must be planned for.

- Allows for partial recovery:

  As discussed earlier in this chapter, most data loss is simple user error and does not require an elaborate failover response. Restoring an entire file server is not an appropriate response to the loss of a single file.

- Must be storable offsite:

  The major point of backup is making a copy of your data. Keeping that copy in an alternate location protects against physical theft, loss, and tampering. That site must be reasonably far away from the origin site, and physical security must be accounted for.

- Backup points must exceed a single point in time:

  Data corruption is usually not noticed right away. A user may need a copy of a file as it was last week. Your organization may be involved in a lawsuit that requires data that was purged months ago. The rule of how long to keep the backup data for a system is called a retention policy. These are organizationally defined.

- **Volume Shadow Copy Services (VSS)** integration:

  VSS is a Microsoft technology that allows data to be backed up without taking the resource offline. A backup application that is VSS-aware can notify the service to initiate its process. VSS, in turn, will notify VSS-aware applications that a backup is about to occur. They can then take the necessary steps to prepare. As an example, Microsoft SQL Server will flush all data to disk and commit its logs. All pending disk operations such as regular file writes are also flushed. VSS takes a snapshot of the volume (this concept is similar to, but not the same as a Hyper-V snapshot). The backup application is then free to read the snapshotted data while the system continues operating normally. The purpose of VSS is to ensure that there are no active transactions in memory. All data is captured in the backup at the moment of the snapshot. This is known as an application consistent backup. Compare this to crash consistent (sometimes called file consistent) backups in which the disk contents are exactly as they were at the moment of the snapshot but active I/O and in-memory data are lost.

- Hyper-V Server awareness:

    Many backup applications cannot work with Hyper-V virtual machines. Some cannot even work with Hyper-V. There are ways to proceed without Hyper-V awareness but your options for backup and restoration are reduced.

- Cluster awareness:

    Even among applications that do understand Hyper-V, not all can interact with a cluster. With advancements in the way that Hyper-V Server and Microsoft Failover Clustering interoperate, this can sometimes be worked around. However, these workarounds are generally more trouble than they're worth.

- CSV/SMB 3.0 Awareness:

    Cluster-awareness should also extend to the storage. Some applications are able to back up virtual machines in a cluster, but only if they are held on a cluster disk. As you'll recall, a cluster disk can only hold the files for a single virtual machine as only one cluster host at a time can access that disk. Prior to Hyper-V Server 2012, a truly cluster-aware backup application needed to be able to back up the contents of a CSV. Now you must also verify that your solution is able to back up virtual machines stored on SMB 3.0 file shares if you are using them.

- Physical backup portability:

    In the event that you do not have the capability to back up to a remote site, the backup data that you have needs to be able to be moved offsite easily in order to ensure that it is protected from building loss. If you are able to back up to a remote destination, you'll need to have the ability to easily bring that data back to a primary site in the event that a rebuild is necessary. Over-the-wire restores during crisis recovery are often too slow. Also, your secondary site could be in danger as well, so being able to move at least some backup data quickly is always a necessity.

- Encryption:

  Encryption is not universally necessary, but usually desirable. Many industries such as finance have regulations that require that all backup data be encrypted. Organizations in lightly regulated industries may also have some legal requirements to encrypt data. For instance, if your employee database contains sensitive personal information, you may be obligated to encrypt its backups. In other cases, you may not be under a legal requirement, but it is beneficial to be able to assure your customers that any data you keep on them is protected, especially if it is on portable media.

The previous items set the ground rules for applications that you'll evaluate as part of your solution. There are a number of packages available on the market today, and their number is increasing. There are very few free offerings, and most that can be had without cost do not cover the entire range of requirements.

Architecting a backup solution

Usually, only small infrastructures can be adequately covered with a simple view: backup everything nightly and keep each month-end backup for a one-year approach. Most organizations employ a tiered backup strategy. There are four foundational criteria: what needs to be backed up, how often does it need to be backed up, how long does the data need to be kept, and where will the backed-up data reside? Answering these questions in order will help you to architect your solution.

Choosing what to back up

The level of backup granularity will vary from organization to organization. If you have very tight budgets and need to watch every megabyte of storage, you may need to specifically exclude things such as page files. In other organization, it's simple to just back up everything. Make sure that you involve the departments who own the data.

If you have applications with data that spans servers, such as a database-dependent application using multiple databases, then search for a backup application that knows how to handle that application. Standard backup solutions will capture data that keeps the data on a single system consistent, but will not coordinate across multiple computers. If all of the systems in such a group are virtualized, you could design a script that shuts them down or places them in a save state and another that wakes them up. Most backup applications provide the capability to call scripts at the start and end of a backup job.

Choosing when to back up

Backups are traditionally taken on a daily basis. Sometimes this is too much. For instance, you may have a server that holds only the frontend web interface for a database-driven application. Except for the logs, it only changes when it is upgraded. Your organization may consider that to be a waste of network bandwidth and disk resources to back up each night. You might elect to only have this system be backed up manually right after an upgrade cycle or automatically at the first of every month.

Other systems may require more frequent backups. Some backup applications even offer continuous updates.

Deciding how long to keep backup data

As mentioned previously, the amount of time to keep data is known as a **retention policy**. Most organizations will not use a single number for this. Financial data may need to be kept for a certain number of years for regulatory compliance. Other data, such as domain controller backups, becomes stale very quickly.

Hybrid solutions

After researching the capabilities of available backup software and your particular needs, you may determine that a single backup application cannot provide everything you need. You may have a single application that can perform all the tasks, but not with a singular approach. In such cases, you may decide upon a hybrid backup strategy. In these cases, some virtual machines will be backed up from within Hyper-V. Others will be backed up as though they were physical systems via an agent installed inside the guest.

The following figure shows how a hybrid solution could be deployed and configured:

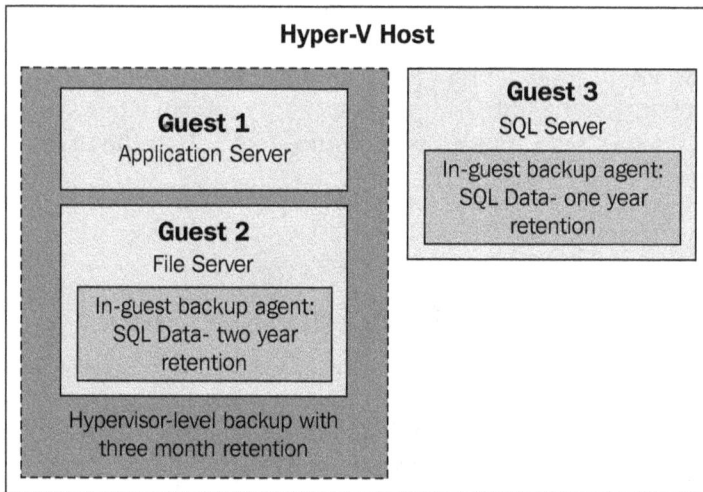

In the previous figure, backup software agents are installed and configured in a way that ensures that all data is backed up according to the organization's frequency and retention policies. In the context of backup applications, an agent is a smaller piece of software that can be installed in an operating system, where its backup operations can be controlled by a central backup server. Not all applications will use these agents. They may require you to install the complete application inside the target computer. Such applications will not be aware of the activities of other installations of the same program, so you're likely to wind up with complicated and overlapping backup schedules that could lead to resource contention.

Storage for backup

With the previous three sections addressed, you are now likely to have an idea of the capacity you'll need for your backups. Most backup applications provide some capability for compressing or deduplicating the stored data, but it's very difficult to predict just how much space this will actually save. The text data generally compresses very well while applications, images, and other binary data generally compresses very poorly. Many vendors will advertise a fifty percent compression ratio, but this is optimistic.

Start with a safer estimate such as thirty percent. Deduplication can often save you much more, but these are usually tracked across copies of the same data and not necessarily across different backed up items. For instance, if you have a daily copy of your file server's virtual machine, your backup application may only keep one copy of any given block of data that is the same in all five copies. If a file is changed in one of those copies, only the different blocks are kept. These changed blocks are known as **deltas**. However, if identical blocks exist in a completely different virtual machine, your application may not deduplicate across the virtual machines. The more thorough a deduplication process is, the more storage savings you can expect to realize. Be aware that space savings come at the expense of processing power and time.

Storage media is a large consideration in backup. Disk-based backup systems are becoming more and more ubiquitous, but the venerable tape drive is still around and is likely to remain for some time. Disk-based systems are much faster and often less expensive, but they have different vulnerabilities. A single tape is quickly and easily carried from location to location and shielded, carrying caddies and briefcases are available for organizations with many tapes. A single disk drive is harder to transport and you always need to be conscious of power supplies. Tape-based systems are generally designed for more simplistic rotation systems that allow you to keep historical backups that do not rely on any particular tape set. Hard-drive systems usually build periodic master images and only track the changes for subsequent backups. What's more, they could require a fairly large chain of data to be available in order to effect a restore. Overall, hard drives are more reliable than tapes, but their dependence upon moving parts and drive controllers also means they have more components that could fail.

You also have the option of paying to use some else's space. Many vendors and third-party hosting providers will allow you to back up to their systems. These are usually marketed as cloud-based backup solutions.

Whatever medium or media you choose, ensure that your backup solution supports it and that you understand how it supports it. Some applications will use both disk and tape, but expect that you will only use them in a disk-to-disk-to-tape configuration. They may not back up directly to tape and they may not retain data on disk for any length of time.

Deploying a backup solution

Virtual machines need to be prepared for backup. By default, they are created with the option for the host's VSS to communicate with the VSS in the guest. This occurs through Hyper-V Integration Services. Access the virtual machine's property sheet in **Hyper-V Manager** or **Failover Cluster Manager** and click on the **Integration Services** tab on the left. In the right pane, the state of the **Backup (volume snapshot)** checkbox indicates whether or not this communication is occurring. It can also be checked via PowerShell:

```
Get-VMIntegrationService -VMName sv-dc1 -Name VSS
```

You can use Enable-VMIntegrationService or Disable-VMIntegrationService with the exact same format as the previous cmdlet to switch its status.

If this checkbox is enabled, Windows guests with a functioning VSS will be backed up in an application-consistent fashion. If the checkbox is cleared, the virtual machine will be suspended while the host takes a VSS snapshot of the containing volume. Behavior varies if the checkbox is checked but the guest does not support VSS. Errors and warnings will be recorded in the host's application event log.

> In Hyper-V Server 2012, Linux guests need to be suspended for backup unless your application has specific methods for handling them. In R2, this is no longer the case depending on the guest's kernel version. However, live Linux backups are always crash consistent; not application consistent.

Deployment of your backup application will be dependent upon that software and will need to be done in accordance with its documentation and support staff. The following sections will discuss built-in Windows tools to perform backups.

Windows Server Backup

Windows Server Backup has the advantage of being a built-in component of Windows Server and Hyper-V Server. Unfortunately, it has a number of limitations, making it mostly appropriate for very small installations or as a stop-gap measure until a more robust application can be deployed. Chief among these limitations is that it is not precisely cluster-aware. It can back up virtual machines on a **Cluster Shared Volume (CSV)**, but not on SMB 3.0 shares. Also, it doesn't match virtual machines to CSVs so you need to be sure you are directly instructing it to back up all locations where your virtual machines reside.

A single backup job can target CSVs or the local file system, but not both. Another limitation is that it can only back up to disk targets or Microsoft's Azure service, and only provides true rotation protection when the disk target is a local disk. At the time of writing this, the Azure service is still considered a preview and is therefore not production-ready.

If you use Windows Server Backup with your cluster, only use one host to backup guests on any single CSV. Non-highly-available virtual machines will need to be backed up by a local installation of Windows Server Backup.

> An enhancement in Windows Server Backup 2012 allows it to directly see and backup virtual machines on a host. However, it cannot follow them if they move from one host to another. Only use this feature for local virtual machines.

Microsoft provides very detailed instructions on setting up and operating Windows Server Backup under multiple conditions. You can view the entire topic on TechNet at `http://technet.microsoft.com/en-us/library/cc770757.aspx`. The sub-item **Configure Automatic Backups with Task Scheduler** is of special interest. If you use Windows Server Backup to target a URL, it can only overwrite existing data. Also, the built-in tool's only scheduling option is daily or less. By leveraging Task Scheduler, you can schedule multiple backups that have the same basic structure but target different locations. For instance, you can set up a file share called **\\sv-backup\Monday** and schedule a backup that runs only on Mondays and targets that folder. This will automatically give you a one-week retention schedule.

Hyper-V Replica

The purpose of Hyper-V Replica is to provide a mechanism for the extremely rapid recovery of a lost virtual machine. As mentioned in the previous sections on backup, it is not a backup solution and does not replace the need for such a solution. The simple description of replica is that it creates another virtual machine on another Hyper-V host that is a ready-to-run clone of the source virtual machine and asynchronously updates the replica's VHDs. Hyper-V Server 2012 allows you to make a single replica; R2 allows you to chain to a second replica system.

Replica works by first duplicating the source system and then actively updating the replica as the source changes. The original copy includes the virtual machine configuration and disk contents. Ongoing replication contains only the changes made to the disk's contents. Replica works at the block storage level and only tracks changes instead of repeatedly copying the entire virtual machine. It does have the power to periodically trigger the guest's VSS component so that some instances of the replica are application consistent; although this can occur no more often than once every hour. All others are crash consistent. Running threads and memory contents are never captured.

> Hyper-V Replica cannot replicate the contents of pass-through disks or R2's shared VHDX files.

Replicas are created by copying the initial and changed block data to a logfile simply called the **Hyper-V Replica Log (HRL)**. This logfile is transmitted to the replica host. Upon arrival, it acknowledges receipt back to the sending host. The receiving host then processes the HRL files as necessary to keep the active replica and its historical recovery points current.

Architecting a Hyper-V Replica solution

Designing your Hyper-V Replica deployment isn't quite as complicated as backup. You need to decide which virtual machines and virtual disks to replicate, where to send them, and how many replicas to track. Unlike backups, the frequency is mostly decided for you. In Hyper-V Server 2012, it is every five minutes and this is not changeable. In R2, you can choose between thirty second, five minute, or fifteen minute intervals.

Choosing where to send replicas

One of the first decisions you'll make is where to send your replicas as that is likely to have the most influence on your other decisions. Unlike backups, replicas are actual virtual machines that need to be ready to run at a moment's notice. The destination hardware needs to be able to run those virtual machines at acceptable performance levels. Your disaster recovery planning may allow for the replicas to support a lighter workload than the active production system. This means you may choose to use hardware that isn't as powerful as your primary systems. It will still need sufficient disk capacity to hold the replica and unprocessed HRL files. If you'll be keeping more than just the most recent replica, you'll also need to plan for additional storage.

The other limiting factor in your destination planning is connection speed. While you can certainly host replicas in the same building or campus as their sources, that doesn't provide the best protection against a disaster. You're definitely advised to have some distance between the sites, preferably enough to eliminate or significantly reduce the probability that both (or all three, if using R2) would be lost in the same catastrophe. Of course, this means you're going to need a connection between the sites.

The three factors that influence this inter-site connection are bandwidth, the amount of data that is being replicated, and link stability. If your sites' links are asynchronous (differing upload versus download speeds) you'll need to ensure that the incoming speed for the replica site is high enough for your projected data transfers. Replica can reconnect if the link drops, but transmission delays equate to replication delays.

Another option for remote sites is to use a third-party hosting site. Be aware that some of these providers will require the use of additional software such as Microsoft System Center. Using a third party can significantly reduce the costs necessary to facilitate a replica, especially if you don't have a secondary site of your own. A provider will likely consolidate multiple customers onto high-grade equipment, meaning that you'll have access to superior hardware at a lower cost to you. Many providers will also have expert staff that can aid you with setup, configuration, maintenance, and failover operations.

> Microsoft also provides a service that allows you to target your replicas to Azure. However, you cannot run them from Azure; in the event of a site failure, you use Azure as the source and replicate back to your own recovery site. At the time of writing this, this service was also still in preview status.

Choosing what to replicate

With an idea of your hardware, storage, and bandwidth limitations; it's easier to decide what needs to be replicated. Bandwidth will be most stressed by systems that change rapidly.

One system type you should not replicate is the domain controller. Replicas are guaranteed to be older than the systems they are protecting which means that the probability of a USN rollback (explained in *Chapter 9*, *Special Cases*) is very high. Instead, set up at least one active domain controller at your replica site(s).

Hyper-V Replica does allow you to choose which of the virtual machines' virtual disk files to include in the replica, so you can reduce the size of your replicas and the necessary bandwidth by choosing not to replicate disks that contain a pagefile. The pagefile can have a significant amount of data churn and none of it would be useful in a replica. Normally, the pagefile is kept on the same disk as the operating system, and excluding that disk would prevent the replica from booting. As an alternative, you can move the pagefile to its own virtual disk and skip it for replication.

We will perform the following steps to change the pagefile disk for a Hyper-V virtual machine running a Windows operating system:

1. The first step is to set up a replica for the virtual machine as normal (a link to the instructions is provided in the next section). Replicate all of the virtual machine's VHDs. Once done, right-click on the virtual machine in Hyper-V Manager and choose **Remove Replication**. Do the same to the replica.

2. If the virtual machine is generation one (generation two is only available in Hyper-V Server 2012 R2), the virtual machine must be shut down. In Hyper-V Manager for a non-highly-available virtual machine or Failover Cluster Manager for a highly-available guest, right-click on the virtual machine and click on **Settings**.

3. For a generation one virtual machine, you must use a disk on an IDE controller. It does not matter which you choose. The only restriction is that it must not currently have two attached disks because two is the maximum for IDE. For a generation two virtual machine (R2 only), your only option is the SCSI controller. Click on the desired controller to highlight it. In the right pane, highlight **Hard Drive** and click on **Add**. The window will change to reflect properties for a new drive on the selected controller as shown in the following screenshot:

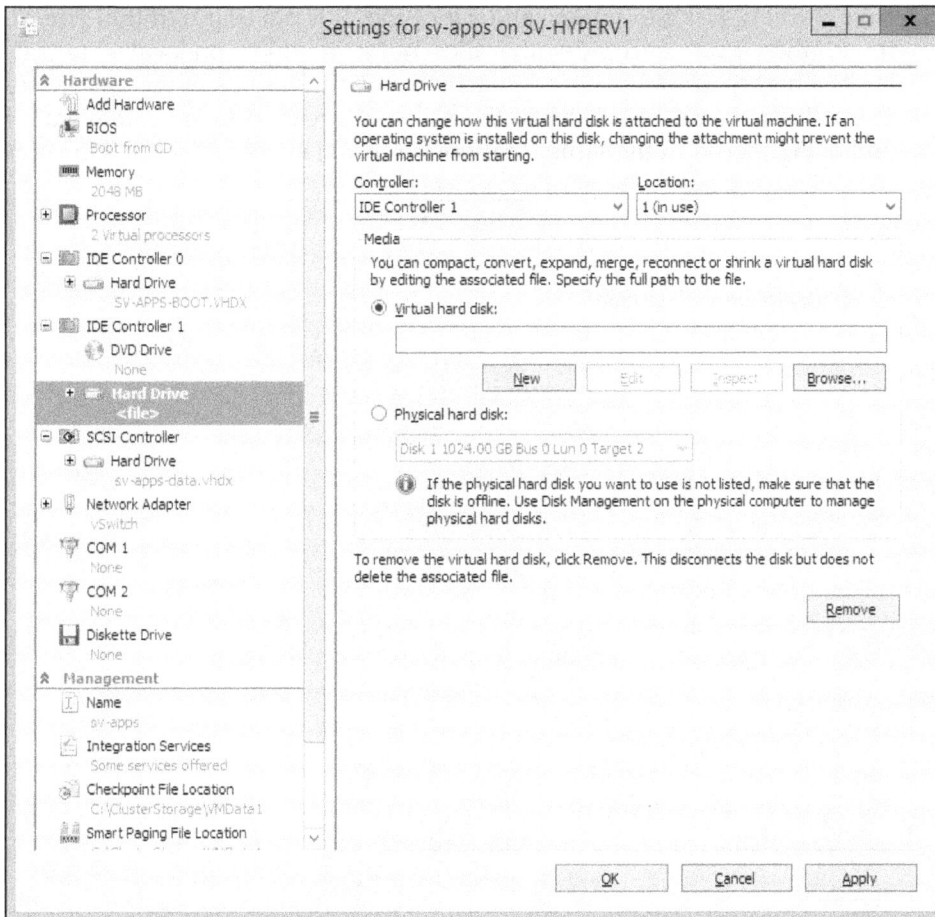

4. Click on the **New** button. Click on **Next** on the introductory tab to be taken to the **Choose Disk Format** screen. It is recommended that you choose VHDX as the drive type. The warning about older operating systems not being able to read VHDX applies to the host. The guest doesn't know what's holding it. Click on **Next**.

5. On the **Choose Disk Type** screen, you may choose either **Fixed** or **Dynamically Expanding**, but not **Differencing**. The fixed disk is slightly faster; but pagefile disks should not be utilized extensively enough for the difference to be meaningful. Because you'll be allocating most of the space all at once and not changing it thereafter, fragmentation of the VHD file will be of little concern no matter which type you use. Make your selection and click on **Next**.

6. Give the new disk file a name and a location. It is not required that you place it with the virtual machine's other files, but it should be on local storage if it is not a highly-available virtual machine and on shared storage otherwise. The following screenshot shows the disk being named to indicate what it is and being placed in the same location as the VM's other files. Click on **Next**.

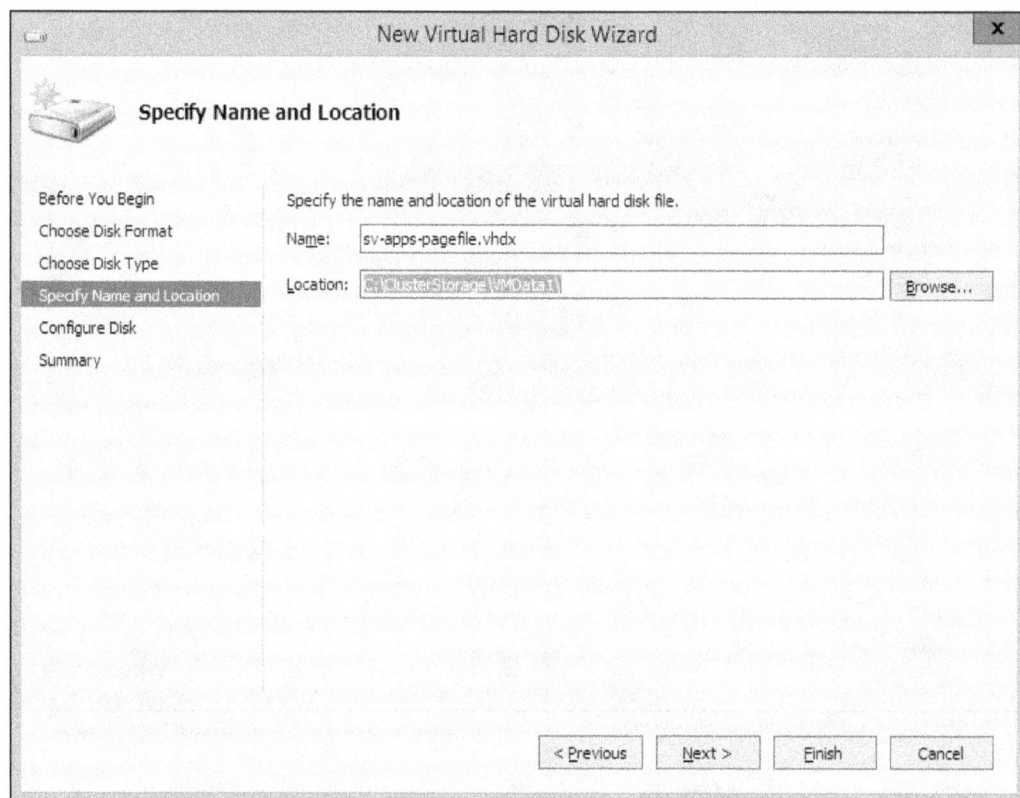

7. This will bring you to the **Configure Disk** screen, where you need to create a new file or clone an existing one. You'll be creating a new disk, so leave the radio button on that option (as shown in the following screenshot) and select a size. The disk should be large enough to contain your pagefile plus at least five percent to keep low disk space warnings from occurring. If you are creating a fixed VHDX, remember that all of the unused space will be completely wasted, so do not oversize this volume. Once you have entered the desired size, click on **Next**.

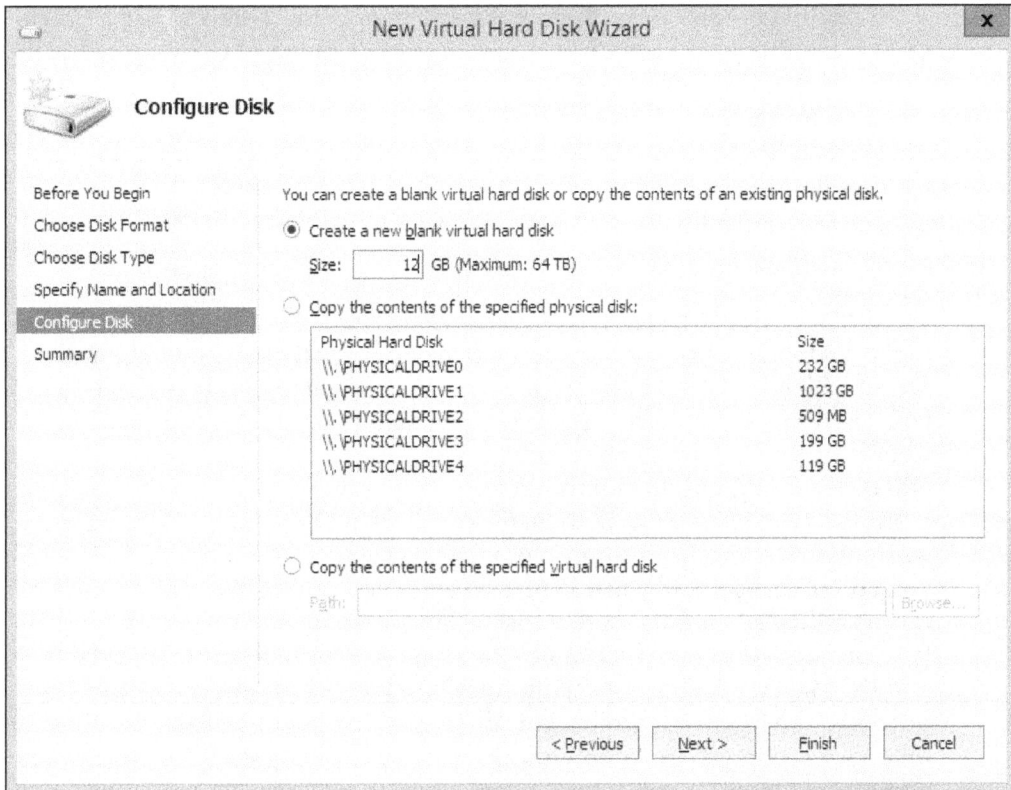

New Virtual Hard Disk Wizard

Configure Disk

Before You Begin

Choose Disk Format

Choose Disk Type

Specify Name and Location

Configure Disk

Summary

You can create a blank virtual hard disk or copy the contents of an existing physical disk.

⦿ Create a new blank virtual hard disk

Size: 12 GB (Maximum: 64 TB)

○ Copy the contents of the specified physical disk:

Physical Hard Disk	Size
\\.\PHYSICALDRIVE0	232 GB
\\.\PHYSICALDRIVE1	1023 GB
\\.\PHYSICALDRIVE2	509 MB
\\.\PHYSICALDRIVE3	199 GB
\\.\PHYSICALDRIVE4	119 GB

○ Copy the contents of the specified virtual hard disk

Path: [   ] Browse...

< Previous   Next >   Finish   Cancel

8. Review your options and click on **Finish**. Click on **OK** in the **settings dialog** and turn the virtual machine on.

9. Inside the guest, access **Disk Management** through **Computer Management** in **Administrative Tools** (or the **Tools** menu of Server Manager in Windows Server 2012 and later). As with any other disk, you must initialize it, bring it online, and format it. You must assign a drive letter.

10. The dialog box to change page file settings is consistent across all current versions of Windows, but the way that you access it varies:

    ° For Windows XP and Windows Server 2003, right-click on the **My Computer** icon and click on **Properties**. When the dialog opens, switch to the **Advanced** tab.

    ○   For Windows operating systems starting with Vista and Server 2008, the **Properties** option is on the right-click menu of **Computer**, which is now **This PC** as of 8.1/Server 2012 R2. This icon is found on the Start menu or Start screen. This opens a screen which displays a large window of system information. At the left of this window, click on the **Advanced Properties** link and you will be taken to the computer properties dialog with the **Advanced** tab already selected.

11. Click on the **Settings** button in the **Performance** group box. In the **Performance Options** dialog, switch to the **Advanced** tab. Click on **Change**.

12. In the **Virtual Memory** dialog, deselect **Automatically manage paging file size** for all drives. Highlight the operating system volume in the list box. Use the radio button to select either **Custom size** or **No paging file**. Generally, you'll want to use a minimal pagefile so that blue screen data will be recorded, but the minimum necessary changes based on the installed RAM. You can enter 16 in both fields then click on **Set** and **OK** to receive a warning that indicates the minimum for this system. Highlight the drive that you added and set it to **Custom size** as well. You can use the **Recommended** size as indicated near the bottom of the box or whatever size you desire. It is considered best practice to use the same size for both the **Initial size** and the **Maximum size**, especially since you have dedicated a disk for this purpose. The following screenshot shows the creation of an 8 GB pagefile following these recommendations. Once you've made your selections, click on **Set** and **OK**.

Virtual Memory

☐ Automatically manage paging file size for all drives

Paging file size for each drive

Drive [Volume Label]	Paging File Size (MB)
C:	200 - 200
E: [sv-apps-data]	None
P: [PageFile]	8192 - 8192

Selected drive: P: [PageFile]
Space available: 12186 MB

◉ Custom size:

Initial size (MB):   8192

Maximum size (MB):   8192

◯ System managed size

◯ No paging file   [Set]

Total paging file size for all drives

Minimum allowed: 16 MB

Recommended: 2047 MB

Currently allocated: 8200 MB

[OK]   [Cancel]

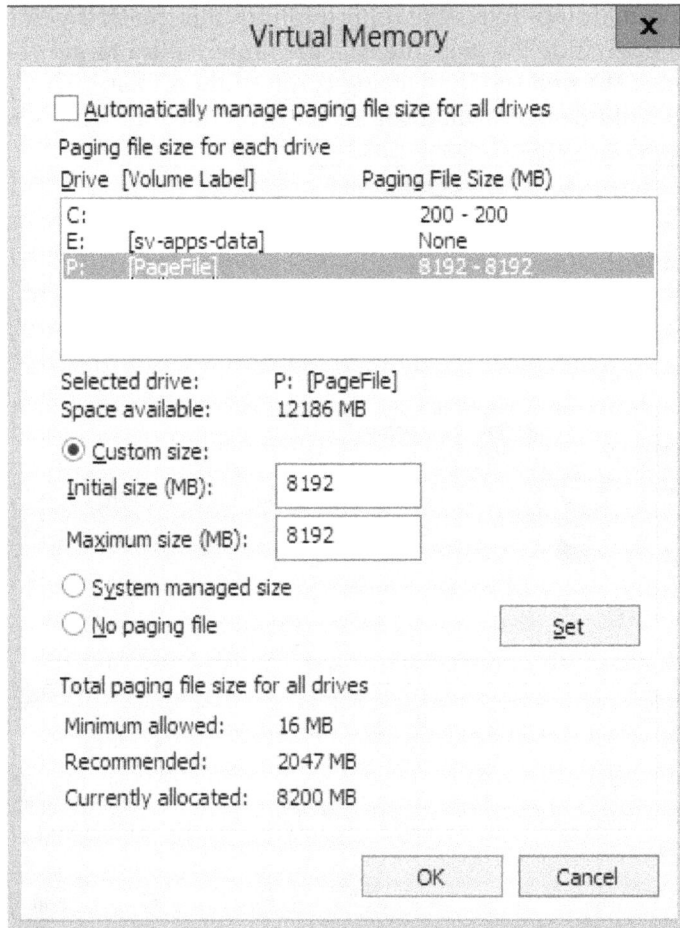

> Older operating systems will not allow a single pagefile to exceed 4 GB.

13. You'll be notified that you need to restart for your changes to take effect. Keep responding **OK** to the dialogs and you'll be given the opportunity to reboot. Once the guest has restarted, the pagefile has been moved.

14. Follow normal steps to enable replication for this guest. If you are recreating a replica to exclude the page file, use the same replica target you did when you created the first replica. During configuration, ensure that you do not select the volume that contains it, as shown in the following screenshot:

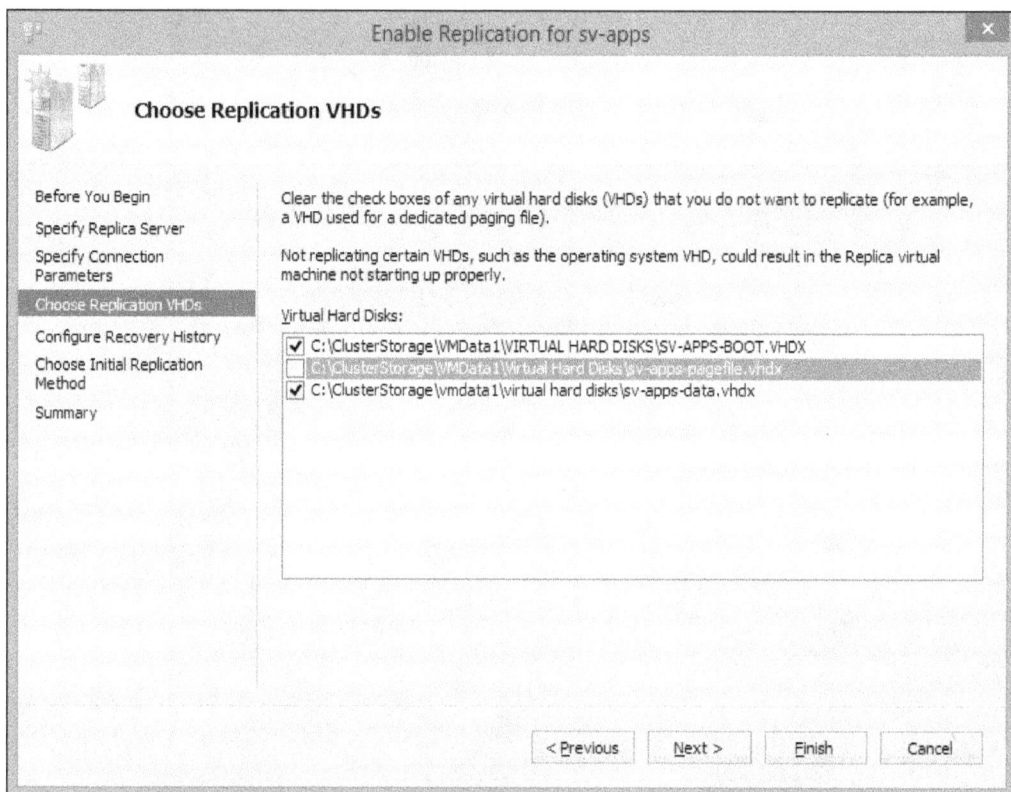

15. If you are re-enabling replication on a virtual machine, ensure that you instruct Hyper-V Replica to use it as the initial seed when reconfiguring, as shown in the following screenshot:

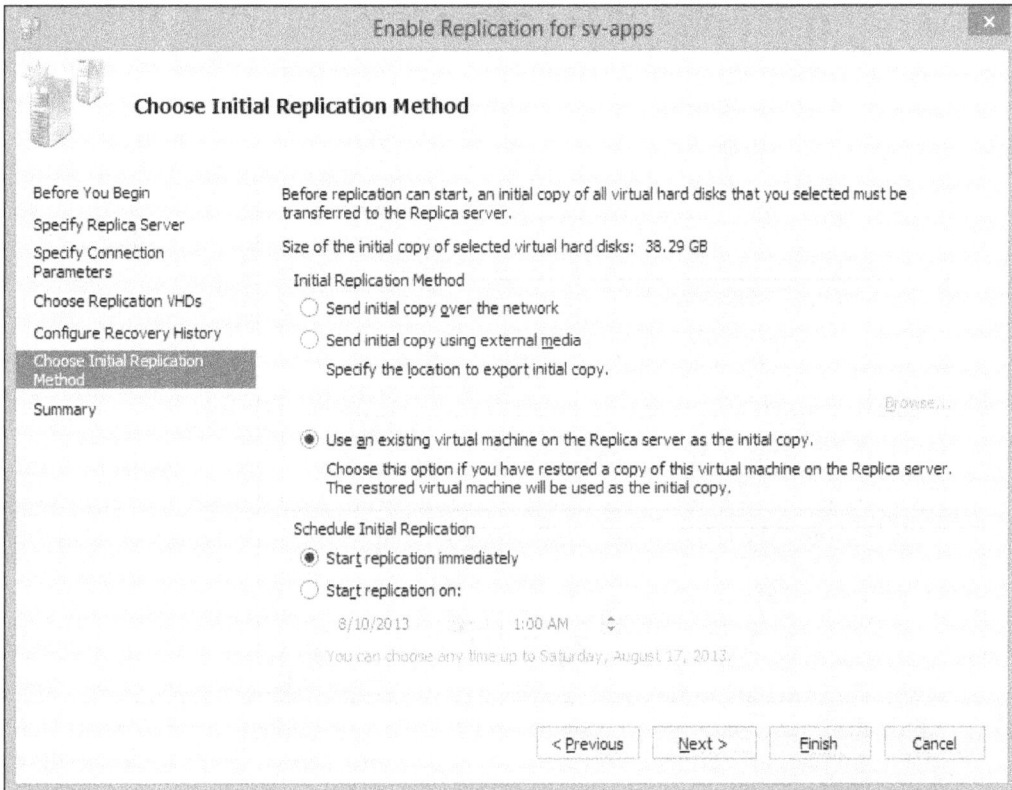

If you perform these steps on a system that has never been replicated, it will be unable to use any pagefile other than the small one that you placed on the system volume. It will still boot, but performance will likely be impacted. This is the reason that the previous procedure recommended that the pagefile VHD be initially replicated with the others.

Deciding how many recovery points to keep

In large part, available storage will dictate how many recovery points to keep. Each one is kept as a complete replica, not simple differencing files such as the logs. The benefit of keeping more than one is to counteract any problems that might arise from corruption. Events that cause outages can cause or be caused by data corruption, and there is a chance that this corruption might be transmitted in an HRL file marked as successfully retrieved.

Deploying Hyper-V Replica

This book will not directly cover the mechanics of replica deployment. Microsoft has provided an extremely detailed walkthrough that would be difficult to substantially improve upon. You can access those directions at the following URL: `http://technet.microsoft.com/en-us/library/jj134207.aspx`. One weak point of the directions relates to configuring the Hyper-V Replica Broker. Like Cluster-Aware Updating, this requires the creation of a computer account in Active Directory. Prestaging does not work. You must give your cluster's computer account sufficient permissions to create computer accounts in its own organizational unit. Refer to the *Configuring Cluster-Aware Updating* in *Chapter 10, Maintaining and Monitoring a Hyper-V Server Cluster*, for more information.

Practical Hyper-V Replica guidance

There are a few items in Microsoft's directions that could use additional explanation and there are some other things to be aware of:

- Because you are protecting a cluster, you must follow the steps to create the Hyper-V Replica Broker role (Step 1.4 in the Microsoft document). This role is assigned its own **Cluster Name Object** (CNO). That object is created by the wizard using the credentials of the current cluster's computer object. Therefore, you must grant that computer object privileges to the Active Directory organizational unit where the current cluster's name object resides. The directions for doing so are the same as for Cluster-Aware Updating. Refer to the *Configuring Cluster-Aware Updating* section in *Chapter 10, Maintaining and Monitoring a Hyper-V Server Cluster*, for more details.

- When transmitting replica data over a connection that is not secure (such as the public Internet), use the certificate-based authentication method as opposed to the Kerberos method to encrypt the transmission. Certificate encryption is asymmetrical, resulting in an encrypted package that is larger than its source, so more bandwidth is used. If your sites are connected by a static VPN, it is likely that they are already using an encrypted tunnel so Kerberos authentication may be sufficient.

> If your sites are connected by MPLS and your routers employ encryption cards, Kerberos will fail. An exception ACL must be set up to allow Kerberos. Consult with your MPLS provider for assistance.

- Even though you are replicating from a cluster, it is not required for the destination system to also be a cluster.

- After configuring the replica host or cluster to accept incoming replicas from the live cluster, you'll also want to configure the live cluster to accept replicas from the replica host or cluster. This will allow you to fail back after a test or impermanent primary site failure.

- If you need to employ port forwarding on your routers, Kerberos replication uses TCP port 80 and certificate-based replication uses 443.

- Hyper-V Replica contains no built-in ability to automatically failover. This is because it has no ability to prevent a **split-brain scenario**. In this situation, a single virtual machine is running in more than one location at a time. It is possible to set up scripts that automatically perform a failover, but it is recommended that you only automate the failover steps, not the trigger that starts them. Replica failover should only occur as an intentional action carried out when an active decision has been made and involved parties are aware of the possibility of the split brain scenario and of the time that will be required to fail back to the primary site once the failover event is resolved.

- R2 introduces the ability to change the amount of time between replica transmissions. The default is still five minutes and can be changed to thirty seconds or fifteen minutes. These settings will reduce or increase your RPO accordingly and individual transmissions will also be larger or smaller.

- When testing a replica in a failover situation, it is possible to encounter network collisions with the source system. To counter this, you have the ability to specify TCP/IP information just for a failover situation. These settings are made on the individual virtual network adapter. When you access the **Settings** dialog for any replicated virtual machine, its network adapters will have a **Failover TCP/IP** sub-tab. This screen and sample settings are shown in the following screenshot:

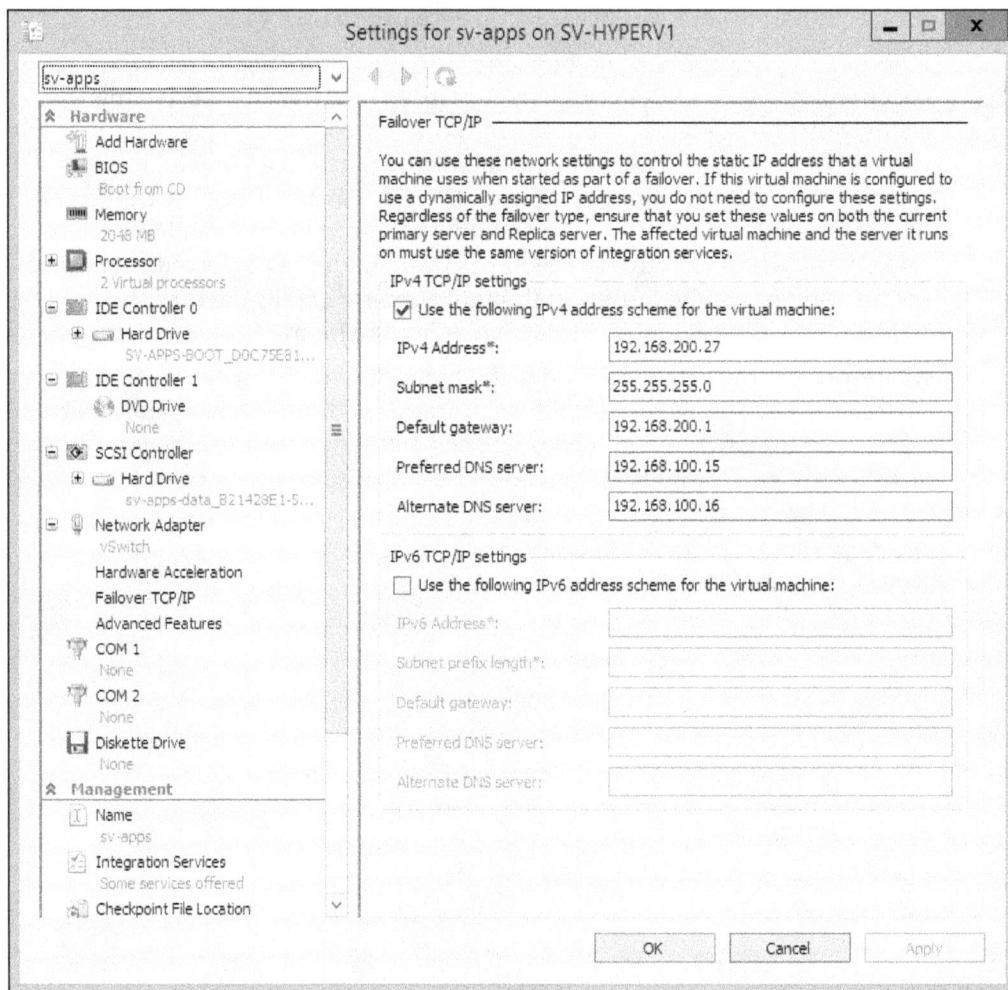

> Depending on the configuration of your replica site, it may still be possible for a replicated virtual machine to register its failover IP address or update its Active Directory information. Carefully design your replica network to avoid this.

- Replicas exist as distinct virtual machines. If replication is removed, the replica host or cluster keeps the replica and all its data. You can use Hyper-V Manager and PowerShell to manage them just as you would any other virtual machine. However, replicas that are still actively receiving changes need to be left offline and the VHDs participating in replication must not be touched.

Verifying your disaster recovery plan

One of the most-ignored activities in disaster recovery is the need to ensure that the plan can actually be used. A good disaster recovery plan should include periodic verification of backup data and failover/failback tests of the replica system. If any systems are not being backed up or replicated, verifications need to be made to ensure that the organization can actually operate without them. If any special activities are required that are not immediately obvious, such as how to failover to the replica site, they need to be fully documented and made available to multiple individuals.

What follows are some simple items that should be included on a disaster recovery checklist:

- Backups are periodically restored and tested.
- Replica failovers are periodically tested.
- The strategy for what, when, and how backups and replicas occur are periodically checked to ensure that they are still relevant.
- Staff are aware of and trained on the organizational procedures to respond to a disaster. Drills are carried out periodically.

Most Hyper-V backup applications have the ability to restore a virtual machine as a clone. Make sure that you don't connect a clone to the network at the same time as the original; but it should be powered on and tested. Windows Server Backup cannot create a clone, but it can place restored files in an alternate location. You can then use the Import feature in Hyper-V Manager or the Import-VM cmdlet. The drawback with this is that the restored item will have the same name as the original, so care must be taken to segregate them so that it is the clone that is deleted when testing is complete.

Step 4 of Microsoft's deployment pages for deploying Hyper-V Replica provide a walkthrough for testing your Hyper-V Replica with a controlled failover. A failover of this type ensures that all data is replicated before initiating the transfer, so this procedure is safe to perform.

Periodic testing of your backups and replica is essential. It ensures that your data protection schemes are functioning properly and verifies that the storage media and locations are performing as expected. These data tests should be part of a larger battery of tests that verify your overall disaster recovery plan.

Summary

This chapter was devoted to explaining the methods you can use to protect the data on your Hyper-V Server Failover Cluster. It examined the basics of disaster recovery planning, discussed backup strategies, and introduced Hyper-V Replica in the context of a cluster. Of all the tasks this book has covered, backup is the most important. This is the only way to provide any reasonable assurance that your data is truly protected.

Index

CSV cache 145

D

data backup time
  deciding 405
database availability groups (DAG) 366
Data Center Bridging. *See* DCB
data corruption 399
data loss 398
DCB
  802.1p tagging 195
  about 58, 59, 193, 194
  applications, assigning to QoS classes 196
  bandwidth, setting on QoS classes 197
  default class 197
  traffic types, assigning to QoS classes 196
deduplication, storage 147
default class 197
deltas 407
design phase
  about 22, 38
  Active Directory domain 29
  adapter teaming 28
  backup 31
  Cluster and Cluster Shared Volumes 26
  Cluster Shared Volumes (CSV) 23
  CSV, mixing 24
  host computers 22
  iSCSI 27
  live migration 26
  management tools 30
  management traffic 25
  networking 25
  Physical adapter, considerations 28
  SMB 3.0, mixing 24
  SMB shares 24
  software, supporting 30
  storage 23
  subnetting 26
  training 31
  Virtualized domain controllers 29
  virtual machine traffic 27
Details mode 92
Device Specific Modules (DSM) 60, 367
Differentiated Service Code Point.
    See DSCP

Direct Memory Access (DMA) 210
disaster recovery
  plan, verifying 423, 424
  planning for 401
disk 329
disk analysis
  IOMeter usage for 274, 275
Disk-based systems 407
Disk I/O testing 271-274
disk management 143, 144
disk measurements 47
Disk Witness option 113
drive bus 122
DSCP 196
Dual Inline Memory Module (DIMM) 223
dynamic memory
  about 242-244
  minimum RAM value, accessing 245, 246
  requirements 244
  restrictions 244
  smart paging 245
  startup RAM 245
dynamic VHD file
  about 129
  versus, fixed VHD file 130, 131
dynamic VHDX file
  about 129
  performance 134, 135
  versus, fixed VHDX file 130, 131

E

ECC 225
Encapsulated Packet Task Offload 215
Enhanced Transmission Selection (ETS) 197
equipment preparation
  BIOS options, setting 78
  hardware, configuring 78
  shared storage system, configuring 78
Error Correcting Code. *See* ECC
event logs 354
existing systems
  planning for 38
expansion, Hyper-V Server storage 133
External Network 93

F

Failback parameter 373
failover
limits 380, 381
Failover Clustering Tools 83
Failover Cluster Management Tools 83
Failover Cluster Manager
about 104, 127, 144, 319
used, for configuring quorum 385, 386
used, for creating highly available virtual
machine 361-364
used, for making existing virtual machine
highly available 364
used, for setting possible owners 282, 283
used, for setting preferred owners 280
validation wizard, running 325-329
Failover Cluster Manager item 112
Fail Over Only (FOO) 143
fault tolerance 361
FB-DIMM 223
FC storage
connecting to 141
Feature Administration Tools 81-83
Fiber Channel Protocol (FCP) 124
Fibre Channel (FC) 59, 122
Fibre Channel over Ethernet (FCoE) 58, 193
file servers 156
File Share Witness option 113
File System Settings page 111
Firewall settings
about 186
Firewall rules 187, 188
PowerShell 187
remote desktop 186, 187
fixed VHD file 129
versus, dynamic VHD file 130, 131
fixed VHDX file 129
versus, dynamic VHDX file 130, 131
force 329
fragmentation, Hyper-V Server storage 133,
134
dynamic VHDX file, performance 134, 135
frames 203

G

geographically distributed cluster
about 312, 313
considerations 312, 313
Get-ClusterNetwork cmdlet 115
Group Policy Management Console
(GPMC) 187
Guest 8
guest virtualization rights
about 63-68
client access licenses 69
example, Hyper-V Replica 68
Software Assurance 69
GUI
used, for enabling CAU 343-345
GUI tools
acquiring 80
enabling 80
enabling, on Windows 8/8.1 80, 81
enabling, on Windows
Server 2012/R2 82-84
enabling, PowerShell used 85
used, for initial node configuration 86
used, for networking configuration 86-95

H

Hard-drive systems 407
hardware-assisted offloading
technologies 215, 216
HAVirtualMachine.mht 336
high availability
about 12, 13, 359
beyond Hyper-V 366
printing 14
removing, from virtual machine 365
highly available virtual machine
converting, PowerShell used 365
creating 361
creating, Failover Cluster Manager used
361-364
creating, PowerShell used 365
making available, Failover Cluster Manager
used 364

virtual machine, networking 317, 318

N

Properties screen 112

Q

QoS
about 189
settings 192
QoS classes
applications, assigning 195, 196
bandwidth, setting 197
traffic types, assigning 195, 196
Quality of Service. *See* QoS
Quick Migration 8
quorum
about 383-385
configuring 113
configuring, Failover Cluster Manager 386
configuring, Failover Cluster Manager used 385, 386
configuring, PowerShell used 387
guidance 388
loss, recovering from 389, 390
R2 Only quorum PowerShell operations 387, 388
QuorumConfiguration.mht 336

R

R2
network protection 381, 382
VHDX, shared in 367, 369
R2 Only quorum PowerShell operations 387, 388
RADIUS 138
RAID 122, 123
RAID-1 122
RAID-5 122
RAID-6 123
RAID-10 122
R-DIMM 223
RDMA 28, 124, 212, 213
real-time monitoring
with Performance Monitor 262, 263
Receive-Segment Coalescing (RSC) 216
receive-side scaling. *See* RSS
recovery points

deciding 419
Redirected Access Mode 162
Remote Direct Memory Access. *See* RDMA
RemoteFX 17
Remote Server Administration Tools.
    See RSAT
Remote tab 103
Rename-Computer cmdlet 97
Rename Network Adapters section 94
replica location
choosing 410
ReportName 330
requirements, existing sustems
disk measurements 47
MAP 39
MAP, using 40-44
memory measurements 46
metrics reading, approaches 46
network measurements 47
Performance Monitor 45
processor measurements 48
requirements, existing systems 39
resource metering 17
Restart-Computer command 97
Restart Needed column 98
restricted virtual machine 294, 295
retention policy 402, 405
risks
about 398
analysis 399
data corruption 399
data loss 398
mitigation 400, 401
physical loss 398
Role Administration Tools 81-83
roles 10
Round Robin (RR) 143
RSAT 80, 81, 83
RSAT, Windows 8
download link 80
RSAT, Windows 8.1
download link 80
RSS
about 210, 211
tuning 211, 212

S

Thank you for buying
Microsoft Hyper-V Cluster Design

About Packt Publishing

Packt, pronounced 'packed', published its first book "Mastering phpMyAdmin for Effective MySQL Management" in April 2004 and subsequently continued to specialize in publishing highly focused books on specific technologies and solutions.

Our books and publications share the experiences of your fellow IT professionals in adapting and customizing today's systems, applications, and frameworks. Our solution based books give you the knowledge and power to customize the software and technologies you're using to get the job done. Packt books are more specific and less general than the IT books you have seen in the past. Our unique business model allows us to bring you more focused information, giving you more of what you need to know, and less of what you don't.

Packt is a modern, yet unique publishing company, which focuses on producing quality, cutting-edge books for communities of developers, administrators, and newbies alike. For more information, please visit our website: www.packtpub.com.

About Packt Enterprise

In 2010, Packt launched two new brands, Packt Enterprise and Packt Open Source, in order to continue its focus on specialization. This book is part of the Packt Enterprise brand, home to books published on enterprise software – software created by major vendors, including (but not limited to) IBM, Microsoft and Oracle, often for use in other corporations. Its titles will offer information relevant to a range of users of this software, including administrators, developers, architects, and end users.

Writing for Packt

We welcome all inquiries from people who are interested in authoring. Book proposals should be sent to author@packtpub.com. If your book idea is still at an early stage and you would like to discuss it first before writing a formal book proposal, contact us; one of our commissioning editors will get in touch with you.

We're not just looking for published authors; if you have strong technical skills but no writing experience, our experienced editors can help you develop a writing career, or simply get some additional reward for your expertise.

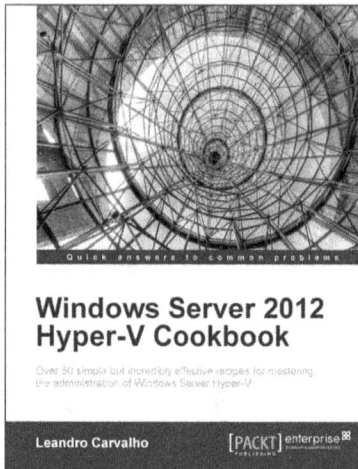

Windows Server 2012 Hyper-V Cookbook

ISBN: 978-1-849684-42-2   Paperback: 304 pages

Over 50 simple but incredibly effective recipes for mastering the administration of Windows Server Hyper-V

1. Take advantage of numerous Hyper-V best practices for administrators

2. Get to grips with migrating virtual machines between servers and old Hyper-V versions, automating tasks with PowerShell, providing a High Availability and Disaster Recovery environment, and much more

3. A practical Cookbook bursting with essential recipes

Instant Hyper-V Server Virtualization Starter

ISBN: 978-1-782179-97-9   Paperback: 58 pages

An intuitive guide to learning Virtualization with Hyper-V

1. Learn something new in an Instant! A short, fast, focused guide delivering immediate results

2. Step-by-step, practical guide to understanding and implementing virtualization for an enterprise environment

3. Learn how to create a virtual machine in three steps

Please check **www.PacktPub.com** for information on our titles

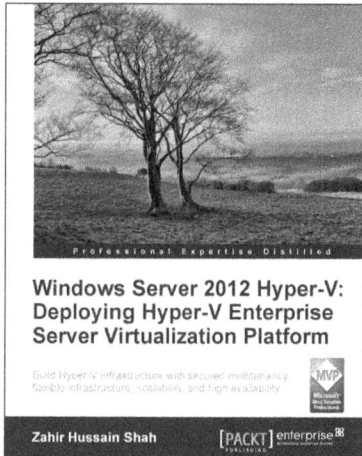

Windows Server 2012 Hyper-V: Deploying Hyper-V Enterprise Server Virtualization Platform

ISBN: 978-1-849688-34-5   Paperback: 410 pages

Building Hyper-V infrastructure with secured multitenancy, fl exible infrastructure, scalability, and high availability

1. A complete step-by-step Hyper-V deployment guide, covering all Hyper-V features for configuration and management best practices

2. Understand multi-tenancy, flexible architecture, scalability, and high availability features of new Windows Server 2012 Hyper-V

3. Learn Hyper-V Replica, Hyper-V Extensible Virtual Switch, Virtual Machine Migration, Hyper-V Storage, Hyper-V Failover Clustering, and also System Center VMM and DPM for management, backup, and recovery

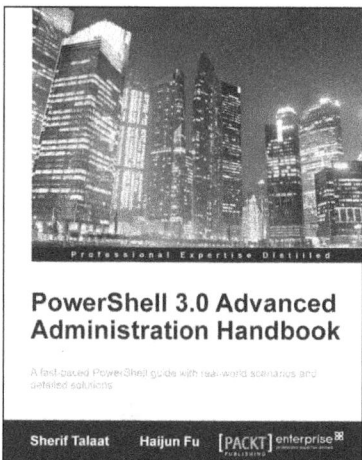

PowerShell 3.0 Advanced Administration Handbook

ISBN: 978-1-849686-42-6   Paperback: 370 pages

A fast-paced PowerShell guide with real-world scenarios and detailed solutions

1. Discover and understand the concept of Windows PowerShell 3.0

2. Learn the advanced topics and techniques for a professional PowerShell scripting

3. Explore the secret of building custom PowerShell snap-ins and modules

Please check **www.PacktPub.com** for information on our titles

www.ingramcontent.com/pod-product-compliance
Lightning Source LLC
Chambersburg PA
CBHW080132220326
41598CB00032B/5034